THE LIFE OF
JESUS CHRIST

and

BIBLICAL REVELATIONS

Volume I

a.C. frmmm put

Blessed Anne Catherine Emmerich
1774-1824
Mystic, Stigmatist, Visionary and Prophet

THE LIFE OF JESUS CHRIST

and

BIBLICAL REVELATIONS

From the Visions of
Blessed Anne Catherine Emmerich
as recorded in the journals of Clemens Brentano

Arranged and edited by the Very Reverend
Carl E. Schmöger, C.SS.R.

Translated by an American Nun

Volume I

TAN Books
Charlotte, North Carolina

Nihil Obstat: Em. De Jaegher
                    Can. lib. cens.
                    Brugis, 14 Februarii 1914

Imprimatur: ✠ A. C. De Schrevel
                    Vicar General
                    Brugis, 14 Februarii 1914

ISBN: Vol. 1 978-0-89555-787-2
ISBN: Vol. 2 978-0-89555-788-9
ISBN: Vol. 3 978-0-89555-789-6
ISBN: Vol. 4 978-0-89555-790-2
ISBN: Set 978-0-89555-791-9

TAN Books
Charlotte, North Carolina
2011

"But there are also many other things which Jesus did; which, if they were written every one, the world itself, I think, would not be able to contain the books that should be written."

—St. John the Evangelist
(John 21:25)

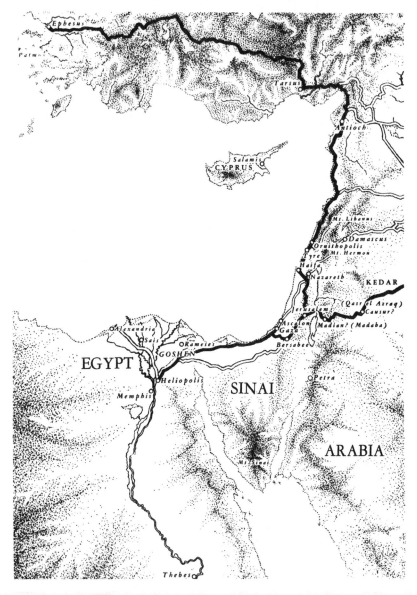

Miles

0   25 50   100   200

0   10   25   50   100

"Hours" or Leagues

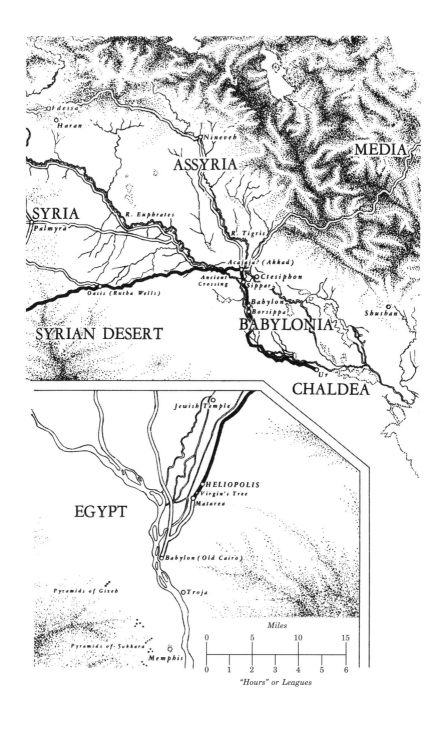

Ö Edessa
Ö Haran
Nineveh
ASSYRIA
MEDIA
SYRIA
Palmyra
R. Euphrates
R. Tigris
Acainia? (Akkad)
Ancient
Crossing
O Ctesiphon
Sippar
Oasis (Rutba Wells)
Babylon
Borsippa
BABYLONIA
Shushan
SYRIAN DESERT
Ur
CHALDEA

Jewish Temple
HELIOPOLIS
Virgin's Tree
Matarea
EGYPT
Babylon (Old Cairo)
Pyramids of Gizeh
O Troja
Pyramids of Sukkara
Memphis

Miles

0		5		10		15

0	1	2	3	4	5	6

"Hours" or Leagues

Anne Catherine Emmerich

Anne Catherine Emmerich was born on September 8th, 1774, at Flamske, near Koesfeld, Westphalia, in West Germany, and became a nun of the Augustinian Order on November 13th, 1803, in the Convent of Agnetenberg at Dülmen (also in Westphalia). She died on February 9th, 1824. Although of simple education, she had perfect consciousness of her earliest days and could understand the liturgical Latin from her first time at Mass.

During most of her later years she would vomit up even the simplest food or drink, subsisting for long periods almost entirely on water and the Holy Eucharist. She was told in mystic vision that her gift of seeing past, present and future was greater than that possessed by anyone else in history.

From the year 1812 until her death, she bore the stigmata of Our Lord, including a cross over her heart and wounds from the crown of thorns. Though Anne Catherine Emmerich was an invalid confined to bed during her later years, her funeral was nevertheless attended by a greater concourse of mourners than any other remembered by the oldest inhabitants of Dülmen.

Her mission in life seems to have been to suffer in expiation for the godlessness that darkened the "Age of Enlightenment" and the era of the Napoleonic wars, a time during which she saw her convent closed and her Order suppressed by Napoleon.

During the last five years of her life the day-by-day transcription of her visions and mystical experiences was recorded by Clemens Brentano, poet, literary leader, friend of Goethe and Görres, who, from the time he met her, abandoned his distinguished career and devoted the rest of his life to this work.

The immense mass of notes preserved in his journals forms one of the most extensive case histories of a mystic ever kept and provides the source for the material found in this book, plus much of what is found in her two-volume definitive biography written by V. Rev. Carl E. Schmöger, C.SS.R.

Preface

This book is the first and only English version of the combined Biblical visions of Blessed Anne Catherine Emmerich. The original was published in 1914 by Desclée, de Brouwer (Bruges, Belgium) as *The Lowly Life and Bitter Passion of Our Lord and Saviour Jesus Christ and His Blessed Mother, together with the Mysteries of the Old Testament*. The text is that of the 4th German edition of the 1881 version of the Very Rev. Carl E. Schmöger, C.SS.R., a compilation of the three classic works: *The Life of Our Lord and Saviour Jesus Christ, The Bitter Passion of Our Lord Jesus Christ,* and *The Life of Mary*. The translation was made by an American nun, since deceased, who wished to remain anonymous.

The first edition was issued with the approval and warm recommendation of the following members of the American hierarchy: Cardinal Gibbons, Archbishops Gross, Feehan and Elder, and Bishop Toebbe. It also included testimonials from Michael Wittman, Bishop of Ratisbon, Dean Overberg, Sister Emmerich's spiritual director, Count Leopold von Stolberg, J. J. Goerres, Dom Prosper Guéranger and several others less well known in our day. To this list might be added the names of Claudel, the Maritains, Huysmans, Father Gerard Manley Hopkins, Leon Bloy . . . to name but a few who have written in glowing terms of the saintly "Bride of the Passion" who was privileged to bear the wounds of Him whose life she beheld in the prophetic eye of her spirit.

The publishers, in reprinting these volumes, do so in complete and willing conformity to the decrees of Pope Urban VIII respecting private revelations, persons not as yet canonized, and the prudence with which all alleged supernatural phenomena not attested to by the Church must properly be regarded. The final decision in all such matters rests with the See of Rome, to which the publishers humbly submit.

Like other private revelations, Sister Emmerich's accounts of the life of Our Lord, His Blessed Mother, and other biblical personages should be treated with that respect and that degree of faith which they seem to merit when compared with the holy dogmas of our Faith as derived from Scripture and Tradition, as well as when compared with our knowledge of history, geography, and science. These revelations are not, of course, guaranteed free from all error, as are the Sacred Scriptures. The *Imprimatur* which these books bear simply means they have been judged by ecclesiastical authority to be free of error in matters of faith and morals. Nevertheless, these revelations show a remarkable harmony with what is known about the history, geography, and customs of the ancient world.

The visions of Anne Catherine Emmerich provide a wealth of information not found in the Bible. In these times of disbelief, when the Sacred Scriptures are so often regarded as symbolical narratives with little historical value, the visions of this privileged soul providentially confirm the Christian's faith in the rock-solid reality of the life of Our Lord Jesus Christ, of His words, His deeds, and His miracles.

In addition, Sister Emmerich's visions show how our sacred religious heritage goes back in an unbroken line all the way to the time of Adam, to the very beginning of the world—a line which no other religion but the Roman Catholic can claim. These revelations show how the Roman Catholic Church faithfully follows the teachings, and administers the Sacraments, of Jesus Christ Himself—which teachings and Sacraments are in turn the perfect fulfillment of the Old Testament religion.

This crucial fact, which has been almost totally

forgotten in our day, is nevertheless all-important in proving which is the one true religion established by Almighty God. The unbroken line of the Roman Catholic Church becomes obvious to all who read these accounts of the marvelous events which Anne Catherine Emmerich was privileged to behold. For this reason alone, they are priceless—a gift of Divine Providence to an unbelieving world.

May God guide these revelations into the hands of those who need them most. May they do immense good for souls, both in time and for eternity.

—The Publishers
January 31, 1986
Feast of St. John Bosco

Contents of Volume I

THE MOST HOLY VIRGIN

THE MOST HOLY INCARNATION

Illustration

Foreword

THE LIFE OF CHRIST contained in these volumes is one of the most complete and one of the most extraordinary works on the subject ever published. It was witnessed in vision by a stigmatized German nun of the early 19th Century, Blessed Anne Catherine Emmerich, and for some periods of Our Lord's life it consists of an almost day-by-day description of the three years of His Public Ministry, combined with a life of Mary, events from the Old Testament and a history of the establishment of the Church by the Apostles.

During the hundred years after it was first published in Germany, *The Life of Our Lord and Saviour Jesus Christ* met with all but total neglect in English. The present version, the only complete translation ever to appear in our language, was out of print for over a generation and extremely rare. The first edition (published in 1914) received a very limited distribution and is not to be found in our libraries, bookstores or at second hand.

Besides dealing with the most profound mysteries of Judaism and Christianity, the narrative synchronizes the major events of the Gospels with the feasts, fasts and Sabbaths of the ancient Jewish calendar and liturgy. It includes biographies of the ancestors and relatives of the Holy Family, John the Baptist, the Apostles and minor disciples, Mary Magdalen, Judas and Lazarus—to mention only a few— as well as a veritable encyclopedia of information regarding the culture, customs, political and religious sects, architecture, geography, agriculture, even the weather conditions of first-century Palestine. Twenty major journeys of Christ are recorded in a detailed itineraria of the cities and towns of Galilee,

Samaria, Judea, Gilead and (in the Third Year) Cyprus, Chaldea and Egypt.

The person to whom this *Summa Biblica* was revealed was a peasant girl born of devout and very poor parents on a farm in Westphalia in 1774. She received little education. For a number of years she worked on the farm, then as a servant girl, and later became a seamstress. At the age of 28 she entered the Augustinian convent at Dülmen, a small country town a few miles from her birthplace, near Münster. Ten years later, in 1811, all religious communities in western Germany were suppressed on the order of Jerome Bonaparte and the nuns forced to separate and find refuge wherever they could.

Shortly before taking her vows, while she was still working in the world, Anne Catherine had received the visible stigmata of the bleeding Crown of Thorns on her head. A few months after the closing of the convent, a cross appeared on her breast, as well as the wounds of the Passion on her hands, feet and side. She was given shelter by charitable persons of the town and for the remaining years of her life was unable to leave her bed. Her life became that of a victim soul, voluntarily dedicated to suffering and acts of mystical reparation. She gradually lost the power to eat food and often could not even drink a few drops of water. Also, toward the end of her life she did not sleep. She became widely known, and the public manner of her life added greatly to her sufferings. Besides the great numbers who came to see her, not always from pious motives, there were two prolonged and scrupulous investigations made of her case, one by a deeply antagonistic civil commission, in which every conceivable—and futile— effort was made to heal her mysterious wounds and expose her as an imposter.

Among those who visited her was one of the leading literary figures of the day in Germany, the poet, Clemens Brentano. He was then at the height of a brilliant and worldly career as the author of various published works. His meeting with Sister Emmerich had a profound and lasting influence on his life. He immediately grasped the importance of keeping a written record of her experiences, abandoned all other projects and, having obtained the permission of her spiritual director, settled himself in Dülmen. For the next five years, from the autumn of 1818 until the day of her death, February 9, 1824, he dedicated himself to the more or less continual daily task of recording her life and visions. The notes preserved in his Journals form one of the most extensive records of its kind ever kept and provided the source for the three published works combined in this version.

The period of the Emmerich revelations was one of the darkest hours in the history of Europe, the so-called Age of Enlightenment and the era of the Napoleonic wars. In the year Anne Catherine was born there appeared in Germany a work destined to be the first attack on Christianity of the rationalist school of historical criticism, Reimarus' *Apologia or Defense for the Reasonable Worshippers of God.* Its theme was the naked denial of the supernatural element in religion and the Bible as revelation. Two years later, in France, Voltaire published his *Bible at last Explained* and his *History of the Establishment of Christianity.* During the following century there continued to appear, for the most part in Germany, a whole flood of similar writings in which, under the appearance of scientific objectivity, Jesus Christ was explained as a minor historical figure, if not actually a myth, and the Church He had founded as the creation of deluded or calculating men.

In light of the period when they were revealed, it is seen that the historical content in the Emmerich visions and their emphasis upon the humanity of the Son of Man was profoundly allied to their spiritual mission. The purpose of private revelations, as defined by St. Thomas, is not to prove or to add anything to the truth of Christian doctrine, but to offer men of a certain period and because of the circumstances of that period a direction for human action.

In this our 20th Century, their principal value lies, it would seem, in their ability to focus our attention on the myriad of explicit detail which Anne Catherine witnessed in vision—details of the various episodes and events of Christ's life which confirm and expand upon what we are given in the Gospels and which reveal many, many additional points which bear directly upon the establishment of our Religion and its many saintly practices, devotions, sacramentals, and liturgical events. The net effect of reading about these events, as the visionary was privileged to see them, is the confirming of our faith in what the Church teaches, as well as in her various practices and devotions. Living, as we are, in the last half of the 20th Century, we are witnessing a continual deterioration of belief in the Catholic Faith. What these revelations of Sister Emmerich achieve for us is to call us back to a firm and committed adherence to all that Holy Mother the Church teaches.

For the men of the 19th Century, on the other hand (and actually, for many in the 20th Century as well), the purpose of these revelations on the life of Christ, insofar as one is humanly able to judge them, was to point out, in authentic terms, the historic reality of the Incarnation and the Redemption. Its striking realism and almost incredible wealth of historical, archaeological, chronological and geographical detail were the necessary means to accomplish this purpose at a time when scholarship and the alleged demonstration of facts were being used to deny the fundamental dogma of Christianity, that God was made Man.

During the century that has passed, and to an even greater extent in the last fifty years, many significant advances have been made in the field of bib-

lical scholarship. Along with the opening up of the
Holy Land to archaeological exploration, the sys-
tematic study of ancient history and languages, new
translations of the Bible and many important discoveries of new evidence, has come a gradual accu-
mulation of accurate information, and with it the
demonstration in scientific terms of the historical
validity of the Gospels and the reliability of early
Christian tradition. Yet despite this invaluable accu-
mulation, unequalled in any previous generation, the
field is admitted by its leaders to be still in its infancy
and in constant need of correction. As in every truly
scientific advance, a great part of the modern achieve-
ment has been, not discoveries alone, but the elim-
ination of earlier errors and the isolation of problems
that yet remain. From the present objective view-
point and with the help of present day knowledge it
is possible, now more than ever before, to evaluate
the historical content in the Emmerich revelations.

It must be noted that the Emmerich revelations
are not directed towards the end of merely supplying us with historical data. Their purpose is also
spiritual, for they are not written in the technical
language of scholarship. They also contain a great
deal of mystical, theological and symbolical material that cannot and ought not to be taken as historical fact. Furthermore, in their published form,
they include many experimental and provisional
arrangements of the material arising from the original problems of the narration and Brentano's later
attempts to put it in proper order.

The narration was attended by many difficulties.
There were interruptions, omissions, repetitions and
an almost infinite complexity in the subject matter
itself. Sister Emmerich's visions of the public life of
Christ did not begin at the beginning of the First
Year, but at a point not clearly defined towards the
end of the Third. There were several gaps, one lasting six months, only partially restored later from

memory or repeated on dates out of sequence with
the biblical period they referred to. In some cases
the order was not determined by the historical
chronology but by the liturgical seasons of the Church,
to which Sister Emmerich's whole life was attuned
in a mysterious manner. Many visions of the Third
Year were repeated annually during the long period
of Septuagesima, thus occurring and recurring on
varying dates in the Christian calendar. Each year
during Passiontide, Advent and Lent, on the feast
days of saints, or in relation to her ceaseless mystical labors of reparation, she saw and related other
scenes of a liturgical or symbolical sort interwoven
with those of the life of the Saviour.

It is not difficult to understand, therefore, that for
some eighteen years following Sister Emmerich's
death, until the day of his own, the Pilgrim (the
familiar name by which she called Brentano) engaged
in repeated and never wholly successful attempts to
organize the immense mass of writing he had preserved. Most of the material was never published by
him. During his lifetime he brought out only *The
Bitter Passion* (also known as *The Dolorous Passion
of Our Lord Jesus Christ),* based largely on a special series of visions witnessed during Lent, 1823.
At the time of his death he had nearly completed
The Life of Mary (also known as *The Life of the
Blessed Virgin Mary),* a work compiled from various
visions, mainly of liturgical origin, which was put
into final form and posthumously published by his
relatives. The longest part of his record, the day-by-
day cycle of the three years of the public life of
Christ, was beyond his power to compose and he
referred to it, significantly, as his "lockjaw." It is
known that he remained dissatisfied with the final
arrangement. As his life drew to a close he sought,
in vain, to find someone qualified to complete the
project, to whom he could impart the full knowledge
of the problems as he alone knew them. After his

death the manuscripts passed into other hands and in 1858/60 the three-volume *Life of Our Lord and Saviour Jesus Christ* was published for the first time at Regensburg by the Very Rev. Carl Erhard Schmöger, C.SS.R., in an edition based on the Journals as Brentano had left them. This edition has remained the standard and the source for the many subsequent editions and translations, including the present English version.

Some Things to Look For in These Volumes

The remarkable visions of Anne Catherine Emmerich light up innumerable aspects of the Faith, bringing to life many things which the reader may not have sufficiently appreciated. Our Lord's manner of healing and exorcising, His teaching on the connection between sin and physical maladies, His teaching on marriage and especially the role of the wife, Our Lord's attitude toward material possessions and the poor, the religious status of pagans and the way in which Our Lord presented His message to them—these are a few of the fascinating topics covered in these pages.

But beyond individual insights into one or another aspect of the Christian traditions, there are two central insights to be gained from these four books—insights of paramount significance regarding the very definition of the Christian religion. These are: 1) The Church which Jesus Christ founded was the Catholic Church, a Church identical in substance and even in detail with the Catholic Church of today; 2) The Church which Our Lord Jesus Christ founded was the perfect fulfillment of the religion of the Old Testament, going back all the way to the time of Adam—thus the Catholic religion is the one true religion established and approved by Almighty God from the very beginning of the world.

Anne Catherine Emmerich saw and heard Our Lord teaching doctrines which are the same as those taught by the Catholic Church of today. As she sets forth these doctrines, the Catholic of today will have no difficulty in recognizing as Catholic Christ's words on penance, marriage, prayer, mercy, the Bread of Life, humility, love of the poor, gratitude to God, faith, avoiding the occasions of sin, amendment of life, Baptism, renunciation of all earthly things to follow Christ, and the punishment in store for those who do not accept Him and His teachings.

Moreover, Sister Emmerich clearly describes Our Lord as establishing a sacrificing priesthood, bishops, Sacraments, blessings, sacramentals (e.g., holy water, holy oils), the power of exorcism, the papacy, the Blessed Sacrament, and even the reservation of the Blessed Sacrament upon the altar. She saw Our Lord bringing His Apostles to His Mother to be adopted as her spiritual children, finally entrusting all Christians to her as He hung on the cross; and she saw Him celebrating the first Mass, on the evening of the Last Supper—with ceremonies strikingly similar to those of Holy Mass of today, including the ablution of the priest's thumb and forefinger after the Consecration, and the placing of a particle of the Sacred Host into the chalice. The reader is also struck by the concrete way in which Our Lord perpetuated His Church; for this purpose He ordained and commissioned the Apostles to preach His word and administer His Sacraments, this commission to begin with the descent of the Holy Ghost on Pentecost. All these elements were present in the Church from the very beginning. They were not added onto Christ's message by human invention at a later date; they came from Our Lord Himself.

These details show most clearly that Our Lord founded a *visible* Church. Truly, the entire Christian religion can be summed up in those words of St. John the Evangelist: "And the Word was made flesh, and dwelt among us." (*John* 1:14). Our Lord's name, "Emmanuel," means "God with us"—a fact which was true not only for the years of His life on earth but is still true today, by His Real Presence in the Holy Eucharist upon our altars.

Yet so many of the elements of Christ's religion, left to us by Our Lord Himself, are disregarded and even attacked by those who claim that "the church" is something purely interior and invisible, existing solely in the hearts of individuals—individuals who want to accept Christ's Word but yet who deny His Sacraments and who base their faith upon their own personal understanding of His Word. Sister Emmerich's accounts, on the other hand, show that Our Lord continually demanded that His listeners accept *His divine interpretation* of the Holy Scriptures—and He sent His Apostles out to continue the true presentation of this teaching. ("He that heareth you, heareth me"—*Luke* 10:16). Indeed, the Pharisees themselves had the same Scriptures (Old Testament) as Our Lord, but they based their religion and teachings on their own human interpretations of them. For this sin Our Lord time and time again rebuked them severely.

Let no one fail to notice that the Catholic Church—and she alone—speaks to her hearers today in the very same terms used by Our Lord: You must hear My living voice telling you *My* divine explanation of the Scriptures. Even though the New Testament, as a book, did not exist in the early Christian days, Christ's Church existed, nourished by the unwritten divine Tradition that had come down through the Apostles from Our Lord Jesus Christ Himself.

A second great insight to be gathered from these revelations is that while Our Lord was indeed the Founder of a new religion, this new religion was itself the accomplishment of the old religion, of the holy expectations of the Chosen People, the Patriarchs and Prophets, back through Noah all the way to the time of Adam, who was the first human being to receive an intimation of God's Promised Redeemer. (*Gen.* 3:15). Our Lord Himself was the fulfillment of God's Promise, and He left a Church, His Mystical Body, to continue that blessed fulfillment until the end of the world.

One of the great proofs that Our Lord came from

God and was the promised Messiah was His accomplishing of the Old Testament prophecies. The Old Covenant (or Old Testament) between God and man, begun with God's Promise to Abraham (*Genesis* 17), had been renewed time and again with animal sacrifices and the shedding of animal blood. But God had promised the Prophets (e.g., *Ezechiel* 37 and *Isaiah* 49) that He would one day establish a new covenant between Himself and His people. Moreover, the Prophet Malachias had prophesied that one day there would be a "clean oblation" *(Mal.* 1:11), a sacrifice offered from the rising to the setting of the sun, a sacrifice offered even among the Gentiles. In addition to Malachias' prophecy in word, the High Priest Melchisedech had foretold this new and perfect sacrifice by means of a deed, by offering to God bread and wine (which sacrifice is still mentioned today in the Holy Sacrifice of the Mass). And of course, Abraham's sacrifice of his son Isaac is the most famous prophetic deed, or "type," foreshadowing the perfect Sacrifice to come—that is, that of the father sacrificing his "only begotten son." (Abraham's sacrifice, too, is mentioned in the Mass today.)

When He came upon earth, Our Lord Jesus Christ, fully conscious of His authority, abolished the Old Covenant between God and man which had existed since Abraham (some 2,000 years before) and established a New Covenant, thus inaugurating an entirely new era in the history of the world. Watching Our Lord unfold this New Covenant through His teachings, and then seeing it draw to its consummation as He, the God-Man, seals it by shedding His Blood, first mystically, after the Last Supper, and then physically on Calvary, is one of the most striking experiences the reader will encounter in these entire four volumes.

With the benefit of hindsight, the Catholic of today watches in awe as Anne Catherine Emmerich describes the momentous events of the first Holy

Thursday and Good Friday, knowing—much more clearly than did the Apostles at that time—that on those two days was carried out the most epochal event in the history of the human race. "A new era, a new sacrifice, are about to begin," Our Lord said on that first Holy Thursday night, "and they shall last till the end of the world." As the reader sees the old religious forms (principally the Paschal supper) giving way to the new (Holy Mass and the Blessed Sacrament), those sonorous and weighty words of the *Tantum Ergo* come to mind: *Et antiquum documentum, Novo cedar ritui* ("Lo! o'er ancient forms departing, newer rites of grace prevail."). To His ordained priests Our Lord gave the power and the command to perpetuate mystically His perfect sacrifice of His Body and Blood, the source and wellspring of all salvation, until He should come again at the end of the world.

The phenomena which accompanied Christ's death on Calvary—the earthquake in Jerusalem and the rending of the Temple veil—were outward signs that the Old Covenant had just come to an end and that the most desired event in the history of mankind, the making of a New Covenant between God and man, a Covenant bringing salvation to all those who would be faithful to it, had finally taken place. For the first time since the sin of Adam, the Gates of Heaven were again opened to the members of the human race.

Henceforth God's Chosen People would no longer be the Jews only; the Chosen People would now be all those, Jews and Gentiles alike, who would accept the New Covenant and its requirements: obedience to the New Law—that is, the teachings of Christ; and the New Sacrifice, that clean and perfect oblation of the Body and Blood of Christ Himself, as perpetuated in the Holy Sacrifice of the Mass. God's Chosen People would now become known as "Christians," and soon they would also begin to be known by the name of "Catholics," that is, those who embrace that religion which is *"katholikos,"* or universal, given by God as the one way of salvation for all men everywhere.

As Anne Catherine Emmerich describes the words and deeds of Our Lord during His public ministry, culminating with the events of Holy Week and Pentecost, one sees that He is clearly conscious of accomplishing the Mysteries of Salvation for which Patriarchs and Prophets had longed during many ages. He speaks of Abraham, of the Promise, the manna in the desert, the destroying angel, and of the prophecy of Malachias regarding the "clean oblation." Our Lord even visited the tomb of Abraham, the first Patriarch, the man with whom God had made the Old Covenant.

By God's Providence there are numerous "coincidences" of time and place, recorded in the visions of Anne Catherine Emmerich, which link the Old Testament events to their fulfillment in the deeds of Jesus Christ. For instance, Anne Catherine states (in agreement with a long Christian tradition) that Our Lord was crucified over the very spot on Mount Calvary where the bones of Adam lay buried; thus, the sin of Adam was repaired, four millenia later, over the very relics of him who had committed the Original Sin and thus brought about the fall of the human race. Likewise, the chalice used by Our Lord at the Last Supper was the very same one used by Melchisedech some 2,000 years previously in his prophetic sacrifice of bread and wine—a chalice which had come with Noah and his family in the Ark.

As one reads Anne Catherine Emmerich's accounts of the events of our salvation, the conviction grows that no aspect was accidental. God's eternal plan was perfect in every detail, and Our Lord carried out to the letter those things which had been foretold of Him. Through these revelations, one sees clearly that man's task is not the foolish one of creating for himself a religion after his own liking, but rather that he must submit in obedience to that religion given him by Almighty God: the Catholic religion—the one religion prepared for man from the time of Adam, brought from Heaven by the Son of God, and guaranteed to endure, to unite men with God, and to lead souls to Heaven, until the very end of time.

Deo Gratias.

GENEALOGY OF THE HOLY FAMILY

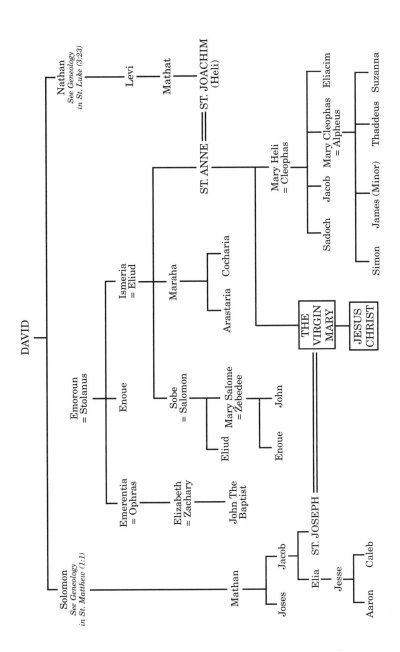

THE LIFE OF JESUS CHRIST

and

BIBLICAL REVELATIONS

Volume I

LIFE OF
OUR LORD JESUS CHRIST

THE CREATION

Introductory Remarks

Of the visions of her childhood Sister Emmerich tells us: When in my sixth year I reflected on the first article of the Apostles' Creed, "I believe in God, the Father Almighty, Creator of Heaven and earth," there passed before my soul innumerable pictures of the creation of Heaven and earth. I saw the Fall of the angels, the creation of the earth and Paradise, that of Adam and Eve, and the Fall of man. I thought everyone saw this as we do other things around us, and I spoke of it freely to my parents, brothers, sisters, and playmates. But they laughed at me. They asked me whether I had a book containing all these things, and so I began to keep silence concerning them. I thought, though without much reflection, that perhaps it was not proper to speak on such subjects.

I had these visions by night and by day, in the fields, in the house, sitting or walking, and when engaged in all kinds of employments. One day at school, I happened to speak of the Resurrection, describing it differently from what we had been taught. I felt certain that everyone knew it just as I did. I did not dream that there was anything peculiar in my account of it. But the children gazed at me in wonder and laughed, while the master reproved me gravely, and warned me not to indulge such imaginations. My visions continued, but I kept them to myself. I was like a child looking at a picture book, explaining the pictures in its own way, but not thinking much about their meaning. They represented the saints or scenes from Sacred History, sometimes in one way, sometimes in another. They produced no change in my faith, they were merely my picture book. I gazed upon them quietly and always with the good thought: All to the greater glory of God! In spiritual things, I have never put faith in anything but what God the Lord has revealed to the Catholic Church for our belief, whether it be written or not. I have never believed so firmly what I have seen in vision. I looked upon the latter as I devoutly regard, here and there, the various Cribs at Christmas. I feel no annoyance at their difference in style, for in each I adore the same dear little Infant Jesus. And so it is with those pictures of the creation of Heaven, earth, and man. In them I adore God the Lord, the Almighty Creator of Heaven and earth.

1. Fall of the Angels

I saw spreading out before me a boundless, resplendent space, above which floated a globe of light shining like a sun. I felt that It was the Unity of the Trinity. In my own mind, I named It the ONE VOICE, and I watched It producing Its effects. Below the globe of light arose concentric circles of radiant choirs of spirits, wondrously bright and strong and beautiful. This second world of light floated like a sun under that higher Sun.

These choirs came forth from the higher Sun, as if born of love. Suddenly I saw some of them pause, rapt in the contemplation of their own beauty. They took complacency in self, they sought the highest beauty in self, they thought but of self, they existed but in self.

At first all were lost in contemplation out of self,

but soon some of them rested in self. At that instant, I saw this part of the glittering choirs hurled down, their beauty sunk in darkness, while the others, thronging quickly together, filled up their vacant places. And now the good angels occupied a smaller space. I did not see them leaving their places to pursue and combat the fallen choirs. The bad angels rested in self and fell away, while those that did not follow their example thronged into their vacant places. All this was instantaneous.

Then rising from below, I saw a dark disc, the future abode of the fallen spirits. I saw that they took possession of it against their will. It was much smaller than the sphere from which they had fallen, and they appeared to me to be closely crowded together.

I saw the Fall of the angels in my childhood and ever after, day and night, I dreaded their influence. I thought they must do great harm to the earth, for they are always around it. It is well they have no bodies, else they would obscure the light of the sun. We should see them floating around us like shadows.

Immediately after the Fall, I saw the spirits in the shining circles humbling themselves before God. They did homage to Him and implored pardon for the fallen angels.

At that moment I saw a movement in the luminous sphere in which God dwelt. Until then it had been motionless and, as I felt, awaiting that prayer.

After that action on the part of the angelic choirs, I felt assured that they would remain steadfast, that they would never fall away. It was made known to me that God in His judgment, in His eternal sentence against the rebel angels, decreed the reign of strife until their vacant thrones are filled. But to fill those thrones seemed to me almost impossible, for it would take so long. The strife will, however, be upon the earth. There will be no strife above, for God has so ordained.

After I had received this assurance, I could no longer sympathize with Lucifer, for I saw that he had cast himself down by his own free, wicked will. Neither could I feel such anger against Adam. On the contrary, I felt great sympathy for him because I thought: It has been thus ordained.

2. Creation of the Earth

Immediately after the prayer of the faithful choirs and that movement in the Godhead, I saw below me, not far from and to the right of the world of shadows, another dark globe arise.

I fixed my eyes steadily upon it. I beheld it as if in movement, growing larger and larger, as it were, bright spots breaking out upon it and encircling it like luminous bands. Here and there, they stretched out into brighter, broader plains, and at that moment I saw the form of the land setting boundaries to the water. In the bright places I saw a movement as of life, and on the land I beheld vegetation springing forth and myriads of living things arising. Child that I was, I fancied the plants were moving about.

Up to this moment, there was only a gray light like the sunrise, like early morn breaking over the earth, like nature awakening from sleep.

And now all other parts of the picture faded. The sky became blue, the sun burst forth, but I saw only one part of the earth lighted up and shining. That spot was charming, glorious, and I thought: There's Paradise!

While these changes were going on upon the dark globe, I saw, as it were, a streaming forth of light out of that highest of all the spheres, the God-sphere, that sphere in which God dwelt.

It was as if the sun rose higher in the heavens, as if bright morning were awakening. It was the first morning. No created being had any knowledge of it, and it seemed as if all those created things had been there forever in their unsullied innocence. As the sun rose higher, I saw the plants and trees growing larger and larger. The waters became clearer and holier, colors grew purer and brighter—all was unspeakably charming. Creation was not then as it is now. Plants and flowers and trees had other forms. They are wild and misshapen now compared with what they were, for all things are now thoroughly degenerate.

When looking at the plants and fruits of our gardens, apricots, for instance, which in southern climes are, as I have seen, so different from ours, so large, magnificent, and delicious, I often think: As miserable as are our fruits compared with those of the South, are the latter when compared with the fruits of Paradise. I saw there roses, white and red, and I thought them symbols of Christ's Passion and our Redemption. I saw also palm trees and others, high and spreading which cast their branches afar, as if forming roofs.

Before the sun appeared, earthly things were puny; but in his beams they gradually increased in size, until they attained full growth.

The trees did not stand close together. Of all plants, at least of the largest, I saw only one of each kind, and they stood apart like seedlings set out in a garden bed. Vegetation was luxuriant, perfectly green, of a species pure, sound, and exempt from decay. Nothing appeared to receive or to need the attention of an earthly gardener. I thought: How is it that all is so beautiful, since as yet there are no human beings! Ah! Sin has not yet entered. There has been no destruction, no rending asunder. All is sound, all is holy. As yet there has been no healing, no repairing. All is pure, nothing has needed purification.

The plain that I beheld was gently undulating and covered with vegetation. In its center rose a fountain, from all sides of which flowed streams, crossing one another and mingling their waters. I saw in

them first a slight movement as of life, and then I
saw living things. After that I saw, here and there
among the shrubs and bushes, animals peeping forth,
as if just roused from sleep. They were very different from those of a later day, not at all timorous.
Compared with those of our own time, they were
almost as far their superior as men are superior to
beasts. They were pure and noble, nimble, and joyous. Words cannot describe them. I was not familiar
with many of them, for I saw very few like those we
have now. I saw the elephant, the stag, the camel,
and even the unicorn. This last I saw also in the
ark. It is remarkably gentle and affectionate, not so
tall as a horse, its head more rounded in shape. I
saw no asses, no insects, no wretched, loathsome creatures. These last I have always looked upon as a
punishment of sin. But I saw myriads of birds and
heard the sweetest notes as in the early morning.
There were no birds of prey that I could see, nor did
I hear any animals bellowing.

Paradise is still in existence, but it is utterly impossible for man to reach it. I have seen that it still
exists in all its splendor. It is high above the earth
and in an oblique direction from it, like the dark
globe of the angels fallen from Heaven.

3. Adam and Eve

I saw Adam created, not in Paradise, but in the
region in which Jerusalem was subsequently situated. I saw him come forth glittering and white from
a mound of yellow earth, as if out of a mold. The
sun was shining and I thought (I was only a child
when I saw it) that the sunbeams drew Adam out
of the hillock. He was, as it were, born of the virgin
earth. God blessed the earth, and it became his
mother. He did not instantly step forth from the
earth. Some time elapsed before his appearance. He
lay in the hillock on his left side, his arm thrown

over his head, a light vapor covering him as with a veil. I saw a figure in his right side, and I became conscious that it was Eve, and that she would be drawn from him in Paradise by God. God called him. The hillock opened, and Adam stepped gently forth. There were no trees around, only little flowers. I had seen the animals also, coming forth from the earth in pure singleness, the females separate from the males.

And now I saw Adam borne up on high to a garden, to Paradise.

God led all the animals before him in Paradise, and he named them. They followed him and gamboled around him, for all things served him before he sinned. All that he named, afterward followed him to earth. Eve had not yet been formed from him.

I saw Adam in Paradise among the plants and flowers, and not far from the fountain that played in its center. He was awaking, as if from sleep. Although his person was more like to flesh than to spirit, yet he was dazzlingly white. He wondered at nothing, nor was he astonished at his own existence. He went around among the trees and the animals, as if he were used to them all, like a man inspecting his fields.

Near the tree by the water arose a hill. On it I saw Adam reclining on his left side, his left hand under his cheek. God sent a deep sleep on him and he was rapt in vision. Then from his right side, from the same place in which the side of Jesus was opened by the lance, God drew Eve. I saw her small and delicate. But she quickly increased in size until full-grown. She was exquisitely beautiful. Were it not for the Fall, all would be born in the same way, in tranquil slumber.

The hill opened, and at Adam's side arose a crystalline rock, formed apparently of precious stones. At Eve's, lay a white valley covered with something like fine white pollen.

When Eve had been formed, I saw that God gave something, or allowed something to flow upon Adam. It was as if there streamed from the Godhead, apparently in human form, currents of light from forehead, mouth, breast, and hands. They united into a globe of light, which entered Adam's right side whence Eve had been taken. Adam alone received it. It was the germ of God's Blessing, which was threefold. The Blessing that Abraham received from the angel was one. It was of similar form, but not so luminous. Eve arose before Adam, and he gave her his hand. They were like two unspeakably noble and beautiful children, perfectly luminous, and clothed with beams of light as with a veil. From Adam's mouth I saw issuing a broad stream of glittering light, and upon his forehead was an expression of great majesty. Around his mouth played a sunbeam, but there was none around Eve's. I saw Adam's heart very much the same as in men of the present day, but his breast was surrounded by rays of light. In the middle of his heart, I saw a sparkling halo of glory. In it was a tiny figure as if holding something in its hand. I think it symbolized the Third Person of the Godhead. From the hands and feet of Adam and Eve, shot rays of light. Their hair fell in five glittering tresses, two from the temples, two behind the ears, and one from the back of the head.

I have always thought that by the Wounds of Jesus there were opened anew in the human body portals closed by Adam's sin. I have been given to understand that Longinus opened in Jesus' Side the gate of regeneration to eternal life, therefore no one entered Heaven while that gate was closed.

The glittering beams on Adam's head denoted his abundant fruitfulness, his glory, his connection with other radiations. And all this shining beauty is restored to glorified souls and bodies. Our hair is the ruined, the extinct glory; and as is this hair of ours to rays of light, so is our present flesh to that of Adam before the Fall. The sunbeams around Adam's mouth bore reference to a holy posterity from God, which, had it not been for the Fall, would have been effectuated by the spoken word. Adam stretched forth his hand to Eve. They left the charming spot of Eve's creation and went through Paradise, looking at everything, rejoicing in everything. That place was the highest in Paradise. All was more radiant, more resplendent there than elsewhere.

4. The Tree of Life and The Tree of Knowledge

In the center of the glittering garden, I saw a sheet of water in which lay an island connected with the opposite land by a pier. Both island and pier were covered with beautiful trees, but in the middle of the former stood one more magnificent than the others. It towered high over them as if guarding them. Its roots extended over the whole island as did also its branches, which were broad below and tapering to a point above. Its boughs were horizontal, and from them arose others like little trees. The leaves were fine, the fruit yellow and sessile in a leafy calyx like a budding rose. It was something like a cedar. I do not remember ever having seen Adam, Eve, or any animal near that tree on the island. But I saw beautiful noble-looking white birds and heard them singing in its branches. That Tree was the Tree of Life.

Just before the pier that led to the island, stood the Tree of Knowledge. The trunk was scaly like that of the palm. The leaves, which spread out directly from the stem, were very large and broad, in shape like the sole of a shoe. Hidden in the forepart of the leaves, hung the fruit clustering in fives, one in front, and four around the stem. The yellow fruit had something of the shape of an apple, though more of the nature of a pear or fig. It had five ribs uniting in a little cavity. It was pulpy like a fig inside, of the color of brown sugar, and streaked with blood-red veins. The tree was broader above than below, and its branches struck deep roots into the ground. I see a species of this tree still in warm countries. Its branches throw down shoots to the earth where they root and rise as new trunks. These in turn send forth branches, and so one such tree often covers a large tract of country. Whole families dwell under the dense foliage.

At some distance to the right of the Tree of Knowledge, I saw a small, oval, gently sloping hill of glittering red grains and all kinds of precious stones. It was terraced with crystals. Around it were slender trees just high enough to intercept the view. Plants and herbs grew around it and they, like the trees, bore colored blossoms and nutritious fruits.

At some distance to the left of the Tree of Knowledge, I saw a slope, a little dale. It looked like soft clay, or like mist, and it was covered with tiny white flowers and pollen. Here too were various kinds of vegetation, but all colorless, more like pollen than fruit.

It seemed as if these two, the hill and the dale, bore some reference to each other, as if the hill had been taken out of the dale, or as if something from the former was to be transplanted into the latter. They were to each other what the seed is to the field. Both seemed to me holy, and I saw that both, but especially the hill, shone with light. Between them and the Tree of Knowledge arose different kinds of trees and bushes. They were all, like everything else in nature, transparent as if formed of light.

These two places were the abodes of our first parents. The Tree of Knowledge separated them. I think that God, after the creation of Eve, pointed out those places to them.

I saw that Adam and Eve were little together at first. I saw them perfectly free from passion, each in a separate abode. The animals were indescribably noble-looking and resplendent, and they served Adam and Eve. All had, according to their kind, certain retreats, abodes, and walks apart. The different spheres contained in themselves some great mystery of the Divine Law, and all were connected with one another.

Sin and Its Consequences

1. The Fall

I saw Adam and Eve walking through Paradise for the first time. The animals ran to meet and follow them, but they appeared to be more familiar with Eve than with Adam. Eve was in fact more taken up with the earth and created things. She glanced below and around more frequently than Adam. She appeared the more inquisitive of the two. Adam was more silent, more absorbed in God. Among the animals was one that followed Eve more closely than the others, It was a singularly gentle and winning, though artful creature. I know of none other to which I might compare it. It was slender and glossy, and it looked as if it had no bones. It walked upright on its short hind feet, its pointed tail trailing on the ground. Near the head, which was round with a face exceedingly shrewd, it had little short paws, and its wily tongue was ever in motion. The color of the neck, breast, and underpart of the body was pale yellow, and down the back it was a mottled brown very much the same as an eel. It was about as tall as a child of ten years. It was constantly around Eve, and so coaxing and intelligent, so nimble and supple that she took great delight in it. But to me there was something horrible about it. I can see it distinctly even now. I never saw it touch either Adam or Eve. Before the Fall, the distance between man and the lower animals was great, and I never saw the first human beings touch any of them. They had, it is true, more confidence in man, but they kept at a certain distance from him.

When Adam and Eve returned to the region of shining light, a radiant Figure like a majestic man with glittering white hair stood before them. He pointed around, and in few words appeared to be giving all things over to them and to be commanding them something. They did not look intimidated, but listened to him naturally. When he vanished, they appeared more satisfied, more happy. They appeared to understand things better, to find more order in things, for now they felt gratitude, but Adam more than Eve. She thought more of their actual bliss and of the things around them than of thanking for them. She did not rest in God so perfectly as did Adam, her soul was more taken up with created things. I think Adam and Eve went around Paradise three times.

Again I saw Adam on the shining hill upon which God had formed the woman from a rib of his side as he lay buried in sleep. He stood alone under the trees lost in gratitude and wonder. I saw Eve near the Tree of Knowledge, as if about to pass it, and with her that same animal more wily and sportive than ever. Eve was charmed with the serpent; she took great delight in it. It ran up the Tree of Knowledge until its head was on a line with hers. Then clinging to the trunk with its hind feet, it moved its head toward hers and told her that, if she would eat of the fruit of that tree, she would no longer be in servitude, she would become free, and understand how the multiplication of the human race was to be effected. Adam and Eve had already received the command to increase and multiply, but I understood that they did not know as yet how God willed it to be brought about. I saw, too, that had they known it and yet sinned after that knowledge, Redemption would not have been possible. Eve now became more thoughtful. She appeared to be moved by desire for what the serpent had promised. Something degrading took possession of her. It made me feel anxious. She glanced toward Adam, who was still quietly standing under the trees. She called him, and he came.

Eve started to meet him, but turned back. There

was a restlessness, a hesitancy about her movements. Again she started, as if intending to pass the tree, but once more hesitated, approached it from the left, and stood behind it, screened by its long, pendent leaves. The tree was broader above than below, and its wide, leafy branches drooped to the ground. Just within Eve's reach hung a remarkably fine bunch of fruit.

And now Adam approached. Eve caught him by the arm and pointed to the talking animal, and he listened to its words. When Eve laid her hand on Adam's arm, she touched him for the first time. He did not touch her, but the splendor around them grew dim.

I saw the animal pointing to the fruit, but he did not venture to snap it off for Eve. But when the longing for it arose in her heart, he broke off and handed her the central and most beautiful piece of the clustering five.

And now I saw Eve draw near to Adam, and offer him the fruit. Had he refused it, sin would not have been committed. I saw the fruit break, as it were, in Adam's hand. He saw pictures in it, and it was as if he and Eve were instructed upon what they should not have known. The interior of the fruit was blood-red and full of veins. I saw Adam and Eve losing their brilliancy and diminishing in stature. It was as if the sun went down. The animal glided down the tree, and I saw it running off on all fours.

I did not see the fruit taken into the mouth as we now take food in eating, but it disappeared between Adam and Eve.

I saw that while the serpent was still in the tree, Eve sinned, for her consent was with the temptation. I learned also at that moment what I cannot clearly repeat; namely, that the serpent was, as it were, the embodiment of Adam and Eve's will, a being by which they could do all things, could attain all things. Here it was that Satan entered.

Sin was not completed by eating the forbidden fruit. But that fruit from the tree which, rooting its branches in the earth thus sent out new shoots, and which continued to do the same after the Fall, conveyed the idea of a more absolute propagation, a sensual implanting in self at the cost of separation from God. So, along with disobedience, there sprang from their indulgence that severing of the creature from God, that planting in self and through self, and those selfish passions in human nature. He that uses the fruit solely for the enjoyment it affords, must accept as the consequence of his act the subversion, the debasement of nature as well as sin and death.

The blessing of a pure and holy multiplying out of God and by God, which Adam had received after the creation of Eve was, in consequence of that indulgence, withdrawn from him; for I saw that the instant Adam left his hill to go to Eve, the Lord grasped him in the back and took something from him. From that *something,* I felt that the world's salvation would come.

Once on the Feast of the Holy and Immaculate Conception, God gave me a vision of that mystery. I saw enclosed in Adam and Eve the corporal and spiritual life of all mankind. I saw that by the Fall it became corrupted, mixed up with evil, and that the bad angels had acquired power over it. I saw the Second Person of the Godhead come down and, with something like a crooked blade, take the Blessing from Adam before he had sinned. At the same instant, I saw the Virgin issuing from Adam's side like a little luminous cloud, and soaring all resplendent up to God.

By the reception of the fruit, Adam and Eve became, as it were, intoxicated, and their consent to sin wrought in them a great change. It was the serpent in them. Its nature pervaded theirs, and then came the tares among the wheat.

As punishment and reparation, circumcision was instituted. As the vine is pruned that it may not run wild, may not become sour and unfruitful, so must it be done to man that he may regain his lost perfection. Once when the reparation of the Fall was shown me in symbolical pictures, I saw Eve in the act of issuing from Adam's side, and even then stretching out her neck after the forbidden fruit. She ran quickly to the tree and clasped it in her arms. In an opposite picture, I saw Jesus born of the Immaculate Virgin. He ran straight to the Cross and embraced it. I saw posterity obscured and ruined by Eve, but again purified by the Passion of Jesus. By the pains of penance must the evil love of self be rooted out of the flesh. The word of the Epistle that the son of the handmaid shall not be joint heir, I always understood to mean the flesh and slavish subjection thereto, typified under the figure of the handmaid. Marriage is a state of penance. It calls for prayer, fasting, almsdeeds, renunciation, and the intention to increase the Kingdom of God.

Adam and Eve before sin were very differently constituted from what we, poor, miserable creatures now are. With the reception of the forbidden fruit, they imbibed a material existence. Spirit became matter; flesh, an instrument, a vessel. At first they were one in God, they sought self in God; but afterward they stood apart from God in their own will. And this self-will is self-seeking, a lusting after sin and impurity. By eating the forbidden fruit, man turned away from his Creator. It was as if he drew creation into himself. All creative power, operations, and attributes, their commingling with one another and with all nature, became in man material things of different forms and functions.

Once man was endowed with the kingship of nature, but now all in him has become nature. He is now one of its slaves, a master conquered and fettered. He must now struggle and fight with nature—but I cannot clearly express it. It was as if man once possessed all things in God, their Creator and their Center; but now he made himself their center, and they became his master.

I saw the interior, the organs of man as if in the flesh, in corporeal, corruptible images of creatures, as well as their relations with one another, from the stars down to the tiniest living thing. All exert an influence on man. He is connected with all of them; he must act and struggle against them, and from them suffer. But I cannot express it clearly since I, too, am a member of the fallen race.

Man was created to fill the choirs of the fallen angels. Were it not for the Fall of Adam, the human race would have increased only till the number of the fallen angels was reached, and then the world would have come to an end. Had Adam and Eve lived to see even one sinless generation, they would not have fallen. I am certain that the world will last until the number of the fallen angels has been filled, until the wheat shall have been reaped from the chaff.

Once I had a great and connected vision of sin and the whole plan of Redemption. I saw all mysteries clearly and distinctly, but it is impossible for me to put all into words. I saw sin in its innumerable ramifications from the Fall of the angels and from Adam's Fall down to the present day, and I saw all the preparations for the repairing and redeeming down to the coming and death of Jesus. Jesus showed me the extraordinary blending, the intrinsic uncleanness of all creatures, as well as all that He had done from the very beginning for their purification and restoration.

At the Fall of the angels, myriads of bad spirits descended to earth and into the air. I saw many creatures under the influence of their wrath, possessed by them in many ways.

The first man was an image of God, he was like Heaven; all was one in him, all was one with him. His form was a reproduction of the Divine Prototype. He was destined to possess and to enjoy earth and all created things, but holding them from God and giving thanks for them. Man was, however, free; therefore was he subjected to trial, therefore was he forbidden to eat of the Tree of Knowledge. In the beginning, all was smooth and level. When the little mound, the shining hill upon which Adam stood arose, when the white, blooming vale by which I saw Eve standing was hollowed out, the corruptor was already near. After the Fall, all was changed. All forms of creation were produced in self, dissipated in self. What had been one became many, creatures no longer looked to God alone, each was concentrated in self.

Mankind at first numbered two, then three, and at last they became innumerable. They had been images of God; but after the Fall, they became images of self, which images originated in sin. Sin placed them in communication with the fallen angels. They sought all their good in self and the creatures around them with all of whom the fallen angels had connection; and from that interminable blending, that sinking of his noble faculties in self and in fallen nature, sprang manifold wickedness and misery.

My Affianced showed me this clearly, distinctly, intelligibly, more clearly than one beholds the things of daily life. At the time, I thought that a child might comprehend it, but now I cannot repeat it. He showed me the whole plan of Redemption with the way in which it was to be effected, as also all that He Himself had done. I saw that it is not right to say that God need not have become man, need not have died for us upon the Cross; that He could, by virtue of His omnipotence, have redeemed us otherwise. I saw that He did what He did in conformity with His own infinite perfection, His mercy, and His justice; that there is indeed no necessity in God, He does what He does, He is what He is!

I saw Melchisedech as an angel and a type of Jesus, as a priest upon the earth; inasmuch as the priesthood is in God, he was an angel priest of the eternal hierarchy. I saw him preparing, founding, building up, and separating the human family, and acting toward them as a guide. I saw too, Enoch and Noe, what they represented, what they effected; on the other side, I saw the ever-active empire of Hell and the infinitely varied manifestations and effects of an earthly, carnal, diabolical idolatry. And I saw in all these manifestations similar pestiferous forms and figures leading, so to say, by a secret, inborn necessity and an uninterrupted process of dissolution to sin and corruption. In this manner, I saw sin and the prophetic, foreshadowing figures of Redemption which, in their way, were images of divine power as man himself in the image of God. All were shown me from Abraham to Moses, from Moses to the Prophets, also the way in which they were connected and their reference to similar types in our own day. Thus, for instance, with these visions of the Old Testament was connected the instruction I received upon the reason priests no longer relieve or cure, why it is either not in their power, or why it is now effected so differently from what it used to be. I saw this gift of the priesthood possessed by the Prophets, and the signification of the form under which it was exercised was shown me. I saw, for example, the history of Eliseus giving his staff to Giezi to lay upon the dead child of the Sunamitess. In this staff lay spiritually Eliseus's mission and power. It was, as it were, his arm, the prolongation of his arm. And here I saw the interior signification and power of a Bishop's crozier and a monarch's scepter. If used with faith, they unite both Bishop and monarch in a certain way with Him from whom they hold their dignity, with God, marking them out at the same time as distinct from all others. But Giezi's faith was not firm, and the mother thought that only through Eliseus himself could help be obtained; and so between Eliseus's power from God and his staff, the questionings of human presumption intervened, and the staff cured not. Then I saw Eliseus praying and stretching himself, hand to hand, mouth to mouth, breast to breast, upon the boy, and the soul of the boy returned to his body. It was explained to me that this manner of healing referred to and prefigured the death of Jesus. In Eliseus, by faith and the power conferred by God, were opened again in man all the avenues of grace and expiation that had been closed after the Fall: viz., the head, the breast, the hands, and the feet. Eliseus stretched himself as a living, symbolical cross upon the dead, closed cross of the boy's form, and through his prayer of faith life was restored. He expiated, he atoned for the sins the parents had committed by their head, heart, hands, and feet—sins that had brought death to their boy. Side by side with the above, I saw pictures of the Wounds of Jesus and of His death upon the Cross, by which I traced the harmony between Jesus and His Prophet. Since the Crucifixion of Jesus, the gift of healing and repairing has existed in full measure among the priests of His Church and in general among faithful Christians; for in the same proportion as we live in Him and are crucified with Him, are those avenues of grace, His Sacred Wounds, opened to us. I learned many things of the imposition of hands, the efficacy of a benediction, and the influence exerted by the hand, even at a distance— all was explained by the staff of Eliseus, which symbolized the hand. That priests of the present day so seldom cure and bless, was shown me in an example significant to that conformity to Jesus upon which depend all such effects. I saw three artists making figures of wax. The first used beautiful white wax, and he was both skillful and intelligent. But he was self-conceited, the image of Christ was not in him, and his work was of no value. The second used wax not so white as that of the first, and his indolence and self-will spoiled all. He did nothing at all. The third was awkward and unskillful; but he worked away in his simplicity and with great diligence on common yellow wax. His work was excellent, a speaking likeness, although the features were coarse. I saw renowned preachers vaunting their worldly wisdom, but effecting nothing; while many a poor, unlettered man exercises by the priestly power alone the gift of healing and blessing. It seemed to me, while all this was shown me, that I was in school. My Affianced made me see how He had suffered from His conception to His death, always expiating, always satisfying for sin. I saw this in distinct visions of His life. I saw too that, by prayer and the offering of sufferings for others, many souls that have done no good upon earth may be converted and saved at the hour of death.

I saw also that the Apostles were sent over the greater part of the earth to crush the power of Satan and to scatter benedictions. It was just those regions into which they went that had been most thoroughly infected by the evil one. Jesus, by His perfect atonement, acquired that power against Satan for such as had received or such as would receive His Holy Spirit, and He secured it to them forever. I was given to understand that the power to withdraw various regions of the earth from Satan's dominion by means of a blessing, is signified by the words: "Ye are the salt of the earth." For the same reason is salt one of the ingredients of holy water.

I saw, too, in this vision that the punctilios of sensual, worldly life are most scrupulously observed. I saw the malediction following the reversed blessing. I saw the pretended miracles in the kingdom of Satan. I saw that the worship of nature, superstition, magic, mesmerism, worldly arts and science, and all the means employed to smooth death over, to make sin attractive, to lull the conscience, are practiced with rigorous exactitude, even with fanaticism by the very men who regard the ceremonies of the Holy Church as superstitious forms, for which any other may be indifferently substituted. And yet these men subject their whole life and all their actions to certain ceremonious observances. It is only of the kingdom of the God-Man that they make no account. The world is served with perfection, but the service of God is shamefully neglected!

2. The Promise of the Redeemer

After the Fall of Man, God made known to the angels His plan for the restoration of the human race. I saw the throne of God. I saw the Most Holy Trinity and a movement in the Divine Persons. I saw the nine choirs of angels and God announcing to them the way by which He would restore the fallen race. I saw the inexpressible joy and jubilation of the angels at the announcement.

I saw Adam's glittering rock of precious stones arise before the throne of God, as if borne up by angels. It had steps cut in it, it increased in size, it became a throne, a tower, and it extended on all sides until it embraced all things. I saw the nine choirs of angels around it, and above the angels in Heaven, I saw the image of the Virgin. It was not Mary in time; it was Mary in eternity, Mary in God. The Virgin entered the tower, which opened to receive her, and she appeared to become one with it. Then I saw issuing from the Most Holy Trinity an apparition which, likewise, went into the tower.

Among the angels, I noticed a kind of ostensorium at which all were working. It was in shape like a tower, and on it were all kinds of mysterious carving. Near it on either side stood two figures, their joined hands embracing it. At every instant it became larger and more magnificent. I saw something from God passing through the angelic choirs and going into the ostensorium. It was a shining Holy Thing, and it became more clearly defined the nearer it drew to the ostensorium. It appeared to me to be the germ of the divine Blessing for a pure offspring which had been given to Adam, but withdrawn when he was on the point of hearkening to Eve and consenting to eat the forbidden fruit. It was the Blessing that was again bestowed upon Abraham, withdrawn from Jacob, by Moses deposited in the Ark of the Covenant, and lastly received by Joachim, the father of Mary, in order that Mary might be as pure and stainless in her Conception as was Eve upon coming forth from the side of the sleeping Adam. The ostensorium, likewise, went into the tower.

I saw too, a chalice prepared by the angels. It was of the same shape as that used at the Last Supper, and it also went into the tower. To the right of the tower, I saw, as if on the edge of a golden cloud, grapevines and wheat intertwining like the fingers of clasped hands. From them sprang a branch, a whole genealogical tree upon whose boughs were little figures of males and females reaching hands to one another. Its highest blossom was the Crib with the Child.

Then I saw in pictures the mystery of Redemption from the Promise down to the fullness of time, and in side pictures I saw counteracting influences at work. At last, over the shining rock, I saw a large and magnificent church. It was the One, Holy, Catholic Church, which bears living in itself the salvation of the whole world. The connection of these pictures one with another and their transition from one to another was wonderful. Even what was evil and opposed to the end in view, even what was rejected by the angels as unfit, was made subservient to the development of Redemption. And so, I saw the ancient Temple rising from below; it was very large and like a church, but it had no tower. It was pushed to one side by the angels, and there it stood slanting. I saw a great mussel shell[1] make its appearance and try to force its way into the old Temple; but it, too, was hurried aside.

I saw appear a broad, lopped-off tower[2] through whose numerous gateways figures like Abraham and

---

1. Symbol of pagan worship and mythology.
2. An Egyptian pyramid.

the children of Israel entered. It was significant of their bondage in Egypt. It was shoved aside, as well as another Egyptian tower in staircase form. The latter was symbolical of astrology and soothsaying. Then appeared an Egyptian temple. It was pushed aside like the others, and remained standing crooked.

At last, I saw a vision on earth such as God had shown to Adam; viz., that a Virgin would arise and restore to him the salvation he had forfeited. Adam knew not when it would take place, and I saw his deep sadness because Eve bore him only sons. But at last she had a daughter.

I saw Noe and his sacrifice at the time in which he received from God the Blessing. Then I had visions of Abraham, of his Blessing, and of the promise of a son Isaac. I saw the Blessing descending from firstborn to firstborn, and always transmitted with a sacramental action. I saw Moses on the night of Israel's departure from Egypt, getting possession of the Mystery, the Holy Thing, of which none other knew save Aaron. I saw It afterward in the Ark of the Covenant. Only the High Priests and certain saints, by a revelation from God, had any knowledge of it. I saw the transmitting of this Mystery through the ancestry of Jesus Christ down to Joachim and Anne, the purest and holiest couple that ever existed, and from whom was born Mary, the spotless Virgin. And then I saw Mary becoming the living Ark of God's Covenant.

3. Adam and Eve Driven from Paradise

After some time, I saw Adam and Eve wandering about in great distress. They were no longer beaming with light, and they went about, one here, the other there, as if seeking something they had lost. They were ashamed of each other. Every step they took led them downward, as if the ground gave way beneath their feet. They carried gloom wherever they went; the plants lost their bright colors and turned gray, and the animals fled before them. They sought large leaves and wove them into a cincture for their loins. They always wandered about separate.

After they had thus fled for a considerable time, the region of refulgent light whence they had come began to look like the summit of a distant mountain. Among the bushes of a gloomy-looking plain, they hid themselves, but apart. Then a voice from above called them, but they would not obey the call. They were frightened, they fled still further, and hid still deeper among the bushes. It made me sad to see that. But the voice became more imperative, and, in spite of their desire to flee and hide, they were compelled to come forth.

The majestic Figure shining with light again appeared. Adam and Eve with bowed head stepped from their hiding places, but they dared not look upon their Lord. They glanced at each other, and both acknowledged their guilt. And now God pointed out to them a plain still lower than the one on which they stood. On it were bushes and trees. On reaching it, they became humble, and for the first time, rightly understood their miserable condition. I saw them praying when left there alone. They separated, fell on their knees, and raised up their hands with tears and cries. I thought as I gazed upon them how good it is to be alone in prayer.

Adam and Eve were at this time clothed in a garment that reached from the shoulders to the knee, and which was girded at the waist by a strip of the inner bark of a tree.

While our first parents were descending lower and lower from the place of their creation, Paradise itself appeared, like a cloud, to be mounting higher and higher above them. Then a fiery ring, like the circle sometimes seen around the sun and moon, came down from Heaven and settled around the height upon which was Paradise.

Adam and Eve had been only one day in Paradise.

I now see Paradise far, far off like a strip of land directly under the point of sunrise. When the sun rises, it mounts up from the right of that strip of land which lies east of the Prophet Mountain and just where the sun rises. It looks to me like an egg hanging over indescribably clear water which separates it from the earth. The Prophet Mountain is, as it were, a promontory rising up through that water. On that mountain, one sees extraordinarily verdant regions broken here and there by deep abysses and ravines full of water. I have, indeed, seen people climbing up the Prophet Mountain, but they did not go far.

I saw Adam and Eve reach the earth, their place of penance. Oh, what a touching sight—those two creatures expiating their fault upon the naked earth! Adam had been allowed to bring an olive branch with him from Paradise, and now he planted it. Later on, the Cross was made from its wood. Adam and Eve were unspeakably sad. Where I saw them, they could scarcely get a glimpse of Paradise, and they were constantly descending lower and lower. It seemed as if something revolved and they came at last, through night and darkness, to the wretched, miserable place upon which they had to do penance.

4. The Family of Adam

It was to the region of Mount Olivet that I saw Adam and Eve come. The country was very different from what it is at present, but I was assured that it was the same. I saw Adam and Eve living and doing penance on that part of Mount Olivet upon which Jesus sweat Blood. They cultivated the soil. I saw them surrounded by sons. They were in great distress, and they implored God to bestow upon them a daughter, for they had received the Promise that the woman's seed should crush the serpent's head.

Eve bore children at stated intervals. After each

birth a number of years was always devoted to penance. It was after seven years of penance that Seth, the child of promise, was born of Eve in the Grotto of the Crib, where, also, an angel announced to Eve that Seth was the seed given her by God in the place of Abel. For a long time, Seth was concealed in that Grotto, likewise in the cave in which Abraham was afterward suckled, for his brothers like those of Joseph sought his life.

Once I saw about twelve people: Adam, Eve, Cain, Abel, two sisters, and some young children. All were clothed in skins thrown over their shoulders like a scapular and girded at the waist. The female dress was large and full around the breast where it served as a pocket. It fell down around the limbs, and was fastened at the sides and once under the arm. The men wore shorter dresses, which had a pocket fastened to them. The skins from which their dresses were made were, from the neck to the elbow, exceedingly fine and white. They all looked very noble and beautiful in their clothing. They had huts in those days, partly sunk in the earth and covered with plants. Their household was quite well-arranged. I saw orchards of low, but tolerably vigorous fruit trees. There was grain also, such as wheat, which God had given to Adam for seed.

I do not remember having seen either grapevines or wheat in Paradise. None of the productions of Paradise had to be prepared for eating. Such preparation is a consequence of sin and, therefore, a symbol of labor and suffering. God gave to Adam whatever it was necessary for him to sow. I remember having seen men who looked like angels, taking something to Noe when he went into the ark. It appeared to me to be a vine branch stuck in an apple.

A certain kind of grain grew wild at that time, and among it Adam had to sow the good wheat. That improved it for awhile, but it again degenerated and became worse and worse. The wild grain was excel-

lent in those early times. It was most luxuriant further to the east, in India or China, where as yet
there were but few inhabitants. It does not thrive
where wine is largely made and fish abound.
The milk of animals was drunk in those days, and
they likewise ate cheese dried in the sun. Among the
animals, I noticed sheep in particular. All that Adam
had named followed him from Paradise, but afterward they fled from him. He had to entice them back
with food, that is the domestic animals, and famil-
iarize them to himself. I saw birds hopping about,
little animals running around, and all sorts of bound-
ing creatures, such as antelopes, deer, etc.

The household order was quite patriarchal. I saw
Adam's children in their separate huts, reclining
around a stone at meals. I saw them also praying
and giving thanks.

God had taught Adam to offer sacrifice; he was
the priest in his family. Cain and Abel also were
priests. I saw that even the preparations for their
sacrifice took place in a separate hut.

On the head, they wore caps made of leaves and
their stalks woven together. They were shaped like
a ship and had a rim in front by which they could
be raised from the head. Those first human beings
had beautiful skin of a yellowish tinge, which shone
like silk, and their hair was reddish-yellow like gold.
Adam wore his hair long. His beard was short at
first, but later he let it grow. Eve at first wore her
long hair hanging around her; but later on she wound
it around her head in a coil like a cap.

Fire I always saw like a hidden flame, and it
appeared to be in the earth. It was given to man
from Heaven, and God Himself taught him the use
of it. They burned for fuel a yellow substance that
looked like earth. I saw no cooking going on. In the
beginning, the food was merely dried in the sun; and
the wheat, after being crushed, was exposed under
twisted covers to the heat of the sun to dry. God

gave them wheat, barley, and rye, and taught them how to cultivate them. He guided man in all things. I saw no large rivers in the beginning as, for instance, the Jordan; but fountains sprang forth whose waters were conducted into reservoirs. Flesh meat was not eaten before Abel's death. I once had a vision of Mount Calvary. I saw on it a prophet, the companion of Elias. The mount was at that time full of caves and sepulchers. The prophet entered one of the caves and from a stone coffin filled with bones he took up the skull of Adam. Instantly an angel appeared before him, saying: "That is Adam's skull," and he forbade its removal. Scattered over the skull was some thin yellow hair. From the prophet's account of what had occurred, the spot was named "The Place of Skulls" (Calvary). Christ's Cross stood in a straight line above that skull at the time of His Crucifixion. I was interiorly instructed that the spot upon which the skull rests is the middle point of the earth. I was told the distance east, south, and west in numbers, but I have forgotten them.

5. Cain. The Children of God. The Giants

I saw that Cain conceived on Mount Olivet the design to murder Abel. After the deed, he wandered about the same spot frightened and distracted planting trees and tearing them up again. Then I saw a majestic Figure in the form of a man refulgent with light appear to him. "Cain," He said, "where is thy brother Abel?" Cain did not at first see the Figure; but when he did, he turned and answered: "I know not. He has not been given in charge to me." But when God replied that Abel's blood cried to Him from the earth, Cain grew more troubled, and I saw that he disputed long with God. God told him that he should be cursed upon the earth, that it should bring forth no fruit for him, and that he should forthwith flee from the land in which he then dwelt. Cain

responded that everywhere his fellow men would seek
to kill him. There were already many people upon
the earth. Cain was very old and had children. Abel
also left children, and there were other brothers and
sisters, the children of Adam. But God replied that
it would not be so; that whoever should kill Cain
should himself be punished sevenfold, and He placed
a sign upon him that no one should slay him. Cain's
posterity gradually became colored. Cham's children
also were browner than those of Sem. The nobler
races were always of a lighter color. They who were
distinguished by a particular mark engendered children of the same stamp; and as corruption increased,
the mark also increased until at last it covered the
whole body, and people became darker and darker.
But yet in the beginning there were no people perfectly black; they became so only by degrees.

God pointed out to Cain a region to which he should
flee. And because Cain said: "Then, wilt Thou let me
starve?"—(the earth was for him accursed)—God
answered no, that he should eat the flesh of animals.
He told him likewise that a nation would arise from
him, and that good also would come from him. Before
this men ate no flesh.

Cain went forth and built a city, which he named
after his son Henoch.

Abel was slain in the valley of Josaphat opposite
Mount Calvary. Numerous murders and evil deeds
took place there at a subsequent period. Cain slew
Abel with a kind of club that he used to break soft
stones and earth when planting in the fields. The
club must have been of hard stone, for it was shaped
like a pickaxe, the handle of wood.

We must not picture to ourselves the earth before
the Deluge as it is now. Palestine was by no means
so broken up by valleys and ravines. Plains were far
more extensive, and single mountains less lofty. The
Mount of Olives was at that time only a gentle rising. The Crib Cave of Bethlehem was as later a wild

cavern, but the surroundings were different. The people of those early times were larger, though not out of proportion. We would regard them with astonishment, but not with fright, for they were far more beautiful in form than people of a later period. Among the old marble statues that I see in many places lying in subterranean caves, may be found similar figures.

Cain led his children and grandchildren to the region pointed out to him, and there they separated. Of Cain himself, I have never seen anything more that was sinful. His punishment appeared to consist in hard, but fruitless labor. Nothing in which he was personally engaged succeeded. I saw that he was mocked and reviled by his children and grandchildren, treated badly in every way. And yet they followed him as their leader, though as one accursed. I saw that Cain was severely punished, but not damned.

One of Cain's descendants was Thubalcain, the originator of numerous arts, and the father of the giants. I have frequently seen that, when the angels fell, a certain number had a moment of repentance and did not in consequence fall as low as the others. Later on, these fallen spirits took up their abode on a high, desolate, and wholly inaccessible mountain whose site at the time of the Deluge became a sea, the Black Sea, I think. They were permitted to exercise their evil influence upon men in proportion as the latter strayed further from God. After the Deluge they disappeared from that region, and were confined to the air. They will not be cast into Hell before the last day.

I saw Cain's descendants becoming more and more godless and sensual. They settled further and further up that mountain ridge where were the fallen spirits. Those spirits took possession of many of the women, ruled them completely, and taught them all sorts of seductive arts. Their children were very large.

They possessed a quickness, an aptitude for everything, and they gave themselves up entirely to the
wicked spirits as their instruments. And so arose on
this mountain and spread far around, a wicked race
which by violence and seduction sought to entangle
Seth's posterity likewise in their own corrupt ways.
Then God declared to Noe His intention to send the
Deluge. During the building of the ark, Noe had to
suffer terribly from those people.

I have seen many things connected with the race
of giants. They could with ease carry enormous stones
high up the mountain, they could accomplish the
most stupendous feats. They could walk straight up
trees and walls just as I have seen others possessed
by the devil doing. They could effect the most wonderful things, they could do whatever they wished;
but all was pure jugglery and delusion due to the
agency of the demon. It is for that reason that I have
such horror of every species of jugglery and fortune-
telling. These people could form all kinds of images
out of stone and metal; but of the knowledge of God
they had no longer a trace. They sought their gods
in the creatures around them. I have seen them
scratch up a stone, form it into an extravagant image,
and then adore it. They worshipped also a frightful
animal and all kinds of ignoble things. They knew
all things, they could see all things, they were skilled
in the preparing of poisons, they practiced sorcery
and every species of wickedness. The women invented
music. I saw them going around among the better
tribes trying to seduce them to their own abominations. They had no dwelling houses, no cities, but
they raised massive round towers of shining stone.
Under those towers were little structures leading
into great caverns wherein they carried on their horrible wickedness. From the roofs of these structures,
the surrounding country could be seen, and by mounting up into the towers and looking through tubes,
one could see far into the distance. But it was not

like looking through tubes made to bring distant objects into view. The power of the tubes to which I here allude, was effected by satanic agency. They that looked through them could see where the other tribes were settled. Then they marched against them, overcame them, and lawlessly carried all before them. That same spirit of lawlessness they exercised everywhere. I saw them sacrificing children by burying them alive in the earth. God overthrew that mountain at the time of the Deluge.

Henoch, Noe's ancestor, opposed that wicked race by his teachings. He wrote much. Henoch was a very good man and one very grateful to God. In many parts of the open fields, he raised altars of stone and there the fruits of the earth flourished. He gave thanks to God and offered sacrifice to Him. Chiefly in his family was religion preserved and handed down to Noe. Henoch was taken up to Paradise. There he waits at the entrance gate, whence with another *(Elias)* he will come again before the last day.

Cham's descendants likewise had similar relations with the evil spirits after the Deluge, and from such connection sprang so many demoniacs and necromancers, so many mighty ones of the world, so many great, wild, daring men.

Semiramis herself was the offspring of demoniacs, consequently she was apt at everything save the working out of her salvation.

Later on, there arose another people esteemed as gods by the heathens. The women that first allowed themselves to be ruled by evil spirits were fully conscious of the fact, though others were ignorant of it. These women had it *(the principle of possession)* in them like flesh and blood, like original sin.

6. Noe and His Posterity. Hom and Dsemschid, Leaders of the People

I saw Noe, a simple-hearted old man, clothed in a long white garment. He was walking about in an orchard and pruning the trees with a crooked bone knife. A cloud hovered over him and in it was a human Figure. Noe fell on his knees. I saw that he was, then and there, interiorly instructed upon God's design to destroy mankind, and he was commanded to build an ark. I saw that Noe grew sad at the announcement, and that he prayed for the punishment to be averted. He did not begin the work at once. Again the Lord appeared to him, twice in succession, commanding him to begin the building, otherwise he should perish with the rest of mankind. At last, I saw Noe removing with all his family to the country in which Zoroaster, the Shining Star, subsequently dwelt. Noe settled in a high, woody, solitary region where he and his numerous followers lived under tents. Here he raised an altar and offered sacrifice to the Lord. Neither Noe nor any of his family built permanent houses, because they put faith in the prophecy of the Deluge. But the godless nations around laid massive foundations, marked off courts, and erected all kinds of buildings designed to resist the inroads of time and the attacks of an enemy.

There were frightful deeds upon the earth in those days. Men delivered themselves up to all kinds of wickedness, even the most unnatural. They plundered one another and carried off whatever suited them best, they laid waste homes and fields, they kidnapped women and maidens. In proportion to their increase in numbers, was the wickedness of Noe's posterity. They even robbed and insulted Noe himself. They had not fallen into this state of base degradation from want of civilization. They were not wild and barbarous; rather, they lived commodiously and had well-ordered households—but they were deeply imbued with wickedness. They practiced the most shameful idolatry, everyone making his own god of whatever pleased him best. By diabolical arts, they sought to seduce Noe's immediate family. Mosoch, the son of Japhet and grandson of Noe, was thus corrupted after he had, while working in the field, taken from them a poisonous beverage which intoxicated him. It was not wine, but the juice of a plant which they were accustomed to drink in small quantities during their work, and whose leaves and fruit they chewed. Mosoch became the father of a son, who was named Hom.

When the child was born, Mosoch begged his brother Thubal to take it, and thus hide his guilt. Thubal did so out of fraternal affection. The child, with the stalks and sprouts of a certain viscous root, was laid by his mother before Thubal's tent. She hoped thereby to acquire a right over his inheritance; but the Deluge was already at hand, and so her plans were fruitless. Thubal took the boy and had him reared in his family without betraying his origin. And so it happened in this way that the child was taken into the ark. Thubal called the boy Hom, the name of the root whose sprouts lay near him as the only sign. The child was not nourished with milk, but with the same root. If that plant is allowed to grow up straight, it will reach the height of a man; but when it creeps along the ground, it sends up shoots like the asparagus, hard with tender tops. It is used as food and as a substitute for milk. The root is bulbous, and from it rises a crown of a few brown leaves. Its stem is tolerably thick and the pith is used as meal, cooked like pap or spread in thin layers and baked. Wherever it thrives, it grows luxuriantly and covers leagues of ground. I saw it in the ark.

It was long before the ark was completed, for Noe often discontinued it for years at a time. Three times did God warn him to proceed with it. Each time Noe would engage workmen, recommence and again discontinue in the hope that God would relent. But at last the work was finished.

I saw that in the ark, as in the Cross, there were four kinds of wood: palm, olive, cedar, and cypress. I saw the wood felled and hewed upon the spot, and Noe bearing it himself upon his shoulders to the place of building, just as Jesus afterward carried the wood of His Cross. The spot chosen for the construction of the ark was a hill surrounded by a valley. First the bottom was put in.

The ark was rounded in the back and the keel, shaped like a trough, was smeared with pitch. It had two stories supported on hollow posts, which stood one above another. These posts were not round trunks of trees; they were in oval sections filled with a white pith which became fibrous toward the center. The trunk was knotty, or furrowed, and the great leaves grew around it without branches. *(Probably a species of palm.)* I saw the workmen punching the pith out with a tool. All other trees were cut into thin planks. When Noe had carried all the materials to the appointed spot and arranged them in order, the building was begun. The bottom was put in and pitched, the first row of posts raised, and the holes in which they stood filled up with pitch. Then came the second floor with another row of posts for the third floor, and then the roof. The spaces between the posts were filled in with brown and yellow laths placed crosswise, the holes and chinks being stuffed with a kind of wool found on certain trees and plants, and a white moss that grows very abundantly around some trees. Then all was pitched inside and outside. The roof was rounded. The entrance between the two windows was in the center of one side, a little more than halfway up. In the middle of the roof likewise was a square aperture. When the ark had been entirely covered with pitch, it shone like a mirror in the sun. Noe went on working alone and for a long time at the different compartments for the animals, as all were to be separate. Two passages extended through the middle of the ark, and back in the oval part, concealed by hangings, stood a wooden altar, the table of which was semicircular. A little in the front of the altar was a pan of coals. This was their fire. Right and left, were spaces partitioned off for sleeping apartments. All kinds of chests and utensils were carried into the ark, and numerous seeds, plants, and shrubs were put into earth around the walls, which were soon covered with verdure. I saw something like vines carried in, and on them large yellow grapes, the bunches as long as one's arm.

No words can express what Noe endured from the malice and ill will of the workmen during the whole time that the ark was building. They mocked him, they insulted him in every way, they called him a fool. He paid them well in cattle, but that did not prevent their reviling him. No one knew why he was building the ark, therefore did they ridicule him. When all was finished, I saw Noe giving thanks to God, who then appeared to him. He told him to take a reed pipe and call all the animals from the four corners of the globe. The nearer the day of chastisement approached, the darker grew the heavens. Frightful anxiety took possession of the whole earth; the sun no longer showed his face, and the roar of the thunder was unceasingly heard. I saw Noe going a short distance north, south, east, and west, and blowing upon his reed pipe. The animals came flocking at the sound and entered the ark in order, two by two, male and female. They went in by a plank laid from the entrance to the ground. When all were safe inside, the plank also was hoisted in. The largest animals, white elephants and camels, went in first. They were restless as at the approach of a storm, and it took several days for them all to enter. The birds flew in through the skylight and perched under the roof on poles and in cages, while the waterfowl went into the bottom of the vessel. The land animals were in the middle story. Of such as are slaughtered, there were seven couples.

The ark, lying there by itself on the top of the hill, shone with a bluish light. At a distance, it looked as if it were descending from the clouds. And now the time for the Deluge drew nigh. Noe had already announced it to his family. He took with him into the ark Sem, Cham, and Japhet with their wives and their children. There were in the ark grandsons from fifty to eighty years old with their children small and large. All that had labored at its construction and who were good and free from idolatry, entered with Noe. There were over one hundred people in the ark, and they were necessary to give daily food to the animals and to clean after them. I must say, for I always see it so, that Sem's, Cham's and Japhet's children all went into the ark. There were many little boys and girls in it, in fact all of Noe's family that were good. Holy Scripture mentions only three of Adam's children, Cain, Abel, and Seth; and yet I see many others among them, and I always see them in pairs, boys and girls. And so too, in *I Peter* 3:20, only eight souls are mentioned as saved in the ark; viz., the four ancestral couples by whom, after the Deluge, the earth was to be peopled. I also saw Hom in the ark. The child was fastened by a skin into a bark cradle formed like a trough. I saw many infants cradled in a similar way, floating on the waters of the Deluge.

When the ark rose on the waters, when crowds of people upon the surrounding mountains and in the high trees were weeping and lamenting, when the waters were covered with the floating bodies of the drowned and with uprooted trees, Noe and his family were already safe inside. Before he and his wife, his three sons and their wives entered the ark, he once more implored God's mercy. When all had entered, Noe drew in the plank and made fast the door. He left outside near relatives and their families who, during the building of the ark, had separated from him. Then burst forth a fearful tempest. The light-

nings played in fiery columns, the rains fell in torrents, and the hill upon which the ark stood soon
became an island. The misery was great, so great
that I trust it was the means of many a soul's salvation. I saw a devil, black and hideous, with pointed
jaws and a long tail, going to and fro through the
tempest and tempting men to despair. Toads and serpents sought a hiding place in the crevices of the
ark. Flies and vermin I saw not. They came into existence later to torment men.

I saw Noe offering sacrifice in the ark upon an
altar covered with red over which was a white cloth.
In an arched chest were preserved the bones of Adam.
During prayer and sacrifice, Noe laid them on the
altar. I saw on the altar, likewise, the Chalice of the
Last Supper which, during the building of the ark,
had been brought to Noe by three figures in long
white garments. They looked like the three men that
announced to Abraham the birth of a son. They came
from a city that was destroyed at the time of the Deluge. They addressed Noe as one whose fame had
reached them, and told him that he should take with
him into the ark a mysterious something that they
gave him, in order that it might escape the waters
of the Deluge. The mysterious thing was that Chalice. In it lay a grain of wheat, large as a sunflower
seed, and a vine branch. Noe stuck both into a yellow apple and put it into the Chalice. The Chalice
had no cover, for the branch was to grow out of it.
After the dispersion of men at the building of the
Tower of Babel, I saw that Chalice in the possession
of one of Sem's descendants in the country of Semiramis. He was the ancestor of the Samanenses, who
were established at Canaan by Melchisedech. Hither
they took the Chalice.

I saw the ark driving over the waters, and dead
bodies floating around. It rested upon a high rocky
peak of a mountain chain far to the east of Syria,
and there it remained for a long time. I saw that

land was already appearing. It looked like mud covered with a greenish mold.

Immediately after the Deluge, fish and shellfish began to be eaten. Afterward, as people multiplied, they ate bread and birds. They planted gardens, and the soil was so fruitful that the wheat which they sowed produced ears as large as those of maize. The root from which Hom received his name was also planted. Noe's tent stood on the spot where, at a later period, was that of Abraham. In the plain and in the surrounding country, Noe's sons had their tents.

I saw the cursing of Cham. But Sem and Japhet received from Noe on their knees the Blessing. It was delivered to them with ceremonies similar to those used by Abraham when giving over the same Blessing to Isaac. I saw the curse pronounced by Noe upon Cham moving toward the latter like a black cloud and obscuring him. His skin lost its whiteness, he grew darker. His sin was the sin of sacrilege, the sin of one who would forcibly enter the Ark of the Covenant. I saw a most corrupt race descend from Cham and sink deeper and deeper in darkness. I see that the black, idolatrous, stupid nations are the descendants of Cham. Their color is due, not to the rays of the sun, but to the dark source whence those degraded races sprang.

It would be impossible for me to say how I beheld the nations increasing and extending and, in many different ways, falling into darkness and corruption. But with all that, many luminous rays streamed forth from them and sought the light.

When Thubal, the son of Japhet, with his own children and those of his brother Mosoch, sought counsel of Noe as to the country to which they should migrate, they were fifteen families in number, Noe's children already extended far around, and the families of Thubal and Mosoch also dwelt at some distance from Noe. But when Noe's children began to quarrel and oppress one another, Thubal desired to remove still farther off. He wanted to have nothing to do with Cham's descendants, who were already thinking of building the Tower. He and his family heeded not the invitation received later to engage in that undertaking, and it was declined also by the children of Sem.

Thubal with his troop of followers appeared before Noe's tent, asking for directions as to whither he should go. Noe dwelt upon a mountain range between Libanus and Caucasus. He wept when he saw Thubal and his followers, for he loved that race, because it was better, more God-fearing than others. He pointed out a region toward the northeast, charged them to be faithful to the commands of God and to the offering of sacrifice, and made them promise to guard the purity of their descent, and not to intermingle with the descendants of Cham. He gave them girdles and breastpieces that he had had in the ark. The heads of the families were to wear them when engaged in divine service and performing marriage ceremonies, in order to guard against malediction and a depraved posterity. The ceremonies used by Noe when offering sacrifice, reminded me of the Holy Sacrifice of the Mass. There were alternate prayers and responses, and Noe moved from place to place at the altar and bowed reverently. He gave them likewise a leathern bag containing a vessel made of bark, in which was an oval golden box enclosing three other smaller vessels. They also received from him the roots or bulbs of that Hom plant, rolls of bark or skins upon which were written characters, and round wooden blocks upon which signs were engraved.

These people were of a bright, reddish-yellow complexion, and very beautiful. They were clothed in skins and woolen garments girdled at the waist, the arms alone bare. The skins they wore were scarcely drawn from the animal when they were clapped, still bloody, on the limbs. They fitted so tightly that my first thought was: Those people are hairy. Not so how-

ever, for their own skin was smooth as satin. With
the exception of various kinds of seed, they did not
take much baggage with them, since they were departing for a high region toward the northeast. I saw no
camels, but they had horses, asses, and animals with
spreading horns like stags. I saw them, Thubal's followers, on a high mountain where they dwelt one
above another in long, low huts like arbors. I saw
them digging the ground, planting, and setting out
trees in rows. The opposite side of the mountain was
cold. Later on the whole region became much colder.
In consequence of this change in the climate, one of
the grandsons of Thubal, the ancestor Dsemschid, led
them further toward the southwest. With a few excep-
tions, all who had seen Noe and had taken leave of
him died in this place, that is, on the mountain to
which Thubal had led them. They who followed Dsemschid were all born on the same mountain. They took
with them the few surviving old men who had known
Noe, carrying them very carefully in litters.

When Thubal with his family separated from Noe,
I saw among them that child of Mosoch, Hom, who
had gone with Thubal into the ark. Hom was already
grown, and later on I saw him very different from
those around him. He was of large stature like a
giant, and of a very serious, peculiar turn of mind.
He wore a long robe, he was like a priest. He used
to go alone to the summit of the mountain and there
spend night after night. He observed the stars and
practiced magic. He was taught by the devil to arrange
what he saw in vision into a science, a religion, and
thereby he vitiated and counteracted the teaching of
Henoch. The evil inclinations inherited from his
mother mingled in him with the pure hereditary teachings of Henoch and Noe, to which the children of
Thubal clung. Hom, by his false visions and revelations, misinterpreted and changed the ancient truth.
He studied and pondered, watched the stars and had
visions which, by Satan's agency, showed him deformed

images of truth. Through their resemblance to truth, his doctrine and idolatry became the mothers of heresy. Thubal was a good man. Hom's manner of acting and his teaching were very displeasing to Thubal, who was greatly grieved to see one of his sons, the father of Dsemschid, attach himself to Hom. I heard Thubal complaining: "My children are not united. Would that I had not separated from Noe!"

Hom conducted the waters of two springs from the higher part of the mountain down to the dwellings. They soon united into one stream which, after a short course, swelled into a broad torrent. I saw Dsemschid and his followers crossing it at their departure. Hom received almost divine homage from his followers. He taught them that God exists in fire. He had also much to do with water, and with that viscous root from which he derived his name. He planted it, and solemnly distributed it as a sacred medicine and nourishment. This distribution at last, became a ceremony of religion. He carried its juice or pap around with him in a brown vessel like a mortar. The axes were of the same material. They got them from people of another tribe that lived far away in a mountainous country and forged such implements by means of fire. I saw them on a mountain from which fire burst forth, sometimes in one place, sometimes in another. I think the vessel which Hom carried around with him was made out of the melted metal or rock that flowed from the mountain, and which was caught in a mold. Hom never married nor did he live to be very old. He published many of his visions referring to his own death. He himself put faith in them as did also Derketo and his other followers at a later period. But I saw him dying a frightful death, and the evil one carried him off body and soul; nothing remained of him. For that reason his followers thought, that, like Henoch, he had been taken up to a holy dwelling place. The father of Dsemschid had been a pupil of Hom, and Hom left him his spirit in order that he might then be the one who would succeed him.

On account of his knowledge, Dsemschid became the leader of his people. They soon became a nation, and were led by Dsemschid still further south. Dsemschid was very distinguished; he was well-educated, and had embraced Hom's teachings. He was unspeakably lively and vigorous, much more active and better also than Hom, who was of a dark, rigid disposition. He practiced the religion formulated by Hom, added many things of his own thereto, and gave much attention to the stars. His followers regarded fire as sacred. They were all distinguished by a certain sign which denoted their race. People at that time kept together in tribes; they did not intermingle then as now. Dsemschid's special aim was to improve the races and maintain them in their original purity; he separated and transplanted them as seemed best to him. He left them perfectly free, and yet they were very submissive to him. The descendants of those races, whom I now see wild and barbarous in distant lands and islands, are not to be compared with their progenitors in point of personal beauty or manly character; for those early nations were noble and simple, yet withal most valiant. The races of the present day are also far less skillful and clever, and possess less bodily strength.

On his marches, Dsemschid laid the foundations of tent cities, marked off fields, made long roads of stone, and formed settlements here and there of certain numbers of men and women, to whom he gave animals, trees, and plants. He rode around large tracks of land, striking into the earth with an instrument which he always carried in his hand, and his people then set to work in those places, grubbing and hacking, making hedges and digging ditches. Dsemschid was remarkably strict and just. I saw him as a tall old man, very thin and of a yellowish-red complexion. He rode a surprisingly nimble little animal with slender legs and black and yellow stripes, very much like an ass. Dsemschid rode around a tract of land just as our poor people go around a field on the heath by night, and thus appropriated it for cultivation. He paused here and there, plunged his grubbing axe into the ground or drove in a stake to mark the sites of future settlements. The instrument, which was afterward called Dsemschid's golden plough share, was in form like a Latin cross. It was about the length of one's arm and, when drawn out, formed with the shaft a right angle. With this instrument, Dsemschid made fissures in the earth. A representation of the same appeared on the side of his robe where pockets generally are. It reminded me of the symbol of office that Joseph and Aseneth always carried in Egypt, and with which they also surveyed the land, though that of Dsemschid was more like a cross. On the upper part was a ring into which it could be run.

Dsemschid wore a mantle that fell backward from the front. From his girdle to the knee hung four leathern flaps, two behind and two before, strapped at the side and fastened under the knee. His feet were bound with leather and straps. He wore a golden shield on his breast. He had several similar breastplates to suit various solemnities. His crown was a pointed circlet of gold. The point in front was higher and bent like a little horn, and on the end of it waved something like a little flag.

Dsemschid constantly spoke of Henoch. He knew that he had been taken away from the earth without undergoing death. He taught that Henoch had delivered over to Noe all goodness and all truth, had appointed him the father and guardian of all blessings, and that from Noe all these blessings had passed over to himself. He wore about him a golden egg-shaped vessel in which, as he said, was contained something precious that had been preserved by Noe in the ark, and which had been handed down to himself. Wherever he pitched his tent, there the golden vessel was placed on a column, and over it, on elegant posts carved with all kinds of figures, a covering was stretched. It looked like a little temple. The cover of the vessel was a crown of filigree work. When Dsemschid lighted fire, he threw into it something that he took out of the vessel. The vessel had indeed been used in the ark, for Noe had preserved the fire in it; but it was now the treasured idol of Dsemschid and his people. When it was set up, fire burned before it to which prayers were offered and animals sacrificed, for Dsemschid taught that the great God dwells in light and fire, and that He has many inferior gods and spirits serving Him.

All submitted to Dsemschid. He established colonies of men and women here and there, gave them herds and permitted them to plant and build. They were now allowed to follow their own pleasure in the matter of marriage, for Dsemschid treated them like cattle, assigning wives to his followers in accordance with his own views. He himself had several. One was very beautiful and of a better family than the others. Dsemschid destined his son by her to be his successor. By his orders, great round towers were built, which were ascended by steps for the purpose of observing the stars. The women lived apart and in subjection. They wore short garments, the bodice and breast of material like leather, and some kind of stuff hung behind. Around the neck and over the shoulders they wore a full, circular cloak, which fell below the knee. On the shoulders and breast, it was ornamented with signs or letters. From every country that he settled, Dsemschid caused straight roads to be made in the direction of Babel.

Dsemschid always led his people to uninhabited regions, where there were no nations to expel. He marched everywhere with perfect freedom, for he was only a founder, a settler. His race was of a bright reddish yellow complexion like ochre, very handsome people. All were marked in order to distinguish the pure from these of mixed descent. Dsemschid marched over a high mountain covered with ice. I do not remember how he succeeded in crossing, but many of his followers perished. They had horses or asses; Dsemschid rode on a little striped animal. A change of climate had driven them from their country. It became too cold for them, but it is warmer there now. Occasionally he met on his march a helpless tribe either escaping from the tyranny of their chief, or awaiting in distress the advent of some leader. They willingly submitted to Dsemschid, for he was gentle, and he brought them grain and blessings. They were destitute exiles who, like Job, had been plundered and banished. I saw some poor people who had no fire and who were obliged to bake their bread on hot stones in the sun. When Dsemschid gave them fire, they looked upon him as a god. He fell in with another tribe that sacrificed children who were deformed or who did not reach their standard of beauty. The little ones were buried up to the waist, and a fire kindled around them. Dsemschid abolished this custom. He delivered many poor children, whom he placed in a tent and confided to the care of some women. He afterward made use of them, here and there, as servants. He was very careful to keep the genealogical line pure.

Dsemschid first marched in a southwesterly direction, keeping the Prophet Mountain to the south on his left; then he turned to the south, the mountain still on his left, but to the east. I think he afterward crossed the Caucasus. At that period, when those regions were swarming with human beings, when all was life and activity, our countries were but forests, wildernesses, and marshes; only off toward the east might be met a small, wandering tribe. The Shining Star (Zoroaster), who lived long after, was descended from Dsemschid's son, whose teachings he revived. Dsemschid wrote all kinds of laws on bark and tables of stone. One long letter often stood for a whole sentence. Their language was as yet the primitive one,

to which ours still bears some resemblance. Dsemschid lived just prior to Derketo and her daughter,
the mother of Semiramis. He did not go to Babel himself, though his career ran in that direction.

I saw the history of Hom and Dsemschid as Jesus
spoke of it before the pagan philosophers, at Lanifa
in the isle of Cyprus. These philosophers had in Jesus'
presence spoken of Dsemschid as the most ancient of
the wise kings who had come from far beyond India.
With a golden dagger received from God, he had divided
off and peopled many lands, and had scattered blessings everywhere. They questioned Jesus about him
and the various wonders related to him. Jesus
responded to their questions by saying that Dsemschid was by nature a prudent man, a man wise according to flesh and blood; that he had been a leader
of the nations; that upon the dispersion of men at the
building of the Tower of Babel, he had led one race
and settled countries according to a certain order; that
there had been other leaders of that kind who had,
indeed, led a worse life than he, because his race had
not fallen into so great ignorance as many others. But
Jesus showed them also what fables had been written about him and that he was a false side picture,
a counterfeit type of the priest and king Melchisedech.
He told them to notice the difference between Dsemschid's race and that of Abraham. As the stream of
nations moved along, God had sent Melchisedech to
the best families, to lead and unite them, to prepare
for them lands and abiding places, in order that they
might preserve themselves unsullied and, in proportion to their degree of worthiness, be found more or
less fit to receive the grace of the Promise. Who
Melchisedech was, Jesus left to themselves to determine; but of one thing they might be certain, he was
an ancient type of the future, but then fast approaching fulfillment of the Promise. The sacrifice of bread
and wine which he had offered would be fulfilled and
perfected, and would continue till the end of time.

7. The Tower of Babel

The building of the Tower of Babel was the work of pride. The builders aimed at constructing something according to their own ideas, and thus resist the guidance of God. When the children of Noe had become very numerous, the proudest and most experienced among them met to resolve upon the execution of some work so great and so strong as to be the wonder of all ages to come and cause the builders to be spoken of as the most skillful, the most powerful of men. They thought not of God, they sought only their own glory. Had it been otherwise, as I was distinctly told, God would have allowed their undertaking to succeed. The children of Sem took no active part in the work. They dwelt in a level country where palm trees and similar choice fruit grow. They were, however, obliged to contribute something toward the building, for they did not dwell so far distant at that period as they did later. The descendants of Cham and Japhet alone were engaged in the work; and because the Semites refused to join them, they called them a stupid race. The Semites were less numerous than the children of Cham and Japhet, and among them the family of Heber and the ancestors of Abraham studiously refrained from encouraging the enterprise. Upon Heber who, as we have said, took no part in the work, God cast His eyes; and amid the general disorder and corruption, He set him and his posterity apart as a holy nation. God gave him also a new and holy language possessed by no other nation, that thereby his race should be cut off from communication with all others. This language was the pure Hebrew, or Chaldaic. The first tongue, the mother tongue, spoken by Adam, Sem, and Noe, was different, and it is now extant only in isolated dialects. Its first pure offshoots are the Zend, the sacred tongue of India, and the language of the Bactrians. In those languages, words may be found exactly similar to the Low German of my native place. The book that I see in modern Ctesiphon, on the Tigris, is written in that language. Heber was still living at the time of Semiramis. His grandfather Arphaxad was the favorite son of Sem. He was a man of great judgment and full of profound wisdom. But a good deal of idolatrous worship and sorcery may have been handed down by him. The Magi derive their origin from him.

The Tower of Babel was built upon rising ground, about two leagues in circumference, around which lay an extensive plain covered with fields, gardens, and trees. To the foundations of the Tower, that is up to its first story, twenty-five very broad stone walks led from all sides of the plain. Twenty-five tribes were engaged in the building, and each tribe had its own road to the Tower. Off in the distance, where these roads began, each tribe had its own particular city that, in time of danger or attack, they might flee to the Tower for shelter. The Tower was intended likewise to serve as a temple for their idolatrous worship. The stone roads were, where they took their rise in the plain, tolerably far apart; but around the Tower, they lay so close that the intervening spaces were not greater than the breadth of a wide street. Before reaching the Tower, they were connected by cross arches, and between every two there opened a gateway about ten feet wide into its base. When these gently inclined roads had reached a certain height, they were pierced by single arcades. Near the Tower the arcades were double, one above the other, so that through them one could make the circuit of the building, even around the lowest part, under all the roads. Above the arches that connected the inclined roads were walks, or streets, running horizontally around the Tower.

Those gently rising roads extended like the roots of a tree. They were designed in part, as supporting counter-pillars to strengthen the foundation of the immense building, and partly as roads for the conveyance from all points of building materials and other loads to the first story of the Tower.

Between these extended bases were encampments upon substructures of stone. In many places the tops of the tents rose above the roads that ran through them. From every encampment, steps cut in the walls led up to the walks. One could go all around the Tower through the encampments and arches and under the stone roads.

Besides the occupants of the encampments, there were others who lived in the vaults and spaces on either side of the stone roads. In and around the whole building swarmed innumerable living beings. It was like a huge anthill. Countless elephants, asses, and camels toiled up and down the roads with their heavy burdens. Although these burdens were far broader than the animals themselves, yet several could with ease pass one another on the roads. On them were halting places for feeding and unloading the animals, also tents on the level spaces and even factories. I saw animals without a guide bearing their burdens up and down. The gateways in the basement of the Tower led into a labyrinth of halls, passages, and chambers. From this lower part of the Tower, one could mount by steps cut out on all sides. A spiral walk wound from the first story around the exterior of the polygonal building. The interior at this point consisted of cellars, immense and secure, covered chambers and passages.

The building was begun on all sides at once. All tended to one central point where at first stood a large encampment. They used tiles, also immense hewed stones, which they hauled to the site. The surface of the walks was quite white, and it glistened in the sun. At a distance, the sight it presented was wonderful. The Tower was planned most skillfully. I was told that it would have been finished and would now be standing as a magnificent monument of human skill, had it been erected to the honor of God. But the builders thought not of God. Their work was the offspring of presumption. The names of those that had contributed to the grandeur and magnificence of the building were inscribed with words of praise in the vaults and on the pillars; in the former by means of different colored stones, and on the latter in large characters. There were no kings, but only the heads of the different families, and they ruled according to common counsel. The stones employed in the building were skillfully wrought. They fitted into one another, held one another together. There were no raised figures on the building, but many parts of it were inlaid with colored stones and, here and there, were figures hewn in niches. Canals and cisterns were constructed for water supplies. All lent a helping hand, even the women trod the clay with their feet. The men worked with breast and arms bare, the most distinguished wearing a little cap with a button. Even in very early times, women kept the head covered.

The building so increased in bulk and height that, on account of the shade it cast, it was quite cold on one side, while on the other the reflection of the sun's rays made it very hot. For thirty years, the work went on. They were at the second story. They had already encircled and walled in the interior with towerlike columns, had already recorded their names and races thereon in colored stones when the confusion broke forth. I saw one sent by God, Melchisedech, going around among the leaders and the masters of the building. He called upon them to account for their conduct, and he announced to them the chastisement of God. And now began the confusion. Many who had up to this time worked on peaceably, now boasted their skill and the great services they had rendered in the undertaking. They formed parties, they laid claim to certain privileges. This occasioned contradictions, animosities, and rebellion.

There were at first only two tribes among the disaffected and these, it was resolved, should be put down; but soon it was discovered that disunion existed among all. They struggled among themselves, they slew one another, they could no longer make themselves understood by one another, and so at last they separated and scattered over the whole earth. I saw Sem's race going farther southward where later on was Abraham's home. I saw one of Sem's race. He was a good man, but he did not follow his leader. On account of his wife, he preferred staying among the wicked ones of Babel. He became the leader of the Samanenses, a race that always held themselves aloof from others. Under the cruel Semiramis, Melchisedech transplanted them to Palestine.

When in my childhood I had the vision of the building of the Tower, I used to reject it because I could not understand it. I had, of course, seen nothing like it, no buildings but our farmhouses *whence the cows go out by the chimney,*[1] and the city of Coesfeld. More than once I thought it must be Heaven. But I had the vision again and again, and always in the same way I see it still, and I have also seen how it looked in Job's time.

One of the chief leaders in the Tower building was Nemrod. He was afterward honored as a deity under the name of Belus. He was the founder of the race that honored Derketo and Semiramis as goddesses. He built Babylon out of the stones of the Tower, and Semiramis greatly embellished it. He also laid the foundation of Ninive, and built substructures of stones for tent dwellings. He was a great hunter and tyrant. At that period savage animals were very numerous, and they committed fearful ravages. The hunting expeditions fitted out against them were as grand as military expeditions. They who slew these wild animals, were honored as gods. Nemrod also

---

1. That is, where the door serves as an egress for the smoke, as well as for the cows.

drove men together and subdued them. He practiced idolatry, he was full of cruelty and witchcraft, and he had many descendants. He lived to be about two hundred and seventy years old. He was of sallow complexion, and from early youth he had led a wild life. He was an instrument of Satan and very much given to star worship. Of the numerous figures and pictures that he traced in the planets and constellations, and according to which he prophesied concerning the different nations and countries, he sought to reproduce representations, which he set up as gods. The Egyptians owe their Sphinx to him, as also their many-armed and many-headed idols. For seventy years, Nemrod busied himself with the histories of these idols, with ceremonial details relative to their worship and the sacrifices to be offered them, also with the forming of the pagan priesthood. By his diabolical wisdom and power, he had subjected the races that he led to the building of the Tower. When the confusion of tongues arose, many of those tribes broke away from him, and the wildest of them followed Mesraim into Egypt. Nemrod built Babylon, subjected the country around, and laid the foundation of the Babylonian Empire. Among his numerous children were Ninus and Derketo. The last-mentioned was honored as a goddess.

8. Derketo

From Derketo to Semiramis, I saw three generations of daughters. Derketo was a tall, powerful woman. I saw her clothed in skins with numerous straps and animals' tails hanging about her. Her head was covered by a cap made of the feathers of birds. I saw her with a great train of followers, male and female, sallying forth from the neighborhood of Babylon. She was constantly in vision, or engaged in prophesying, offering sacrifice, founding cities, or roving about. She and her followers drove before them scattered tribes with their herds, prophesied on the subject of good dwelling places, piled up stones some of which were immense, offered sacrifice, and practiced all kinds of wickedness. She drew all to herself. She was sometimes here, sometimes there. She was everywhere honored. She had in her old age a daughter, who played a part similar to her own. I saw this vision in a plain, by which was signified the origin of the abomination. Lastly, I saw Derketo as a frightful old woman in a city by the sea. She was again carrying on her sorcery by the seashore. She was in a state of diabolical ecstasy, and she was proclaiming to her people that she must die for them, give her life for them. She told them that she could remain with them no longer, but that she would be transformed into a fish and as such be always near them. She gave directions for the worship to be paid her and, in presence of the assembled multitude, plunged into the sea. Soon after a fish arose above the waves, and the people saluted it with sacrifices and abominations of all kinds. Their divinations were full of mysteries, signs, etc., connected with water. Through Derketo's instrumentality, an entire system of idolatry arose.

After Derketo, I saw another woman, the daughter of Derketo. She appeared to me on a low mountain, which signified that her position was more powerful than that of her mother. This was still in Nemrod's time, for they belonged to the same age. I saw this daughter leading a life even wilder and more violent than her mother's had been. She was engaged most of her time in hunting, attended by crowds of followers. She often went to a distance of three hundred miles, pursued wild animals, offered sacrifice, practiced witchcraft, and prophesied. In this way numerous places were founded and idolatrous worship established. I saw this woman fall into the sea while struggling with a hippopotamus.

Her daughter Semiramis I saw upon a lofty mountain surrounded by all the kingdoms and treasures of the world, as if Satan were showing them to her, giving them to her. I saw that Semiramis put the finishing touch to every abomination of the Babylonian race.

In the earliest times power over others was held more peaceably and was vested in many; later on unlimited jurisdiction was possessed by single individuals. These latter then became the leaders, the gods of their followers, and they formulated various systems of idolatrous worship, each according to his own ideas. They could also perform wonders of skill, valor, and invention, for they were full of the spirit of darkness. Thence arose whole tribes, first rulers and priests combined, later of priests alone. I have seen that, in those days, women of this stamp were more numerous than men. They were all in interior communication, connected with one another by feelings, thoughts, and influence. Many things narrated of them are imperfect recitals of their ecstatic, or mesmeric expressions relative to themselves, their origin, their doings uttered sometimes by themselves, at others by their devilish clairvoyants. The Jews also had many secret arts in Egypt. But Moses, the seer of God, rooted them out. Among the rabbis, however, many such things existed as points of learning. Later on these secret arts became low, vulgar practices among wandering tribes, and they still exist in witchcraft and superstition. But they have all sprung from the same tree of corruption, from the same low kingdom of darkness. I see the visions of all that engage in such practices either just above or entirely under the earth. There is an element of the same in magnetism.

Water was held specially sacred by those early idolaters. It entered into all their service. Whether divinations or ecstasies, they always began by a gazing into water. They had ponds consecrated to that purpose. After some time, their ecstatic state became habitual, and even without the aid of water they had their evil visions. I have seen the way in which they had those visions and it was indeed singular. The whole earth with all that it contains seemed to be once more under water, but veiled as in a dark sphere. Tree stood under tree, mountain under mountain, water under water. I saw that those enchantresses beheld all that was going on: wars, nations, perils, etc., just as is done at the present day, only with this difference that the former put what they saw into effect, made good what they saw. Here was a nation to be subdued, here one to be taken by surprise, there a city to be built. Here were famous men and women, and there was the plan by which they might be outwitted; in fine, every item of their diabolical worship was seen before reduced to practice by those females. Derketo saw in vision that she should cast herself into the sea and be transformed into a fish, and what she saw, she hesitated not to carry into effect. Even the abominations practiced in their worship, were all mirrored in the water before they put them into execution.

In the age in which Derketo's daughter lived, dykes and roads began to be constructed. She raided down into Egypt itself. Her whole life was one series of movings and hunting expeditions. Her adherents belonged to the tribe that had plundered Job in Arabia. The diabolical worship of Derketo's people became systematized first in Egypt. Here it took such hold that, while the witches sat in the temples and in chambers on strange-looking seats before various kinds of mirrors, their visions, communicated while actually seen, were reported by the priests to hundreds of men who engraved them upon the stone walls of caverns.

Strange that I should see all those abominable chief instruments of darkness always in unconscious communion with one another! I saw similar actions and things going on in different places among similar instruments of the evil one. The only difference among them was that which arose from the diversity of manners and customs among the several nations and the different degrees of depravity into which they had fallen. Some had not as yet sunk so deep in these abominations, and were not so far removed from the truth; those, for instance, from whom the family of Abraham and the races of Job and the Three Kings sprang, as also the star worshippers of Chaldea, and they that had the Shining Star *(Zoroaster)*.

When Jesus Christ came upon earth, when the earth was soaked with His Blood, the fierce influence of such practices was considerably diminished, and witchcraft lost much of its power. Moses was a seer from his cradle, but he was according to God and he always practiced what he saw.

Derketo, her daughter, and her granddaughter Semiramis lived to be very old, according to the general age of that time. They were tall, powerful, mighty, such as would almost frighten us in our day. They were inconceivably bold, fierce, shameless, and they carried out with astonishing assurance whatever the evil one had shown them in vision. They felt their own power, they thought themselves divinities; they were facsimiles of those furious sorcerers on the high mountain that perished in the Deluge.

It is touching to see how the holy patriarchs, although they had frequent revelations from God, had nevertheless to suffer and to struggle unremittingly in order to keep clear of the abominations that surrounded them. And again, is it affecting to remember in what secret, what painful ways salvation at last came upon earth, while all went well with demonolatry, while all things were made to subserve its interests.

When I saw all this, the immense influence exercised by those goddesses and the high worship they received over all the earth; and, on the other side, when I contemplated Mary's little band with whose symbolical picture in the cloud of Elias, the philosophers of Cyprus sought to couple their lying abominations; when I saw Jesus, the Fulfillment of all promises, poor and patient, standing before them teaching and afterward going to meet His Cross—ah, that made me inexpressibly sad! But after all, this is the history of the truth and the light ever shining in the darkness, and the darkness not comprehending it. And so it has been and so it is still, the same old story even down to our own day.

But the mercy of God is infinite. I have seen that at the time of the Deluge, many, very many were saved from eternal punishment. Fright and anguish converted them to God. They went to Purgatory, and Jesus freed them on His descent into hell.

Numbers of trees escaped being uprooted by the waters of the Deluge. I saw them thriving again, but most of them were covered, choked up by mud.

9. Semiramis

The mother of Semiramis was born in the region of Ninive. Outwardly demur, in secret she was cruel and dissolute. The father of Semiramis was a native of Syria and, like her mother, sunk in the most detestable idolatry. He was put to death after the child's birth, his murder being in some way connected with, or in consequence of their divinations. Semiramis was born far away at Ascalon, in Palestine, and then taken by pagan priests to some shepherds in a wilderness. She spent much of her time during her childhood alone on a mountain. I saw her mother and the pagan priests turning aside, when on their hunting expeditions, to visit her. I saw too the devil under various forms playing with her, like John in the desert going around with angels. I saw near her birds of brilliant plumage. They brought her all kinds of curious toys. I do not remember all that went on connected with her, but it was the most horrible idolatry. She was beautiful, full of intelligence and seductive arts, and everything succeeded with her. In obedience to certain divinations, she became the wife of one of the chief shepherds of the King of Babylon, and later on she married the King himself. This King had conquered a nation far to the north, and had dragged a part of them to his own country as slaves. Some time after when Semiramis reigned alone, many of them were oppressed by her and forced to labor at her extravagant buildings. Semiramis was looked upon as a goddess by her nation.

The hunting expeditions carried on by Semiramis's mother were wilder than those which she herself conducted. She, the mother, went about with a little army mounted on camels, striped asses, and horses. Once I saw them in Arabia toward the Red Sea, on a great hunt, at the time when Job dwelt in his city there. The huntresses were very dexterous, and they sat on horseback like men. They were fully clothed to the knee, below which the limbs were laced with straps. On the feet they wore soles with two high heels upon which were colored figures. They wore short, closely fitting jackets made of fine feathers of the most diverse hues and patterns. Crossed over the arms and breast were straps trimmed with feathers. The shoulders were covered with a cape, likewise of feathers, and set with glittering stones and pearls. On the head, they wore a kind of hat of red silk or wool. Over the face fell a veil in two halves, either of which could be used as a protection from wind and dust. A short mantle completed their costume. Their hunting weapons consisted of spears, bows, and arrows; at their side hung a shield. The savage animals had multiplied astonishingly. The hunters drove them together from all parts of immense districts and slew them. They also dug pits and covered them as snares. When the beasts fell into them, they were soon dispatched with hatchets and clubs. I saw the mother of Semiramis hunting the animal described by Job

under the name of behemoth, also tigers, lions, etc.
I saw no monkeys in those early times. I saw similar hunts upon the water, upon which idolatry and
numerous abominations were generally practiced.
The mother was outwardly not so dissolute as Semiramis, but she possessed a diabolical nature with
amazing strength and temerity. What a frightful
thing, to plunge into the sea in her struggle with that
mighty monster![1] Mounted on a dromedary, she pursued the animal, until dromedary and rider plunged
into the waves. She was honored as the goddess of
the chase and a benefactress to mankind.

Semiramis returning home from Africa after one
of her hunting or military expeditions, went to Egypt.
This kingdom had been founded by Mesraim, the
grandson of Cham, who at his coming had found there
already several scattered tribes of degenerate neighboring races. Egypt was peopled by several races, and
ruled sometimes by one, sometimes by another. When
Semiramis went to Egypt four cities were in existence. The oldest was Thebes where a lighter, a more
slender, and agile race lived than in the city of Memphis, whose inhabitants were short and thickset. It
lay upon the left bank of the Nile, over which was a
long bridge. On the right bank was the place where
in Moses's time Pharao's daughter lived. The darker
inhabitants with woolly hair were even in those first
ages, slaves, and they had never ruled in Egypt. They
that first went thither and built Thebes came, I think,
from Africa; the others from over the Red Sea and
from where the Israelites entered. A third city was
called Chume, later Heliopolis. It lies toward the north
below Thebes.

When Mary and Joseph fled to Egypt with Jesus,
I saw extraordinarily large buildings still around
this city. Lower down than Memphis, not very far
from the sea, lay the city of Sais. I think it is still

---

1. A hippopotamus.

older than Memphis. Each of these four cities had
its own king.

Semiramis was very highly honored in Egypt where,
by her intrigues and diabolical arts, she greatly contributed to the spread of idolatry. I saw her in Memphis, where human sacrifices were common, plotting
and practicing magic and astrology. I did not at this
period see the bull Apis, but I saw idols with tails
and a head like the sun. It was Semiramis who here
planned the first pyramid; it was built on the eastern bank of the Nile, not far from Memphis. The
whole nation had to assist at its construction. When
it was completed, I saw Semiramis again journeying
thither with about two hundred followers. It was for
the consecration of the building, Semiramis was honored almost as a divinity.

The pyramid happened to be constructed on marshy
ground; consequently a foundation of stupendous pillars was built for it. It was like an immense broad
bridge. The pyramid was raised upon it. One could
go around under it, as if into an immense temple
formed of columns. It was divided off into innumerable rooms, dungeons, and spacious halls. The pyramid itself up to the very summit also contained
numerous apartments, large and small, with openings like windows from which I saw flags of cloth
hanging and waving. All around the pyramid were
baths and gardens. This building was the real center of Egyptian idolatry, astrology, witchcraft, and
abominable impurity. Here children and the aged were
offered in sacrifice. Astrologers and necromancers
dwelt in the pyramid and there had their diabolical
visions. Near the baths was immense machinery for
purifying the muddy waters of the Nile. The baths
witnessed the most infamous horrors of idol worship.
I saw later on Egyptian women practicing the greatest abominations in them. This pyramid did not long
exist; it was destroyed.

The nation was frightfully superstitious. The pagan

priests were in darkness so great and so given to divination that in Heliopolis, even the dreams of the people were collected, recorded, and referred to the stars. Numerous mesmerists arose who, in their diabolical visions, confounded truth with falsehood. According to their visions, idolatry was formulated, and even the cycles of time computed. I saw that the idols Isis and Osiris were no other than Joseph and Aseneth whose coming into Egypt the astrologers foresaw in their demoniacal visions. They consequently incorporated them into their religion. When they did come, they were honored as divinities. I saw that Aseneth wept over such impiety, and wrote against it.

The scholars of the present day who write about Egypt are in gross error. They accept so many things concerning the Egyptians as history, science, and learning, which nevertheless have no other foundation than astrology and false visions. That any nation could remain as stupid and beastly as the Egyptians is a proof of it. But these savants reject such demoniacal inspirations and practices as impossible. They esteem the Egyptians more ancient than they really are, because in those early times they appear to have possessed such knowledge of abstruse and hidden things.

But I saw that, even at the coming of Semiramis to Memphis, these people, in their pride had designedly confused their calendar. Their ambition was to take precedence of all other nations in point of time. With this end in view, they drew up a number of complicated calendars and royal genealogical tables. By this and frequent changes in their computations, order and true chronology were lost. That this confusion might be firmly established, they perpetuated every error by inscriptions and the erection of great buildings. For a long time they reckoned the ages of father and son, as if the date of the former's demise were that of the latter's birth. The kings, who waged constant war with the priests on the subject of chronology, inserted among their forefathers the names of persons that never existed. Thus the four kings of the same name who reigned simultaneously in Thebes, Heliopolis, Memphis, and Sais, were in accordance with this design, reckoned one after the other. I saw too that once they reckoned nine hundred and seventy days to a year, and again, years were computed as months. I saw a pagan priest drawing up a chronological table in which for every five hundred years, eleven hundred were set down.

I saw these false computations of the pagan priests at the same time that I beheld Jesus teaching on the Sabbath at Aruma. Jesus, speaking before the Pharisees of the Call of Abraham and his sojourn in Egypt, exposed the errors of the Egyptian calendar. He told them that the world had now existed 4028 years. When I heard Jesus say this, He was Himself thirty-one years old.

I saw in those times, also, a people who honored Seth as a god. They made distant and perilous journeys into Arabia where they supposed his grave to be. It seems to me that the descendants of this people are still in existence, and that the Turks suffer them to pass freely through their territory on their pilgrimages to that grave.

10. Melchisedech

I have often seen Melchisedech, but never as a human being. I have always seen him as a being of another nature, as an angel, as one sent by God. I have never at any time seen any determinate dwelling place, any home, any family, any associates connected with him. I never saw him eating, drinking, or sleeping, and never did the thought occur to me that he was a mortal. He was clothed as no priest at the time on the earth, but like the angels in the heavenly Jerusalem. His robes were such as Moses, upon the command of God, afterward ordained the priestly vestments should be. I have seen Melchisedech appearing here and there, interposing and legislating the affairs of nations; as, for instance, at the celebration of victories after war, at that time waged with such cruelty. Wherever he appeared, wherever he was, he exercised an irresistible influence by his mere presence. No one opposed him, and yet he never resorted to harsh measures; even the idolaters cheerfully accepted his decisions and acted upon his advice. He had no companion of his own nature; he was entirely alone. Sometimes he had two hired couriers. They were clothed in short white garments, and they ran on before him to announce his coming. He dismissed them when their mission was over. All that he needed, he had without trouble of acquiring. They from whom he received anything could always spare what they gave. They bestowed it upon him with joy. They regarded him with reverential fear, but esteemed themselves happy to be in his company. Although the wicked found fault with him, yet they humbled themselves in his presence. Melchisedech, that being of a higher order, was regarded by the great ones of the pagan world, those sensuous, godless men, in much the same light that an extraordinarily holy man would be looked upon at the present day, if he suddenly appeared amongst us as a stranger doing good to all around.

Thus I saw Melchisedech at the court of Semiramis in Babylon, where she reigned with indescribable grandeur and magnificence. She caused immense buildings to be erected by her slaves, whom she oppressed far more severely than did Pharao the children of Jacob in Egypt. The most horrible idolatry was practiced among the Babylonians. Human victims were buried up to the neck in the earth, and thus offered in sacrifice. It is hardly credible to what a degree all kinds of luxury, magnificence, opulence, and the arts were carried. Semiramis also waged great wars; her armies were composed of countless warriors. But these wars were almost always against na-

tions off toward the east. She went not much westward. The nations toward the north were dark and
sinister-looking people.

As time went on, there arose in the kingdom of
Semiramis a numerous people of the Semitic race.
After the building of the Tower, their ancestors had
remained in Babylon. They lived as a little pastoral
tribe under tents, raised cattle, and celebrated their
religious ceremonies by night, either in an open tent
or under the starry sky. Many blessings attended them,
they were prosperous in all things, and their cattle
was always remarkably fine. Semiramis, the diabolical woman, resolved to exterminate this tribe and she
had already destroyed a great many belonging to it.
She knew from the blessing attending them that God
had merciful designs over them; therefore would she,
as an instrument of the devil, oppress them. When
the distress of these people was at its height,
Melchisedech appeared. He went to Semiramis,
demanded permission for them to depart, and rebuked
her for her cruelty. Semiramis yielded to his desires,
and he led them in different bands toward Palestine.
Melchisedech dwelt in a tent near Babylon, and here
he broke that bread to the good people from which
they received strength to depart. He pointed out to
them, here and there in Canaan, places suitable for
settlements, and they received from him lands of various quality. He divided them off according to their
purity in order that they should not mix with others.
Their name sounded like Samanen, or Semanen.
Melchisedech pointed out to some of them as suitable
for a settlement the region which was afterward the
site of the Dead Sea, but their city was destroyed
with Sodom and Gomorrha.

Semiramis received Melchisedech with great reverence. She secretly dreaded him on account of his
wisdom. He appeared before her as the King of the
Morning Star, that is of the most distant eastern land.
She fancied that he might perhaps woo her for his

bride. But he spoke to her sternly, reproached her with her cruelty, and foretold to her the destruction of her pyramid at Memphis. Semiramis grew speechless from terror, and I saw the punishment that fell upon her. She became like a beast. She was for a long time penned up, and they cast to her in derision grass and straw in a manger; only one servant was faithful to her and furnished her with food. She was freed from the chastisement, but she carried on her disorders anew. She came at last to a frightful end, her intestines being torn from her body. She was aged one hundred and seventeen years.

Melchisedech came to be regarded as a prophet, as a teacher, as a being from a higher sphere, with whom all things succeeded. There were at that time, as also later, many such apparitions of beings of a higher order. They were to the people of that age as familiar as were the angels in Abraham's time. But diabolical apparitions also were frequent, in the same way as false prophets rose up by the side of the true. The departure of the Semitic race from Babylon bears some analogy to that of the Israelites from Egypt, although the former were by no means so numerous as the latter.

Of the Samanenses whom Melchisedech settled in Palestine, I saw long before the coming of Abraham three men on the so-called Bread Mountain, in the neighborhood of Thabor. They lived in caves. They were of a browner complexion than Abraham, and were clothed in skins. They bound a great leaf on their head to protect them from the sun. Their life, modeled on that of Henoch, was a holy one. Their religion was simple, though full of mysterious signification, and they had visions and revelations which they easily interpreted. Their religion taught that God would unite Himself with man and for that union they must prepare in every possible way. They also offered sacrifice. A third part of their daily allowance they exposed to the sun, either to be consumed by it or, perhaps, for the benefit of other needy creatures. That the latter was the case, I also saw. These people lived quite solitary, apart from the rest of the inhabitants of the country. The latter were not yet numerous and lived scattered, here and there, in abodes built in the style of fortified tent cities. I saw those three men going through the country digging wells, cutting down forests, and laying the foundations of subsequent cities. I saw them driving the evil spirits from the air around whole regions and banishing them to other places, to poor, swampy, foggy districts. I saw again that the wicked spirits prefer such wretched abodes. I often saw these men wrestling with them. At first, I wondered how cities could arise where they laid stones, which so soon became overgrown, and then I had another vision in which I was shown a number of places built on these sites; for instance, Saphat, Bethsaida, Nazareth (where those three men worked on the spot upon which afterward stood the house in which the angel delivered the message to Mary); Gathepher, Sephoris (in the region near Nazareth, where Anne's house afterward stood); Mageddo, Naim, Ainon, the caves of Bethlehem and Hebron. I also saw them founding Machmethat and many other places that I have now forgotten.

I saw them every month assembling on this mountain where Melchisedech broke a large four-cornered loaf (three feet square, perhaps, and tolerably thick) into numerous little pieces which he divided among them. The loaf was of a brownish color and had been baked in the ashes. I saw that Melchisedech always went to them without a companion. Sometimes he bore the loaf quite lightly, as if it merely floated above his hand; and again when he drew near to the mountain, I saw it as a weight upon his shoulders. I think he took this precaution on approaching them that they might look upon him as merely a man. Still they met him with great reverence, prostrating before him. He taught them how to plant vines on Thabor. He also gave them all kinds of seeds, which they scattered in many parts of the country and which now grow wild there. I saw these people every day cutting a piece off the loaf with the brown spades they used at work. They also ate birds, which flew toward them in great numbers. They had festival days, and they were familiar with the stars. They celebrated the eighth day with prayer and sacrifice, also some days in the course of the year. I saw them also making numerous roads through the still wild country to the places where they had laid foundations, dug wells, and sowed seed. This they did that the people coming after them might, by following these roads, make settlements near the wells and fertile places prepared for them. I saw these three men often surrounded while at work by crowds of evil spirits, whom they could see. I saw these spirits, by prayer and the word of command, banished to swampy wastes. They departed instantly, and the men went quietly on with their work, clearing and purifying.

They made roads to Cana, Mageddo, and Naim, and in this way they prepared the birthplace of most of the Prophets. They laid the foundations of Abelmahula and Dothain, and dug out the beautiful baths at Bethulia. Melchisedech still scoured the country alone and as a stranger; no one knew where he lived.

The three Samanenses were old, but still very active. On the site of the Dead Sea and in Judea, cities already existed. There were some also further north but none as yet in the central regions.

The Samanenses dug their own graves and sometimes stretched themselves in them; one made his near Hebron, another on Thabor, and the third in the caves not far from Saphet. They were, in a certain sense, for Abraham what John was for Jesus. They purified the country, they prepared the land and the ways, they sowed good fruit, and they brought water for the leader of God's people. But John prepared the heart for penance and for a second birth in Jesus

Christ. The Samanenses did for Israel what John did for the Church. I have seen such men in other places also, where they had been introduced by Melchisedech.

I often saw Melchisedech as he appeared in Palestine long before the time of Semiramis and Abraham, when the country was still a wilderness. He seemed to be laying it out, marking off and preparing certain districts. I saw him entirely alone, and I thought: What is this man doing here so early? There is not a human being in this place! I saw him near a mountain, boring a well. It was the source of the Jordan. He had a long fine instrument which, like a ray of light, pierced the mountainside. I saw him in the same way opening fountains in different parts of the earth. In those early times, that is, before the Deluge, I never saw the rivers gushing forth and flowing as they do now, but I saw volumes of water pouring down from a high mountain in the east.

Melchisedech took possession of many parts of Palestine by marking them off. He measured off the site for the Pool of Bethsaida, and long before Jerusalem existed he laid a stone where the Temple was to stand. I saw him planting in the bed of the Jordan the twelve precious stones upon which the priests stood with the Ark of the Covenant at the departure of the children of Israel. He planted them like seeds, and they increased in size.

I always saw Melchisedech alone, save when he had to busy himself with the uniting, the separating, or the guiding of nations and families.

I saw that Melchisedech built a castle at Salem. But it was rather a tent with galleries and steps around it, like the castle of Mensor, in Arabia. The foundation alone was solid, for it was of stone. I think the four corners where the principal posts stood, were still to be seen even in John's time. It had only a very strong foundation of stone, which looked like a fortification overrun with verdure. John had there his little hut of rushes.

That tent castle was a resort for strangers and travellers, a kind of safe and convenient inn near the pleasant waters. Perhaps Melchisedech, whom I have always seen as the guide and counselor of the still unsettled races and nations, kept this castle as a place in which to harbor and instruct them. But even at that time, it bore some reference to Baptism.

This was Melchisedech's central point. From it he started on his journeys to lay out Jerusalem, to visit Abraham, and to go elsewhere. Here also he gathered together and distributed families and peoples, who settled in various places. All this took place previously to the offering of bread and wine which, I think, was made in a valley south of Jerusalem. Melchisedech built Salem before he built Jerusalem. Wherever he labored and constructed, he seemed to be laying the foundation of a future grace, to be drawing attention to that particular place, to be beginning something that would be perfected in the future.

Melchisedech belongs to the choir of angels that are set over countries and nations, that brought messages to Abraham and the other Patriarchs. They stand opposite the archangels Michael, Gabriel, and Raphael.

11. Job

The father of Job, a great leader of the nations, was brother to Phaleg, the son of Heber. Shortly before his time occurred the dispersion of men at the building of the Babylonian Tower. Job was the youngest of thirteen sons. They dwelt north of the Black Sea near a mountain chain which was warm on one side, and on the other cold and covered with ice. Job was forefather of Abraham. Abraham's mother was a great granddaughter of Job, who had married into the family of Heber. Job may have still been alive at the time of Abraham's birth. He dwelt in different places, and his afflictions came upon him in three different abodes. Between the first and the second, there intervened a

period of nine years' prosperity; between the second
and the third, seven years; and after the third, twelve
years. His sufferings always befell him in a different
dwelling place. But he never was so absolutely ruined
as to have nothing left; he merely became quite poor
when compared with his former circumstances. He
always had enough left to pay all his debts.

Job could not remain in his parents' house. His
ideas and inclinations did not accord with theirs. Job
adored in nature the one only God, especially in the
stars and in the change from day to night. He spoke
frequently of God's wonderful works, and offered to
Him a worship purer than that of those around him.
He moved with his followers northward from the Caucasus to a very miserable swampy region. I think it
is now inhabited by a nation distinguished by their
flat noses, high cheekbones, and small eyes. Here Job
first settled, and things went well with him. He gathered around him all kinds of poor, abandoned creatures who dwelt in caves and bushes, and who lived
exclusively upon the raw flesh of birds and animals
taken in hunting. Job was the first who taught them
how to cook their food. With their help he dug up
and cultivated the land. He and his people wore at
that time but little clothing and they dwelt in tents.
Job soon found himself the owner of immense herds
in this place, among them numerous striped asses
and spotted animals. Once three sons were born to
him at one birth, and three daughters at another. He
had as yet no city here, but went around among his
fields which extended to a distance of seven leagues.
No grain was cultivated in those marshy districts;
but they raised a large sedge, which grows also in
water, and whose pith was eaten either boiled or
roasted. They dried their meat in holes dug in the
earth, and exposed to the sun, until Job taught them
how to cook it. They planted many species of gourds
for food.

Job was unspeakably gentle, affable, just, and benevolent. He assisted all in need. He was, too, exceedingly pure and very familiar with God, who communicated with him through an angel, or "a white man," as the people of that period expressed it. These angelic apparitions were like radiant, but beardless, youths in long white garments that fell in heavy folds or strips around them, I could not distinguish which. They were girded, and they took food and drink. God consoled Job during his sufferings by means of these apparitions, and they passed sentence on his friends, his nephews, and his other relatives. He did not, like the nations around him, worship idols. They made for themselves images of all kinds of animals and adored them. But Job fabricated for himself a representation of the Almighty God, the figure of a child crowned with rays. The hands were held one above the other, and in one was a globe upon which was depicted a little vessel riding on the waves. I think it was to represent the Deluge of which, as well as of the wisdom and mercy of God, Job often spoke to his two confidential servants. The figure was portable and shone like metal. Job prayed before it, and burned grain before it as a sacrifice. The smoke arose from the top of it as through a funnel. It was in this place that Job's first affliction befell him. The time that intervened between the different misfortunes recorded of him, was not for him a time of peace. He always had to combat and struggle against the wicked races by whom he was surrounded. After his first affliction, he removed further up the mountain range, the Caucasus, where he again began anew and where prosperity again followed him. He and his followers now began to clothe themselves less scantily, and their mode of life exhibited more refinement.

From this, his second dwelling place, Job went, accompanied by a numerous train of followers, to Egypt where at that time strangers called shepherd kings, and who were from his own native land, governed a part of the country. These shepherd kings were afterward expelled by an Egyptian monarch. Job's mission to Egypt was to conduct thither one of his own relatives, who was to be the bride of one of the shepherd kings. He took with him rich presents, about thirty camels, and many servants. When I saw him in Egypt, Job was a large, powerful man of agreeable appearance; he had a yellowish-brown complexion and reddish hair. Abraham was fairer. The Egyptians were of a dirty brown. Job was not contented in Egypt. I used to see him looking back longingly toward the east, toward his fatherland which lay more to the south than the most distant country of the Three Kings. I heard him complaining bitterly to his servants telling them that he would rather live with wild beasts than with the people of Egypt. The horrible idolatry that everywhere prevailed in that country afflicted him. The Egyptians worshipped a frightful idol with an upraised head, like that of an ox, and broad open jaws. They heated it intensely, and laid living children as offerings on its glowing arms.

The shepherd king, for whose son Job conducted the bride into Egypt, would fain have kept him there, and he assigned to him Matarea as a dwelling place. The region was at that time very different from what it was at a later period when the Holy Family sojourned there. Still I saw that Job dwelt on the spot afterward occupied by them, and that the Fountain of Mary was already shown him by God. When Mary discovered this well, it was already lined with stone, though still covered over. Job used the stone by the well for religious worship. By prayer he freed the country around his dwelling place from wild and venomous animals. Visions referring to man's salvation were vouchsafed him here, and he saw, too, the trials in store for him. With burning zeal he exclaimed against the infamous practices of the Egyptians and their human sacrifices. I think these latter were in consequence abolished.

When Job had returned to his native country, his

second misfortune overtook him; and when, after twelve years of peace, the third came upon him, he was living more toward the south and directly eastward from Jericho. I think this country had been given to him after his second calamity, because he was everywhere greatly revered and loved for his admirable justice, his knowledge, and his fear of God. This country was a level plain, and here Job began anew. On a height, which was very fertile, noble animals of various kinds were running around, also wild camels. They caught them in the same way as we do the wild horses on the heath.

Job settled on this height. Here he prospered, became very rich, and built a city. The foundations were of stone; the dwellings were tents. It was during this period of great prosperity that his third calamity, his grievous distemper, overtook him. After enduring this affliction with great wisdom and patience, he entirely recovered, and again became the father of many sons and daughters. I think Job did not die till long after, when another nation intruded itself into the country.

Although in the Book of Job this narrative is given very differently, yet many of Job's own words are therein recorded. I think I could distinguish them all. Where the story says that the servants came quickly one after another to Job with news of his losses, it must be remarked that the words: "And as he still spoke of it," signify, "And while the last calamity was not yet effaced from the mind of men," etc.

That Satan appeared before God with the sons of God and brought an action against Job, is told in this way only for the sake of brevity. There was at that time much communication between the evil spirits and idolaters to whom they appeared in angelic form. In this way, Satan incited his wicked neighbors against Job, and they calumniated him. They said that he did not serve God properly, that he had a superfluity of possessions, and that it was very easy for him to be good. Then God resolved to show that afflictions are often only trials, etc.

The friends who spoke around Job symbolized the reflections of his kinsmen upon his fate. But Job longingly awaited the Saviour, and he was one of the ancestors of the race of David. He was to Abraham, through the mother of the latter (who was one of his descendants), what the ancestors of Anne were to Mary.

The history of Job, together with his dialogues with God, was circumstantially written down by two of his most trusty servants who seemed to be his stewards. They wrote upon bark, and from Job's own dictation. These two servants were named respectively Hai and Uis, or Ois. These narratives were held very sacred by Job's descendants. They passed from generation to generation down to Abraham. In the school of Rebecca, the Canaanites were instructed in them on account of the lessons of submission under trials from God that they inculcated.

Through Jacob and Joseph, they descended to the children of Israel in Egypt. Moses collected and arranged them differently for the use of the Israelites during their servitude in Egypt and their painful wanderings in the wilderness; for they contained many details that might not have been understood, and which would have been of no service in his time. But Solomon again entirely remodelled them, omitting many things and inserting many others of his own. And so, this once authentic history became a sacred book made up of the wisdom of Job, Moses, and Solomon. One can now only with difficulty trace the particular history of Job, for the names of cities and nations were assimilated to those of the land of Canaan, on which account Job came to be regarded as an Edomite.

12. Abraham

Abraham and his forefathers belonged to a very peculiar type of a mighty race. They led a pastoral life. They were not really natives of Ur, in Chaldea, but they had removed there. They exercised special authority and jurisdiction. Here and there, they took possession of certain regions where good pasturage was found. They marked off the boundaries, erected an altar of stones, and the land thus enclosed became their property. Something happened to Abraham in his early childhood similar to that which occurred to the child Moses by which his nurse saved his life. It had been prophesied to the ruler of the country that a wonderful child would be born whose birth would be very fatal to his interests. The ruler took measures accordingly, on which account Abraham's mother concealed herself before his birth in the same cave in which Seth had been hidden by Eve. There Abraham was born, and there secretly reared by his nurse, Maraha. She passed for a poor slave who worked in the wilderness. Her hut was near this cave, which was named after her the *Milk Cave*. She was, after her death and in accordance with her own request, buried there by Abraham.

Abraham was a remarkably large child. When, on account of his unusual size, he was of an age to pass for a child born before the prophecy alluded to, his parents took him home. But his precocious wisdom exposed him to danger, so the nurse fled with him, and again concealed him a long time in the same cave. Many children of his age were massacred at that time. Abraham tenderly loved Maraha, his nurse. In after years, in all his peregrinations he took her with him on a camel. She also dwelt with him at Socoth. She died at the age of one hundred years. Abraham hewed out a tomb for her in the white stone which, like a hill, enclosed the cave in which he was born. The cave became a place of devotion, especially for mothers. Throughout the whole of this history, we discover a mysterious prefiguring of the early persecutions which Mary with the Child Jesus had to endure. It was, too, in this same cave that they hid

from Herod's soldiers when they sought the Child.
The father of Abraham received great graces from
Heaven, and understood many mysteries. His race
possessed the gift of discovering gold in the earth,
and he fabricated out of it little idols similar to those
that Rachel purloined from Laban. Ur is a place in
the north of Chaldea. I perceived in many parts of
this region, on mountains and plains, white flames
arising, as if the ground were on fire. I know not
whether this fire was spontaneous or kindled by man.
Abraham was a great astronomer. He understood
the properties of things, and the influence of the
stars upon birth. He saw all kinds of things in the
stars, but he turned all to God. He followed God in
all things and served Him alone. He imparted his
knowledge to others in Chaldea, but he traced all
back to God.

I saw that in a vision he received from God the
order to depart from his own country. God showed
him another land, and Abraham next morning, without asking any questions, led forth all his people and
departed. I afterward saw him pitching his tent in a
region of Palestine which seemed to me to lie around
the place where Nazareth subsequently stood. Abraham himself erected here an oblong altar of stone
with a tent over it. Once when kneeling before the
altar, a light descended from Heaven upon him. An
angel, a messenger from God, appeared, said something to him, and presented to him a shining, transparent gift. The angel spoke with Abraham, and the
latter received the mysterious Blessing, the Holy
Thing from Heaven; he opened his garment and laid
it upon his breast. I was told that this was the Sacrament of the Old Testament. Abraham, as yet, knew
not what it contained. It was hidden from him, as
from us is concealed the substance of the Most Holy
Sacrament. But it was given to him as a sacred thing,
as a pledge of the promised posterity. The angel was
exactly of the same kind as the one that announced

to the Blessed Virgin the conception of the Messiah. He was also as gentle and tranquil as Gabriel in the execution of his commission, not so hasty and rapid as I see other angels under similar circumstances. I think Abraham always carried the mysterious gift about with him. The angel spoke to him of Melchisedech who was to celebrate before him the sacrifice which, after the coming of the Messiah, would be accomplished, and which should be continued forever.

Abraham then took from a casket five large bones which he laid upon the altar in the form of a cross. A light burned before it, and he offered sacrifice. The fire burned like a star, the center white and the rays red.

I also saw Abraham with Sara in Egypt. He went thither in obedience to a command from God; first, on account of the famine; and, secondly, to take possession of a treasure which had been carried there by one of Sara's relatives. The treasure consisted of triangular pieces of gold strung together to form a genealogical table of the children of Noe, and especially of Sem down to Abraham's own time. It had been taken into Egypt by a daughter of Sara's maternal aunt, who had gone thither with a pastoral tribe, some of Job's lateral descendants, who afterward degenerated into a wild state. She had there hired herself as a servant. She had stolen that treasure as later on Rachel did the gods of Laban. The genealogical table was made like the scales of a balance hanging on cords. The latter consisted of small triangular pieces strung together, and from them depended single collateral strings. On the gold pieces were figures and letters denoting Noe's, and especially Sem's descendants. When the cords were let down, the various pieces all lay together in the dish. I heard, but I have forgotten, the number of shekels (so the sum is called) to which the whole amounted. This family register had fallen into the hands of Pharao and the priests. They made on it various reckonings connected with their own unending chronological calculations, but they never rightly understood it.

When Pharao was visited by heavy afflictions he consulted with his idolatrous priests, and granted to Abraham all he demanded.

Upon Abraham's return to Palestine, I saw Lot by him in a tent. Abraham was pointing all around with his hand. In his bearing there was something of the deportment of the Three Kings. He wore a long white, woollen garment with sleeves; a plaited white girdle with tassels; and a sort of cowl hanging down the back. On his head was a small cap, and upon his breast a shield in the shape of a heart made of metal or precious stones. His beard was long. I have no words to say how kind and generous Abraham was. If he had anything that pleased another, especially if it were cattle, he offered it to him at once, for he was a declared enemy to envy and covetousness. Lot's clothing was almost like that of Abraham, but he was not so tall, nor so noble-looking. He was indeed, good, but at the same time a little covetous. I often saw the servants of the two disputing, and I saw Lot separating from Abraham. But as he went, I saw him enveloped in fog. Over Abraham, I saw light. I saw him take down his tents and wander about. He built an altar of field stones, and raised a tent over it. The people of that time were skillful in building out of rough stones, and the master with the servant put his hand to the work. The altar just mentioned was in the region of Hebron, the subsequent dwelling place of Zacharias, the father of the Baptist. The region to which Lot removed was very good, as was all this part of the country toward the Jordan. I saw the cities around Lot's dwelling place plundered, and Lot himself with all his goods and chattels carried off. I saw a fugitive bear the news to Abraham, who immediately invoked the aid of Heaven. Then gathering his servants together, he surprised the enemy and freed his brother. The latter thanked him gratefully, and was full of regret for having separated from him. The enemy and the warriors in general, especially the giants, were not clothed like Abraham's followers. Their garments were narrower and shorter; their dress was in many pieces, covered with buttons, stars, and other ornaments. The giants were extraordinarily large people. They brutally and insolently carried off all they could lay their hands upon, but they were often obliged to yield their booty to others who plundered them in turn.

13. Melchisedech's Sacrifice of Bread and Wine

I often saw Melchisedech with Abraham. He appeared to him in the same way as did the angels at different times. Once he commanded him a triple sacrifice of doves and other birds, and he prophesied concerning Sodom and Lot. He told him that he would come to him again to sacrifice bread and wine, and he indicated to him, also, for what he should pray to God. Abraham was full of reverence before Melchisedech, and he eagerly awaited the promised sacrifice. As a preparation for it, he built a very beautiful altar and surrounded it with an arbor. When about to come for the sacrifice of bread and wine, Melchisedech sent messengers to command Abraham to make his coming known and to announce him as the King of Salem. Abraham went out to meet him. He knelt before him and received his blessing. This took place in a valley southward from the fertile vale that lies toward Gaza.

Melchisedech came from the region where Jerusalem afterward stood. He had with him a very nimble animal of a gray color. It had a short, broad neck, and it was laden on both sides. On one was a vessel of wine, flat on the side that lay against the beast; on the other, was a box containing rows of flat, oval loaves, likewise the Chalice that I afterward saw

used at the Last Supper for the institution of the
Blessed Sacrament. It had cups in the shape of little barrels. These vessels were neither of gold nor silver, but transparent as of brownish precious stones.
They did not appear to me to have been fabricated
by man, they looked as if they had grown. The impression made by Melchisedech was similar to that produced by the Lord during His teaching life. He was
very tall and slight, remarkably mild and earnest.
He wore a long garment so white and shining that
it reminded me of the white raiment that surrounded
the Lord at His Transfiguration. Abraham's white
garment was quite dingy compared with it. He wore
also a girdle with letters similar to that worn later
by the Jewish priests, and like them his head was
covered with a small gothic miter during the sacrifice. His hair was shining yellow like long glittering
strands of silk, and his countenance was luminous.

Upon Melchisedech's arrival, he found the King of
Sodom already with Abraham in his tent, and around
were numbers of people with animals, sacks, and
chests. All were very grave and solemn, full of reverence for Melchisedech whose presence inspired awe.
He stepped to the altar, which was a kind of tabernacle, wherein he placed the Chalice. There was also
a recess in it, I think for the sacrifice. Abraham had
laid upon the altar the bones of Adam which Noe had
had in the Ark. They now prayed before them that
God would fulfill the Promise made to Adam of a
future Messiah. Melchisedech spread upon the altar
first a red cover, which he had brought with him, and
over that a white transparent one. The ceremony
reminded me of the Holy Mass. I saw him elevate
the bread and wine, offer, bless, and break. He reached
to Abraham the Chalice used afterward at the Last
Supper in order that he might drink. All the rest of
those present drank from the little vessels which were
handed around by Abraham and the most distinguished personages. The bread, too, was passed around

in morsels larger than those given at Holy Communion in the early times. I saw these morsels shining. They had only been blessed, not consecrated. The angels cannot consecrate. All that partook of the food were filled with new life and drawn nearer to God.

Melchisedech gave bread and wine to Abraham, the former more luminous than that received by the others. Abraham derived from it great strength and such energy of faith that later on at the command of God, he did not hesitate to sacrifice his child of promise. He prophesied in these words: "This is not what Moses upon Sinai gives the Levites." I know not whether Abraham also offered the sacrifice of bread and wine, but I do know that the Chalice from which he drank was the same used by Jesus at the institution of the Most Holy Sacrament.

When Melchisedech at the sacrifice of bread and✓ wine blessed Abraham, he at the same time ordained him a priest. He spoke over him the words: "The Lord said to my Lord, sit thou at My right hand. Thou art a priest forever according to the order of Melchisedech. The Lord hath sworn, and He will not repent."

He laid his hands upon Abraham, and Abraham gave him tithes. I understood the deep signification of Abraham's giving tithes after his ordination. But the reason of its importance, I no longer recollect.[1]

I saw also that David, when composing this Psalm, had a vision of Abraham's ordination by Melchisedech, and that he repeated the last words prophetically. The words, "Sit thou at my right hand," have a peculiar signification. When the eternal generation of the Son from the Father was shown me in vision, I saw the Son issuing from the right side of the Father as a luminous form surrounded by a triangle, as the Eye of God is depicted, and in the upper corner I saw the Holy Ghost. But it is inexpressible!

I saw that Eve came from the right side of Adam,

---

1. See *Heb.* 7.

that the Patriarchs carried the Blessing in their right side, and that they placed the children to whom they delivered it upon their right. Jesus received the stroke of the lance in His right side, and the Church came forth from the same right side. When we enter the Church, we go into the right side of Jesus, and we are in Him united to His Heavenly Father.

I think that Melchisedech's mission upon earth was ended with this sacrifice and the ordination of Abraham, for after that I saw him no more. The Chalice with the six cups he delivered to Abraham.

14. Abraham Receives the Sacrament of the Old Covenant

Abraham sat in front of his tent under a large tree by the roadside. He was in prayer. He often sat thus waiting to show hospitality to travellers. As he prayed, he raised his eyes to Heaven and saw, as in a sunbeam, an apparition from God that announced to him the coming of the three *white men.* He arose and sacrificed a lamb on the altar, before which I saw him kneeling in ecstasy begging for the Redemption of mankind. The altar stood to the right of the large tree in a tent open at top. Further on was a second tent in which the vessels and other utensils for sacrifice were kept. It was to this last that Abraham generally retired when superintending the shepherds who dwelt around here. Still further on, and on the opposite side of the road, was the tent of Sara and her household. The females always lived apart.

Abraham's sacrifice was almost accomplished when he beheld the three angels appear on the high road. On they came in their girded garments, one after another, an even distance between them. Abraham hurried out to meet them. Bowing low before God, he saluted them, and led them to the tent of the altar. Here they let down their garments and commanded Abraham to kneel. I saw the wonderful things

that now happened to Abraham through the ministry of the angels. He was in ecstasy, and all the
actions were rapid, as is usual in such states. He
heard the first angel announce to Abraham as he
knelt that God would bring forth from his posterity
a sinless, an immaculate maiden who, while remaining an inviolate virgin, should be the mother of the
Redeemer, and that he was now to receive what Adam
had lost through sin. Then the angel offered him a
shining morsel and made him drink a luminous fluid
out of a little cup. After that he blessed him, drawing his right hand in a straight line down from Abraham's forehead, then from the right and the left
shoulder respectively down under the breast, where
the three lines of the blessing united. Then with both
hands the angel held something like a little luminous cloud toward Abraham's breast. I saw it entering into him, and I felt as if he were receiving the
Blessed Sacrament.

The second angel told Abraham that he should
before his death impart the Mystery of this Blessing to Sara's firstborn, in the same way that he had
himself received it. He informed him also that his
future grandson, Jacob, would be the father of twelve
sons from whom twelve tribes should spring. The
angel told him also that this Blessing would be withdrawn from Jacob; but that after Jacob had become
a nation, it should be again restored and placed in
the Ark of the Covenant as a Holy Thing belonging
to the whole nation. It should be theirs as long as
they gave themselves to prayer. The angel explained
to Abraham that, on account of the wickedness of
men, the Mystery would be removed from the Ark
and confided to the Patriarchs and that at last it
would be given over to a man who would be the
father of the promised Virgin. I heard also in this
promise that by six prophetesses and through star
pictures it had been made known to the heathens
that the Redemption of the world should be ac-

complished through a virgin.

All this was made known to Abraham in vision, and he saw the Virgin appear in the heavens, an angel hovering at her right and touching her lips with a branch. From the mantle of the Virgin issued the Church.

The third angel foretold to Abraham the birth of Isaac. I saw Abraham so full of joy over the promised holy Virgin and the vision he had had of her that he gave no thought to Isaac, and I think that this same promise made the command he subsequently received to sacrifice Isaac easy to him. After these holy communications, I saw first the entertainment of the angels and then the laughing of Sara. I saw Abraham escorting the angels at their departure, and I heard him supplicating for Sodom.

When Abraham awoke from ecstasy, he led the angels under the tree and placed stools around it. The angels sat down, and he washed their feet. Then Abraham hurried to Sara's tent to tell her to prepare a meal for his guests. This she did and, veiling herself, she carried it halfway to them. The meal over, Abraham accompanied the angels a short distance on their journey. It was then that Sara heard them speak to him of the birth of a son. She had approached them behind the enclosure of the tent. She laughed. I saw numbers of doves tame as hens before the tents. The meal consisted of the same kind of birds, round loaves, and honey.

Abraham at his departure from Chaldea had already received the Mystery of the Blessing from an angel, but it was given to him in a veiled manner, and was more like a pledge of fulfillment of the promise that he should be the father of an innumerable people. Now, however, the Mystery was resuscitated in him by the angels, and he was enlightened upon it.

15. Jacob

Rebecca knew that Esau had no share in the Divine Mystery. Esau was dull, rough, and slothful; Jacob was very active and shrewd, more like his mother. Isaac, however, was more partial to Esau as his first-born. Esau was often away from home hunting. Rebecca often pondered how she could procure the birthright, the Blessing, for Jacob, and she taught him how to go about buying it. The mess of pottage for which Esau sold it was composed of vegetables, meat, and green leaves like lettuce. Esau came home tired from the chase. Jacob coaxed him, and received the surrender of the birthright.

Isaac was at this time very old and blind. He feared he would soon die, and consequently he was anxious to give his Blessing over to Esau. Rebecca, who knew that Jacob should and must have it, could not persuade Isaac to give it to him. She was on that account very much afflicted, and went around quite anxious. When she found that Isaac would no longer be withheld from imparting the Blessing, and that he called to him Esau who was in the neighborhood, she laid her plans. She told Jacob to hide when his brother came in that he might not be seen. Isaac ordered Esau to go bring him something of his hunting. Then Rebecca sent Jacob to get a kid from the flock, and hardly was Esau gone when the dish for Isaac was prepared.

Esau's best clothes, which Rebecca now put upon Jacob, consisted of a jacket very like Jacob's own, only stiffer and embroidered on the breast in colors. Esau's arms and breast were covered with thick, black hair like wool, his skin being like the skin of an animal; therefore Rebecca wrapped a part of the kid's skin around Jacob's arms and put a piece upon his breast where the jacket lay open. This jacket differed from the one usually worn only by the amount of work upon it. It was slit at the sides, and passed over the head by a hole which was bound with soft, brownish leather. The side slits were fastened together with leather strings, and when a girdle was worn over it, the fullness around the breast served as a pocket. No garment was worn under this jacket, which was sleeveless and left the breast bare. The headgear and apron worn with the jacket were brownish, or gray.

I saw Isaac feeling Jacob's breast and hands where Esau was full of hair. I saw that he wavered a little, he was troubled and doubting. But then came the thought that, notwithstanding his doubts, it was certainly Esau and that God willed him to have the Blessing. And so he made over to Jacob that Blessing which he had received from Abraham, and Abraham from the angel. He had, with Rebecca's assistance, previously prepared something mystical which was connected with it; viz., a drink in a cup.

The other children of the Patriarchs knew not of it. Only the one that received the Blessing knew of the Mystery which, however, still remained to him, as to us the Blessed Sacrament, a mystery. The cup was rather flat on one side. It was transparent and shone like mother-of-pearl. It was filled with something red, something like blood, and I felt that it was Isaac's blood. Rebecca had helped to prepare it.

When Isaac blessed Jacob, they were alone. Jacob bared his breast and stood before his father. Isaac drew the hand with which he gave the Blessing from Jacob's forehead straight down to the abdomen, from the right shoulder to the same point, and the same from the left shoulder. Then he laid his right hand on Jacob's head and his left upon the pit of his stomach, and Jacob drank the contents of the little cup. And now it seemed as if Isaac delivered to him all things, all power, all strength, while with both hands he took, as it were, something out of his own person and placed it in that of Jacob. I felt that this something was his own strength, that it was the Blessing. All this time, Isaac was praying aloud. While giving over the Blessing, Isaac sat erect on his couch; he became animated, and rays of light streamed from him. When Isaac drew his hand down in giving the Blessing, Jacob held both of his open and half-raised, as the priest does at the *Dominus vobiscum;* but when the father merely prayed, Jacob kept them crossed on his breast. When Isaac delivered the Blessing to Jacob, the latter received it and crossed his hands under his breast like one who is holding something. At the close of the ceremony, Isaac laid his hands upon Jacob's head and upon the region of the stomach, and then Jacob received the cup out of which he had drunk.

When the imparting of the Blessing had been accomplished, I saw Isaac swooning, either from exertion or from having actually given over and parted with his strength. But Jacob was radiant, quickened, full of life and strength. And now came Esau from the hunt.

When Isaac discovered that the Blessing had been transferred to the wrong one, he had no regret, he recognized it to be God's will. But Esau was mad with rage, he tore his hair. Still, in his fury there seemed to be more envy of Jacob than grief for the lost Blessing.

Both Esau and Jacob were full-grown men, over forty years old at the time of the transfer of the Blessing. Esau already had two wives who were not much liked by his parents. When Rebecca saw Esau's rage, she sent Jacob away secretly to her brother Laban. I saw his departure. He wore a jacket that reached to the waist, an apron as far as the knees, sandals on his feet, and a band wrapped round his head. In his hand was a shepherd's staff, a small sack containing bread hung from his shoulder, and under his arm was a flask. This was all he took with him. I saw him hurrying off followed by the tears of his mother. Isaac had blessed him a second time, and commanded him to go to Laban, and to take a wife in his new home.

Isaac and Rebecca had much to endure from Esau. Rebecca especially had much sorrow.

I saw Jacob, on his journey to Mesopotamia, lying asleep on the spot where Bethel afterward stood. The sun had set. Jacob lay stretched on his back, a stone under his head, his staff resting on his arm. Then I saw the ladder that Jacob beheld in his dream, and which in the Bible is described as "standing upon the earth, and the top thereof touching heaven." I saw this ladder rising up to heaven from Jacob where he lay upon the earth. It was like a living genealogical tree of his posterity. I saw below on the earth, just as those genealogical trees are represented, a green trunk as if growing out of the sleeping Jacob. It divided into three branches which arose in the form of a triangular pyramid whose apex reached the heavens. The three branches were connected by other smaller ones that formed a three-sided pyramidal ladder. I saw this ladder surrounded by numerous apparitions. I saw on it Jacob's descendants, one above another; they formed the ancestry of Jesus according to the flesh. They often crossed over from side to side, stepping past and even before one another. Some stood back and others from the opposite side stepped before them, according as the germ of the Sacred Humanity was clouded by sin and then again purified by continence until at last the pure flower, the Holy Virgin in whom God willed to become Man appeared on the highest point of the ladder touching the heavens. I saw Heaven open above her and disclose the splendor of God. God spoke thence to Jacob.

I saw Jacob awake the next morning. First, he built a round foundation of stone on which he laid a flat stone, then he raised upon this the stone which he had placed under his head the preceding night. Lastly he made a fire and offered something in sacrifice; he also poured something into the fire on the stone. He knelt while praying, and I think he kindled the fire as the Three Kings did, that is, by friction.

I saw Jacob in many other places also, at Bethel for instance, as he journeyed to Laban, staff in hand. I saw him at Ainon where he had been before and where he repaired a cistern which later on became John's fountain of baptism. I saw him even at that early period, praying at the spot Mahanaim. He begged Almighty God to protect him and also to keep his clothes from becoming shabby lest, on his arrival in Mesopotamia, his uncle Laban on account of his miserable appearance might not acknowledge him. Then he beheld two troops of angels hovering on either side of him like two armies. This was shown him as a sign of God's protection over him, and of the power which should be given unto him. The fulfillment of this vision, he saw on his return journey.

Then I saw him going further eastward, along the south side of the river Jabok, and passing a night on the spot where he afterward wrestled with the angel. Here too, he had a vision.

On Jacob's return from Mesopotamia, his encampment lay east of the encampment of the subsequent Jabesh Gilead. I saw Laban, his father-in-law, following him in pursuit of his lost idols. He overtook him, and words ran high between them on the score of the idols, for Jacob did not know that Rachel had secretly brought them with her. When Rachel saw that her father, who had been searching the whole encampment for his lost treasures, would soon reach her tent, she took the stolen idols and hid them under a heap of fodder not far from her own tent. The idols were metal dolls, about two and a half arms long in swaddling clothes. The heaps of fodder were on a slope of the valley south of the Jabok, and were for the use of the camels. Rachel muffled herself up and sat down on one of them, as if she were sick and had retired for awhile. Many other women sat like her on the other heaps. On a similar, though somewhat larger straw heap, I have seen the leprous Job sitting. That on which Rachel sat was of the size of a full harvest wagon. They brought quantities of fodder with them on the camels, and on the way often laid in fresh supplies of it. These idols had long been a subject of scandal to Rachel, and she carried them off merely to disengage her father from them.

Jacob had sent messengers to Esau, of whom he was in dread. They returned with the news that Esau was at hand with four hundred men. Then Jacob divided his whole train into two bands. His best flocks he divided into several and sent them on to Esau. He led his followers to Mahanaim where he had for the second time the vision which he had seen on his setting out; viz., the vision of the angelic armies. He said: "With my staff did I set out, but I am now richer by two armies." He now understood the signification of that first vision.

When his whole train had crossed the Jabok, Jacob sent his wives and children over by night, and remained alone. Then he ordered his tent to be erected on the spot where, on his journey from Palestine, he had seen the face of God. He wanted to pray there by night. He ordered his tent to be closed on all sides, and bade his servants retire to some distance. Then I saw him crying with his whole heart to God. He laid all things before Him, especially his great anxiety with regard to Esau. The tent was open above, that he might better send forth his sighs to Heaven.

Then I saw him wrestling with the angel. It took place in a vision. Jacob arose and prayed. Then there descended from above a light in which was a great luminous figure, which began to wrestle with Jacob, as if wanting to push him out of the tent. They wrestled here and there, up and down, in all directions through the tent. The apparition acted as if wanting to draw Jacob toward all the cardinal points, but Jacob always faced about to the center of the tent. This struggle prefigured the fact that Israel, though pressed on all sides, should not be forced from Palestine.

But when Jacob once again faced to the middle of the tent, the angel grasped him by the hip. I saw this took place when Jacob, who was wrestling in vision, wanted to cast himself upon his couch, or sink back upon it. When the angel touched Jacob's hip and at the same time did what he wanted to do, he said to the latter who was holding him fast: "Let me go, for the dawn is breaking!" Then Jacob ceased struggling and awoke from his vision. Seeing the angel of God still standing before him, he cried: "No, I will not let thee go until thou bless me!" He felt the need of God's blessing, for he knew that strength had departed from him and that Esau was at hand. Then spoke the angel: "How art thou called?" (This belonged to the Blessing. Abram also at his Blessing was named Abraham). He answered: "Jacob." Then said the angel: "Thou shalt be called Israel, for thou hast wrestled with God and men and hast not been vanquished." Then Jacob said: "How art thou called?" And the angel answered: "Why dost thou ask me how I am called?"— which words signified: "Dost thou not know me? Hast thou not already learned who I am?" And Jacob knelt before him, and received the blessing. The angel blessed him as Abraham had been blessed by God, as Abraham had imparted the blessing to Isaac, and Isaac to Jacob; viz., in three lines. This blessing was especially to ensure patience and perseverance. And now the angel vanished. Jacob saw that the dawn was breaking, and he named the place Phanuel. He ordered his tent to be taken down, and he crossed the Jabok to his family. And now the sun arose upon him. He limped on the right side, for he had there been deprived of strength.

When Esau turned off, Jacob went with all his family, his servants, and his herds, to Mahanaim and took possession of the country from Socoth to the hill Ainon. He dwelt ten years at Ainon. He afterward extended his settlement westward from Ainon and over the Jordan to Salem. His tents reached to where Sichem dwelt, for there he bought a field.

I saw Dina walking around there with her maids, and conversing out of curiosity with the Sichemites. I saw Sichem caressing her, for which reason her maids went away, and he took her with him into the city. This was the cause of great sorrow to Dina while bloodshed and slaughter accrued from it to the Sichemites. Sichar[1] at that time was not yet a great city. It was built of large, square stones and had only one gate.

The Patriarchs, Abraham, Isaac, and Jacob, had more strength in their right side than in their left; it was not, however, noticeable, for their garments were wide and full. There was in their right side a certain fullness like a swelling. It was the Holy Thing, the Blessing, the Mystery. It was luminous, in shape like a bean, and it contained a germ. The firstborn received it from the father, hence the prerogatives of primogeniture. Jacob received it instead of Esau, because Rebecca knew that he was the one destined for it. In his struggle with the angel, it had been taken away from Jacob, though without producing a wound. It was like a drying up of the swelling. But after the removal of the Blessing, Jacob no longer lived so securely, so immediately under God's protection. While he possessed the Blessing, he was like one strengthened by a Sacrament; afterward, however, he felt himself humiliated, he was careworn and he experienced great troubles. He was conscious of the Blessing's having been withdrawn from him, therefore he would not let the angel go until, by a benediction, he had strengthened him. Joseph later on, when in the prison of Pharao, in Egypt, received that same Blessing from an angel.

---

1. Sichem.

16. Joseph and Aseneth

Joseph was sixteen years old when he was sold into Egypt. He was of middle height, very slender and agile, active both in body and mind. He was indeed very different from his brothers, and all felt drawn to love him. Were it not for the marked preference shown him by his father, his brothers also would have loved him. Reuben was of a more lively disposition than the others. Benjamin was a large, ungainly man, but very good-natured, easily led. Joseph wore his hair divided into three, one part on either side of his head, the third falling down behind in long curls. When ruler over Egypt, he wore it short, but afterward allowed it again to grow.

When Jacob bestowed the many-colored coat upon Joseph, he gave over to him also some of the bones of Adam, without telling him, however, what they were. Jacob gave them to Joseph as a precious talisman, for he knew well that his brothers did not love him. Joseph carried the bones on his breast in a little leathern bag rounded on top. When his brothers sold him, they took from him only the colored coat and his customary outer garment, but left the band and a sort of scapular on his breast beneath which he had hung the little bag.

The colored coat was white with broad red stripes. It had on the breast three rows of black cord crossing one another, in the center of which were yellow ornaments. It was full around the breast. When bound at the waist, the fullness served as a pocket. It was narrower toward the lower part of the skirt and had slits at the side, to render motion easier. It fell below the knee, was somewhat longer in the back and open in front. Joseph's ordinary dress did not reach to the knees.

Joseph was known to Pharao and his wife before his imprisonment. Putiphar's affairs were so flourishing under Joseph's management, Putiphar himself was so blessed during Joseph's stay under his roof, since he conducted all things so well for Pharao, that the latter was eager to see the faithful servant. Pharao's wife, who was religiously inclined and very desirous of salvation and who had, at the same time, like all the Egyptians, a great hankering after new gods, was so astounded at the wise, intelligent, extraordinary young stranger, that she honored him interiorly as a divinity. She said repeatedly to Pharao: "This man has been sent by our gods. He is not a human being like ourselves." Hence it came to pass that he was thrown, not into the common dungeon, but into the prison reserved for the nobility, and there he was made the overseer. Pharao's wife sincerely deplored his conviction as a malefactor, and thought that she had been mistaken in him. But when he was liberated and again appeared at court, she treated him with great distinction. The cup that Joseph ordered to be placed in Benjamin's sack was the first present the queen had made to him. I know it well; it had two handles, but no foot. It seemed to have been cut out of one precious stone or one solid transparent mass, I know not which, and was in shape exactly like the upper part of the Chalice used at the Last Supper. It was also among the vessels that the children of Israel took away with them from Egypt, and it was afterward preserved in the Ark of the Covenant.

Joseph was seven years in prison. During his greatest affliction, he received the mysterious Blessing of Jacob in the same manner as the Patriarchs had done. He had a vision also of a numerous posterity.

I know all about Putiphar's wife. I saw how desirous she was to pervert Joseph, but after his elevation, she did penance and became chaste and devout. She was a tall, powerful woman, her skin of a yellowish-brown and shining like silk. She wore a colored robe over which was one of figured gauze. The lower one shone through it as if through lace.

Joseph was thrown much with her, since his master's affairs were all entrusted to him. But when he became aware of the fact that she had grown more familiar in her manner toward him, he no longer remained in the house overnight during his master's absence. She often intruded herself upon him when he was busy at his writing. Once I saw her enter his presence in immodest attire. He was standing writing in one corner of a hall. (In those days, they used to write upon rolls of parchment which hung on the wall. The writer either sat or stood before them). She addressed him and he replied. Then she grew bolder, seeing which he turned hurriedly away. She grasped his mantle, but he fled leaving it in her hand.

I saw Joseph with Putiphar's pagan priests at Heliopolis. Aseneth, the daughter of Dina and the Sichemite, lived with them as a prophetess and a decorator of the idols. Seven other maidens were her companions. Putiphar had bought her from her nurse in her fifth year. This nurse had fled with her to the Red Sea by order of Jacob, that the child might not be murdered by his sons. Aseneth possessed the spirit of prophecy, and was esteemed by Putiphar as a prophetess. Joseph knew her, but he knew not that she was his niece. She was of a very earnest character, she sought seclusion, and in spite of her great beauty, she abhorred the society of men. She was favored with significant visions, was familiar with the Egyptian star worship, and had a secret presentiment of the religion of the Patriarchs. I saw no witchcraft connected with her. She saw in vision the whole mystery of life, the transplanting, the coming to, and the departure of Israel from Egypt, even the long journey through the wilderness. She wrote many rolls on the leaves of a water-plant or on skin. The letters were strange-looking, they were like the heads of birds and animals. These writings were, even during her lifetime, misunderstood by the Egyptians and

misconstrued into a sanction for their wicked abominations. Aseneth grieved deeply over this misconception brought about by the evil one, and she shed
many tears. She had more numerous visions than
any other of her time, and she was filled with won-
drous wisdom. She conducted herself gravely, and
refused advice to none. She could weave also and
embroider. Her enlightened spirit detected man's corruption of truth, therefore was she grave, reserved,
retiring, and silent.

I saw that the misconception of Aseneth's visions
and writings led to her being worshipped under the
name of Isis, and Joseph under that of Osiris. This
perhaps was the cause of her abundant tears. She
also wrote against their erroneous conception of her
visions which had led to their proclaiming her the
mother of all the gods.

When Putiphar offered sacrifice, Aseneth ascended
a tower upon which she seemed to be, as it were, in
a little garden. Here she gazed upon the stars by
moonlight. She fell into ecstasy, and read all things
clearly in the stars. The truth was shown her in pictures, because she was chosen of God. I have seen
the pagan priests introduced into strange, diabolical
worlds where they beheld the most abominable
things. By such diabolical visions were the secret
communications of Aseneth disfigured and made to
contribute to the abominations of idolatry.

Aseneth introduced many useful arts and domestic animals into Egypt, among the latter, for instance,
the cow. She taught the art of making cheese, that
of weaving, and many others hitherto unknown to
the inhabitants. She also healed many diseases. The
plow was introduced by Joseph, who was himself
skilled in its use. There was one thing that seemed
truly wonderful to me. Aseneth ordered the flesh of
the numerous animals slaughtered for sacrifice to be
boiled down until it became a gelatinous mass, which
served for food on campaigns and in times of scar-

city. The operation was carried on in the open air and
in caldrons in the earth. The Egyptians were rejoiced
and amazed at this new mode of procuring food.
When Joseph met Aseneth at the pagan priest's
dwelling, she approached to embrace him. This she
did not through boldness, but impelled by the Spirit.
It was in her a kind of prophetic action, and took
place in presence of the pagan priest. Aseneth was
looked upon as holy. But I saw Joseph keep her off
with outstretched hand and address earnest words
to her. Then Aseneth, deeply agitated, retired to her
own room where she remained in tears and penance.

I saw her in her chamber. She stood concealed by
a curtain, her wealth of long and beautiful hair falling
around her and curling at the ends. There was
impressed on the skin of the pit of her stomach a
wonderful sign. In a figure like a heart-shaped shell
stood a child with outstretched arms, holding in one
hand a small dish, in the other a cup, or chalice. In
the dish, were three young ears of corn that appeared
to be just breaking out of the husk, and the figure
of a dove which seemed to peck after the grapes in
the cup held by the child. Jacob knew of this sign;
but notwithstanding, he had to send the child away
in order to shield her from the rage of his sons. But
when he came down into Egypt, and Joseph told him
all things, he recognized his granddaughter by this
mark. Joseph, too, had a mark of the same kind upon
his breast, a very full bunch of grapes.

Now I saw an angel appear in resplendent raiment, holding a lotus in his hand. He saluted Aseneth.
She glanced at him and drew her veil around her.
He commanded her to dry her tears, to adorn herself in festal robes, and he also requested her to
bring him food. She left the room and returned
adorned as directed, bringing with her a low table,
small and light, upon which were wine and little flat
loaves that had been baked in ashes. Aseneth evinced
no fear. She was not shy, but simple and humble,

just like Abraham and the other Patriarchs when treating with apparitions. When the angel now spoke to her, she unveiled. He asked her for some honey, but she replied that, unlike other maidens who are fond of it, she had none. Thereupon the angel told her that she would find some among the idols that stood in the chamber. These idols were of various forms; they had heads of animals and for bodies serpents coiled downward.

Aseneth looked, and found a beautiful, coarse-celled honeycomb, white as the Host of our altars. She set it before the angel, who bade her eat of it. He blessed it, and I saw it shining and flashing between them. I cannot now express the signification of this heavenly honey; for when one sees such things, it is just as they actually are, one knows all. But now, when I try to recall it, the honey appears to be what is called honey, yet I know not what the flowers, the bees, and the honey properly signified. I can only say this much: Aseneth really possessed in herself only bread and wine (or that which is typified by bread and wine), but she had no honey. By the reception of this honey, she issued from idolatry into the light of Israel, into salvation through the Old Law. It signified also that she should aid many souls, that many like bees should build around her. I heard her say that she would drink no more wine, for that now she was more in need of honey. I saw numbers of bees and vast stores of honey in Midian near Jethro.

In blessing the honeycomb, the angel directed his finger toward all regions of the world, which signified that, by her presence, her types, and the mystery of its own, the honey's signification, Aseneth should be a mother and a leader. When later on she was honored as a divinity and represented with numerous breasts, it was in consequence of the misconception of her vision that she should nourish many.

The angel told her that she was destined to be

united with Joseph, that she should be his bride, and he blessed her as Isaac had blessed Jacob and as the angel had blessed Abraham. The three lines that constituted the formula of the blessing, were drawn upon her twice, once to the pit of the stomach and once to the abdomen.

After this, I saw in vision Joseph going to Putiphar to demand Aseneth for his wife; but I can only remember that, like the angel, he carried a lotus in his hand. Joseph knew of Aseneth's wonderful wisdom, but their mutual relationship was hidden from both.

I saw that Pharao's son likewise was in love with Aseneth, on which account she had to remain secluded. He had persuaded Dan and Gad to espouse his cause, and all three lay in ambush to slay Joseph. But Juda (obeying a divine inspiration, I think) warned Joseph to take another route. Benjamin also conducted himself nobly in this affair, and defended Aseneth. Dan and Gad were punished by the death of their children; for even before it was known to anyone, they had been warned not to enlist in the murderous design.

When Joseph and Aseneth appeared in public, like the pagan priests of Putiphar, they bore in their hand a sign regarded as sacred and emblematic of the highest authority. The upper part was a ring; the lower, a Latin cross, a T. It served as a seal, and when grain was measured and divided the heaps were marked with it. It was used in the same way for the building of granaries and canals, also for the rising and falling of the Nile. Writings were sealed with it after they had first been marked with a red vegetable juice. When Joseph discharged any official duty, this symbol of authority, the cross being clasped in the ring, lay on a cushion at his side. It seemed to me also like a distinctive sign of the mystery of the Ark of the Covenant still enclosed in Joseph.

Aseneth also had an instrument like a wand. When in vision, she followed wherever it led. Where it quivered she struck the earth, and so discovered springs and water. It was made under the influence of the stars.

In the processions of high festivals, Joseph and Aseneth rode upon a glittering chariot. Aseneth wore an ancient shield which enclosed the whole person from below the arms. On it were numerous signs and figures. Her dress reached to her knees, below which the limbs were tightly laced. A wide mantle fell over the back, the sides of which were clasped together over the knees. The toes of her shoes were turned up like skates, and her headdress of colored feathers and pearls was shaped like a helmet.

Joseph wore a tight-fitting coat with sleeves, and over it a golden breastplate covered with figures. Straps with golden knots were crossed around the hips, and from his shoulders fell a mantle. His head ornament was of feathers and precious stones.

When Joseph went to Egypt, New Memphis was being built about seven leagues north of Old Memphis. Between the two cities, built on a dyke, was a highway with walks. Scattered among the trees were idols with grave, sad female faces and bodies of dogs. They sat upon stone slabs. There were as yet no beautiful buildings, only great, long ramparts and artificial stone mountains *(pyramids)* full of vaults and chambers. The dwellings were slight with a superstructure of wood. There were still great forests and morasses all around. At the flight of Mary into Egypt, the Nile had already changed its course.

The Egyptians worshipped all kinds of animals: toads, serpents, crocodiles. They looked on quite coolly while a person was being devoured by a crocodile. At Joseph's coming, the worship of the bull had not yet come into practice. It was introduced in consequence of Pharao's dream of the seven fat and the seven lean cows. They had numerous kinds of idols; some like swaddled children, others like coiled serpents, some of which could be made longer or shorter at pleasure.

A great many of the idols were adorned with breast-plates on which the plans of cities and the course of the Nile were curiously inscribed. These shields were made in accordance with the pictures which the pagan priests traced in the stars, and after whose plan they built cities and canals. New Memphis was founded in this way.

The evil spirits at that time must have possessed a different, a more material power, for I saw that Egyptian sorcery came out of the earth, out of the abyss. When a pagan priest began his enchantments, I saw figures of all kinds of ugly animals arise out of the ground around the sorcerer and enter his mouth in a current of black vapor. He became thereby entranced and clear-sighted. It was as if, at the entrance of each spirit, a world hitherto closed was opened up to him and he saw things far and near, the abysses of the earth, countries, human beings, in fine, all things over which each particular spirit exerted an influence. Modern witchcraft always appears to me to be more under the influence of the spirits of the air. What the wizard saw by the aid of these spirits appeared like a delusion, a mirage, which they conjured up before him. I could see far beyond these pictures, for they were like shadows. It was as if one looked behind a curtain.

When the Egyptian pagan priests intended to read the stars, they fasted as a preparation, performed certain purifications, clothed themselves in sackcloth, and sprinkled themselves with ashes. While they gazed upon the stars from their tower, sacrifices were offered. The pagans of those times had a confused knowledge of the religious mysteries of the true God which had been handed down from Seth, Henoch, Noe, and the Patriarchs to the chosen people, there-fore were there so many abominations in their idol-atry. The devil made use of them, as later on of heresy, to weave the pure, unclouded, authentic revelations of God into a snare for man's destruction. Therefore

God enveloped the Mystery of the Ark of the Covenant in fire in order to preserve it. The women of Egypt in Joseph's time were still clothed like Semiramis.

When Jacob went into Egypt to Joseph, he pursued the same route through the wilderness by which later on Moses journeyed to the Promised Land. Jacob knew that he would see Joseph again; he always had a presentiment of this in his heart. He had even on this journey to Mesopotamia at the place upon which he erected the altar (not where he saw the ladder) a vision of his future sons. One he saw, in the region where Joseph was sold, sink from sight and like a star rise again in the south. He exclaimed therefore when they brought him the bloodstained coat, the foregoing circumstance almost forgotten recurring to him: "I shall weep for Joseph until I find him again."

Jacob had, through Reuben, made many inquiries as to whom Joseph had married, but had not yet been entirely enlightened on the point that Joseph's wife was his own niece. Reuben and Putiphar were old acquaintances. Owing to the influence of the former, the latter received circumcision and served the God of Jacob.

Jacob dwelt about a day's journey distant from Joseph. When he fell sick, Joseph drove in a chariot to see him. Jacob questioned him closely about Aseneth and, when he heard of the sign on her person, he exclaimed: "She is flesh of thy flesh. She is bone of thy bone!" and he revealed to Joseph who she was. Joseph was so deeply affected that he almost lost consciousness. On his return home, he told his wife, and both shed tears to their heart's content over the news.

Some time after, Jacob grew worse, and Joseph was again by his side. Jacob put his feet from the couch to the floor, and Joseph had to lay his hand under his father's hip, and swear to bury him in Canaan. While Joseph swore, Jacob adored the Blessing hidden in him, for he knew that Joseph had received from an angel the Blessing that had been withdrawn from himself. Joseph bore this Blessing in his right side until death. Even after death, it lay enclosed in his body until the night before the departure of the Israelites, when Moses took possession of it and placed it in the Ark of the Covenant, together with the remains of Joseph, as the Sacred Thing of the chosen people.

Three months after his visit, Jacob died. Both Jews and Egyptians celebrated his obsequies and sounded his praises, for he was greatly loved.

Aseneth bore to Joseph first Manasses and Ephraim, then other children, in all eighteen, among them several twins. She died three years before Joseph, and was embalmed by Jewish women. As long as Joseph lived, her body stood in his own monument. But the ancients of the people had taken some part of her intestines which they preserved in a little golden figure; and as the Egyptians also aspired to its possession, it was entrusted to the Jewish midwives. One of these women placed it in a reed box smeared with pitch and concealed it in the bulrushes near the canal. On the night of the Departure, a nurse of the tribe of Aser brought this secret thing to Moses. The woman's name was Sara.

Joseph, at his death, was embalmed by the Jews in presence of the Egyptians. Then were placed together the remains of Joseph and Aseneth in compliance with the notes that the latter had made from her visions and had left to the Jews. The Egyptian priests and astrologers had placed Joseph and Aseneth among their own divinities. They had some inkling of the notes left by Aseneth and a presentiment of the high influence, the blessing that she and Joseph would be for Israel. But that blessing they coveted for themselves, and therefore, they sought to oppress Israel. It was on this account that the Israelites, who multiplied astonishingly after Joseph's death, were so harrassed by Pharao. The Egyptians knew well that the Israelites would not leave the country without the bones of Joseph; consequently at several different times they stole some of the remains of Joseph and at last got entire possession of them. The Jewish people at large knew only of Joseph's corpse, but not of the Mystery that it contained. That was known to only a few. But the entire nation grieved deeply when the ancients found out and made known to them that the Holy Thing upon which the Promise rested had been stolen. Moses, who had been reared at Pharao's court in all the Egyptian wisdom, visited his people and learned the cause of their grief. When he murdered the Egyptian, God ordained that as a fugitive he should go to Jethro, since the latter by his connection with Syble Segola would be able to help him to discover the purloined Mystery. Moses had, also, at the command of God, married Sephora in order to incorporate that family into the house of Israel.

Segola was the natural daughter of Pharao by a Jewish mother. Although reared in the Egyptian star worship, she was very fond of the Jews. It was she that had divulged to Moses while still at court that he was not a son of Pharao.

Aaron, after the death of his first wife, had to marry a daughter of this Segola, in order that the mother's influence with the Israelites might be increased. The children of this marriage went with the Israelites at their departure from Egypt. But Aaron was obliged to separate from his wife that the Aaronic priesthood might spring from a purely Jewish stock. Segola's daughter, after her separation from Aaron, married again. Her descendants, at the time of the Saviour, dwelt at Abila whither her mummy had been brought by them.

Segola was very enlightened and possessed great influence over Pharao. She had on her forehead a bump such as many of the Prophets had in olden times. She was led by the Spirit to procure numerous favors and gifts for the Israelites.

On the night upon which the angel of the Lord struck the firstborn of the Egyptians, Segola, wrapped in her veil, accompanied Moses, Aaron, and three other Israelites to two sepulchral mounds which were separated by a canal over which lay a bridge. The canal flowed between Memphis and Gosen into the Nile. The entrance into the mounds was under the bridge and below the surface of the water. Steps led from the bridge down to it. Segola descended alone with Moses. She cast into the water a scrap of paper upon which was inscribed the name of God. The water retreated and left the entrance to the monument free. They struck on the stone door and it opened inward. Then they called to the others to come down. When they did so, Moses bound their hands together with his stole and made them swear to protect the Mystery. After the oath, he loosed their hands, and all entered the vault where they struck a light, which showed all kinds of passages with images of the dead standing therein.

Joseph's body, with the remains of Aseneth, lay in an Egyptian tauriform, metal coffin, which shone like polished gold. The back formed a cover. This they lifted off, and Moses took the Mystery out of the hollow body of Joseph, wrapped it in cloths, and handed it to Segola who carried it in her arms concealed under her garments. The remaining bones were placed together upon a stone, wrapped in cloths, and carried away by the men. Now that they had gained possession of the Sacred Thing, Israel could depart from the country. Segola wept, but Israel was full of joy.

Moses concealed a relic of Joseph's body in the top of his staff. This top was in form like a medlar, or persimmon; it was yellowish and surrounded by leaves. It was different from the shepherd's staff that Moses was commanded to cast on the ground before God and which was there changed to a serpent. It was a reed, the upper and the lower end could be pushed in and drawn out. With the lower point, which appeared to me to be of metal and which was in form like a sharp pencil, Moses touched the rock as if tracing words upon it. The rock opened under the point, and water gushed forth. Water flowed also from the sand wherever Moses made signs upon it with this staff. The upper part of the reed staff, in shape like a medlar, could be pushed in and drawn out; before it the Red Sea divided.

From Joseph's death to the departure of Israel from Egypt, there were about one hundred and seventy years according to our manner of reckoning. But they had at that time another way of reckoning, other weeks and years. This was often explained to me, but I cannot now recall it.

While the Israelites lived in Egypt, they had no temple, but only tents. They piled up stones, poured oil over them, sacrificed grain and lambs, sang, and prayed.

17. The Ark of the Covenant

On the same night that Moses took possession of the Holy Thing, a golden casket shaped like a coffin was prepared, in which at their departure the Israelites took it with them. It must have been large enough for a man to rest in it, for it was to become a church, a body. This was the night upon which the doorposts were signed with blood. As I witnessed the rapid working at the chest, I thought of the Holy Cross which, too, was hurriedly put together on the night before the death of Jesus. The chest was of gold plate and shaped like an Egyptian mummiform coffin, broad above and narrow below. On the upper part was a picture of a face surrounded by beams. On the sides were marked the length of the arms and the position of the ribs.

In the center of this coffin-like chest, was placed

a little golden casket wherein was contained the Holy Thing which Segola had taken out of the sepulchral vault. In the lower part of the chest were sacred vessels, among them the chalice and cups of the Patriarchs which Abraham had received from Melchisedech and which with the Blessing had been entailed upon the firstborn. This was the first form of the Ark of the Covenant, and these were its first contents. It had two covers, the lower one red, the upper one white.

Only afterward on Mount Sinai, was made the chest inlaid with gold inside and outside, and in it the golden mummiform coffin with the Holy Thing was placed. The coffin did not fill the chest. It reached only about halfway up the chest and it was not so long; for at the head and foot there was still room for two small compartments in which were placed relics of Jacob's and Joseph's family and later on the rod of Aaron. When the Ark of the Covenant was placed in the Temple upon Sion, its interior had undergone a change. The golden mummiform coffin had been removed, and in its place was a little mass of whitish substance shaped like the coffin.

Even when a child, I often saw the Ark of the Covenant. I saw it inside and outside, and I knew of all that was put into it from time to time. All the precious holy things that the Israelites preserved were kept in it, but it could not have been heavy, since it was easily carried.

The chest was longer than broad, its height being equal to its width. It had below a projecting ledge. The top was wrought skillfully in gold for about half an ell in breadth: flowers, scrolls, faces, suns, and stars, all in different colors. All was magnificent, although the ornamentation was not very much raised. The apex and leaves arose only a little above the top of the chest. At the corners below this border, at either end, were the two rings through which ran the bars for carrying it. The whole chest was of setim wood covered with gold and beautifully inlaid with figures of different colors.

In the middle of the Ark was a small but unnoticeable door, by which the High Priest, when alone in the Most Holy, could take out the Holy Thing for blessing or for prophesying. It opened in two parts toward the interior right and left, and was large enough to admit of the High Priest's reaching in easily. Where the bars for carrying it extended over these doors, they were slightly curved. When the doors were opened, the golden casket, in which was preserved the Holy Thing in its precious coverings, also opened like a book.

Above the top of the Ark arose the Throne of Grace. It consisted of a hollow table covered with gold-plate, and in it lay holy bones. It was as large as the roof of the Ark, but only deep enough to rise a little above it. It was fastened to the Ark by eight setim wood screws, four at either end. It did not rest exactly on the Ark; there was space enough between them to afford a sight from side to side. The heads of the screws were of gold and shaped like fruit. The four outer ones fastened the table to the four corners of the Ark, the four inner ones ran into the interior. Each end of the Throne of Grace was concave, and in each cavity was securely fastened a golden cherub about the size of a boy. In the center of the Throne was a round opening by which a tube ran through the roof of the Ark. One could see it in the space between the roof and the hollow table. This basket-shaped opening was surrounded by a golden crown. Four transverse pieces fastened the crown to the rod, which from the Holy Thing in the Ark arose through the tube and the crown and, like the petals of a flower, spread out into seven points. The right hand of one of the cherubs and the left of the other clasped the rod, while their outspread wings, the right of the one and the left of the other, met behind it. The two other wings, only slightly expanded, did not meet, but left the sight of the crown from the front of the Ark free. Under these wings, the cherubs extended their arms with warning hands. One knee only of each cherub touched the Ark; the other limb was in a hovering attitude. The cherubs turned their face a little to one side with a slightly agitated expression, as if they felt a holy awe before the radiant crown. They were clothed around the middle portions of the body only. On long journeys, they were removed and carried separately.

I saw on the petal-like points of the rod, flames burning, which had been enkindled by the priests. The substance used for these lights was brown. I think it was a sacred resin. They kept it in boxes. But I have often seen great streams of light shooting up out of the crown, and similar streams descending from Heaven into it, also oblique currents breaking out of it in fine rays. These last signified the route by which the people should journey.

On the lower end of the rod inside the Ark, were hooks from which hung the two Tables of the Law and below them the Holy Thing. Below the latter, though not resting on the floor of the Ark, was a ribbed vessel of gold containing manna. When I looked sidewise into the Ark, I could not see the altar, nor the Holy Thing. I always regarded the Ark of the Covenant as a church, the Holy Thing as the altar with the Most Blessed Sacrament, and the vessel of manna as the lamp before the altar. When I entered a church in my childhood, I used to associate its different parts with the corresponding parts of the Ark of the Covenant. The Mystery, the Holy Thing of the Ark, was to me what the Blessed Sacrament is to us, only not so full of grace, although it was something full of strength and reality. It made upon me a more obscure, a more awe-inspiring impression, but still one very sacred and full of mystery. It always seemed to me that all in the Ark of the Covenant was holy, that all our salvation was in it, as if rolled up in a ball, as if in a germ. The Holy Thing of the Ark was more mysterious than the Most Blessed Sacrament. The former seemed to be the germ of the latter; the latter, the fulfillment of the former. I cannot express it. The Holy Thing of the Ark was a mystery as hidden as is Jesus in the Most Holy Sacrament to us. I felt that only a few of the High Priests knew what it was, that only the pious among them knew it by divine enlightenment and made use of it. To many it was unknown and they profited not by it, just as with us so many graces and wonders of the Church pass unheeded. They are lost as all salvation would be, were it founded on human will and intellect, instead of upon a rock.

I could weep over the sad state, the blindness of the Jews. They once possessed all in the germ; but the fruit, they would not recognize. First, they had the Mystery, the Holy Thing; it was the pledge, the promise. Then came the Law and afterward the grace. When I saw the Lord teaching in Sichar, the people questioned Him as to what had become of the Holy Thing of the Ark of the Covenant. He answered them that mankind had already received a great deal of it, that it was even then among them. The fact of their no longer possessing it as they once did, was a proof that the Messiah was born.

I saw the Mystery, the Holy Thing, in a form, in a kind of veil, as a substance, as an essence, as strength. It was bread and wine, flesh and blood; it was the germ of the Blessing before the Fall. It was the sacramental presence of that holy propagation of man before he fell. It was preserved to man by religion. It was possible for it to be ever more and more realized in subsequent generations by a continuous purification through piety, which purification was perfected in Mary thus rendering her fit to receive through the Holy Spirit the long-looked-for Messiah. Noe, in planting the vineyard, had made the preparation; but here in the Holy Thing were contained already the reconciliation and protection. Abraham had received it in that blessing which I saw bestowed upon him as something tangible, as a substance. It was a Mystery intrusted to one family, therefore the great prerogative of the firstborn.

Before the Departure from Egypt, Moses took possession of the Holy Thing. As before this it had been the religious Mystery of one family, so now it became the Mystery of the whole nation. It was placed in the Ark of the Covenant as the Most Holy Sacrament in the tabernacle and in the ostensorium.

When the children of Israel worshipped the golden calf and fell into gross errors, Moses doubted the power of the Holy Thing. For this he was punished by not being allowed to enter into the Promised Land. When the Ark fell into the hands of the enemy, the Holy Thing, the bond of union among the Israelites, was removed by the High Priest, as was always done when danger threatened. And yet was the Ark still so sacred that the enemy under the pressure of God's chastising anger were forced to restore it. Few comprehended the Holy Thing or the influence it exerted. It often happened that one man by his sins could interrupt the stream of grace, could break the direct genealogical line that was to end in the Saviour, or rather in that pure vessel that was to receive Him from God. In this way, the Redemption of the human race was long delayed. But penance could again restore continuity to that line. I do not know for certain whether this Sacrament were in itself divine, whether it came forth simply and purely what it was, directly from God, or whether it owed its sacred character to a kind of priestly, supernatural consecration. I think, however, that the first proposition is the true one, for I know for certain that priests often opposed its action and thus retarded Redemption. But they were heavily punished for it, yes, oftentimes even with death itself. When the Holy Thing operated, when prayer was heard, it became bright and increased in size, shining through the cover with a reddish glow. The blessing proceeding from it increased and diminished at different times according to the purity and piety of mankind. By prayer, sacrifice, and penance, it appeared to grow larger.

I saw Moses expose it before the people only twice: at the passage through the Red Sea and at the worshipping of the golden calf, but even then it was covered. It was removed from the golden casket and veiled as the Blessed Sacrament is on Good Friday. Like It, it was carried before the breast, or raised up for a blessing or a malediction, as if exerting its influence even at a distance. By it, Moses restrained many of the Israelites from idolatry and saved them from death.

I often saw the High Priest making use of it when he was alone in the Holy of Holies. He turned it in a certain direction, as if to strengthen, to protect, to shield, sometimes to shower a blessing, to grant a petition, sometimes even to punish. He never touched it with uncovered hands.

The Holy Thing was also plunged by him into water. This he did with a religious intention, and the water was given as a sacred draught. Deborah, the Prophetess, Anna the mother of Samuel in Silo, and Emerentia, the mother of St. Anne, drank of this water. By this holy drink, Emerentia was prepared for the conception of St. Anne. St. Anne drank not of this water, since the Blessing was in her.

Joachim, through an angel, received the Holy Thing out of the Ark of the Covenant, and Mary was conceived under the Golden Gate of the Temple. At her birth, she herself became the Ark of the Holy Thing which then reached its destination, and the wooden Ark in the Temple was deprived of its presence.

When Joachim and Anne met under the Golden Gate, they were surrounded by dazzling light, and the Blessed Virgin was conceived without original sin. A wonderful sound was heard; it was like a voice from God.

Men cannot comprehend this mystery of Mary's sinless conception in Anne, therefore is it hidden from them. The ancestors of Jesus received the germ of the Blessing for the Incarnation of God; but Jesus Christ Himself is the Sacrament of the New Covenant, the Fruit, the Fulfillment of that Blessing, to unite men again to God.

When Jeremias at the time of the Babylonian Captivity hid the Ark of the Covenant and other precious objects on Mount Sinai, the Mystery, the Holy Thing, was no longer in it; only its coverings were buried by him with the Ark. He knew, however, what it had contained and how holy it was. He wanted, therefore, to speak of it publicly and of the abomination of treating it irreverently. But Malachias restrained him, and took charge of the Holy Thing himself. Through him it fell into the hands of the Essenians, and afterward was placed by a priest in the second Ark of the Covenant. Malachias was like Melchisedech an angel, one sent by God. I saw him not as an ordinary man. Like Melchisedech, he had the appearance of a man, differing from him only inasmuch as was suited to his time.

Shortly after Daniel's being led to Babylon, I saw Malachias as a boy of seven years, wearing a reddish garment, and wandering around with a staff in his hand. He seemed to have lost his way, and he took shelter with a pious couple at Sapha of the tribe of Zabulon. They thought him a lost child of one of the captive Israelites, and they kept him with them. He was very amiable, and so extraordinarily patient and meek that everyone loved him; he could therefore teach and do what he pleased without molestation. He had much intercourse with Jeremias, whom he assisted with advice when in the greatest perils. It was through him also that Jeremias was freed from prison in Jerusalem.

The ancient Ark of the Covenant, hidden by Jeremias on Mount Sinai, was never again discovered.

The second one was not so beautiful as the first, and it did not contain so many precious things. Aaron's rod was in possession of the Essenians on Horeb, where also a part of the Holy Thing was preserved. The family that Moses appointed as the immediate protectors of the Ark of the Covenant, existed till the time of Herod.

All will come to light on the last day. Then will the Mystery become clear, to the terror of all that have made a bad use of it.

THE MOST HOLY VIRGIN

1. Genealogy, Birth, and Marriage of St. Anne

The ancestors of St. Anne were Essenians. These extraordinarily pious people were descended from those priests who, in the time of Moses and Aaron, carried the Ark, and who received precise rules in the days of Isaias and Jeremias. They were not numerous in the beginning. Later on in Palestine they lived in communities occupying a tract about forty-eight miles long and thirty-six wide.[1] Some time after, they migrated to the region of the Jordan where they dwelt chiefly on Mount Horeb and on Mount Carmel.

In early times, before Isaias gathered them together, the Essenians lived scattered as pious, ascetic Jews. They neither changed nor repaired their garments until they actually fell to pieces. They married, but observed great continence in the married state. With mutual consent, husband and wife frequently lived apart in distant huts. They also ate apart, first the husband and on his departure the wife. Even in those early times some of the forefathers of Anne and of other members of the Holy Family were found among them. From them sprang those that are called the children of the Prophets. They dwelt in the desert and around Mt. Horeb. There were many of them likewise in Egypt. For a long time war drove them from Mt. Horeb, but they were gathered together again by their Superiors. The Maccabees belonged to this sect. They greatly revered Moses. They had a piece of his garment. He had given it to Aaron, and through

---

1. A German mile equivalent to four and one-half English miles.

the latter it came into the possession of the Essenians. They preserved it as a sacred thing, and I had a vision in which I saw that fifteen of the Essenians had perished in its defense. Their Superiors knew of the Mystery, the Holy Thing, in the Ark of the Covenant. The unmarried among the Essenians formed a special congregation like a religious order. They had to undergo a probation of long years before being admitted to it, and then they were received for a longer or a shorter time as the prophetical inspiration of Superiors might dictate. The married Essenians, who exercised strict vigilance over their children and household, bore to the real Essenian Community the same spiritual relationship that the Franciscan Tertiaries do to the Franciscan Order. In all affairs they were guided by the counsel of their spiritual Superior on Horeb.

The unmarried Essenians were unspeakably chaste and devout. They wore long white garments, which they kept scrupulously clean. They received children to educate. The aspirant to their rigid life had to be fourteen years old. Postulants of advanced piety were kept only one year on probation; others, two years. They lived in perfect chastity and carried on no kind of business; they exchanged their agricultural products for the various necessaries of life. If anyone of their number were so unfortunate as to sin grievously, he was excommunicated, which excommunication was followed by consequences such as attended St. Peter's malediction against Ananias—he died. The Superior of the Essenians knew by divine inspiration whenever anyone had fallen into sin. I saw also some who lived only to do penance; one, for instance, stood in a sort of stiff coat, with outstretched, inflexible sleeves, lined with prickles.

They had caves on Mt. Horeb which served as cells. Attached to them by wicker-work was a large cave for general assembly. At the eleventh hour all met here for a meal. Each had before him a small loaf and cup. The Superior went around and blessed the loaf of each. The meal over, all returned to their own cells. In the large hall was an altar upon which lay blessed loaves. They were covered and intended for distribution to the poor. There were numbers of tame pigeons around which fed out of the hand. The Essenians used these doves for food, also for religious ceremonies. They uttered some words over them, and they let them fly away. I saw them also performing the same ceremony over lambs; they spoke some words over them and then let them run into the wilderness. I saw that they went three times every year to the Temple of Jerusalem. They had among them priests, whose special care was the preservation of the sacred vestments; they cleaned them and prepared new ones, to the purchase of which they had contributed. I saw these people engaged in agriculture, in cattle raising, and especially in gardening. That part of Mt. Horeb which lay around their cells was covered with gardens and fruit trees. I saw many of them engaged likewise in weaving and platting, and in embroidering the sacerdotal garments. I saw that they did not manufacture the silk themselves. It came in bundles for sale, and they exchanged their products for it.

In Jerusalem, they had a special dwelling place, also a particular part of the Temple assigned to them. They were objects of dislike to the other Jews. I saw them sending offerings to the Temple for sacrifice, huge bunches of grapes that two men carried between them on a pole, and lambs. But these lambs were not slaughtered; they were allowed to run. I never saw them bringing offerings for slaughter. Before going up to the Temple, they prepared themselves by prayer, rigid fasting, disciplines, and other penitential exercises. He who, with unatoned sins, ventured to the Temple, might fear a sudden death; and indeed, this happened to some. If on their way to the Temple they met a person sick or helpless, they paused and went no further until they had in some manner assisted him. I saw them gathering herbs and preparing teas. They healed the sick by the imposition of hands, or by stretching themselves upon them with extended arms. I saw them also exerting their healing power at a distance. If a sick person could not go himself to the Essenians, he sent to them another as his representative. All that would have been done for the sick person himself, had he really been present, was done for his representative, and the sick man was cured at the same hour.

The Superior at the time of Anne's grandparents was a Prophet named Archos. He had visions in the cave of Elias on Horeb, which visions referred to the coming of the Messiah. Archos knew from what family the Messiah would come and, when he prophesied to Anne's grandparents concerning their posterity, he saw that the time was drawing near. He knew not exactly how far off it was nor how it might still be retarded by sin; but he exhorted to penance and sacrifice.

Anne's grandfather, an Essenian, was before his marriage called Stolanus; but by his wife and in consideration of her dowry, he received the name Garescha, or Sarziri. Anne's grandmother was of Mara in the desert. Her name was Moruni, or Emorun, that is, *noble mother.* She married Stolanus upon the advice of Archos, the Prophet, who was the Superior of the Essenians for about ninety years. He was a very holy man with whom counsel was always taken by those intending to enter upon the married state, that they might make a good choice. It seemed to me strange that this divinely enlightened Superior always prophesied respecting the female descendants, and that the ancestors of Anne, as well as Anne herself, always had daughters. It was as if the religious education of the pure vessels that were to conceive the holy children destined to be the precursors of the disciples, of the Apostles, and of the Lord Himself, devolved upon them.

I saw Emorun going to Archos before her marriage. She entered the hall on Horeb, passed thence into a side apartment, and conferred with the Superior through a grating like that of a confessional. Then Archos went up a long flight of steps to the summit of the mountain where was found the cave of the Prophet Elias. The entrance was narrow, and a few steps led down into the cave, which was neatly hollowed out. The light fell through an opening in the vaulted roof. I saw by the wall a small stone altar, upon which was the rod of Aaron and a shining chalice as of one precious stone. In this chalice lay a portion of the Ark of the Covenant. The Essenians had come into possession of it at a time when the Ark had fallen into the hands of the enemy. The rod of Aaron stood in a little tree as in a box. The tree had yellowish leaves wreathed in spirals. I cannot say whether this little tree was really growing or whether it was artificial. It was, for instance, something like a root of Jesse. If the Superior prayed concerning a marriage, he took the rod of Aaron into his hand. If the union in question would contribute to Mary's lineage, the rod put forth a bud from which sprang one or more blossoms bearing the sign of the choice. The forefathers of Anne were legitimate descendants of this lineage, and their chosen daughters had been by such signs designated. New blossoms burst forth whenever a chosen daughter was to enter the married state. The little tree with its spiral leaves was like a genealogical table, like the root of Jesse, and by it could be seen how far the advent of Mary was distant. There were on the altar, also, some small bunches of herbs in pots. Their flourishing or withering denoted something. I saw all around on the walls grated compartments wherein were preserved ancient holy bones very beautifully encased in silk and wool. They were the bones of Prophets and holy Israelites who had lived upon the mountain and in its vicinity. I saw such bones in the cells or caves of the Essenians.

They used to place lighted lamps and flowers before them, and there offer prayers.

When Archos prayed in this cave, he was vested precisely like the High Priest in the Temple. His clothing consisted of about eight pieces: First, he placed upon his breast a kind of broad scapular such as Moses used to wear next to his person. It had an opening in the middle for the neck and fell in equal length before and behind. Over this, he wore a white alb of twisted silk bound by a cincture that fastened also the wide stole which, crossing on the breast, reached down to the knee. Over the alb was a kind of chasuble of white silk. It reached to the ground behind, and had two little bells at the lower edge. Around the neck was a standing collar buttoned in front. The beard was parted over this collar. Last of all came a small, shining mantle of white untwisted silk. It was fastened in front by three stone clasps upon which something was engraved, From either shoulder toward the breast ran a row of six precious stones, upon which also signs were engraved. On the back of it and in the center, was a shield upon which were inscribed some letters. This mantle was also adorned with fringes, tassels and artificial fruit. On one arm he wore a short maniple. The headdress was of white silk rolled in puffs one above another and ending in a silken tuft. Over the forehead was a plate of gold set with precious stones.

Archos prayed prostrate on the earth before the altar. I saw that he had a vision of a rose tree with three branches springing from Emorun. On each branch was a rose, and that of the second was marked with a letter. He saw also an angel writing letters on the wall. In consequence of this vision, Archos told Emorun that she should marry her sixth suitor, that she should bring forth a chosen child who would bear a sign and who would be a vessel of the approaching Promise. The sixth suitor was Stolanus. The married pair did not dwell long in Mara; they removed to Ephron. Again I saw their daughters, Emerentia and Ismeria, consulting with Archos. He commanded them to embrace the married state, for they also were cooperating vessels of the Promise. The elder one, Emerentia, married a Levite named Aphras, and became the mother of Elizabeth, who gave birth to John the Baptist. A third daughter was named Enue. Ismeria was the second daughter of Stolanus and Emorun. She had at her birth the mark that Archos, in his vision of Emorun, had seen on the rose of the second branch. Ismeria married Eliud, of the tribe of Levi. They were wealthy, as I judged from their great household. They owned many herds, but they kept nothing for themselves, they gave all to the poor. They dwelt in Sephoris, four leagues from Nazareth, where they possessed property. They had property also in the valley of Zabulon whither they used to remove in the warm season. After Ismeria's death, Eliud took up his abode there permanently. Joachim's father with his family had likewise settled in the same valley.

The eminent chastity and mortification of Stolanus and Emorun had descended to Ismeria and Eliud. Ismeria's first daughter was called Sobe. She married Solomon, and became the mother of Mary Salome who married Zebedee and gave birth to the future Apostles, James the Greater and John. When at Sobe's birth, the sign of the Promise was not found on her, her parents were greatly troubled. They journeyed to the Prophet on Horeb. He exhorted them to prayer and sacrifice, and promised them consolation. For about eighteen years they were without children, and then Anne was born. Both father and mother had the same vision one night upon their couch. Ismeria saw an angel near her writing on the wall. On awakening she told her husband, who also had had the same vision, and both still saw the written character on the wall. It was the letter M. At her birth Anne brought with her into the world the same sign upon the region of the stomach.

Anne was especially dear to her parents. I saw her
as a child. She was not strikingly beautiful, though
prettier than some others. Her beauty was not to be
compared with Mary's, but she was extraordinarily
pious, childlike, and innocent. She was the same at
every age, as I have seen, as a maiden, as a mother,
and as a little old grandmother. Whenever I happened
to see a very childlike old peasant woman, I always
thought: "She is like Anne."

When in her fifth year, Anne was taken to the Temple as Mary was later. There she remained twelve
years, returning home in her seventeenth year. Meantime, her mother had had a third daughter, whom
she named Maraha, and Anne found also in the paternal house a little son of her eldest sister Sobe, who
was called Eliud. Maraha afterward inherited the
paternal property of Sephoris and became the mother
of the subsequent disciples, Arastaria and Cocharia.
The young Eliud was afterward the second husband
of Maroni, of Naim.

One year later, Ismeria fell sick and died. She called
her household around her deathbed, gave them her
parting advice, and appointed Anne as their future
mistress. Then she spoke alone with Anne, saying
that she must marry, for that she was a vessel of the
Promise. About eighteen months after, Anne, then in
her nineteenth year, married Heli, or Joachim, This
she did in obedience to the spiritual direction of the
Prophet. On account of the approach of the Saviour's
advent, she married Joachim of the House of David,
for Mary was to belong to the House of David; otherwise she would have had to choose her spouse from
among the Levites of the tribe of Aaron, as all of her
race had done. She had had many suitors and, at the
time of the Prophet's decision, she was not yet acquainted with Joachim. She chose him only upon
supernatural direction.

Joachim was poor and a relative of St. Joseph.
Joseph's grandfather Mathan had descended from

David through Solomon. He had two sons, Joses and Jacob. The latter was Joseph's father. When Mathan died, his widow married a second husband named Levi, descendant of David through Nathan. The fruit of this marriage was Mathat, the father of Heli, or Joachim. Joachim was a short, broad, spare man. St. Joseph, even in his old age, was very handsome compared with him. However, in disposition and morals, Joachim was a superior man. Like Anne, he had something very distinguished about him. Both were true Israelites; but there was something in them that they themselves knew not, a yearning, a wonderful earnestness. I have rarely seen either of them laugh, although in the early part of their married life they were not particularly grave. Both possessed a calm, uniform disposition; even in early youth, they were something like sedate old people.

They were married in a small town that possessed only one obscure school, and only one priest presided at the ceremony. Courtship in those days was carried on very simply. The lovers were very reserved. They consulted each other on the subject and regarded their marriage merely as something inevitable. If the young girl said yes, her parents were satisfied; if no, and could she give good reasons for her refusal, they looked upon the affair as ended. First the matter was settled before the parents, and then the promises were made before the priest in the synagogue. The priest prayed in the sanctuary before the rolls of the Law, the parents in their accustomed place, while the young couple in an adjoining apartment deliberated in private over their intention and contract. When they had taken their determination, they declared it to their parents. The latter again conferred with the priest, who now went to meet the couple outside the sanctuary. The nuptial ceremony was celebrated the next day.

Joachim and Anne lived with Eliud, Anne's father. There reigned throughout his household the severe usages and discipline of the Essenians. The house lay

in the environs of Sephoris. It formed one of a group
of houses of which it was the largest. Here Joachim
and Anne dwelt seven years.

Anne's parents were in good circumstances. They
had numerous herds and a house handsomely furnished with beautiful carpets, table furniture, etc. The
servants, men and women, were many. I never saw
them engaged in agriculture, but herding cattle on the
pasture grounds. Ismeria and Eliud were pious, devout,
charitable, and just. They frequently divided their herds
and other possessions into three parts: one part for
the Temple, whither they drove it themselves and where
it was received by the servants of the Temple; a second part they gave to the poor or to their needy relatives, some of whom were generally present to receive
it; and the third part they reserved for their own use.
They lived very frugally and gave to all that asked
help. When I saw all this, even in childhood, I thought:
Giving lasts long. He who gives gets back double, for
I perceived that the third part again rapidly increased.
It was soon so large that it could be again divided
into three parts as before. They had many relatives
who upon all solemn occasions assembled at their
house. But I never even on those occasions saw much
feasting. Food was indeed distributed among the poor,
but grand entertainments I never saw. At these assemblies the guests generally reclined in circles on the
ground, and conversed of God with earnest expectancy.
It frequently happened that some of these relatives
were bad people. They looked angry and displeased
when Eliud and Ismeria, full of heavenly longing,
glanced upward as they spoke of God. But to these
evil-minded people, the holy couple were ever kind;
they never omitted to invite them to their reunions,
and they gave twice as much to them as to others. I
used to see that they, with bitter feelings, impatiently
coveted what Eliud and Ismeria gave them with so
much good will. It was no uncommon thing for the
holy couple to give sheep, sometimes one, sometimes

more, to the poor belonging to them.

Here in her father's house, Anne gave birth to her first daughter, who was called Mary. I saw her full of joy over her newborn babe. It was a lovely child. I saw it growing stout and strong. It was gentle and pious, and the parents loved it. But yet, there was something about the child that I could not understand, something that indicated that it was not the one looked forward to by the parents as the fruit of their union. There was always a shade of trouble and anxiety about them, as if they had offended God, therefore they did penance, lived in continence, and multiplied their good works. I often saw them going apart to pray.

They had lived in this way with their father, Eliud, seven years (which I could guess by the age of their first child), when they resolved to withdraw from the paternal house. Their design was to live in privacy, to begin their married life anew and, by performing actions pleasing to God, to draw down His benediction upon their union. I saw them take this resolution in the paternal home and I also saw Eliud setting aside a portion of his riches for them. The herds were divided, oxen, asses, and sheep set apart for the new household. The animals named were much larger than those of our country. On the asses and oxen were packed all kinds of movables, furniture and clothing. The good people were as skillful in packing as were the animals ready to receive and carry away their loads.

We do not pack our goods so skillfully on our wagons as these people could upon their beasts. They had beautiful vessels, all more highly ornamented than those of the present day. Beautiful, fragile, curiously-shaped pitchers, upon which were all kinds of ornamentation like carving, were stuffed with moss, enveloped in wrappings, fastened to the ends of a strap, and hung over the back of the animals upon which were laid bundles of colored covers and garments. Some of the covers were embroidered in gold and were very costly. Father Eliud gave the departing couple a small, but heavy lump of something in a bag; it was like a lump of gold, of precious metal. When all was ready, the servant men and maids formed in procession and drove the herds and beasts of burden before them toward the new dwelling, about five or six leagues distant.

The house stood upon a hill between the vale of Nazareth and the valley of Zabulon. A terebinthine walk led to it. In front of it, on a bare, stony foundation, was a courtyard surrounded by a low stone wall, upon or behind which grew a hedge. On one side of this courtyard were sheds for the cattle. The door of the house, which was tolerably large, was in the center of the building and hung upon hinges. Through it one entered a kind of anteroom, which extended the whole breadth of the house. Right and left of the hall were small apartments cut off by lightly woven partitions, or screens, that could be removed at pleasure. It was in this hall that the principal meals were laid on feasts as, for instance, when Mary was taken to the Temple. Opposite the entrance, a light wicker door led from the hall into a passage upon either side of which were four apartments lying right and left. They were separated by movable wicker partitions, the upper part ending in gratings. These partitions were so placed as to form a rounded, or rather a kind of triangular space, in the middle of whose central side, just opposite the door, was the fireplace. Behind the two oblique sides, right and left, were other chambers. In the center of this kitchen there hung from the ceiling a many-branched lamp. Around the house were fields and orchards.

When Joachim and Anne entered their new abode, they found everything in order, owing to the diligence of the domestics who had preceded them. They had unpacked all things as nicely and carefully as they had packed them, and everything was in its place. Anne's servants were so handy, they did everything quietly and intelligently. They were not like the servants of our day, who have to be told every single thing. And now the holy couple began here a new married life. They made a sacrifice to God of all the preceding years, and began again as if they had only just now been united. Their only aim was by a life pleasing to God, to attract upon themselves that blessing for which alone they sighed. I saw them both going to and fro among their herds. They divided them into three parts, and drove the best to the Temple. The poor received the second part, and the worst was retained for themselves. They acted in the same manner with all that belonged to them.

2. The Holy and Immaculate Conception of Mary

Anne had the assurance, the firm belief that the coming of the Messiah was very near, and that she herself would be of the number of His relatives according to the flesh. Her prayer was continuous and she constantly aimed at greater purity. It had been revealed to her that she was to bring forth a child of benediction. Her firstborn daughter, who had remained with her grandfather Eliud, Anne recognized and loved as her own and Joachim's child; but she felt certain that she was not the child whom, by interior enlightenment, she knew that she was to bear. For nineteen years and five months after the birth of this first child, Joachim and Anne were childless. They lived in continued prayer and sacrifice, in mortification and continency. I frequently saw them dividing their herds, which rapidly multiplied again. Joachim often remained far away with his flocks in humble supplication to God.

The anxiety of both and their longing after the promised blessing had reached their height. Many of their acquaintances upbraided them because of their sterility, which they attributed to some wickedness. They said that the child living with Eliud was not really Anne's daughter, otherwise she would have it with her. When Joachim, absent with the herds, went again to the Temple to offer sacrifice, Anne used to send servants out to the fields to him with numbers of things, doves, and other birds in baskets and cages. Joachim loaded two asses from the meadow with them, also with three little long-necked animals, white and nimble, and lambs and kids in wicker baskets. He carried a lantern at the end of a stick; it looked like a light in a scooped-out gourd. I saw him with his offerings journeying over a beautiful green field between Bethania and Jerusalem. I often saw Jesus in the same spot. Toward evening, Joachim reached the Temple. The asses were stabled in the same place as subsequently at Mary's Presentation, and the offerings were carried up the steps of the Mount that led to the Temple. When they had been received by the attendants, Joachim's servants returned while he himself went on into the hall in which were the water basins for the cleansing of the gifts. Thence he passed through a long corridor to a hall upon the left of the Sanctuary where were the altar of incense, the table of show bread, and the seven-branched candlestick. The hall was filled with those that had brought offerings. Joachim was received in a very contemptuous manner by a priest named Reuben, who would scarcely admit him. He was shoved into a corner behind a grating, and his offerings were not, like those of others, conspicuously placed behind the gratings to the right of the courtyard, but indifferently set on one side. The priests were around the altar of incense, upon which an offering was being made. Lamps were burning, and lights were lit on the seven branched candlestick, but not all seven at once. I have often noticed that different arms of the candlestick were lighted on different occasions.

I saw Joachim leaving the Temple in great trouble. He went from Jerusalem through Bethania, and into the country of Macharus, where he sought consolation in the house of an Essenian. The Prophet Manahem had once dwelt here, and also in the family of an Essenian at Bethania. This Prophet had foretold to Herod while still a child his future kingdom and wickedness. From this place, Joachim went to his most distant herds on Mount Hermon. The way led through the wilderness of Gaddi and over the Jordan. Hermon is a long, narrow, unbroken mountain whose sunny side is green and blooming when the other is still covered with snow. Joachim was so dejected, so mortified that he would not allow his people to inform Anne where he was staying, while the trouble of the latter when she heard how things had gone at the Temple and saw that Joachim did not return home, was indescribable. For five months Joachim thus remained in concealment on Hermon. I saw him praying and weeping. When he went to look after his flocks and his lambs, he was often so overcome by sadness that he cast himself with covered face prostrate on the ground. His servants questioned him upon the cause of his grief. But he did not tell them that it was because he was childless. Again he divided his magnificent herds into three parts. The best he sent to the Temple, the second to the Essenians, and the least he kept for himself.

Anne, in the midst of her anxiety, had much to endure also from an insolent maid servant who bitterly taunted her with her sterility. She bore with her a long time, but at last she sent her from the house. The maid had requested permission to go to a feast. This was not in accordance with the strict discipline of the Essenians. Anne refused the permission, and then the maid reproached her, telling her that she deserved to be sterile and abandoned by her husband on account of her harsh and unreasonable temper. Then Anne sent her, with gifts and accompanied by two servants, back to her parents, that they might receive her safe and sound as she had come to her. She sent them also the message that she could no longer take charge of their daughter. After the girl's departure, Anne went in sadness to her chamber and prayed. When evening closed, she threw a long scarf over her head and enveloped herself entirely in it, took a covered light beneath her mantle, went out under a spreading tree that stood in the courtyard, lit the lamp and prayed. This tree was one of those whose branches strike root again and again, and thus form a whole tract of covered walk under their foliage. Its leaves are very large. I think it was with such that Adam and Eve clothed themselves in Paradise. The whole tree had the characteristics of that of the forbidden fruit. The pear-shaped fruit hung usually in fives at the end of the branches. It was fleshy inside with blood-colored veins; in its center was a hollow space in which reposed the kernel. The Jews made use of the large leaves chiefly at the Feast of Tabernacles. They adorned the walls with them, laying them like the scales of a fish, so that their edges closely fitted together. The tree was surrounded by groves and seats.

When Anne had long besought God not to separate her from Joachim, her pious husband, although He had been pleased to deprive her of children, an angel appeared to her. He hovered above her in the air. He told her to set her heart at rest, for the Lord had heard her prayer; that she should on the following morning go with two of her maid servants to the Temple of Jerusalem; that there under the Golden Gate, entering by the side of the valley of Josaphat, she should meet Joachim, who was even now on his way thither, that Joachim's offering would be accepted, that his prayer would be heard, that he (the angel) had appeared also to him. The angel likewise directed Anne to take some doves with her as an offering, and promised that the name of the child she was soon to conceive should be made known to her. Anne thanked the Lord and returned to the house. When, after her lengthy prayer, she lay on her couch asleep I saw light descending upon her. It surrounded her, yes, even penetrated her. I saw her, upon an interior perception, tremblingly awake and sit upright. Near her, to the right, she saw a luminous figure writing on the wall in large, shining Hebrew characters. I read and understood the writing word for word. It was to this effect: that she should conceive, that the fruit of her womb should be altogether special, and that the Blessing received by Abraham was to be the source of this conception. I saw Anne's anxiety as to how she should communicate all that to Joachim; but the angel reassured her by telling her of Joachim's vision. I received then a clear explanation of Mary's Immaculate Conception. I saw that, in the Ark of the Covenant, a sacrament of the Incarnation, of the Immaculate Conception, a Mystery for the restoration of fallen humanity was contained. I saw Anne, with surprise and joy, reading the red and golden letters of this luminous writing. Her gladness increased to such a degree that, when she arose to set out for Jerusalem, she looked far younger than before. I saw on Anne's person at the instant the angel appeared to her a beam of light and in her a shining vessel. I cannot better describe it than by saying that it was like a cradle, or a tabernacle which had been closed but was now opened, and made ready to receive a holy thing. How wonderfully I saw this, is not to be expressed; for I saw it as if it were the cradle of salvation for the whole human race, and also as a kind of sacred vessel now opened, and the veil withdrawn. I saw it quite naturally as if one and the same holy thing.

I saw, too, the apparition of the angel to Joachim. The angel commanded him to take his offering up to the Temple, promised that his prayer should be heard, and told him that he should pass under the Golden

Gate. At this announcement, Joachim was troubled. He felt very timid about going again to the Temple. But the angel assured him that the priests had already been enlightened with regard to him. It was the time of the Feast of Tabernacles. Joachim and his shepherds had already erected their tabernacles. With a large herd of cattle as an offering, Joachim reached Jerusalem on the fourth day of the feast, and put up near the Temple. Anne arrived in Jerusalem also on the fourth day of the feast. She stopped with the family of Zacharias near the fish market, and met Joachim for the first time only at the end of the feast.

When Joachim approached the Temple, two of the priests came out to meet him. They did this acting upon a divine inspiration. Joachim had brought with him two lambs and three kids. His offering was accepted, slaughtered, and burned at the customary place in the Temple. But a part of it was taken and burned at another place to the right of the entrance porch, in the center of which stood the large teacher's desk.

When the smoke arose, I saw a beam of light descend upon Joachim and the officiating priest. There was a pause, the beholders looked on in amazement, and I saw two priests go out to Joachim and lead him through the side apartments into the Sanctuary before the altar of incense. Then the priests laid incense upon the altar, not in grains but in the lump; it kindled of itself. The priests immediately retired to a distance and left Joachim alone before the altar. I saw him on his knees, his arms extended, while the incense offering slowly consumed itself. He remained shut up in the Temple all night, praying with great and ardent desires. I saw that he was in ecstasy. A luminous figure appeared to him in the same manner as to Zachary, and gave him a roll written in shining letters. On it were the three names: Helia, Hanna, Mirjam, and near the last one the picture of a little Ark of the Covenant, or a tabernacle. Joachim laid the roll on his breast under his garment. The angel spoke: "Anne will conceive an immaculate child from whom the Redeemer of the world will be born." The angel told him moreover not to grieve over his sterility which was not a disgrace to him, but a glory, for that what his spouse would conceive should not be from him but through him, a fruit from God, the culminating point of the Blessing given to Abraham. I saw that Joachim could not comprehend these words. Then the angel led him behind the curtain that concealed the grating before the Holy of Holies. The space between the curtain and the grating afforded standing room. Then the angel held up before Joachim's face a shining ball that reflected like a mirror. Joachim breathed upon it and gazed into it. When I saw the angel holding the ball so close to Joachim's face, I thought of a custom in use at our country weddings, where one kisses a painted head and gives fourteen pennies to the sexton. And now, as if called up by the breath of Joachim, appeared all kinds of pictures in the globe. He saw them clearly, for his breath did not dim them. It seemed to me that the angel then said to him that Anne should conceive although remaining just as unsullied by him as this ball. The angel then took it from Joachim and raised it on high. I saw it hovering in the air and, as if through an opening, innumerable and wonderful pictures went into it. They were like a whole world, one picture growing out of another. Up in the highest point appeared the Most Holy Trinity, and below, to one side, were Paradise, Adam and Eve, the Fall, the Promise of a Redeemer, Noe, the Ark, scenes connected with Abraham and Moses, the Ark of the Covenant, and numerous symbols of Mary. I saw cities, towers, gateways, flowers, all wonderfully connected together by beams of light like bridges. They were all assaulted and combated by beasts and spirits, which, however, were everywhere beaten back by the streams of light that burst upon them.

I saw also a garden enclosed by a dense thorn-hedge. All kinds of horrible animals were trying to enter, but could not. I saw a tower stormed by numerous warriors who were, however, always repulsed. And in this way I saw innumerable pictures all bearing some reference to Mary. They were bound together by passages or bridges. In them I saw obstacles, hindrances, struggles, all of which were overcome, and the pictures disappeared successively on the opposite side of the globe, as if they had entered into the Heavenly Jerusalem. But as I gazed at them dissolving in the interior of the globe, the globe itself mounted on high and I saw it no more.

The angel now removed something from the Ark of the Covenant, though without opening the door. It was the Mystery of the Ark, the Sacrament of the Incarnation, the Immaculate Conception, the Consummation of the Blessing of Abraham. I beheld it under the appearance of a luminous body. The angel blessed or anointed Joachim's forehead with the tip of his thumb and forefinger; then he slipped the shining body under Joachim's garment and it entered into him, how I cannot say. He also gave him something to drink out of a glittering chalice which he held supported by two fingers. The chalice was of the same shape as that used at the Last Supper, but without a foot. Joachim was directed to take it with him and keep it at his home.

I understood that the angel forbade Joachim to reveal anything about this Holy Mystery; and then, too, I understood why Zacharias, the father of the Baptist, was struck dumb after receiving the blessing and the promise of Elizabeth's fruitfulness through the Mystery of the Ark of the Covenant. Not till later was this Mystery missed from the Ark by the priests. Then were they at first confounded; afterward they became altogether pharisaical. The angel now led Joachim out of the Holy of Holies and vanished. Joachim lay on the ground like one stupefied.

I saw the priests enter the Sanctuary, lead Joachim out reverently, and place him upon a seat that stood on a raised platform where usually only priests sat. The seat was almost like that used by Magdalen in her grandeur. They bathed his face, held something to his nose, and gave him to drink; in short, they treated him as one in a swoon. Joachim was, by virtue of what he had received from the angel, quite radiant. He looked as if he had returned to the bloom of youth.

Joachim was afterward conducted by the priests to the entrance of the subterranean passage that ran under the Temple and under the Golden Gate. This was a passage set aside for special purposes. Under certain circumstances, penitents were conducted by it for purification, reconciliation, and absolution. The priests parted from Joachim at the entrance, and he went alone into the narrow, gradually widening, and almost imperceptibly descending passage. In it stood pillars twined with foliage. They looked like trees and vines, and the green and gold decorations of the walls sparkled in the rosy light that fell from above. Joachim had accomplished a third part of the way when Anne met him in the center of the passage directly under the Golden Gate, where stood a pillar like a palm tree with hanging leaves and fruit. Anne had been conducted into the subterranean passage through an entrance at the opposite end by the priest to whom she and her maid had brought the offering of doves in baskets, and to whom also she had told what the angel had revealed to her. She was also accompanied by some women, among them the Prophetess Anna.

I saw Joachim and Anne embrace each other in ecstasy. They were surrounded by hosts of angels, some floating over them carrying a luminous tower like that which we see in the pictures of the Litany of Loretto. The tower vanished between Joachim and Anne, both of whom were encompassed by brilliant light and glory. At the same moment the heavens above them opened, and I saw the joy of the Most

Holy Trinity and of the angels over the Conception of Mary. Both Joachim and Anne were in a supernatural state. I learned that, at the moment in which they embraced and the light shone around them, the Immaculate Conception of Mary was accomplished. I was also told that Mary was conceived just as conception would have been effected, were it not for the fall of man.

After this, Joachim and Anne, praising God, turned toward the outer gate of the passage. They went under an arch into a space like a chapel where numerous lights were burning. Thence they passed to the gate where they were received by the priests who accompanied them back. The Temple was all thrown open and decorated with garlands of leaves and fruit. Divine service was performed under the open sky. In one place stood eight pillars at some distance from one another, and over them were twined garlands of green.

Joachim and Anne went for awhile to one of the priests' houses in Jerusalem, and then immediately journeyed homeward. I saw them in Nazareth holding an entertainment at which many of the poor were fed and presented with alms. Joachim received numerous congratulations upon the acceptance of his offering.

Upon their arrival home, the holy couple published the mercy of God with feeling, joy, and devotion. From that time they lived in perfect continence and in great fear of God. I received at this time an instruction upon the great influence exerted upon children by the purity, the continence, and the mortification of parents.

Four and one-half months less three days after St. Anne had conceived under the Golden Gate, I saw the soul of Mary, formed by the Most Holy Trinity, in movement. I saw the Divine Persons interpenetrating one another. It became a great shining mountain, and still like the figure of a man. I saw something from the midst of the Three Divine Persons rising toward the mouth and issuing from it like a beam of light. This beam hovered before the face of God and assumed a human shape, or rather it was formed to such. As it took the human form, I saw it, as if by the command of God, most beautifully fashioned. I saw God showing the beauty of this soul to the angels, and from it they experienced unspeakable joy.

I saw that soul united to the living body of Mary in Anne's womb. Anne lay asleep upon her couch. I saw a light hovering over her and from it a beam descending toward the middle of her side. I saw that beam enter into her in the form of a small, luminous, human figure. At the same instant Anne sat up. She was entirely surrounded by light, and she had a vision. She saw her own person, open as it were and in it, as if in a tabernacle, a holy, luminous virgin from whom proceeded all salvation. I saw, too, that this was the instant that Mary first moved in her mother's womb.

Anne arose and announced to Joachim what had taken place. Then she went out to pray under the tree beneath which a child had been promised to her. I learned that Mary's soul animated her body five days earlier than is customary with ordinary children, and that she was born twelve days sooner.*

3. Symbols of the Mystery of the Immaculate Conception

I saw the whole earth parched and dried up. I saw Elias with two servants climbing up Mt. Carmel. They first crossed a high ridge, then went up steps cut in the rock to a terrace; from this terrace they ascended by similar steps to a level place from which arose a hill. The hill contained a cave, and up to this Elias mounted alone. He left his servants on the borders of

---

* "The terms 'quickened' and 'animation' in present usage are applied to the child after the mother can perceive its motion, which usually happens about the one hundred and sixteenth day after conception." *(The Catholic Encyclopedia,* 1907, Vol. 1, p. 49). —*Publisher,* 2004.

the level place, that they might look down upon the Sea of Galilee. Its waters were dried up, and its bed lay full of holes, mud, and putrified carcasses. Elias sat down, his head resting upon his knees, covered himself with his mantle and prayed earnestly to God. Seven times did he call to his servants as to whether no cloud out of the sea had yet arisen. At last I saw in the middle of the sea a white vapor out of which came a little black cloud. In the latter was a small, shining figure which, rising on high, gradually increased in size. As the cloud rose, Elias perceived in it the figure of a radiant virgin. Her head was surrounded by rays, her arms were outstretched in the form of a cross, one hand grasping a victor's wreath, and her long garments fell as if bound below her feet. She appeared to be hovering over Palestine. In this vision, Elias learned four mysteries relative to the Blessed Virgin. One was that she would come in the seventh age, and another was the family to which she should belong. He also saw on one shore of the sea a low, spreading tree, and on the other a very lofty one whose summit drooped over upon the lower one.

I saw the cloud break up and fall in fleecy vapors upon certain holy places and upon the abodes of certain pious people who were in prayer. These vapors were bordered by rainbow edges, and in them was the blessing like a pearl in its shell. I was told that this, though typical, was a true representation of how the preparation for the coming of the Blessed Virgin would develop from those various blessed points.

Soon after this vision, Elias enlarged the cave in which he was accustomed to pray. He made new regulations for the prophet children, of whom from that time some in that cave constantly supplicated for the coming of Mary and honored her advent.

Elias had by his prayer called up the clouds, and he directed them according to interior enlightenment; otherwise a sudden and destructive rain gust might have resulted from them. At first I saw these clouds dropping down dew, settling in white plains, forming eddies with rainbow-colored edges, and finally dissolving in drops. I recognized some connection between them and the manna in the desert which in the morning lay brittle and thick like a skin upon the ground. It could be gathered in rolls. I saw the vapors floating along the Jordan. They did not fall in all places indiscriminately, but only here and there, at Salem, for instance, where John baptized at a later period, and at the spot where subsequently his pool of baptism stood. I asked for the signification of the colored edges, and it was explained to me by a certain shell of the sea which, too, has shining colored margins. The shell under the sun's rays absorbs the light, reflects its colors at the edges, thus purifying the ray as it were, until in its own center the pure, white pearl is formed. I cannot express it, but I understood that that dew and the rain following it did more than what is commonly signified by a refreshing, a watering of the earth. I received the clear assurance that, without this dew, Mary's advent would have been delayed one hundred years longer; while through that watering and blessing of the earth, the different families living on its produce were quickened and enlivened. Thus their flesh received a new blessing by which it became more purified and ennobled by propagation. The vision of the pearl in its shell bore reference to Jesus and Mary.

The drought that I saw was not confined to the earth alone; there was also a great drought, great sterility among men. But the spray of the fructifying dew descended from generation to generation down to the flesh of Mary. I cannot express it. At times, there appeared upon the colored edges of the cloud, one or several pearls, and upon these a human figure, breathing forth something spirit-like which again seemed to amalgamate in the others.

I saw also that, by the great mercy of God, the pious heathens of that age knew that the Messiah would be born of a virgin of Judea. This knowledge was imparted to the star worshippers of Chaldea by the appearance of a vision either in a star or in the heavens. They prophesied concerning it. I saw the same tidings of salvation proclaimed in Egypt.

Elias was commanded by God to bring together into Judea several pious families scattered to the north, east, and south. He sought for three prophet scholars suited to the mission, and he implored a sign from God by which he might recognize them, for it was a distant and very hazardous undertaking.

One went north; the second, east; and the third, south. This last route led to Egypt where Israelites could not enter without risk. I saw the third messenger journeying along the road subsequently traversed by the Holy Family, and also at Heliopolis. He came, at last, to a great pagan temple surrounded by numerous buildings and situated in a wide plain. A live bull was worshipped in this temple, and in it were also the image of a bull and other idols. Deformed children were sacrificed to the animal. As the prophet was passing the temple, he was seized and led before the priests. Fortunately for him, they were exceedingly inquisitive, else perhaps they would have murdered him at once. They questioned him as to whence he came. He answered fearlessly, telling them that a virgin would be born from whom should proceed the salvation of the world, then would all their idols be shattered. They were amazed and impressed by what they heard, and allowed him to go on his way. But they afterward took counsel together and resolved to make the image of a virgin. When it was finished, they placed it high in the center of the temple roof, and in a position as if in the act of floating down. The virgin's headdress was like that of so many of the other idols, half-woman, half-lion, that were in the temple. The upper part of the arms was close to the body, the forearms extended as if warding off something. Feathers radiated from both upper and lower arms, two clasping together like crests, or combs; similar feathers ran down the sides and the middle of the body to the tiny feet.

The Egyptians honored this image and offered sacrifice to it, that thereby the virgin might not destroy their god Apis and their other idols. But they still continued in their usual abominations. The only change the prophet's communication wrought was that they thenceforth invoked the image of the virgin and honored it according to the various interpretations they put upon his words.

I saw much of the history of Tobias and the marriage brought about by the angel, between young Tobias with Sara. The latter was a type of St. Anne. The old Tobias represented the race of pious Jews that yearned after the Messiah. His blindness signified that he was to be the father of no more children, and that he should devote himself entirely to meditation and prayer. His quarrelsome wife was an image of the vain and troublesome ceremonies of the pharisaical doctors of the Law. The swallow, a messenger of spring, heralded the coming salvation. Tobias's blindness chiefly betokened the faithful, though obscure waiting and longing for salvation and the ignorance of whence it should come. The angel had indeed spoken truly when he said that he was Azarias, the son of Ananias, for this word signifies *the help of the Lord out of the cloud of the Lord*. This angel was the guide of the races, the protector and administrator of the Blessing even unto the Conception of the Blessed Virgin. In the prayer offered together by young Tobias and Sara, and which I saw carried by angels to the throne of God where it was favorably received, I recognized the supplications of the pious Israelites and the daughters of Sion for the coming of the Saviour, also the simultaneous prayers of Joachim and Anne for the child promised to them. The blindness of Tobias and the reproaches of his wife signified also the contempt shown to Joachim and the slighting of his offerings. The seven murdered husbands of Sara represented those among the ancestors of Mary who had placed obstacles to her coming and, consequently, to the salvation of man. They likewise denoted the suitors dismissed by Anne before her marriage with Joachim. The reproaches of Sara's maid signified the derision of pagans, of unbelievers, and of godless Jews upon the delay in the coming of the long-looked-for Messiah. Such impious taunts drove the pious to still more earnest prayer. It was also and very particularly a symbol of the scorn that Anne endured from her maid, at which being confused, she had recourse to prayer with so great earnestness that she was heard. The fish about to devour the young Tobias typified the prolonged sterility of Anne; but the removal of its heart, liver, and gall denoted good works and mortification. The little kid brought home by Tobias's wife as the wages of her work, was really a stolen one that the people had given to her cheap. Tobias knew the people as well as the whole transaction, and that was the reason that they despised him. It bore also some signification to the relations that existed between the pious Jews and the Essenians on the one hand, and the Pharisees and merely ceremonious Jews on the other, also the scorn felt by the latter for the former; but what that signification was, I cannot now recall. The gall, by which the blind Tobias was restored to sight, symbolized the suffering and bitterness by which the elect among the Jews arrived at the knowledge of salvation and attained to a participation in the same. It signified the entrance of light into darkness, Jesus entering upon His bitter Passion from His very birth.

4. Symbolical Vision

I saw a slender pillar arise out of the earth. It was like the stalk of a flower, and like the calyx, or the capsule, of the poppy, I saw the octagonal church upon the top of this pillar. The pillar arose through the center of the church and there, like a tree, divided into several branches. Upon these branches stood the members of the Holy Family and their relatives. They were indeed the central objects of veneration in this vision. They stood as if on the stamens of flowers. Anne stood above between two holy men, Joachim and her father, or some other member of her family. Below St. Anne's breast I saw a brilliant space almost in the shape of a heart. In this light, I saw the figure of a shining child unfolding as it were, becoming larger. Its hands were clasped upon its breast, its head inclined, and it constantly shed toward one quarter of the globe numerous rays of light. I noticed with surprise that the rays did not stream in all directions. On the surrounding branches and inclining toward this middle one, were adorers, and all around in the church, in groups and choirs innumerable, were saints inclining in prayer toward the holy central point. The sweetness, fervor, and simplicity of this sacred service can be compared to nothing but a flowery field swayed toward the sun by a gentle breeze, and sending its perfumes and colors to those beams to which all flowers owe their gifts, yes, their existence itself. Above this picture of the Immaculate Conception, arose the stem of grace. It extended above Anne, and upon this stem, crownlike sat Mary and Joseph. Below them in adoration sat Anne. But above them all, on the very summit of the tree sat the Child Jesus in unfading splendor, the imperial globe in His hand. In adoration around these groups, were first the choirs of the Apostles and disciples and, in more distant circles, those of the other saints. High above all, I saw in the brightest light, figures and powers of indeterminate form, and over them something like a half-sun rayed out its beams. This second picture seemed to signify the advent. First I saw the region below and around the pillar, then I saw the church and its adorers, and lastly the child developing in the shining heart. I received at the same time an unspeakable assurance of the sinless Conception. I read it plainly as if in a book, and I comprehended it. I was also informed that a church had once stood on this spot, but on account of its being the scene of many scandalous disputes on the subject of the Immaculate Conception, it had been given over to destruction. The Church Triumphant, however, still celebrates the feast on its site. I heard also the words: "Every vision contains some mystery until its fulfillment."

5. Eve of Mary's Birth

What gladness throughout all nature! Birds are singing, lambs and kids are gamboling, and swarms of doves are fluttering with joy around the spot upon which once stood Anne's abode. I see only a wilderness there at the present day . . . But I had a vision of pilgrims in the far-off times who, girded and with long staves in their hands, wended their way through the country to Mount Carmel. On their head they wore a covering wound around like a turban. They, too, participated in the joy of nature. And when in their astonishment they asked the hermits that dwelt in the neighborhood the cause of this remarkable exultation, they received for answer that such manifestations of gladness were customary. They were always observed upon the eve of the anniversary of Mary's birth around that spot where once stood Anne's house. The hermits told them of a holy man of the early times who had been the first to notice these wonders in nature. His account gave rise to the celebration of the feast of Mary's Nativity which soon became general throughout the Church. And now I, too, beheld how this came to pass.

I saw a pious pilgrim, two hundred and fifty years after Mary's death, traversing the Holy Land, visiting and venerating all places connected with the actions of Jesus while on earth. He was supernaturally guided. Sometimes he tarried several days together in certain places in which he tasted extraordinary consolation. There he prayed and meditated, and there also he received revelations from on high. For several years he had, from the seventh to the eighth of September, noticed a great jubilation in nature and heard angelic voices singing in the air. He prayed earnestly to know the meaning of all this, and it was made known to him in a vision that that was the birthnight of the Blessed Virgin Mary. He was on his way to Mount Sinai when he had this vision. In it he was informed also of the existence of a chapel built in Mary's honor in a cave of the Prophet Elias. He was told to reveal this, as well as the circumstance of Mary's birthnight, to the hermits on Mount Sinai.

I saw him again when he arrived at the mount. Where the convent now stands there dwelt, even at that early period, hermits scattered here and there. It was then as inaccessible from the valley as it is now. To reach the top of the mountain from that side, hoisting machines were used. I saw that in consequence of the pilgrim's communication, the eighth of September was here first celebrated in the year 250, and that later it was introduced into other parts of the Church.

I saw hermits accompanying the pilgrim to the cave of Elias to visit the chapel that had been built therein to Mary's honor. But it was not easy to find, for the mountain was covered with gardens that still produced magnificent fruits, though long allowed to run wild, and there were numerous caves of hermits and Essenians. The pilgrim who had had the vision told them to send a Jew into the different caves, and that the one out of which he should be thrust would be the cave of Elias. He had been thus instructed in vision. I then saw them sending an old Jew into the caves; but, as often as he tried to enter a certain one that had a narrow entrance built up before it, he was repulsed. By this miracle the cave of Elias was recognized. On entering it they found another cave, the entrance to which had been closed by masonry; this was the chapel in which the Prophet Elias had in prayer honored the future Mother of the Saviour. Many holy relics were still preserved in it, bones of the Prophets and Patriarchs, screens and vessels that had once been used in ceremonies of the Old Law. These latter were appropriated to the use of the Church.

The spot upon which the thornbush had stood was called in the language of that country: *The Shadow of God*. It was entered only barefoot. The Elias chapel was walled up with beautiful large stones through which ran flowerlike veinings. They were afterward employed for the erection of the church. In the vicinity is a mountain entirely of red sand on which, nevertheless, there is very beautiful fruit.

I learned from St. Bridget that if pregnant women fast on the eve of Mary's birth and say fervently nine Hail Marys to honor the nine months she passed in Anne's womb; if they frequently repeat these prayers during their pregnancy, and especially on the eve of their delivery, receiving then the holy Sacraments devoutly, she will offer their prayer to God herself and bring them through even very critical circumstances to a happy delivery.

I saw the Blessed Virgin on the eve of her nativity. She said to me: "Whoever says this evening," (Sept. 7th) "nine times the Hail Mary lovingly and devoutly to honor the nine months spent in my mother's womb as also my birth, and continues the same devotion for nine consecutive days, daily gives to the angels nine flowers for a bouquet. This bouquet they bear to Heaven and offer to the Most Holy Trinity to obtain some favor for the one that prays."

I was transported to a high place between Heaven and earth. I saw the earth below me gray and somber, and above me Heaven where, among the choirs of angels and the orders of the blessed, was the Blessed Virgin before the throne of God. I saw prepared for her two thrones of honor, two buildings of honor, which finally became churches, yet, whole cities, and they were formed out of the prayers of earth. They were built entirely of flowers, leaves, garlands, the various species typical of the different value and characteristics of the prayers of individuals and of whole congregations. Angels and saints took them from the hands of those that offered them and bore them up to Heaven.

6. Birth of Mary

Several days previously, Anne informed Joachim that the time of her delivery was at hand. She sent messengers to her sister Maraha, at Sephoris, also to the widow Enue, Elizabeth's sister, in the valley of Zabulon, and to her sister Sobe's daughter Salome, the wife of Zebedee, of Bethsaida. The sons of Sobe and Zebedee, James the Greater and John, were not yet born. Anne sent for these three women to come to her. I saw them on their journey. Two of them were accompanied by their husbands, who returned, however, when they had reached the neighborhood of Nazareth. Joachim had sent the men servants off to the herds, and had otherwise disposed of the domestics not absolutely needed in the house. Mary Heli, Anne's eldest daughter, now the wife of Cleophas, took charge of the household affairs.

On the evening before the birth of the child, Joachim himself went to his herds in the field nearest his home. I saw him with some of his servants who were related to him. He called them brothers, but they were only his brother's children. The pasture grounds were beautifully divided off and hedged in. In the corners were huts wherein the servants were provided with food supplied from Anne's house.

There was also a stone altar before which they prayed. Steps led down to it, and the space around it was neatly paved with triangular stones. Behind the altar was a wall with steps at the sides. The whole place was surrounded by trees.

Joachim, after praying here awhile, selected the finest lambs, kids, and bullocks from his herds, and sent them by his servants to the Temple as offerings. He did not return to his home before night.

I saw the three women approaching Anne's abode toward evening. When they arrived, they went straight to her apartment back of the fireplace. Anne embraced them, told them that her time drew near, and standing entoned with them a Psalm. "Praise God, the Lord. He has had pity on His people and has freed Israel. Truly, He has fulfilled the promise that He made to Adam in Paradise: "The seed of the woman shall crush the serpent's head." I do not remember all, verse for verse, but Anne rehearsed the different types of Mary, and said: "The germ that God gave to Abraham has ripened in me. The promise made to Sara and the blossom of Aaron's rod are fulfilled in me." During all this time, Anne was shining with light. The room was full of glory, and over Anne hovered Jacob's ladder. The women around her were amazed, entranced. I think they too saw the ladder.

And now a slight refreshment was placed before the visitors. They ate and drank standing and toward midnight lay down to rest. But Anne remained up in prayer. After awhile, she went and roused the women. She felt that her time was near, and she desired them to pray with her. They all withdrew behind a curtain that concealed an oratory. Anne opened the doors of a little closet built in the wall. In it was a box containing sacred treasures, and on either side lights so contrived that they could be raised in their sockets at pleasure, and rested on upright supports. These lamps were now lighted. At the foot of the little altar was a cushioned stool. The box contained some of Sara's hair, which Anne held in great reverence; some of the bones of Joseph, which Moses had brought with him out of Egypt; something belonging to Tobias, relics of clothing, I think; and the little, white, shining, pear-shaped cup from which Abraham drank when he received the Blessing from the angel, and which was later on taken from the Ark of the Covenant and given to Joachim along with the Blessing. This Blessing was like wine and bread, like a sacrament, like a supernatural, invigorating food. Anne knelt before the shrine, one of the women on either side, and the third behind her. Again I heard them reciting a Psalm. I think that the burning bush on Horeb was mentioned in it. And now a supernatural light began to fill the chamber and to hover around Anne. The three women fell prostrate as if stunned. Around Anne the light took the exact form of the thornbush on Horeb, so that I could no longer see her. The flame streamed inward, and all at once I saw Anne receiving into her arms the shining child Mary. She wrapped it in her mantle, pressed it to her heart, laid it on the stool before the relics, and went on with her prayer.

Then I heard the child crying, and I saw Anne drawing forth some linen from under the large veil that enveloped her. She swathed the child first in gray and then in red, leaving the breast, arms, and head bare, and then the luminous thornbush vanished. The holy women arose and in glad surprise received the newborn child into their arms. They wept for joy. All entoned a hymn of praise while Anne held the child on high. I saw the chamber again filled with light and myriads of angels. They announced the child's name, singing: "On the twentieth day, this child shall be called Mary." Then they sang *Gloria* and *Alleluia*. I heard all these words.

Anne went to her chamber, and lay down upon her couch. The women bathed and swathed the child, and laid it by the mother. Next to the bed was a little portable basket-crib furnished with wooden pegs, by means of which it could be stuck into holes on the right or left, or at the foot of the bed as might be desired. One of the women went and called Joachim. He entered, knelt by Anne's couch, and his tears fell in torrents over the child. Then he took it up, held it aloft, and entoned a canticle of praise like unto that of Zachary. He spoke words expressive of his longing now to die, and he alluded to the germ given by God to Abraham and perfected in himself, also to the root of Jesse. I noticed, though not till afterward, that Mary Heli was not among the first to see the child. She must at this time have been for some years the mother of Mary Cleophas. Still she was not present at Mary's birth, because the Jewish custom does not permit the daughter to be with the mother at such a time.

When Mary was born, I saw her at one and the same time before the Most Holy Trinity in Heaven and on earth in Anne's arms. I saw the joy of the whole heavenly court. I saw all her gifts and graces in a supernatural way revealed to her. I often have such visions, but they are for me inexpressible, for others unintelligible, therefore am I silent with regard to them. Mary was also instructed in innumerable mysteries. As this vision ended, the child cried upon earth.

I saw the news of Mary's birth announced also in Limbo, and I beheld the transports of joy with which it was received by the Patriarchs, especially by Adam and Eve who rejoiced that the Promise made them in Paradise was now fulfilled. I saw also that the Patriarchs increased in grace, their abode became lighter and less constrained, and that they began to exercise a greater influence on earth. It was as if all their good works, all their penance, all the efforts of their life, all their desires and aspirations had at last brought forth fruit.

All nature, animate and inanimate, men and beasts were stirred to joy, and I heard sweet singing. But sinners were filled with anguish and remorse. I saw, especially around Nazareth and in other parts of Palestine, many possessed souls who at the hour of Mary's birth became perfectly furious. They uttered horrible cries, and they were tossed and dashed about. The devils cried out of them: "We must withdraw! We must go out!"

My greatest delight was to see the old priest Simeon in the Temple on this night of Mary's birth. He was aroused by the fearful cries of the possessed confined in one of the streets on the Temple mountain. Simeon with others had charge of them. He went that night to the house in which they were, and asked the cause of those shrieks that roused everyone from sleep. The possessed man nearest to the entrance cried out fiercely that he must get out. Simeon released him, and then the devil cried out: "I must go forth! We must go forth! A virgin is born, and there are upon earth so many angels who torment us. We must go forth, and never again shall we dare possess a human being!" Then I saw the poor creature horribly tossed to and fro by the devil, who at last went out of him. Simeon was in prayer. I rejoiced greatly at seeing old Simeon then.

I saw, too, Anna, the Prophetess, and another one of Mary's future teachers in the Temple aroused and instructed in vision upon the birth of the child. They told each other what had happened. I think they knew of Anne.

In the country of the Three Holy Kings, certain prophetesses had visions of the birth of the Blessed Virgin. They told their priests that a Virgin was born, to welcome whom many spirits had come down upon earth, but that other spirits were troubled. The stargazing Kings also saw pictures of it in their stars.

In Egypt, on the night of the birth, an idol was hurled from its temple into the sea, and another fell from its place and was dashed to pieces.

Next morning I saw a great crowd from the neighborhood around the house along with Anne's servants, male and female. The women in charge showed the child to them. Many of them were very much affected, and many wicked hearts were changed. They had gathered around the house because they had seen a light over it during the night and also because the birth of Anne's child was looked upon as a great blessing.

Later on other relatives of Joachim from the valley of Zabulon arrived, also the servants from a distance. The child was shown to all, and a repast was prepared in the house.

On the following days people flocked in numbers to see the child Mary. Her little cradle, which was in the form of a boat, was placed upon a raised pedestal, something like a sawing-jack, in the front apartment. The lower coverlet was red, the upper one white, and on them lay the child swathed up to the armpits in red and transparent white. She had tiny, golden curls.

I saw also Mary Cleophas, the child of Mary Heli and Cleophas, the grandchild of Anne. She was then a little girl of only a few years. She was playing with the infant Mary and caressing her. She was a stout, healthy child. She wore a little white, sleeveless dress bordered with red from which hung tiny red balls, like apples. Around her little bare arms were twined rows of white stuff, maybe feathers or silk or wool. The child Mary had also a little transparent scarf around her neck.

7. The Child Receives the Name of Mary

I saw a great feast in Anne's house; all was gladness. The wicker partitions in the front of the house had been taken away, and a large room was thusly made ready. All around it ran a low table upon which stood plates, glasses, etc., but as yet no eatables. In the middle of the room was an altar covered with red and white, and a stand upon which scrolls were laid. A small basket-cradle stood on the altar. It was shaped like a shell, and woven in white and red; the coverlet was sky-blue. Priests from Nazareth were present in their sacred vestments; among them was one robed more magnificently than the rest. Many of the female guests, relatives of Anne, were also in their holiday garments. Among them were Anne's eldest daughter Mary Heli, espoused to Cleophas, Anne's sister from Sephoris, and others. Several of Joachim's relatives also were present. Anne was up, but she did not appear. She remained in her chamber behind the fireplace. Enue, Elizabeth's sister, brought the infant Mary, swathed as described in red and transparent white, and gave her to Joachim. The priests approached the altar, the attendants bearing the chief priest's train, and prayed from the scrolls. Joachim placed the child on the arms of the chief priest, who held her aloft, prayed for awhile, and then laid her in the little cradle on the altar. Then he took a pair of scissors, furnished with a little box at the end for catching the clippings, (something like a pair of snuffers), and cut a little hair from both sides and from the middle of the child's head. The hair thus removed, he burned it upon a pan of coals. Then he took a box of oil and anointed the five senses of the child. With his thumb, he pressed the ointment upon the ears, the eyes, the nose, the mouth, and the heart of the child. He wrote the name Mary on a scrap of parchment, and laid it on the child's breast. Then the little Mary was, by Joachim, given back to Enue, who took her to Anne. The women stood back during the ceremony, at the end of which other Psalms were sung. I saw then all kinds of table furniture, dishes, etc., that I had not before noticed. There were vessels on the table that were quite light, their covers pierced with holes. I think they were baskets into which flowers were put.

On a side table, I saw numbers of little white rods, as if of bone, also spoons. There were also bent tubes lying on it, but I know not for what use. I saw no more of the meal itself.

8. Preparations for Mary's Presentation

Mary was three years and three months old when she made the vow to join the virgins in the Temple. She was very delicately built and had golden hair inclined to curl at the ends. She was already as tall as a child of five or six here in our country. Mary Heli's daughter was a few years older than Mary, and much stronger and stouter. I saw in Anne's house the preparations for Mary's admittance into the Temple. It was made the occasion of a great feast. Five priests had assembled from Nazareth, Sephoris, and other places, among them Zachary and a son of the brother of Anne's father. They were about to perform a sacred ceremony over the child Mary, a kind of examination as to whether she was sufficiently mature in mind to be admitted to the Temple. Besides the priests, there were present Anne's sister from Sephoris with her daughter Mary Heli and her child, and several other little girls and relatives.

The robes worn by the child at this feast were cut out by the priests themselves and the different parts quickly sewed together by the women present. The child was clothed in them at certain periods when subjected to a series of interrogatories. The ceremony was in itself very grave and solemn, although the faces of the aged priests were at times lit up by smiles of admiration at the expressions and answers of the little Mary, and it was frequently interrupted by the tears of Joachim and Anne. Three entire suits were prepared for Mary and put on her at different times during the ceremony, the questioning and answering going on in the meantime. All this took place in a large room next to the dining hall. Light entered through a square opening in the center of the roof, which opening was often covered by a net. The floor was covered with a red carpet. In the middle of the room stood a table, intended for an altar, with a red cover, and over that a white transparent one. Upon it lay a case with rolls of writings and a curtain upon which the picture of Moses was either embroidered or laid on and sewed down. He was represented in the large mantle in which he used to pray, the tables of the Law hanging on his arm. I have always seen Moses represented as a tall, broad-shouldered man. He had a high, somewhat pyramidal head, a large hooked nose, and upon his broad, high forehead, were two bumps inclining toward each other and giving him a very remarkable appearance. In his childhood, they were like little warts. His complexion was brown, bright and ruddy, his hair inclined to red. I saw many such protuberances as those possessed by Moses on the foreheads of the ancient Prophets and hermits; sometimes only one such excrescence appeared upon the middle of the forehead.

On the altar lay the three outfits for the child Mary along with various materials, etc., presented by the relatives for her dowry. A kind of throne stood upon steps before the altar. The priests entered the hall with naked feet. Three of them only proceeded to the examination and blessed the child, who was as yet in her usual clothing. Joachim and Anne were present with their relatives; the women stood back, the little girls at Mary's side. One of the priests took the garments from the altar, explained their signification, and handed them to Anne's sister, from Sephoris, who put them on the child.

First came a little, yellow, knitted robe, and then a colored, laced bodice, which was put on over the head and fastened around the body. It had on the breast something like cords. Over that came a brownish mantle with armholes, from the upper part of which hung lappets. It was cut out around the neck, and closed under the breast. On her feet were brown sandals with thick, green soles. Her reddish-yellow curls were arranged, and a silken crown with feathers in it placed upon them. The feathers were a finger in length, and they bent over toward the inside of the crown. I know to what bird in that country they belonged. A large square, ash-colored kerchief was thrown over her head like a large veil. It could be drawn together under the arms in such a way that they might rest in it as in slings. It appeared to be a mantle used in time of prayer and penance, also in travelling.

The priests now put to the child all sorts of questions relative to the discipline enforced in the Temple. Among other things, they said to her: "Thy parents, having promised thee to the Temple, have made a vow that thou shouldst drink no wine nor vinegar, shouldst eat no grapes nor figs. Now what wilt thou add to this vow? Think upon this during thy meal." The Jewish people, and especially the young maidens were accustomed to drink vinegar. Mary, too, was fond of it. On these and similar things, was she interrogated.

And now the second suit was put upon the child, It consisted of a sky-blue body, a mantle of the same color, but of a lighter shade, a richer bodice, and a white veil, glossy like silk, which fell behind in folds something like the consecrated veil of a nun. Over this was a fine, closely-fitting wreath of colored flower-buds made of silk and intermixed with small green leaves. Then the priests threw over her face a white veil gathered on top like a cap. It was caught by three clasps, one below the other, by means of which the veil could be raised upon the head, either one third, or one half, or even the whole.

The child was instructed upon the use of this veil, when to be raised or lowered in eating or answering questions. In this array, Mary went to table where she sat between two of the priests, the third oppo-

site to her. The women and children sat at one end
of the table apart from the men. During the meal,
the priests practiced the child in many points upon
the use of the veil, asking questions and receiving
her answers, and also in many other of the customary ceremonies. They reminded her that she still
could partake of everything, and they offered her different dishes, tempting her in order to see how far
her abstinence would go. But Mary excited their admiration by all that she did and said. She tasted sparingly of only a few dishes, and answered all their
questions with simplicity and wisdom. During the
meal and the whole of the examination, I saw angels
hovering around her, directing and assisting her in
all things.

After the repast, she was clothed anew before the
altar in the next room. Anne's sister from Sephoris
assisted the priest in the ceremony, during which
the latter explained the signification of the garments
and spoke of spiritual things. The robes now put on
the child were the most beautiful of all. A violet-blue
bodice, and over it a breast-piece embroidered in colors. The latter was now fastened to the piece that
covered the back, caught to the plaited skirt, and
fell below in a point. Over this fell a violet-blue mantle, full and magnificent, rounded in the back very
much like a chasuble. When it was closed on the
breast, it formed puffs on the arms, like arches,
wherein they could rest, and yet be exposed to view.
It had five rows of gold embroidery down the front,
the middle one furnished with the buttons or hooks
that fastened the mantle. It was also embroidered
around the edge. A large changeable-colored veil was
then put on, which glanced from white to violet-blue.
Upon this veil rested a crown, closed on top by five
clasps. It was a thin, broad circlet lined with gold,
the upper edge spreading into points tipped with little balls. A network of silk covered the outside, which
was ornamented with small roses of the same mate-

rial in whose center were fastened five pearls. The
five points also were of silk and surmounted by a
ball. The breastpiece was fastened behind, yet had
cords also in front as if for lacing. Her mantle was
caught first over the breast by a crossband, which
was prevented from pressing upon the breast ornament by a button with a long shank; it closed again
under the bodice and fell behind the arms in folds.

In this festive attire, Mary was placed upon the
steps before the altar, the little girls at her side. She
now repeated her resolve to abstain from flesh, fish,
and milk, to make use of only a certain drink prepared from the pith of a reed soaked in water. This
was much used by the poor of Palestine, just as here
in our own country rice or barley water is drunk by
them. To this beverage, Mary proposed to add occasionally some terebinthine juice. This juice is like a
white, viscid oil and is very refreshing, though not
in the same degree as balsam. Mary expressed her
resolution to refrain also from spices and fruits, with
the exception of a kind of yellow berry that grows
in bunches. I know them well. Children and poor
people eat them in that country. She said also that
she would lie on the bare ground and nightly rise
three times to pray. The other maidens rose but once.

Upon hearing this, Anne and Joachim shed tears,
and the aged Joachim pressed his child in his arms,
saying: "Ah, my child, that is too hard! If thou livest
so mortified a life, I, thy poor old father, shall never
see thee again." This scene was very affecting.

But the priests replied to the child that she should,
like the others, rise once only during the night, and
they laid down other and milder conditions for her.
Finally, they said, "Many of the other virgins enter
the Temple without a dowry or even wherewith to
pay their board. On this account and with their parents' consent, they engage to wash the blood-besprin-
kled garments of the priests and the rough woollen
cloths. This is a very heavy work, and not accom-

plished without bleeding hands. But thou wilt never be called upon for such services, since thy parents are able to maintain thee at the Temple."

But Mary quickly replied that she was ready even for this work, were she esteemed worthy to perform it. At this speech, Joachim again betrayed his emotion. During these holy ceremonies, I beheld Mary becoming at times so tall that she even rose above the heads of the priests. This was for me a sign of her wisdom and grace. The priests were filled with amazement, at once solemn and joyful.

At last, Mary was blessed by the priests. I saw her radiant with light as she stood on the little altar throne, two priests on either side of her and one opposite. They held rolls of writing, and prayed over the child, their hands outstretched above her. At that moment, I saw a wonderful vision in the child Mary. She seemed, by virtue of the blessing, to become transparent. In her was a glory, a halo of unspeakable splendor, and in that halo appeared the Mystery of the Ark of the Covenant, as if in a glittering crystal vessel. I saw Mary's heart open like the doors of a temple, and the Holy Thing of the Ark of the Covenant, around which a tabernacle of precious stones of multiplied signification had been formed like a heavenly throne, going into her heart through that opening, like the Ark of the Covenant into the Holy of Holies, like the ostensorium into the tabernacle. I saw that by this the child Mary was glorified; she hovered above the earth. With the entrance of this Sacrament into Mary's heart, which immediately closed over It, the vision faded, and I saw the child all penetrated by glowing fervor. During this wonderful vision, I saw that Zachary received an interior assurance, a heavenly monition that Mary was the chosen vessel of the Mystery. From it he had received a ray that had appeared figuratively in Mary.

And now the priests led the child to her parents. Anne caught her child to her breast and kissed her, but Joachim—deeply affected—reverenced Mary and only took her hand. The elder sister Mary Heli embraced the favored child with much more gaiety than did Anne, who was a very serious, practical, moderate, and self-possessed woman. The little niece, Mary Cleophas, acted as any child would, and fondly embraced the little Mary.

Then the priests took the child again, disrobed her, and led her forth in her customary dress. I saw them standing drinking out of a cup, and then departing.

9. The Journey to the Temple

I saw Joachim, Anne, and their elder daughter busied during the night packing and preparing for a journey. A lamp with several wicks was burning, and I saw Mary Heli busily going about with a light. Some days before, Joachim had sent his servants up to the Temple with offerings of cattle, five of the finest of every kind. They made a nice herd. Now he saddled two of the beasts of burden, and loaded them with all kinds of baggage: clothes for the child and presents for the Temple. A broad package was laid on the back of each beast, and formed a comfortable seat. The baggage was all in bundles. On both sides of one of the beasts platter-shaped baskets with arched covers were fastened. In them were birds as large as partridges. There were also oval baskets containing fruit. A cover with heavy tassels was thrown over the whole load.

Two of the priests were still present. One was very old. He wore a cap pointed on the forehead and with lappets over the ears. His upper garment was shorter than the under one, and over it was a kind of stole. He had much to do with the child. The other priest was younger.

I saw also two boys present. They were not human. They appeared there supernaturally and with a spiritual signification. They carried long standards rolled upon staffs furnished with knobs at both ends. The larger of the two boys came to me with his standard unfurled, read, and explained it to me. The writing appeared entirely strange to me, the single, golden letters all inverted. One letter represented a whole word. The language sounded unfamiliar, but I understood it all the same. He showed me in his roll the passage referring to the burning thornbush of Moses. He explained to me how the thornbush burned, and yet was not consumed; so now was the child Mary inflamed with the fire of the Holy Spirit, but in her humility she knew nothing of it. It signifies also the Divinity and Humanity in Jesus, and how God's fire united with the child Mary. The putting-off of the shoes, he explained thus: "The Law will now be fulfilled. The veil is withdrawn and the essence appears." By the little standard on his staff was signified, as he told me, that Mary now began her course, her career, to become the Mother of the Redeemer. The other boy seemed to be playing with his standard. He jumped about and ran around with it. By this was signified Mary's innocence. The great Promise is to be fulfilled in her, rests upon her, and yet she plays like a child in this holy destiny. I cannot express the loveliness of those boys. They were different from all others present, and these latter did not appear to see them.

There were besides Anne about six female relatives with their children and some men who accompanied them. Joachim guided the beast, upon which the child Mary sometimes rode. He carried a light, for it was still dark when they set out. A servant led the other. The little procession was also accompanied by the other apparitions of the Prophets. As Mary hastened from the house, they pointed out to me a place in their rolls, wherein it was declared that, although the Temple was indeed magnificent, yet Mary contained in herself still greater magnificence. Mary wore the little yellowish gown and the large veil so fastened around her that her arms could rest in it. When she rode, the Prophet boys followed behind her; but when she walked, they were at her side, singing the *Psalms 44* and *49*. I knew that the same would be sung at her reception in the Temple. The child Mary saw those boys, but she said nothing about it. She was perfectly silent, wholly recollected in self.

The journey was difficult, over mountain and valley. In the latter lay chilling mists and dew. Once I saw the travellers resting at a fountain under some balsam trees, and again stopping overnight at an inn at the foot of a mountain.

Twelve leagues from Jerusalem, they came up at an inn with the herd that had been sent on in advance as an offering, and which was just about starting anew. Joachim was well known here, and was quite at home. When taking his offerings up to Jerusalem, he had always stopped at this inn; and when, from his penitential stay among the shepherds he returned to Nazareth, he had also put up here.

I again saw the holy travellers in the city Bethoron, six leagues from Jerusalem. They had crossed a rivulet, had passed Gophna and Ozensara, and were still distant about two leagues from a road whence Jerusalem could be descried. At Bethoron, they put up at a Levitical school. Relatives of Joachim and Anne from Nazareth, Sephoris, Zabulon, and the country around, had come hither with their daughters, and there was quite a little festival in Mary's honor. She was conducted with many other children to a hall in which a special place had been prepared for her on an elevated seat like a throne. She was then crowned. The teachers questioned her, and were struck with all her answers. Mention was made of the wisdom of another maiden who not long since had returned from the Temple to her home at Gophna. She was called Susanna, and I think that it was her place Mary was going to take in the Temple. Susanna was then fifteen; later, she joined the holy women that followed Jesus.

Mary rejoiced at being now so near to the Temple. Joachim embraced her, weeping and saying, "I shall never see thee again!" During the repast, Mary went here and there. Several times she reclined by Anne's side at table, or stood behind her with her arm around her neck.

On the following day, accompanied by the teacher of the Levitical school and his family, they started very early for Jerusalem. The young girls carried beautiful fruits and garments as presents for the child. It looked to me as if there was going to be a real feast in Jerusalem. The nearer they approached the Holy City, the more eager and desirous became Mary. She generally ran on before her parents.

I saw the arrival of the procession in Jerusalem, and also beheld the roads and paths and buildings more distinctly than I had done for a long time. Jerusalem was a very singular-looking city. We must not represent it to ourselves with its streets thronged as the great cities of the present day. Many steep and hilly streets ran around behind the city walls, from which no gates led. The houses lying high behind those walls faced the opposite side, for many parts of the city were built at subsequent periods, new ridges of hills being taken in accordingly. The old city walls, however, were always allowed to remain standing. Many of the deep valleys were spanned by massive stone arches. The courtyards and rooms of the houses all opened toward the back of the building, the entrance only being on the street. The walls were surmounted by terraces or balconies. The houses were kept closed the greater part of the time. When the inhabitants had no affairs to call them to the public places of the city or to the Temple, they remained for the most part in their own houses and courts. It was tolerably quiet on the streets, except-ing in the neighborhood of the markets and palaces where there was much going to and fro of soldiers and travellers. On certain days, at the time when all were gathered in the Temple for worship, the city in many localities was entirely deserted. On this account and the seclusion of the people in their houses, Jesus and His disciples were enabled to go undisturbed through the solitary streets and deep valleys. Water was not plentiful in the city; one often sees high buildings to and from which it was conveyed, also towers in which it was pumped. They were very careful of water at the Temple where such quantities were needed for washing and purifying the various vessels, etc. They had great engines for pumping it up. There were numbers of shopkeepers and merchants in the city; they had their booths all together in the markets and open squares. So stood, for instance, not far from the sheepgate, many dealers in all kinds of gold trinkets and shining stones. Their booths were round and light, and quite brown as if streaked with something, pitch or resin, probably. Though light, they were very strong. There they carried on their business and, under tents stretched from one to another, they exposed their different wares. There were also certain localities, near the palaces for instance, where there was more life in the streets, where it was more brisk. Old Rome was indeed more pleasantly situated. It was not so steep, and its streets were more lively. On one side of the mountain upon which the Temple was situated, the declivity was more gentle. Here there were several streets upon terraces and on top of the thick walls, where some of the priests and servants of the Temple dwelt, as did some laboring people who performed the lowest services, such as purifying the ditches wherein was thrown the offal of the cattle slaughtered for the Temple. On the other side, the mountain was very steep, and the ditch quite black. Around the summit of the mountain was a green ledge whereon the priests had all kinds of little gardens.

Even in Christ's time, there was upon certain parts of the Temple work constantly going on.

There were quantities of ore in the mountain upon which stood the Temple, and much was dug out and used in the building. Inside the meadow were numbers of smelting vaults and furnaces. I never felt at home in the Temple, for I never could find in it a place well-suited for prayer. It was all so immensely solid, so massive, so high, the numerous courts were so narrow, dark, and obstructed by so many elevated platforms and seats, that, when the people were in it, it presented a somewhat frightful spectacle, and even looked confined with its high, massive walls and lofty pillars. The constant slaughtering going on and the quantities of blood flowing in consequence, I found most repulsive, though words cannot express the wonderful order and cleanliness that reigned in everything connected with it.

10. The Entrance into Jerusalem

I saw the caravan that conducted Mary approaching Jerusalem from the north, and winding toward the east around the outlying gardens and palaces of the city. They crossed the valley of Josaphat and, leaving the road to Bethania on the left, entered the city by the sheepgate leading to the cattle market. There was a pool here in which the sheep were washed. Thence their way turned to the right and ran between walls to another section of the city. Then they followed a long road through a valley, and at last reached the neighborhood of the fish market at the west side of the city. Here stood the house at which Zachary, when engaged in the service of the Temple, always put up. Out of this inn came men, women, and children with garlands to meet the caravan and to conduct them in ceremony to the house, about a quarter of an hour's distance, at which they were to stop. Zachary was not present, but I saw a very old man there, his father's brother I think; and among those that came out to welcome Mary, were relatives with their children from the country around Hebron and Bethlehem. There was a fine feast prepared for them in the house at which they stopped. The child Mary wore the second festival suit with the little blue mantle.

Zachary called here for them, in order to take them to the feast inn that he had hired for them. This was an inn which could be hired on festival occasions like the present. There were four such inns on the northeast side of the mountain on which stood the Temple. That hired by Zachary was very large. Four halls surrounded a large court, along whose walls were sleeping places and long, low tables. A spacious saloon and a kitchen were also prepared for the guests. On two sides of this feast inn, dwelt some of the servants of the Temple, whose duty it was to see to the animals intended for sacrifice. The court wherein was placed the herd that Joachim had brought as an offering, lay hard by.

A procession was formed when Zachary was about to lead the travellers into the inn hired for the feast. He himself walked first with Joachim and Anne; then came Mary surrounded by four little girls in white, and followed by the other children and relatives. Their way led to Herod's palace and passed that of the Roman governor, leaving the citadel of Antonia behind; at last they reached a high wall, up which there was a flight of more than fifteen steps. Mary, to the astonishment of all, mounted them without assistance. Her friends wanted to help her, but she refused. Upon their entrance into the inn, their feet were washed. Then they were shown into a large hall in the center of which a lamp was suspended from the ceiling over a large, metal basin of water. Here they washed their face and hands.

Joachim and Anne then went up with Mary to the dwelling of some of the priests. Here, likewise urged by an interior spirit, the child hurried to mount the steps. The two priests cordially received them into the house. Both had been present at Mary's examination in Nazareth. They called one of the women belonging to the Temple, where she executed all kinds of works common to females, and educated little girls. Her abode was at some distance from the Temple, among the added rooms forming the sleeping apartments of the Temple virgins. Out of these rooms, one could—unseen—look down into the sanctuary. The widow was so enveloped in her mantle that one could see only a little of her face. The priests and the parents delivered the child Mary over to her as her future pupil. She received her gravely, but cordially, while the child was all submission and reverence. She (the widow) accompanied the party to the feast inn, and received a package as the child's dowry.

The following day was taken up with preparations for Joachim's sacrifice and for Mary's entrance into the Temple.

Joachim went early with his offering of cattle to the Temple, in front of which the animals for the sacrifice were selected. Those not chosen were at once led back to the cattle market. Joachim had to lay his hand upon the head of each animal before it was slaughtered and he afterward received some of the flesh and blood of each. There were in this place many pillars, tables, and vessels, where the sacrifices were cut up, divided, and arranged. The scum of the blood was put aside; the fat, the spleen, and the liver separated, and all parts were salted. The entrails of the lambs were cleaned, filled with something, and again restored to the animal so that it looked like a whole lamb. The feet were bound crosswise. A great portion of the meat was taken to a court in which were some of the Temple virgins. They seemed to have something to do connected with it; perhaps they had to prepare it either for themselves or for the priests. All was carried on with inde-

scribable order. The priests and Levites came and
went, two and two; and during the difficult and multi-
farious work, all progressed as if by line and level.
The pieces prepared for sacrifice lay over till the
next day.

In the inn was held a feast, and there was also a
repast, at which about one hundred people assisted
along with the children, among them twenty-four
girls of different ages. Among others, I saw Seraphia,
who was called Veronica after the death of Jesus.
She was already well-grown, probably from ten to
twelve years old. They prepared garlands and wreaths
for Mary and her companions, and ornamented for
them seven scepter-shaped lamps on whose summit
burned a flame. During the feast many priests and
Levites went in and out of the inn, taking part also
in the repast. When they expressed surprise at the
greatness of Joachim's offering, he bade them recall
the ignominy he had endured at the Temple when
his former offerings were rejected, and the great
mercy of God who had heard his supplications, and
he asked them whether he should not now express
his gratitude according to the extent of his power. I
saw the child Mary and the other girls taking a walk
in the neighborhood of the house.

11. Mary's Entrance into the Temple and her Offering

Zachary and the other men had already gone to
the Temple, and now Mary was led thither by the
women and the virgins. Anne and her elder daughter Mary Heli, with the little daughter of the latter,
Mary Cleophas, walked first; then came Mary in her
second suit, the sky-blue dress and mantle, her neck
and arms adorned with garlands, and the flower-
wreathed candlestick in her hand. On either side
walked three little maidens with similarly trimmed
candlesticks. They were dressed in white embroidered

with gold, and wore bluish mantles. They were quite covered with garlands, even their arms were twined with flowers. Then followed the other virgins and little girls, about twenty in number, all dressed beautifully, but somewhat differently though all wore mantles. Then came the elderly females. They could not proceed straight to the Temple from this point; they had to take a circuitous route of nearly half an hour. They passed through some streets and before Veronica's house. From many of the dwellings the procession was saluted, the spectators gazing in wonder at the child and her beautiful train of attendants. There was something very extraordinary in Mary's appearance. At the Temple, men were busy opening a large and wonderfully beautiful gate upon which were carved grapevines, ears of wheat, and heads of various kinds. It was the Golden Gate. The priests led the Holy Virgin up numerous steps to this gate. Joachim and Zachary met them at the gate, which opened into a long archway, and led them through several passages into a hall. Here Mary was again questioned by the priests, after which she was clothed in the third holiday suit, the violet-blue, embroidered one.

And now Joachim went with the priests to offer sacrifice. He took fire from a certain place and stood between two priests at the altar. The approach to the altar from three sides was free, but not so on the fourth. At the four corners of the altar, stood small copper pillars and a pipe of the same metal, shaped like a large inverted funnel, which ended in a spiral tube. By this arrangement the smoke from the burning sacrifice rose and escaped over the head of the priest. On three sides of the altar a shelf could be drawn out to receive what was to be laid on the middle of it, since to reach that far would be impossible.

When the sacrifice was kindled, Mary went with the women and children to her place of prayer in the women's porch, where she and her young companions stood in the front row. The porch was separated from the court of the altar of burnt offerings by a wall, in which was a gate with a grating above. Through this gate Joachim entered the subterranean passage when, upon the day of Mary's Immaculate Conception, he met Anne under the Golden Gate. The women back in the court could see the altar better, when mounted on steps raised in tiers. In another court was standing a crowd of white-robed boys belonging to the Temple, playing upon flutes and harps.

After the sacrifice, a portable altar was set up under the arched gateway, and before it were placed a couple of steps. Zachary and Joachim, with some priests and two Levites, entered from the court of the altar of burnt offerings, carrying rolls and writing materials, while Anne led Mary to the steps before the altar. Mary knelt upon the steps, while Joachim and Anne, laying their hands on her head, uttered some words bearing reference to the offering of their child, which words were written down by the two Levites. Then one of the priests cut a lock of hair from the child's head, and cast it upon a pan of live coals, after which he threw around her a brown veil. During this ceremony, the girls sang *Psalm 44, Eructavit cor meum;* the priests, *Psalm 49, Deus deorum Dominus;* and the boys played on their musical instruments.

And now the priests led the Holy Virgin up a long flight of steps in the wall that separated the sanctuary from the rest of the Temple. They stood her in something like a niche, from which she could see into the Temple where were ranged numbers of men who seemed to be consecrated to its service. Two priests stood at Mary's side, and several others on the steps praying and reading aloud from rolls. Behind Mary and on the other side of the wall, a priest was standing at the altar of incense, only half of his person visible from the point at which Mary and her attendants were placed. Through an opening contrived for the purpose, one could cast incense upon the altar without entering the court. The priest now at the incense altar was a holy old man. While he offered sacrifice and the cloud of incense arose around Mary, I saw a vision, which grew in magnitude until at last it filled the whole Temple and obscured it. I saw above the heart of Mary the glory and the Mystery of the Ark of the Covenant. At first it looked exactly like the Ark of the Covenant; and lastly like the Temple itself. Out of the Mystery and before Mary's breast, arose a chalice similar to that of the Last Supper; above it and just in front of her mouth appeared bread marked with a cross. Beams of light radiated around her, and in them shone her various types and symbols. The mysterious pictures of the Litany of Loretto and the other names and titles of Mary, I saw ranged up the whole flight of steps and around her.

From her shoulders, right and left, stretched an olive and a cedar branch crosswise above an elegant palm tree with a small tuft of leaves that stood directly behind her. In the intervening spaces of this verdant cross, appeared all the instruments of Christ's Passion. Over the vision hovered the Holy Spirit, a figure winged with glory, in appearance more human than dovelike. The heavens opened above Mary and the central point of the Heavenly Jerusalem, the City of God, floated over her with all the gardens, the palaces, and the dwellings of the future saints. Angels in myriads hovered around, and the glory that encircled her was full of angelic faces.

Ah, who can express it! Infinite variety, unceasing change, all these pictures following quickly upon and, as it were, growing out of one another. Innumerable points of this vision, I have forgotten. All the splendor and magnificence of the Temple, the richly ornamented wall before which Mary was standing—all grew dark and somber. The whole Temple disappeared, for Mary and her glory alone was visible.

In this vision, symbolical of Mary's spiritual

signification, I saw her not as a child, but full-grown. She hovered in the air. And through and through the vision, I still saw the priests, the incense offering, and everything else. Then the priest at the altar appeared to prophesy, and to call upon the people to thank God and to pray, for that great things were to come upon the child. The crowd in the Temple, greatly awed—although they had not seen the vision that I saw—maintained a solemn stillness. The vision faded away just as gradually as it had unfolded. At last, the Mystery of the Ark of the Covenant shone again in its glory over her heart, and the child once more stood there alone in her rich attire.

Then the priests, among whom Zachary was one of those standing on the lower steps, led Mary down by the hand. One of them took the light from her and the little garlands off her arms, and handed them to the other girls. Mary was then led through a door into another hall where six other Temple virgins, their mistress Noemi, (who was the sister of Lazarus's mother) Anna, and another female met them and scattered flowers before her. To them the priest delivered the child.

When the singing was ended, Mary look leave of her parents. Joachim was especially affected. He took the little child up in his arms, pressed her to his heart, and said weeping: "Remember my soul before God."

Mary now accompanied the women and children belonging to the Temple to their dwelling on the north side, from which passages and winding stairs led up to little chambers adjoining the sanctuary and the Holy of Holies, where they went to pray. The others (that is, Mary's relatives and friends) returned to the apartments near the entrance, and took a repast with the priests, the women apart. There were still in the Temple some devout adorers. Many had followed the procession to the entrance. There were numbers among those present who knew that Mary was a child of promise in her family. I remember, though not distinctly, that Anne had dropped some such expressions to her friends as: "Now does the vessel of the Promise enter the Temple. Now is the Ark of the Covenant in the Temple." It was by a special manifestation of the Divine Will that this feast was so solemnly and magnificently celebrated.

Joachim and Anne were indeed wealthy, but they lived very frugally. They gave all to the Temple and to the poor. I do not now remember how long it was that Anne took for herself nothing but cold victuals, but she treated her domestics generously and provided them with dowries. I think she and Joachim returned that same day with their whole company to Bethoron.

I saw also a feast among the Temple children. They had a meal at which Mary had to question first the mistresses and then the maidens separately as to whether they were willing to have her among them. This was the custom. Then the girls had a dance among themselves. They stood two and two opposite one another and danced, changed places across, and formed figures in and out. There was no leaping, but certain swaying movements of the whole person, which seemed somewhat expressive of the Jewish character. Some of the girls accompanied the dance with the music of flutes, triangles, chimes, and an instrument that gave forth sounds at once strange and agreeable. It consisted of a little box with oblique sides, over which were stretched strings which the players touched with their fingers. The center of the box contained bellows out of which projected several pipes, some crooked, others straight. The performer pressed sometimes here, sometimes there on the center of the bellows which mingled its sounds with those of the strings. The instrument was rested either upon the knee of the performer, or upon a stool under which the knee was placed. In the evening, Noemi took Mary to her cell, from which she could see down into the Temple. Here Mary mentioned to Noemi her desire to get up more frequently in the night to pray, but Noemi refused her request for the present. The women belonging to the Temple wore white robes, long and wide, girdled at the waist. Their flowing sleeves were turned up when at work.

Far back in the Temple were numerous chambers built in the wall and connected with the dwellings of the women. Mary's cell was one of the most distant, one nearest the Holy of Holies. From the passage that led to it, one raised a curtain and stepped into an apartment, a sort of antechamber separated from the cell by a light, semicircular, movable screen. Here in the corners right and left, were shelves for clothing and other things. Opposite the door in the screen that led into the cell was an opening hung with gauze and tapestry, and looking down into the Temple. It was rather high in the wall; one had to mount upon steps to reach it. On the left of the cell, lay a cover rolled into a bundle, which Mary unrolled at night for a couch. A branched lamp stood in a niche of the wall. I saw the holy child standing on a stool near it and praying out of a roll with red knobs on the rod. It was indeed a touching sight. The child wore a little coarsely woven, striped dress, blue and white, with yellow flowers. A small round table like a stool stood in the room, and on it I saw Anna setting a dish of fruit the size of beans, and a little jug. The child was skillful far beyond her years. She could already work on little white cloths for the service of the Temple. The wall of her cell was inlaid with colored, triangular stones.

I often saw the child Mary seized with holy longing for the Messiah and saying to Anna: "Oh, will the promised Child be born soon? Oh, if I could only see that Child! Oh, if only I am living when He is born!" Then Anna would give this reply: "Think how old I am and how long I have waited for that Child! And you—you are still so young!" And Mary would shed tears of longing for the promised Saviour.

The maidens reared in the Temple under the care of the matrons occupied themselves with embroidery, with all kinds of ornamental work, and with cleansing the priestly garments and the vessels belonging to the Temple. From their cells, they could see into the Temple, pray and meditate. They were, by the fact of their parents' having placed them there, entirely dedicated to the Lord. Upon reaching a certain age, they were given in marriage, for there was among the more enlightened Israelites the pious, though secret hope that from such a virgin dedicated to God, the Messiah would be born.

I never saw that Herod built the Temple anew. Under him there were indeed many changes made in it; but at the time of Mary's entrance, eleven years before the Birth of Christ, the Temple itself had not been touched. The additions and changes had been made as heretofore on the outbuildings alone.

12. A Glance at the Obduracy of the Pharisees

How obdurate and obstinate the priests and the Pharisees of the Temple were, may be discovered from the small esteem in which they held the distinctions bestowed upon the Holy Family.

First Joachim's offering was rejected; but after some months both his own and his wife's were, by God's command, received. Joachim was admitted even into the presence of the Holy of Holies and he, as well as Anne, was—though unknown to each other—led into the passage under the Temple. There they met, Mary was conceived, and priests awaited them at the entrance of this cave under the Temple—all that took place by God's command. I have seen that sometimes, though not often, the sterile were commanded to be led in there.

Mary entered the Temple in her fourth year, and in all things was she distinguished and remarkable.

The sister of Lazarus's mother was her teacher and nurse. Her whole manner of acting was so remarkable, so marvelous, that I have seen great rolls written by aged priests about her. I think they still lie hidden with other writings.

Then came the wonderful manifestations at Joseph's espousals and the blossoming of his rod, the accounts of the Three Kings and of the shepherds, the Presentation of Jesus, Anna's and Simeon's testimony, and the teaching of Jesus at the age of twelve in the Temple.

But all this, the priests and Pharisees noticed not. Their mind was preoccupied by business and court affairs. Because the Holy Family lived in voluntary retirement and poverty, they were forgotten in the crowd. The more enlightened, however, such as Simeon, Anna, and others, knew of them.

But when Jesus appeared and John bore witness to Him, the teaching of the Pharisees was so directly contradictory that, even if the signs of His coming had not been forgotten by them, they would certainly not have made them known. Herod's reign and the Roman yoke had so involved them in quarrels and intrigues that their taste for spiritual things was weakened. They did not esteem John's testimony, and they soon forgot him after he was beheaded. They cared little for the teaching and miracles of Jesus, and their ideas of the Prophets and the Messiah were altogether erroneous. It is not surprising, therefore, that they so shamefully treated Jesus, and put Him to death, that they disavowed His Resurrection, the wonderful signs that followed it, and even the fulfillment of His prophecy respecting the destruction of Jerusalem. Nor is it to be wondered at that they neglected the signs that heralded His advent, since He had not at that time either taught or wrought miracles. Were the blindness, the obduracy of these men not so incomprehensibly great, could it have lasted even to this day?

When I go over the Way of the Cross in Jerusalem of the present day, I frequently see under a certain ruined building a large vault, or many adjoining vaults, which are partly fallen in and filled with water. Standing in the midst of the water, which rises almost to a level with it, is a table. From the center of the table to the roof of the vault, rises a pillar around which are hung little coffers filled with rolls of writings. Under the table also I saw rolls lying in the water. Perhaps these vaults were once burial places. They lie under Mount Calvary. I think the ruined building is the house wherein Pilate once dwelt, and the treasure will after some time be discovered.

13. John Promised to Zachary

I saw Zachary conversing with Elizabeth. He was telling her how sad he was because his turn to offer sacrifice in the Temple was drawing near, and how he dreaded the contempt that would there await him on account of his being childless. Zachary went twice a year to the Temple. He did not live at Hebron itself, but at a place called Juta about fifteen minutes' walk from Hebron. The ruins of former buildings still lay between the two places, leading one to fancy that they had once been connected. Many such ruins were to be found on the other side of Hebron, for the place was once as large as Jerusalem. At Hebron dwelt priests of a lower degree; in Juta, those of a higher rank. Zachary seemed to be the Superior of them all. He and Elizabeth were regarded with extraordinary veneration from the fact of both having descended in a direct line from the race of Aaron.

I saw Zachary with many people of this locality, going to a little property that he owned in the neighborhood of Juttah.[1] It consisted of a house, an orchard,

---

1. Juta.

and a spring. I saw him there also with the Holy
Family at the time of Mary's Visitation. At the period
of which I am speaking, Zachary was teaching the
people and praying with them. It seemed to be a
preparation for a feast. He told them of his great
dejection, and of his presentiment that something
remarkable was going to happen to him.

Again I saw Zachary with the same people going
to Jerusalem, where he had to wait four days before
his turn to sacrifice came round. Until that time, he
prayed in the forepart of the Temple. At last when
his turn came, he went into the sanctuary outside
the entrance to the Holy of Holies. The roof over the
altar of incense was opened so that the sky could be
seen. The priest offering sacrifice was not visible to
those outside. A partition concealed him, but the
smoke of the incense could be seen rising. I think
Zachary told the other priests that he must be left
alone, for I saw them leaving the sanctuary. Zachary
went into the Holy of Holies where it was dark. It
appeared to me that he took the Tables of the Law
out of the Ark of the Covenant, and laid them upon
the golden altar of incense. When he kindled the
incense, I saw to the right of the altar a light coming down on him and in it a luminous figure. Zachary,
frightened, stepped back and sank, as if in ecstasy,
at the right side of the altar. The angel raised him
up and spoke some words to him. Zachary replied.
Then I saw something like a ladder let down from
Heaven, and two angels ascending and descending
to him. One took something from him; but the other—
after Zachary had opened his garment—inserted a
shining little body in his side. Zachary had become
dumb. I saw him before leaving the Holy of Holies,
writing on a little tablet that lay there. This tablet
he sent at once to Elizabeth, who likewise had had
a vision at that same hour.

I saw that the people outside were troubled and
anxious on account of Zachary's remaining so long

in the sanctuary. They were even moving toward the door to open it, when Zachary replaced the Tables in the Ark and came forth. The crowd questioned him about his long stay in the sanctuary. He tried to answer, but could not. He signified to them by signs that he had become dumb, and went away. Zachary was a tall and exceedingly majestic old man.

THE MOST HOLY INCARNATION

1. Mary Espoused to St. Joseph

Joseph was the third of six brothers. His parents dwelt in a large mansion outside of Bethlehem. It was the ancient birthplace of David, but in Joseph's time only the principal walls were in existence. His father's name was Jacob. In front of the house was a large courtyard, or garden. In it was a stone spring house built over a spring whose waters gushed forth out of faucets, each of which represented some animal's head. The garden was enclosed by walls and surrounded by covered walks of trees and shrubbery.

The lower story of the dwelling had a door, but no windows. In the upper story there were circular openings, over which ran around the whole top of the house a broad gallery with four little pavilions capped by cupolas. From these cupolas, a view far into the surrounding country was afforded. David's palace in Jerusalem was provided with similar towers and cupolas. It was out of one of them that he saw Bethsabee. Above the center of the flat roof arose another smaller story, likewise crowned by a tower and cupola.

Joseph and his brothers occupied that last story with an aged Jew, their preceptor. The latter occupied the highest room in the story, while the brothers slept in one chamber, their sleeping places separated from one another by mats, which in the daytime were rolled up against the walls. I have seen them playing up there, each in his own separate space. They had toys shaped like animals, like little pugs. Their preceptor gave them all sorts of strange instructions that I could not understand. He laid sticks on the ground in various figures and stood the boys in them. The latter stepped into other figures which they had formed by rearranging the sticks. They laid sticks also in various positions, as if for measurement. I saw too the father and mother of the boys. They did not appear to trouble themselves much about their children, for they paid very little attention to them. They, the parents, appeared to me to be neither good nor bad.

Joseph was perhaps eight years old. He was very different from his brothers, very talented, and he learned quickly; but he was simple in his tastes, gentle, pious, and unambitious. The other boys used to play him all kinds of tricks and knock him around at will. They had little enclosed gardens, at whose entrance there stood on pillars covered images like swaddled infants. I often saw similar figures on the curtains of oratories, those of Anne and the Blessed Virgin, for instance. The only difference was that Mary's picture held in its arms a chalice above which something arose. In Joseph's parental home these images were like swathed infants with round faces environed by rays of light. There were many such pictures in Jerusalem, especially in the olden times, and also among the decorations of the Temple. I have seen them in Egypt also; and among the idols that Rachel purloined from her father, were similar figures though smaller. Many of the Jews had swathed puppets like them lying in little chests and baskets. They were intended to represent the child Moses in his little basket, and the swathing signified the binding power of the Law. When gazing at these figures, I used to think: The Jews honored the little image of the child Moses, but we have the images of the Child Jesus.

In the boys' little gardens grew bushes, small trees, and plants. I saw that his brothers often slyly trod down and tore up the plants in Joseph's little garden. They always treated him roughly, but he bore all patiently. Sometimes, when kneeling in prayer in the colonnade that ran around the courtyard, his face turned to the wall, his brothers would push him over. Once I saw one of them, when Joseph was thus praying, kick him in the back; but Joseph appeared not to notice it. The other repeated his blows, until at last Joseph fell to the ground. Then I saw that he had been absorbed in God. But he did not revenge himself; he merely turned away quietly and sought another secluded spot.

Outside and adjoining the garden wall, were some small, low dwellings. In them dwelt two elderly, veiled females, as is often the case near the schools. They were servants. I saw them carrying water into the house. The domestic arrangements were similar to those of Joachim and Anne's house, the beds rolled up and wicker partitions before them. I often saw Joseph's brothers talking with the servant maids and helping them in their work; but Joseph never interchanged words with them; he was always very reserved. I think there were also some daughters in the family.

Joseph's parents were not well-satisfied with him. They would have wished him, on account of his talents, to fit himself for a position in the world. But he was too unworldly for such aims, he had no desire whatever to shine. He may have been about twelve years old when I often saw him beyond Bethlehem opposite the Crib Cave, praying with some very pious, old, Jewish women. They had an oratory hidden in a vault. I do not know whether these women were relatives of Joseph or not; I think that they were connected with Anne. Joseph often went to them in his troubles and shared their devotions. Sometimes he dwelt in their neighborhood with a master carpenter, to whom he lent a helping hand. The carpenter taught him his trade, and Joseph found his geometry of use. The hostility of his brothers at last went so far that, when eighteen, Joseph fled from his father's house by night. A friend, who lived outside of Bethlehem, had brought him clothes in which to make his escape. I saw him in Lebona carrying on carpentry. He worked for his living in a very poor family. The man supported himself by making such rough wicker partitions as those Joseph knew how to put together. The latter humbly assisted the family as far as he could. I saw him gathering wood and carrying it to the house. His parents, in the meantime, believed that he had been kidnapped; but his brothers discovered him, and then he was again persecuted. Joseph, however, would not leave the poor people nor desist from the humble occupation of which his family was ashamed. I saw him afterward in another place (Thanach). There he did better work for a well-to-do family. Though a small place, it had a synagogue. Joseph lived very piously and humbly, loved and esteemed by all. At last he worked for a man in Tiberias, at which place he lived alone near the water.

Joseph's parents were long since dead, and his brothers scattered; only two of them still dwelt in Bethlehem. The paternal mansion had passed into other hands, and the whole family had rapidly declined. Joseph was deeply pious; he prayed much for the coming of the Messiah. I noticed, too, his great reserve in the presence of females. Shortly before his call to Jerusalem for his espousals with Mary, he entertained the idea of fitting up a more secluded oratory in his dwelling. But an angel appeared to him in prayer, and told him not to do it; that, as in ancient times, the Patriarch Joseph became by God's appointment the administrator of the Egyptian granaries, so now to him was the granary of Redemption to be wedded. In his humility Joseph could not comprehend the meaning of this and so he betook himself to prayer. At last he was summoned to Jerusalem to be espoused to the Blessed Virgin.

There were seven other virgins who were with Mary to be dismissed from the Temple and given in mar-

riage. On this account St. Anne went to Jerusalem
to be with Mary, who grieved at the thought of leaving the Temple. But she was told that she must be
married. I saw one of the distinguished old priests,
who was no longer able to walk, borne into the Holy
of Holies. An incense offering was enkindled. The
priest prayed sitting before a roll of writings, and in
vision his hand was placed upon that verse in the
Prophet Isaias (*Is.* 11:1) in which it is written that
there shall come forth a rod out of the root of Jesse
and a flower shall rise up out of his root. Thereupon
I saw that all the unmarried men in the country of
the House of David were summoned to the Temple.
Many of them made their appearance in holiday attire,
and Mary was conducted to their presence. I saw one
among them, a very pious youth from the region of
Bethlehem, who had always ardently prayed to be
allowed to minister to the advent of the Messiah.
Great was his desire to wed Mary. But Mary wept;
she wished not to take a husband. Then the high
priest gave to each of the suitors a branch which was
to be held in the hand during the offering of prayer
and sacrifice. After that, all the branches were laid
in the Holy of Holies with the understanding that
he whose branch should blossom, was to be Mary's
husband. Now when that youth who so ardently
desired to wed Mary found that this branch, along
with all the others, had failed to blossom, he retired
to a hall outside the Temple and, with arms raised
to God, wept bitterly. The other suitors left the Temple, and that youth hurried to Mount Carmel where,
since the days of Elias, hermits had dwelt. He took
up his abode on the mount, and there spent his days
in prayer for the coming of the Messiah.

I saw the priests, after this, hunting through different rolls of writing in their search for another
descendant of the House of David, one that had not
presented himself among the suitors for Mary's hand.
And there they found that, among the six brothers

of Bethlehem, one was unknown and ignored. They sought him out and so discovered Joseph's retreat, six miles from Jerusalem, near Samaria. It was a small place on a little river. There Joseph dwelt alone in a humble house near the water, and carried on the trade of a carpenter under another master. He was told to go up to the Temple. He went, accordingly, arrayed in his best. A branch was given him. As he was about to lay it upon the altar, it blossomed on top into a white flower like a lily. At the same time I saw a light like the Holy Spirit hovering over him. He was then led to Mary, who was in her chamber, and she accepted him as her spouse.

The espousals took place, I think, upon our 23rd of January. They were celebrated in Jerusalem, on Mount Zion in a house often used for such feasts. The seven virgins that were to leave the Temple with Mary, had already departed. They were recalled to accompany Mary on her festal journey to Nazareth, where Anne had already prepared her little home. The marriage feast lasted seven or eight days. The women and the virgins, companions of Mary in the Temple, were present, also many relatives of Joachim and Anne, and two daughters from Gophna. Many lambs were slaughtered and offered in sacrifice.

I have had a clear vision of Mary in her bridal dress. She wore a colored, woollen underdress without sleeves, her arms encircled by white, woollen fillets. On the breast and as high as the neck, lay a white collar ornamented with jewels, pearls, etc. Then came a kind of gown open in front, wide like a mantle from top to bottom, and with flowing sleeves. This gown was blue, embroidered with large red, white, and yellow roses and green leaves, something like the ancient vestments worn at Mass. It fastened around the neck on the white collar, and the lower border was edged with fringes and tassels. Over this was a kind of scapular of white-and gold-flowered silk, set over the breast with pearls and shining

stones. It lay upon the front opening of the dress,
and reached to the edge of the same; it was about
one-half an ell wide and was fringed with tassels and
balls. A corresponding strip hung down the back,
while shorter and narrower ones fell over the shoulders and arms. These lappets were caught under the
arms from front to back with the gold cords, or delicate chains, with which the broad upper piece of the
bodice was fastened, as also the breastpiece that was
placed over the upper body. By this arrangement, the
flowered stuff of the dress was puffed out between
the cords. The wide sleeves were tightly fastened in
the middle of the upper and the lower arm by buck-
les, puffing out around the shoulders, the elbows, and
the wrists.

Over this costume fell a long sky-blue mantle. It
was fastened at the neck by an ornament, and over
it was a white ruffle seemingly of feathers or silk
dots. The mantle fell back from the shoulders, forming a large fold on the sides, and hung behind in a
pointed train. It was embroidered around the edge
in flowers of gold.

Mary's hair was arranged with such skill as is difficult to describe. It was parted on top of the head
and divided into numerous fine strands, which were
caught together with pearls and white silk. It formed
a large net that fell over the shoulders and down the
back to the middle of the mantle. It looked like a
web. The ends of the hair were rolled in, and the
whole net edged with fringe and pearls.

On her head was placed, first a wreath of white
raw silk or wool, closing on top with three bands of
the same meeting in a tuft. On this rested a crown
about the breadth of one's hand, set with many colored jewels. Three pieces arose from the circlet and
met together in the center, where they were surmounted by a ball.

In her left hand Mary carried a little garland of
red and white roses made of silk, and in the right

a beautiful candlestick covered with gold. It had no foot, but was furnished like a scepter with knobs above and below the point at which it was to be grasped by the hand. The stem began to swell out in the middle and ended in a little dish upon which burned a white flame.

On her feet she wore heavy sandals about two fingers in thickness under which, before and behind, was a support like a heel. They were green, and gave the foot the appearance of standing upon sods. Two straps, white and gold, went over the foot and held them in their place.

The virgins at the Temple arranged Mary's skillfully woven hairnet. I saw them thus engaged. There were many busied with it, and the work went more swiftly than one could imagine.

Anne brought all the beautiful clothes, but Mary was so modest that it was only with reluctance that she allowed herself to be arrayed in them.

After the nuptial ceremony, her braided hair was wound around her head, a milk-white veil reaching up to the elbows thrown over her, and the crown placed upon it.

The Blessed Virgin had auburn hair, dark eyebrows, fine and arched, a very high forehead, large downcast eyes with long, dark lashes, a straight nose, delicate and rather long, a lovely mouth around which played a most noble expression, and a pointed chin. She was of medium height, and she moved very gently and gravely, looking very bashful in her rich attire. After the marriage feast, she wore another dress. It was striped and less magnificent than the one described. I have a scrap of it among my relics. This striped dress she wore at Cana and on other holy occasions. She wore her wedding suit once again in the Temple.

The very wealthy among the Jews changed their dress three or four times during a marriage feast. Mary in her magnificent apparel presented an appearance somewhat similar to the richly adorned women of a much later period, the Empress Helena, for instance, and even Cunegundis herself. The usual clothing of the Jewish women enveloped them closely, giving them an appearance of being wrapped up; but Mary's wedding dress was very different; it was something on the Roman style.

Joseph wore a long, wide blue coat fastened from the breast down with loops and buttons. The wide sleeves were laced at the sides, a broad cuff turned up at the wrist, the inside provided, as it were, with pockets. Around the neck was something like a brown collar, over which lay a kind of stole, and upon the breast hung two white bands.

After the marriage, Joseph went to Bethlehem on some business, and Mary with twelve or fifteen women and maidens went to Anne's house near Nazareth. They made the journey on foot. When Joseph returned, I saw at Anne's house a feast at which, besides the usual household, there were about six guests and several children present. Cups were on the table. The Blessed Virgin wore a mantle embroidered with red, white, and blue flowers. Her face was covered with a transparent veil over which was a black one.

I afterward saw Joseph and Mary in the house of Nazareth. Joseph had a separate apartment in the front of the house, a three-cornered chamber this side of the kitchen. Both Mary and Joseph were timid and reserved in each other's presence. They were very quiet and prayerful.

Once I saw Anne making preparations to go to Nazareth. Under her arm she carried a bundle that contained some things for Mary. To reach Nazareth, which lay in front of a hill, she had to go over a plain and through a grove. Mary wept very much when Anne was leaving and accompanied her a part of the way. Joseph was alone in his apartment in the front of the house.

Mary and Joseph had, properly speaking, no regular housekeeping affairs; they received from Anne all that they needed. I saw Mary spinning and sewing too, but yet with wide stitches. The clothes then worn had not many seams and were entirely in strips. I saw her embroidering also, and with little white sticks knitting or working. The cooking she did was very simple and, while it was going on, the bread was baking in the ashes. They used sheep's milk, and of meat generally pigeons only.

2. The Holy House of Nazareth

The little house at Nazareth which Anne fitted up for Mary and Joseph, belonged to Anne. From her own dwelling, she could, unnoticed, reach it in about half an hour by a crosspath. It lay not far from the gate. It had a small courtyard in front and nearby was a well, a couple of steps leading down to it. It was near a hill, but not built on it. A narrow path dug out of the hill separated it from the back of the house, in which there was one little window. It was darker on this side of the house than on the other. The back part was triangular and built on higher ground than the front. The foundations were cut in the rock; the upper part was a light masonry. Mary's sleeping compartment was in the back, and there it was that the angelic Annunciation took place. This chamber had a semicircular form, on account of the movable partitions placed around the walls and which were of coarser wickerwork than that ordinarily used for the light screens. The patterns in which these screens were woven were similar to wafers, and the colors used were designed to bring the figures out. Mary's sleeping place was on the side just behind a wicker screen. On the left was a little closet with a small table and stool. This was the Blessed Virgin's oratory.

This back room was separated from the rest of the house by a fireplace, which consisted of a graded wall from whose center over the slightly raised hearth, a chimney rose up to the roof and ended in a tube above it. Over the opening through which the tube projected was built a little roof. On top of the chimney, I saw in after years two little bells hanging. To the right and left of the chimney and opening into Mary's rooms were doors up to which three steps led. In the chimney wall were all kinds of nooks in which stood the little vessels that I still see at Loretto. Behind was a rafter of cedarwood, upon which the wall of the chimney rested. From this upright rafter ran a crossbeam to the center of the back wall, and into this there were others dovetailed from the two side walls. These beams were of a bluish cast with yellow ornaments. Between them one could see up through the roof, which was hung with large leaves and matting, and in three places, namely in the three corners, adorned with stars. The star in the middle corner was large like the morning star. Later on the ceiling was adorned with numerous stars. Over the horizontal rafter, which extended from the chimney to the back of the wall, was an opening in the center for the window, and under this was hung a lamp. There was a rafter under the chimney also. The roof was not high and pointed, but so level that one might walk around the edge. It was flat on top, and there rose the chimney with its tubes, protected by the little roof.

When after Joseph's death the Blessed Virgin removed to the neighborhood of Capharnaum, the Holy House was left beautifully adorned like a sacred shrine. Mary often went from Capharnaum to visit the scene of the Incarnation and to pray there. Peter and John, whenever they went to Palestine, visited the House of Nazareth and celebrated Mass in it. An altar was erected where the fireplace used to be. The little cupboard once used by Mary was placed as a tabernacle upon the altar.

I have often in vision witnessed the transporting

of the Holy House to Loretto. For a long time, I could not believe it, and yet I continued to see it. I saw the Holy House borne over the sea by seven angels. It had no foundation, but there was under it a shining surface of light. On either side was something like a handle. Three angels carried it on one side and three on the other; the seventh hovered in front of it, a long train of light after him.

I remember that it was the back of the house, the part that contained the fireplace, the altar of the Apostles, and the little window, that was transported to Europe. It seems to me when I recall it that the rest of the building was in some danger of falling. I see in Loretto the Crucifix also that the Blessed Virgin had when in Ephesus. It was formed of different kinds of wood. Later on, it came into the possession of the Apostles. Many miracles take place before that Crucifix.

The wall of the Holy House of Loretto is entirely the original one. Even the rafter under the chimney is still in its place. The miraculous picture of the Mother of God stands on the altar of the Apostles.

3. Mary's Annunciation

On the day upon which the Church celebrates the feast, I had a vision of Mary's Annunciation.

I saw the Blessed Virgin a short time after her marriage in the house of Nazareth. Joseph was not there. He was at that moment journeying with two beasts of burden on the road to Tiberias, whither he was going to get his tools. But Anne was in the house with her maid and two of the virgins who had been with Mary in the Temple. Everything in the house had been newly arranged by Anne. Toward evening, they all prayed standing around a circular stool from which they afterward ate vegetables that had been served. Anne seemed to be very busy about the household affairs, and for a time she moved around here

and there, while the Blessed Virgin ascended the
steps to her room. There she put on a long, white,
woollen garment, such as it was customary to wear
during prayer, a girdle around her waist, and a yellowish-white veil over her head. The maid entered,
lighted the branched lamp, and retired. Mary drew
out a little, low table, which stood folded by the wall,
and placed it in the center of the room. It had a
semicircular leaf, which could be raised on a movable support so that when ready for use the little
table stood on three legs. Mary spread upon it a red
and then a white, transparent cover, which hung
down on the side opposite the leaf. It was fringed at
the end and embroidered in the center. A white cover
was spread on the rounded edge. When the little
table was prepared, Mary laid a small, round cushion before it and, resting both hands on the leaf, she
gently sank on her knees, her back turned to her
couch, the door of the chamber to her right. The floor
was carpeted. Mary lowered her veil over her face,
and folded her hands, but not the fingers, upon her
breast. I saw her praying for a long time with intense
fervor. She prayed for Redemption, for the promised
King, and that her own supplications might have
some influence upon His coming. She knelt long, as
if in ecstasy, her face raised to Heaven; then she
drooped her head upon her breast and thus continued her prayer. And now she glanced to the right
and beheld a radiant youth with flowing, yellow hair.
It was the archangel Gabriel. His feet did not touch
the ground. In an oblique line and surrounded by an
effulgence of light and glory, he came floating down
to Mary. The lamp grew dim, for the whole room was
lighted up by the glory.

The angel, with hands gently raised before his
breast, spoke to Mary. I saw the words like letters of
glittering light issuing from his lips. Mary replied,
but without looking up. Then the angel again spoke
and Mary, as if in obedience to his command, raised

her veil a little, glanced at him, and said, "Behold the handmaid of the Lord. May it be done unto me according to thy word!" I saw her now in deeper ecstasy. The ceiling of the room vanished, and over the house appeared a luminous cloud with a pathway of light leading up from it to the opened heavens. Far up in the source of this light, I beheld a vision of the Most Holy Trinity. It was like a triangle of glory, and I thought that I saw therein the Father, the Son, and the Holy Ghost.

As Mary uttered the words: "May it be done unto me according to thy word!" I saw an apparition of the Holy Ghost. The countenance was human and the whole apparition environed by dazzling splendor, as if surrounded by wings. From the breast and hands, I saw issuing three streams of light. They penetrated the right side of the Blessed Virgin and united into one under her heart. At that instant Mary became perfectly transparent and luminous. It was as if opacity disappeared like darkness before that flood of light.

While the angel and with him the streams of glory vanished, I saw down the path of light that led up to Heaven, showers of half-blown roses and tiny green leaves falling upon Mary. She, entirely absorbed in self, saw in herself the Incarnate Son of God, a tiny, human form of light with all the members, even to the little fingers perfect. It was about midnight that I saw this mystery.

Some time elapsed, and then Anne and the other women entered Mary's room, but when they beheld her in ecstasy they immediately withdrew. The Blessed Virgin then arose, stepped to the little altar on the wall, let down the picture of a swathed child that was rolled above it, and prayed standing under the lamp before it. Only toward morning did she lie down. Mary was at this time a little over fourteen years old.

An intuitive knowledge of what had taken place was conferred upon Anne. Mary knew that she had conceived the Redeemer, yes, her interior lay open before her, and so she already understood that her Son's kingdom should be a supernatural one, and that the House of Jacob, the Church, would be the reunion of regenerate mankind. She knew that the Redeemer would be the King of His people, that He would purify them and render them victorious; but that in order to redeem them He must suffer and die.

It was explained to me likewise why the Redeemer remained nine months in His mother's womb, why He was born a little child and not a perfect man like Adam, and why also He did not take the beauty of Adam in Paradise. The Incarnate Son of God willed to be conceived and born that conception and birth, rendered so very unholy by the Fall, might again become holy. Mary was His Mother, and He did not come sooner because Mary was the first and the only woman conceived without sin. Jesus when put to death was thirty-three years, four months, and two weeks old.

I thought all the while: Here in Nazareth, things are different from what they are in Jerusalem. There the women dare not set foot in the Temple, but here in this church at Nazareth, a virgin is herself the Temple and the Most Holy rests in her.

4. Mary's Visitation

Mary's Annunciation took place before Joseph's return. He had not yet settled at Nazareth when, with Mary, he started on the journey to Hebron. After the Conception of Jesus, the Blessed Virgin experienced a great desire to visit her cousin Elizabeth. I saw her travelling with Joseph toward the south. Once I saw her passing the night in a hut made of wickerwork and which was all overrun with vines and beautiful white blossoms. From that point to Zachary's house, it was a journey of about twelve hours. Near Jerusalem they turned off to the north in order to take a more solitary route. They made the circuit of a little city two leagues from Emmaus, and took a road traversed by Jesus in after years. Although it was a long journey, they made it very quickly. They now had to cross two hills. I saw them resting between them, eating some bread and refreshing themselves with some balsam drops which they had collected on the way, and which they mingled with their drinking water. The hill was formed of overhanging rocks and caves. The valleys were very fertile. I remarked on the road one particular flower. It had fine green leaves and a cluster of nine tiny bell-shaped blossoms, white, lightly flushed with red.

Mary wore a brown, woollen underdress over which was a gray one with a girdle, and a yellowish covering on her head. Joseph carried in a bundle a long brownish garment with a cowl, and bands in front. It was one that Mary was accustomed to wear whenever she went either to the Temple or the synagogue.

Zachary's house stood upon a solitary hill, and other dwellings were scattered around. Not far from it, a tolerably large brook flowed down from the mountain.

Elizabeth had learned in vision that one of her race was to give birth to the Messiah; she had dwelt in thought upon Mary, had very greatly desired to see her, and had indeed beheld her journeying to Hebron. In a little room, to the right of the entrance to the house, she placed seats, and here she tarried, often looking long and anxiously down the road, in the hope of catching the first glimpse of Mary. When Zachary was returning from the Passover, I saw Elizabeth, urged by an impetuous desire, hurrying from the house and going a considerable distance on the road to Jerusalem. When Zachary met her, he was alarmed to find her so far from home and that, too, in her present condition. But she told him of her anxiety and that she could not help thinking that her cousin Mary was coming from Nazareth to see her. Zachary, however, thought it improbable that the newly married couple would at that time undertake so great a journey. On the following day, I saw Elizabeth taking the road again under the influence of the same impression, and now I saw the Holy Family coming to meet her.

Elizabeth was advanced in years. She was tall, her face small and delicate, and she wore something wrapped around her head. She was acquainted with Mary only by hearsay. As soon as the Blessed Virgin saw Elizabeth, she knew her and hurried on to meet her, while Joseph purposely held back. Mary had already reached the houses in the neighborhood of Zachary's home. Their occupants were enraptured at her beauty, and filled with such reverence by her demeanor that they stood back modestly. When the cousins met, they saluted each other joyfully with outstretched hands. I saw a light in Mary and issuing from her a ray which entered into Elizabeth, who thereby became wonderfully agitated. They did not pause long in sight of the beholders, but arm in arm passed up the courtyard to the door of the house, where Elizabeth once more bade Mary welcome. Joseph went around to the side of the house and into an open hall where sat Zachary. He respectfully saluted the aged priest, who responded in writing on his tablet.

Mary and Elizabeth entered the room in which was the fireplace. Here they embraced, clasping each other in their arms and pressing cheek to cheek. I saw light streaming down between them. Then it was that Elizabeth, becoming interiorly inflamed, stepped back with uplifted hands, and exclaimed, "Blessed art thou among women, and blessed is the Fruit of thy womb.

"And whence is this to me, that the Mother of my Lord should come to me?

"For behold, as soon as the voice of thy salutation sounded in my ears, the infant in my womb leaped for joy.

"And blessed art thou that hast believed, because

those things shall be accomplished that were spoken to thee by the Lord."

At these last words, Elizabeth took Mary into the little room prepared for her that she might sit down and rest. It was only a few steps from where they then were. Mary released her hold upon Elizabeth's arm, crossed her hands on her breast, and divinely inspired, uttered her canticle of thanksgiving: "My soul doth magnify the Lord, and my spirit hath rejoiced in God, my Saviour.

"Because He hath regarded the humility of His handmaid; for behold from henceforth all generations shall call me blessed.

"Because He that is mighty hath done great things to me: and holy is His name.

"And His mercy is from generation unto generations, to them that fear Him.

"He hath showed might in His arm: He hath scattered the proud in the conceit of their heart.

"He hath put down the mighty from their seat, and hath exalted the humble.

"He hath filled the hungry with good things: and the rich He hath sent empty away.

"He hath received Israel his servant, being mindful of His mercy.

"As He spoke to our fathers, to Abraham, and to His seed forever."

I saw Elizabeth, moved by similar emotion, reciting the whole canticle with Mary. Then they seated themselves on low seats. A small goblet was on the little table. And, oh, I was so happy! I sat nearby and prayed with them the whole time.

I saw Joseph and Zachary still together. They were conversing by means of the tablet, and always about the coming of the Messiah. Zachary was a tall, handsome old man clothed like a priest. He and Joseph sat together at the side of the house that opened on the garden, in which Mary and Elizabeth were now sitting on a rug under a high, spreading tree. Behind the tree was a fountain from which gushed water when a spigot was pressed. I saw grass and flowers around, and trees bearing little, yellow plums. Mary and Elizabeth were eating rolls and small fruits out of Joseph's travelling pouch. What touching simplicity and moderation! Two maids and two men servants were in the house. They prepared a table under the tree. Joseph and Zachary came out and ate something. Joseph wanted to return home at once, but they persuaded him to stay eight days. He knew not of Mary's conception. The women were silent on that subject. They had a secret understanding together about their interior sentiments.

When all, Mary and Elizabeth, Joseph and Zachary, were together, they prayed making use of a kind of litany. I saw a cross appear in their midst, and still there was no cross at that time. Yes, it was as if two crosses visited each other.

In the evening they all sat together again in the garden near a lamp under the tree. A cover like a tent was stretched under the tree, and low stools with backs stood around. After that I saw Joseph and Zachary going to an oratory, while Mary and Elizabeth retired to their little chamber. They were inflamed with divine ardor, and together they recited the Magnificat. The Blessed Virgin wore a transparent white veil which she lowered when speaking to men.

Zachary took Joseph on the following day to another garden at some distance from the house. He was in all things most exact and methodical. This second garden was set out with beautiful bushes and trees full of fruit. In the center was an avenue of trees, and at the end of it a small house whose entrance was on the side. Above were openings with slides like windows. A woven couch filled with moss or some other fine plant, stood in one room in which there were also two white figures as large as children. I have no clear knowledge of how they came there nor what they signified, but they appeared to me to be very like Zachary and Elizabeth, only much younger. I saw Mary and Elizabeth much together. Mary helped with everything around the house and prepared all kinds of necessaries for the child. Both she and Elizabeth knit on a large coverlet for the latter, and they worked also for the poor. During Mary's absence, Anne frequently sent her maid to see after Mary's house at Nazareth, and once I saw her there herself.

I saw Zachary and Joseph spending the night of the next day in the garden at some distance from the house. They slept part of the time in the little summer house, and prayed during the other part in the open air. They returned quite early in the morning to the house where Mary and Elizabeth had passed the night. Mary and Elizabeth recited together morning and evening the hymn of thanksgiving, the Magnificat, which Mary had received from the Holy Ghost at the salutation of Elizabeth. During its recital they stood opposite each other against the wall, as if in choir, their hands crossed upon their breast, the black veil of each covering her face. At the second part, which refers to God's promise, I saw the previous history of the Most Holy Incarnation and the mystery of the Most Holy Sacrament of the Altar, from Abraham down to Mary. I saw Abraham sacrificing Isaac, also the Mystery of the Ark of the Covenant, which Moses received on the night before the departure from Egypt, and by which he was enabled to escape and conquer. I recognized its connection with the holy Incarnation, and it seemed to me as if this Mystery were now fulfilled or living in Mary. I saw also the Prophet Isaias and his prophecy of the Virgin, and from him to Mary visions of the approach of the Most Blessed Sacrament. I still remember that I heard the words: "From father to father down to Mary, there are more than fourteen generations." I saw also Mary's blood taking its rise in her ancestors and flowing nearer and nearer to the Incarnation. I have no words to describe this clearly. I can say only that I saw, sometimes here, sometimes there, the people of different races. There seemed to issue from them a beam of light which always terminated in Mary as she appeared at that moment with Elizabeth. I saw this beam issuing first from the Mystery of the Ark of the Covenant and ending in Mary. Then I saw Abraham and from him a ray, which again ended in Mary, etc. Abraham must have dwelt quite near to Mary's abode at that time; for during the Magnificat I saw that the beam which proceeded from him came from no great distance, while those from persons nearer to the Mother of God in point of time seemed to come from afar. Their rays were as fine, as clear as those of the sun when they shine through a narrow opening. In such a beam, I beheld Mary's blood glancing red and bright, and it was said to me: "Behold, as pure as this red light must the blood of that Virgin be from whom the Son of God will become incarnate."

Once I saw Mary and Elizabeth going in the evening to Zachary's country place. They took with them rolls and fruit in little baskets, for they intended to stay overnight. Joseph and Zachary followed them later. I saw Mary going to meet them as they entered. Zachary had brought his little tablet, but it was too dark for writing. I saw Mary speaking to him. She was telling him that he should speak on that night. He laid aside his tablet and conversed orally with Joseph. I saw all this to my own great astonishment. Then my guide said to me: "Why, what is that?" and he showed me a vision of St. Goar, who hung his mantle on the sunbeams as on a hook. I received then the instruction that lively, childlike confidence makes all things real and substantial. These two expressions gave me great interior light upon all kinds of miracles, but I cannot explain it.

They, Mary, Elizabeth, Joseph, and Zachary, all

spent the night in the garden. They sat or walked two by two, prayed now and then, or retired into the little summer house to rest. I heard them say that Joseph would return home on the evening of the Sabbath, and that Zachary would go with him as far as Jerusalem. The moon shone bright in a starry sky. It was indescribably calm and lovely near those holy souls.

Once also I had a peep into Mary's little chamber. It was night, and she was at rest. She was lying on her side with one hand under her head. Over her brown under-dress she wound from head to foot a strip of white, woollen stuff about an ell in width. When preparing for rest, she took one end of this strip under her arm and wound it tightly around her head and the upper part of her person, then down to the feet and up again; so that she was entirely enveloped, and could not take a long step. She did this near the couch, at the head of which was a little roll of something for a pillow. The arms from the elbow down were left free, and the veiling of the head opened on the breast.

I often saw under Mary's heart a glory in whose center burned an indescribably clear little flame, and over Elizabeth's womb a similar glory, but the light in it was not so clear.

When the Sabbath began, I saw in Zachary's house, in a room that I had not before seen, lamps lighted and the Sabbath celebrated. Zachary, Joseph, and about six other men from the neighborhood were standing and praying under a lamp and around a little chest upon which lay rolls of writing. They had on their heads something like a small veil. They did not make so many distorted movements of the body as do the latter-day Jews, although like them they frequently bowed the head and raised the arms.

Mary, Elizabeth, and two other women stood apart in a grated partition from which they could see into the oratory. They were entirely enveloped, their prayer mantles over their heads. Zachary wore his festive robes the whole of the Sabbath. They consisted of a long, white garment with rather narrow sleeves. He was girdled with a broad cincture, wound many times around him. On it were letters, and from it hung straps. This garment was provided with a cowl, which hung in plaits from the head down the back like a folded veil. When he moved or performed any action, he threw this garment rolled together with the ends of the girdle up over one shoulder, and stuck it into the girdle under his arm. His lower limbs were loosely bound, and the strip enveloping them fastened by the straps that kept the soles in place upon his naked feet. He showed his priestly mantle to Joseph. It was sleeveless, wide and heavy and very beautiful, flashing with white and purple intermixed. It was closed on the breast with three jeweled clasps.

When the Sabbath was over, I saw them eating again for the first time. They took their repast together under the trees in the garden near the house. They ate green leaves previously dipped into something, and sucked little bunches of herbs which too had been soaked. There were little bowls of small fruits on the table and other dishes, from which they partook of something with brown, transparent spatulas. It may have been honey that they were eating with horn spatulas. There were also little rolls, and I saw them eating them.

After the meal, Joseph accompanied by Zachary started on his journey home. The night was calm, the moon shining, and the sky studded with stars. Before parting, all prayed separately. Joseph took with him his little bundle in which were a few rolls and a small jug of something. Both the travellers had staves; but Joseph's was hooked on top, while Zachary's was long and ended in a knob. Both had travelling mantles which they wore over their head. Before starting, they embraced Mary and Elizabeth, alternately pressing them to their heart. But I saw no kissing at that time. The parting was calm and cheerful. The two women accompanied them a short distance, and then the travellers proceeded alone. The night was unspeakably lovely.

Mary and Elizabeth now returned to the house and went into Mary's chamber. A lamp was burning upon a bracket on the wall, as was usual while Mary slept or prayed. The two women stood facing each other, and recited the Magnificat. They spent the whole night in prayer, for what reason I cannot now say. Through the day I saw Mary busy with all kinds of work, weaving covers, for instance.

I saw Joseph and Zachary still on the road. They spent the night under a shed. They took very circuitous roads and, I think, visited many people, for they were three days on their journey.

Again I saw Joseph at Nazareth. Anne's maid took charge of the house for him, going to and fro between the two houses. With this exception, Joseph was entirely alone.

I also saw Zachary returning home, and I saw Mary and Elizabeth reciting as usual the Magnificat, and doing all kinds of work. Toward evening, they used to walk in the garden. There was a well in it, a rare occurrence in this part of the country; therefore travellers always took with them in a little jug some kind of juice to drink. Sometimes also, and generally toward evening when it grew cool, Mary and Elizabeth walked some distance from the house, for it stood alone in the midst of fields. They usually retired about nine o'clock, and always rose again before the sun.

The Blessed Virgin remained with Elizabeth three months, until after the birth of John, but she returned to Nazareth before his circumcision. Joseph went to meet her halfway on the journey, and for the first time noticed that she was pregnant. But he gave no sign of his knowledge, and struggled with his doubts.

Mary, who had feared this, was silent and preoccupied, thus increasing his uneasiness. When arrived in Nazareth, Mary went to the parents of the deacon Parmenas and remained some days with them, Joseph's anxiety had meanwhile increased to such a degree that, when Mary returned home, he determined to flee from the house. Then the angel appeared to him and consoled him.

5. Feast Pictures

I saw a wonderful and almost indescribable vision of a feast. I saw a church that looked like a slender, delicate, octangular fruit, the roots of whose stem touched the earth over a bubbling fountain. The stem was not high, one could just see between the church and the earth. The entrance was over the spring which bubbled and bubbled, casting out something white like earth or sand, and rendering all around green and fruitful. There were no roots over the spring in front of the church. The center of the interior was like the capsule in an apple, the cells formed of many delicate white threads. In these cells were little organs like the kernels of an apple. Through an opening in the floor, one could look straight down into the bubbling spring. I saw some kernels that looked withered and decayed, falling into it. But while I gazed, the fruit seemed to be developing more and more into a church; and the capsule at last appeared something like a piece of machinery, like a loose artificial nosegay in the center of it. And now I saw the Blessed Virgin and Elizabeth standing on that nosegay and looking again like two tabernacles, the one the tabernacle of a saint, the other that of the Most Holy. The two blessed women turned toward each other and offered mutual felicitations. Then there issued from them two figures, Jesus and John. John, the larger of the two, lay coiled on the earth, his head in his lap; but Jesus was like a tiny child formed of light, just as I so often see Him in the Blessed Sacrament. Upright and hovering, He moved toward John and passed over him like a white vapor as he lay there with his face upon the earth. The reflection from the snowy vapor glanced through the opening in the floor down into the spring, and by it was swallowed up. Then Jesus raised the little John and embraced him, after which each returned to the womb of his mother, who meantime had been singing the Magnificat.

I saw also during that singing, Joseph and Zachary issuing from the walls on opposite sides of the church and followed by an ever-increasing flow of people, while the whole building continued unfolding, as it were, taking more and more the appearance of a church and the occasion that of a sacred festival. Vines with luxuriant foliage were growing around the church, and they became so dense that they had to be trimmed.

The church now rested on the earth. In it was an altar, and through an opening over the bubbling spring arose a baptismal font. Many people entered by the door, and there was at last a grand and perfect festival. All that took place therein, both in form and in action, was a silent growth. I cannot relate all; words fail me.

On John's feast, I had another vision of a festival. The octangular church was transparent, as if formed of crystal or jets of water. In the center was a well spring above which arose a little tower. I saw John standing by it and baptizing. The vision changed. Out of the spring grew a flower stalk, around which arose eight pillars supporting a pyramidal crown. Upon the crown stood the grandparents of Anne, Elizabeth, and Joseph; a little distant from the main stem were Mary and Joseph with the parents of the latter and those of Zachary. Up on the central stem stood John. A voice seemed to proceed from him, and I saw nations and kings entering the church and receiving the Blessed Eucharist from the hands of a Bishop. I heard John saying that their happiness was greater than his.[1]

6. The Blessed Virgin's Preparations for the Birth of Christ.
Journey to Bethlehem

I saw the Blessed Virgin for many days with Anne, while Joseph remained alone in Nazareth, one of Anne's maids taking charge of the house for him. They, Mary and Joseph, received their principal support from Anne's house as long as she lived. I saw the Blessed Virgin near Anne sewing and embroidering bands and tapestry. They seemed to be very busy in the house. Joachim must long since have been dead, for I saw Anne's second husband there and a little girl of from six to seven years old. She was helping Mary and being taught by her. If not a daughter of Anne, it must have been one of Mary Cleophas's children also called Mary.

I saw Mary sitting in a room with other women and preparing covers large and small. Some were embroidered with gold and silver. There was one large coverlet in a box in the midst of the women, at which all were working, knitting with two little wooden needles and balls of colored wool. Anne was very busy. She went around from one to another, receiving and giving wool. All expected Mary to be delivered in Anne's house, and these covers and other things were being prepared partly for the birth of the Child and partly as gifts for the poor. Everything was of the best, and all abundantly, and richly provided. They knew not that Mary would, of necessity, have to journey to Bethlehem.

Joseph was at that moment on his way to Jerusalem with cattle for sacrifice.

---

1. John never received the Blessed Sacrament.

I saw Joseph returned from Jerusalem. He had taken thither cattle for sacrifice, and had put up at the house before the Bethlehem gate. It was at this same inn that he and Mary stopped later on, before Mary's Purification. The keeper of the inn was an Essenian. Joseph went from there to Bethlehem, but did not visit his relatives. He was looking around after a place to build, also for some means of procuring lumber and tools, for in the spring after Mary's delivery, which he thought would take place in Nazareth, he intended to remove with her to Bethlehem, as he did not care for Nazareth. He wanted to get a place near the inn of the Essenian. From Bethlehem he went again to Jerusalem, to offer sacrifice. When he was returning from this journey to Jerusalem, and about midnight was crossing the field of Chimki, six hours from Nazareth, an angel appeared to him and said that he should set out at once with Mary for Bethlehem, as it was there that her Child was to be born. The angel told him, moreover, that he should provide himself with a few necessaries, but no laces nor embroidered covers, and he mentioned all the other things he was to take. Joseph was very much surprised. He was told also that, besides the ass upon which Mary was to ride, he was to take with him a little she-ass of one year which had not yet foaled. This little animal they were to let run at large, and then follow the road it would take.

I saw Joseph and Mary in their house at Nazareth; Anne too was present. Joseph informed them of the commands he had received, and they began to prepare for the journey. Anne was very much troubled about it. The Blessed Virgin had had all along an interior admonition that she should bring forth her child in Bethlehem; but in her humility she had kept silence. She knew it, also, from the Prophecies. She had all the Prophecies referring to the birth of the Messiah in her little closet at Nazareth; she read them very often and prayed for their fulfillment. She

had received them from her teachers at the Temple,
and by the same holy women had been instructed
upon them. Her prayer was always for the coming of
the Messiah. She esteemed her happy of whom the
Child should be born, and she desired to serve her
as her lowest handmaid. In her humility, she had
never conceived the thought that she herself was to
be the one. From those Prophecies she knew that the
Saviour would be born in Bethlehem, therefore she
lovingly submitted to the Divine Will and began her
journey. It was a very painful one for her, since at
that season it was cold among the mountains. Mary
had an inexpressible feeling that henceforth she must
and could be only poor. She could possess no exterior
goods, for she had all in herself. She knew that she
was to be the Mother of the Son of God. She knew
and she felt that, as by a woman sin had entered
into the world, so now by a woman the Expiation was
to be born. It was under the influence of this feeling
that she had exclaimed: "Behold the handmaid of the
Lord!" I understood, likewise, that Jesus was conceived of the Holy Ghost about the hour of midnight,
and about midnight should be born.

I saw Joseph and Mary with Anne, Mary Cleophas,
and some servants silently setting out upon their
journey. They started from Anne's. An ass bore a
comfortable cross-seat for Mary and her baggage.
On the field of Chimki, where the angel had appeared
to Joseph, Anne had a pasture ground; and here the
servants went to get the little she-ass of one year
which Joseph had to take with him. She ran after
the Holy Family. Anne, Mary Cleophas, and the servants now parted from Joseph and Mary after a
touching leave-taking. I saw the two travellers going
some distance further and putting up at a house
that lay on very high ground. They were well received.
I think the proprietor was the lease holder of a
farm called the House of Chimki and to which the
field belonged. From it one could see far into the

distance, yes, even to the mountains near Jerusalem. I again saw the Holy Family in a very cold valley, through which they were making their way toward a mountain. The ground was covered with frost and snow. It was about four hours from the House of Chimki. Mary was suffering exceedingly from the cold. She halted near a pine tree, and exclaimed: "We must rest. I can go no farther." Joseph arranged a seat for her under the tree, in which he placed a light. I often saw that done at night by travellers in those parts. The Blessed Virgin prayed fervently, imploring God not to allow them to freeze; and at once so great a warmth passed into her that she stretched out her hands to St. Joseph that he might warm himself by them. She took some food to renew her strength. The little ass, their guide, came up with them here and stood still. The actions of the little animal were truly astonishing. On straight roads, between mountains, for instance, where they could not go astray, she was sometimes behind, sometimes far ahead of them; but where the road branched, she was sure to make her appearance and run on the right way. Whenever they reached a spot at which they should halt, the little creature stood still. Joseph here spoke to Mary of the good lodgings that he expected to find in Bethlehem. He told her that he knew the good people of an inn at which, for a moderate sum, they could get a comfortable room. It was better, he said, to pay a little than to depend upon free quarters. He praised Bethlehem in order to console and encourage her.

After that, I saw the Holy Family arrive at a large farmhouse, about two hours' distance from the pine tree. The woman was not at home, and the man refused St. Joseph admittance, telling him that he might go on further. On they went until they came to a shepherd's shed where they found the little ass, and where they too halted. There were some shepherds in it; but they soon vacated after showing themselves most friendly and supplying straw and faggots, or bundles of reeds for a fire. The shepherds then went to the house from which Mary and Joseph had been sent away. They mentioned having met them, and said: "What a beautiful, what an extraordinary woman! What an amiable, pious, benevolent man! What wonderful people those travellers are!" The man's wife had now returned home, and she scolded at their having been sent away. I saw her going to the shepherd's hut at which they had put up, but she was timid and dared not enter. This hut was on the north side of that mountain on whose southern declivity lay Samaria and Thebez. Toward the east of this region and on this side of the Jordan, Salem and Ainon are situated, and on the opposite side, Socoth. It was about twelve hours from Nazareth. The woman came again with her two children. She was quite friendly, and seemed to be very much touched by what she saw. The husband also came and begged pardon. After Mary and Joseph had refreshed themselves a little, he showed them to an inn about an hour further up the mountain.

The host, however, excused himself to Joseph, pleading the numbers already there. But when the Blessed Virgin entered and begged for shelter, the wife of the innkeeper, as also the innkeeper himself, changed their bearing toward them. The man at once arranged a shelter for them under a neighboring shed, and took charge of the ass. The little she-ass was not with them. She was running around the fields; for when not needed, she did not make her appearance. This inn was a tolerably fine one, and consisted of several houses. Although situated on the north side of the mountain, it was surrounded by orchards, pleasure gardens, and balsam trees. Mary and Joseph remained overnight and the whole of the next day, for it was the Sabbath.

On the Sabbath the hostess with her three children visited Mary, also the woman of that other house with her two children. Mary talked to the little ones and instructed them. They had little rolls of parchment from which they read. I, too, made bold to speak confidently to Mary. She told me how extremely well it was with her in her present condition. She felt no weight. But sometimes, she experienced a sensation of being so immensely large internally and as if she were hovering in her own person. She felt that she encompassed God and man, and that He whom she encompassed carried her.

Joseph went out with the host to his fields. Both host and hostess had conceived great love for Mary; they sympathized with her condition. They pressed her to remain, and showed her a room which they would give her. But very early the next morning she started with Joseph on their journey. They went forward, a little more to the east, along the mountain and into a valley, increasing the distance between them and Samaria to which they seemed at first to be going. The temple upon Garizim was in sight. On the roof were numerous figures like lions or other animals, which shone with a white light in the sun.

The road led down into a plain, or the field of Sichem. After a journey of about six leagues, they came to a solitary farmhouse where they were made welcome. The man was an overseer of fields and orchards belonging to a neighboring city. It was warmer here and vegetation more luxuriant than at any place they had been, for it was the sunny side of the mountain, and that makes a great difference in Palestine at this season. The house was not exactly in the valley, but on the southern declivity of the mountain which stretches from Samaria to the east. The occupants belonged to those shepherds with whose daughters later on, the servants remaining behind from the caravan of the Three Kings had married. In after years also Jesus often tarried here and taught. Before departing, Joseph blessed the children of the family.

I saw him and Mary journeying over the plain beyond Sichem. The Blessed Virgin sometimes went on foot. They rested occasionally and refreshed themselves. They had with them little rolls and a cool, strengthening drink in nice little jugs, brown and shining like metal. The seat that Mary used on the ass was furnished with a pad on either side as a support for the limbs, which were thereby brought more into a sitting posture. The support was over the neck of the ass, and Mary sat sometimes to the right, sometimes to the left. Berries and other fruits were still hanging on the bushes and trees that were exposed to the sun, and these they gathered on the way. The first thing that Joseph always did on arriving at an inn, was to prepare a comfortable seat or couch for Mary; then he washed his feet, as did Mary also. Their ablutions were frequent.

It was quite dark one evening when they reached a lonely inn. Joseph knocked and begged for shelter, but the owner would not open the door. Joseph explained to him his position, telling him that his wife could go no farther. But the man was inflexible; he would not interrupt his own rest. And when Joseph told him that he would pay him, he received for answer: "This is not an inn, I will not have that knocking." The door remained closed. Mary and Joseph went on for a short distance and found a shed. He struck a light, and prepared a couch for Mary, she herself assisting him. He brought the ass in, and found some straw and fodder for it. Here they rested a few hours. I saw them departing early the next morning while it was still dark. They may now have been distant from their last halting place about six hours, about six and twenty from Nazareth, and ten from Jerusalem. The last house stood on level ground, but the road from Gabatha to Jerusalem began again to grow steep. Up to this time Mary and Joseph travelled no great highroads, though they crossed several commercial routes which ran from the Jordan to Samaria and to the roads that lead from Syria down into Egypt. So far, the roads by which they came, with the exception of that single broad one, were very narrow and ran over the mountains. One had to be very cautious in walking, but the ass could tread its way securely.

Now I saw the travellers arrive at a house whose owner was at first uncivil to Joseph. He threw the light on Mary's face, and twitted Joseph on having so young a wife. But the man's wife took them in, gave them shelter in an outhouse, and offered them some little rolls.

When they left this place, they next sought lodging in a large farmhouse where also they were not received in a manner especially cordial. The innkeepers were young, and paid little heed to Mary and Joseph. They were not simple shepherds, but rich farmers, such as we have here, mixed up with the world, with trade, etc. I saw one old man going about the house with a walking stick. From here they had still seven hours' journey to Bethlehem, but they did not take the direct route thither, because it was mountainous and at this season too difficult. They followed the little she-ass across the country between Jerusalem and the Jordan. I saw them arrive about noon at a large shepherd's house, about two hours from John's place of baptism on the Jordan. Jesus once passed a night there after His baptism. Near the house was another for the farm and sheep utensils, and in the yard was a spring from which the water was conducted through pipes to the bathtubs. There was a large public house here; and numbers of servants who took their meals at it were going and coming. The host received the travellers very kindly and he was very obliging. He insisted upon one of the servant's washing Joseph's feet at the spring. He also supplied him with fresh garments while he aired and brushed those he took off. A maidservant rendered the same services to Mary, for the mistress of the house was backward in making her appearance; she lived retired. She is the same that Jesus afterward healed of a thirty years' sickness. He told her that her malady had come upon her as a punishment for her want of hospitality toward His relatives. But I know the reason of her nonappearance to Mary and Joseph. She was young and rather frivolous. She had caught a glance of the Blessed Virgin, had spoken a word to her, perhaps, (I do not now recall all the circumstances) and had conceived a feeling of jealousy on account of her beauty. It was for that reason that she kept herself secluded on this occasion. There were some children in the house.

At their departure about noon, Mary and Joseph were accompanied part of the way by some of the people belonging to the inn. They proceeded westward toward Bethlehem, and arrived after a journey of about two hours at a little village consisting of a long row of houses with gardens and courts lying on both sides of a broad highroad. Joseph had connections here such as spring from the second marriage of a stepfather or stepmother. Their house was finely situated and very handsome. But Mary and Joseph did not enter. They passed through the place and went straight on toward Jerusalem for half an hour, when they came to a public house in which a crowd was gathered for a funeral. The frame partitions in the house had been removed from before the chimney and hearth. The fireplace was draped with black, and before it rested a coffin enveloped in the same somber hue. The male mourners wore long black robes with short, white ones over them and some had rough, black maniples on their arms. All were praying. In another apartment sat the women entirely enveloped in their large veils. There was in the yard a large fountain with several faucets. The proprietors of the house, who were taken up with the charge of the obsequies, left to the servants the duty of receiving Mary and Joseph. This was done, accordingly, and the customary services rendered the holy travellers. Tapestry, or mats, were let down from their rollers near the ceiling, and a curtained space arranged for them. After some time, I saw the people of the house in conversation with them. The white garments had been laid aside. I saw a great many beds rolled up against the walls. They could be entirely separated from one another by means of the mats let down from the ceilings. Early the following morning, Mary and Joseph again started off. The good wife of the house told them they might stay, because Mary appeared in hourly expectation of her delivery. But Mary said with lowered veil that she had yet six or eight and thirty hours. The woman was anxious to keep them, though not in her own house. I saw the husband, as Joseph and Mary were departing, talking to the former about his beasts. Joseph praised the ass very much, and told him that he had brought the other with him in case of necessity. When the people spoke of the difficulty of getting lodgings in Bethlehem, Joseph replied that he had friends there and that Mary and he would certainly be well received. This made me feel so sorry. Joseph always spoke of this with so much confidence. I heard him again making the same remark to Mary on their way.

It so happened on the last days of the journey, when they were nearing Bethlehem, that Mary sighed longingly for rest and refreshment. Joseph turned aside from the road for half an hour to a place where, upon a former occasion, he had discovered a beautiful fig tree laden with fruit. It had seats around it for weary wayfarers to rest upon. But when they reached it they found, to their great disappointment, that it was at that time quite destitute of fruit. In after years something connected with Jesus happened near that tree. It nevermore had fruit, though it continued green. Jesus cursed it, and it withered.

7. The Arrival in Bethlehem

The distance from the last public house to Bethlehem may have been three hours. Mary and Joseph went around by the north and approached the city on the west. A short distance outside the city, about a quarter of an hour's walk brought them to a large building surrounded by courtyards and smaller houses. There were trees in front of it, and all sorts of people encamped in tents around it. This house was once the paternal home of Joseph, and ages before it had been the family mansion of David. It was at this period used as the custom house of the Roman taxes.

Joseph still had in the city a brother, who was an innkeeper. He was not his own brother, but a stepbrother. Joseph did not go near him. Joseph had had five brothers, three own-brothers and two stepbrothers. Joseph was five and forty years old. He was thirty years and, I think, three months older than Mary. He was thin, had a fair complexion, prominent cheekbones tinged with red, a high, open forehead, and a brownish beard.

The little she-ass was not with them here. She had run away around the south side of the city, where it was somewhat level, a kind of valley.

Joseph went straight into the custom house, for all newcomers had to present themselves there and obtain a ticket for entrance at the city gate. The city had properly no gate, but the entrance lay between two ruined walls that looked like the remains of a gate. Although Joseph was somewhat late in presenting himself for assessment, he was well received.

Mary remained in a small house in the courtyard among the women, who were very attentive to her, and offered her something to eat. These women cooked for the soldiers. The latter were Romans, as I could tell by the straps hanging around their hips. The weather was lovely, not at all cold, the sun lighting up the mountain between Jerusalem and Bethania. One can see it very well from here. Joseph went up to a large room in an upper story, where he was interrogated, who he was, etc., and his questioners examined long rolls of writing, numbers of which were hanging on the walls. They unrolled them and read to him his ancestry, also that of Mary. Joseph knew not before that through Joachim, Mary had descended in a straight line from David. The official asked him, "Where is thy wife?"

For seven years the inhabitants of this part of the country were not regularly assessed, owing to various political troubles. I saw the numbers V and II, and that certainly makes seven. The tax collecting had already been going on for many months, but two payments were still to be made. The people had to remain almost three months. They had indeed paid something here and there during those seven years, but there had been no regular collection of taxes. Joseph did not pay anything on that first day, but his circumstances were inquired into. He told the official that he possessed no real estate, that he lived by his trade and the assistance of his wife's parents. Mary also was summoned to appear before the clerk, but not upstairs. She was interrogated in a passage on the first floor, and nothing was read to her.

There were numbers of clerks and functionaries in the house, scattered throughout the different rooms, and a great many Romans and soldiers were to be met in the upper stories. There were also Pharisees and Sadducees, priests and elders, and all sorts of clerks and officials of both Jewish and Roman extraction. There was no such payment of taxes going on in Jerusalem. But in many other places, in Magdalum on the Sea of Galilee, for instance, taxes were being received. The Galileans had to pay there, and the people from Sidon, too, partly on account of their commercial intercourse, I think. Only those that had no establishments, that possessed no estates, had to report at their birthplace. The receipts for the next three months were to be divided into three parts. The Emperor Augustus, Herod, and another king who dwelt in the neighborhood of Egypt, had a share in them. The king near Egypt, having gained some advantage in war, had a claim upon a certain district far up the country; consequently, they had to give him something. The second payment had some reference to the building of the Temple; it was something like a payment on money advanced. The third was for the poor and for widows, who had received nothing for a long time. But it all went as such things do in our own day—little to the right man. Good reasons were easily found for its remaining in the hands of the great. Incessant writing and moving to and fro were kept up.

Joseph then went with Mary straight to Bethlehem on whose outskirts the houses stood scattered, and into the heart of the city. At the different streets they met, he left Mary and the ass standing while he went up and down in search of an inn. Mary often had to wait long before Joseph, anxious and troubled, returned. Nowhere did he find room; everywhere was he sent away. And now it began to grow dark. Joseph at last proposed going to the other side of the city, where they would surely find lodgings. They proceeded down a street, which was more of a country road than a regular street, for the houses stood scattered along the hills, and at the end of it reached a low, level space, or field. Here stood a very beautiful tree with a smooth trunk, its branches spreading out like a roof. Joseph led Mary and the beast under it, and there left them to go again in quest of an inn. He went from house to house, his friends, of whom he had spoken to Mary, unwilling to recognize him. Once during his quest, he returned to Mary, who was waiting under the tree. He wept, and she consoled him. He started afresh on his search. But whenever he brought forward the approaching delivery of his wife as a pressing reason for receiving hospitality, he was dismissed still more quickly. Meantime it had grown dark. Mary was standing under the tree, her ungirdled robe falling around her in full folds, her head covered with a white veil. The ass was nearby, its head turned toward the tree, at the foot of which Joseph had made a seat for Mary with the baggage. Crowds were hurrying to and fro in Bethlehem, and many of the passersby gazed curiously at Mary, as one naturally does on seeing a person standing a long time in the dark. I think also that some of them addressed her, and asked her who she was. Ah, they little dreamed that the Saviour was so near! Mary was so patient, so tranquil, so full of hope. Ah, she had indeed long to wait! At last she sat down, her hands crossed on her breast, her head lowered. After a long time, Joseph returned in great dejection. I saw that he was shedding tears and, because he had failed again to find an inn, he hesitated to approach. But suddenly he bethought him of a cave outside Bethlehem used as a storing place by the shepherds when they brought their cattle to the city. Joseph had often withdrawn thither to conceal himself from his brothers and to pray. It was very likely to be deserted at that season or, if any shepherds did come, it would be easy to make friends with them. He and Mary might there find shelter for awhile, and after a little rest he would go out again on his search.

And now they went around to the left, as if through the ruined walls, tombs, and ramparts of a country town. They mounted a rampart or hill, and then the road began again to descend. At last, they reached a hill before which stood trees, firs, pines, or cedars, and trees with small leaves like the box tree. In this hill was the cave or vault spoken of by Joseph. There were no houses around. One side of the cave was built up with rough masonry through which the open entrance of the shepherds led down into the valley.

Joseph opened the light wicker door and, as they entered, the she-ass ran to meet them. She had left them near Joseph's paternal house, and had run around the city to this cave. She frolicked around and leaped gaily about them, so that Mary said: "Behold! It is surely God's will that we should be here." But Joseph was worried and, in secret, a little ashamed, because he had so often alluded to the good reception they would meet in Bethlehem. There was a projection above the door under which he stood the ass and then proceeded to arrange a seat for Mary. It was quite dark, about eight o'clock when they reached this place. Joseph struck a light and went into the cave. The entrance was very narrow. The walls were stuffed with all kinds of coarse straw, like rushes, over which hung brown mats. Back in the vaulted part were some airholes in the roof, but here also everything was in disorder. Joseph cleared it out and prepared as much space in the back part as would afford room for a couch and seat for Mary, who had seated herself on a rug with her bundle for a support. The ass was then brought in, and Joseph fastened a lamp on the wall. While Mary was eating, he went out to the field in the direction of the Milk Cave, and laid a leathern bottle in the rivulet that it might fill. He went also to the city where he procured some little dishes, a bundle of other things, and I think, some fruit. It was, indeed, the Sabbath but, on account of the numerous strangers in the city and their need of various necessaries, provisions and utensils were exposed for sale on tables placed at the street corners. The price was paid down on the spot. I think servants or pagan slaves guarded the tables, but I cannot remember for certain.

When Joseph returned, he brought with him a small bundle of slender sticks beautifully bound up with reeds, and a box with a handle in which were glowing coals. These he poured out at the entrance of the cave to make a fire. He next brought the water bottle, which he had filled at the rivulet, and prepared some food. It consisted of a stew, made of yellow corn, some kind of large plant that contained a great many seeds, and a little bread. After they had eaten and Mary had lain down to rest upon her rush couch over which was spread a cover, Joseph began to prepare his own resting place at the entrance of the cave. When this was done, he went again into the city. Previously to setting out, he had stopped up all the openings of the cave, in order to keep out the air. Then for the first time, I saw the Blessed Virgin on her knees in prayer, after which she lay down upon the carpet on her side, her head resting on her arm, her bundle serving for a pillow.

This cave lay at the extremity of the mountain ridge of Bethlehem. A clump of beautiful trees stood in front of the entrance, and thence could be descried some of the towers and roofs of the city. Over the entrance, which was closed by a door made of wickerwork, was a shed. From the door, a moderately wide passage led into the cave, an irregularly formed vault, half-round, half-triangular. On one side of the passage was a recess rather lower than the general surface, and this Joseph had enclosed by curtains for his own sleeping place. The rest of the passage, from the recess to the entrance, he cut off by hangings, and there had a kind of storeroom.

The passage was not so lofty as the cave itself, which was vaulted by nature. The inner walls of the cave, where they were formed entirely by nature, though not perfectly even, yet were pleasing and clean; indeed to my eye, there was something about them quite charming. They pleased me more than did those parts upon which some attempts had been made at masonry, for these latter were coarse and rough. The foundation of the right side of the entrance appeared for some distance to have been hewn out of the rock; only the upper part seemed to have been made by the hand of man. There were also some holes in this passage. In the middle of the vaulted roof was an opening and, I think, three others cut obliquely halfway up the same. These oblique openings presented a smoother appearance than the topmost one; they looked like the handiwork of man. The floor of the cave was deeper than that of the entrance, and was on three sides surrounded by a stone seat somewhat raised, broad in some places, in others narrow. At one of the broad parts, the ass took its stand. It had no trough, but a large leathern bag was placed before it or hung in the corner. Behind was a small side cave just large enough to allow the animal to stand upright. There the fodder was stored. A gutter ran along by this corner, and I saw Joseph cleaning the cave out every day.

Where Mary reposed before the birth of the Child and where I beheld her elevated above the ground at the moment of her delivery, there was a similar seat of stone. The spot in which the Crib stood was a deep recess, or side vault. Near it was a second entrance into the cave, which was in the ridge of a hill that ran toward the city. In the rear, the hill sank into a very charming valley planted with rows of trees. This valley led to the Suckling Cave of Abraham, situated in a projection of the opposite hill. The valley may have been one-eighth of an hour in width, and through it flowed that little rivulet from which Joseph had procured the water.

Besides the real Crib Cave, there were in the same hill, but lying somewhat deeper, two other caves, in one of which the Blessed Virgin often remained hidden.

When in after years St. Paula laid the first foundation of her convent at Bethlehem, I saw a small, lightly-built chapel erected in the valley and on the east side of the cave. It was so constructed as to be contiguous to the rear of the Crib Cave and directly back of the spot upon which Jesus was born. This little chapel of wood and wicker walls was hung inside with tapestry. Four rows of cells opened into it, which were built as lightly as the shepherd's cots generally are in Palestine. In every row were separate cells, each surrounded by its own little garden, and all connected by covered passages leading to the chapel. Here Paula and her daughter gathered around them their first companions. In the chapel and free from the wall, stood an altar with its little tabernacle. Behind it hung a red and white silk curtain, which concealed the facsimile of the Crib Cave that St. Paula had caused to be made. It was separated from the real cave, from the exact spot upon which Jesus was born, only by the rocky wall. This crib was made of white stone, and was a faithful imitation of that of Jesus. The manger also was represented, and even the hay hanging through its sides. The infant in it was likewise of white stone, and closely swathed in a blue veil. The figure was hollow and not very heavy. I saw St. Paula often taking it up into her arms while she prayed. Upon the wall over this crib, hung a banner upon which was represented the ass with its head turned toward the crib. It was embroidered in colors, and the hair made of thread, so natural that it looked like real hair. Above the crib was a hole in which a star was fastened. I saw that the Child Jesus often appeared here to St. Paula and her daughter. In front of the curtain and right and left of the altar were hanging lamps.

8. Birth of the Child Jesus

I saw Joseph on the following day arranging a seat and couch for Mary in the so-called Suckling Cave of Abraham, which was also the sepulcher of Maraha, his nurse. It was more spacious than the cave of the Crib. Mary remained there some hours, while Joseph was making the latter more habitable. He brought also from the city many different little vessels and some dried fruits. Mary told him that the birth hour

of the Child would arrive on the coming night. It
was then nine months since her conception by the
Holy Ghost. She begged him to do all in his power
that they might receive as honorably as possible this
Child promised by God, this Child supernaturally
conceived; and she invited him to unite with her in
prayer for those hard-hearted people who would afford
Him no place of shelter. Joseph proposed to bring
some pious women whom he knew in Bethlehem to
her assistance; but Mary would not allow it, she
declared that she had no need of anyone. It was five
o'clock in the evening when Joseph brought Mary
back again to the Crib Cave. He hung up several
more lamps, and made a place under the shed before
the door for the little she-ass, which came joyfully
hurrying from the fields to meet them.

When Mary told Joseph that her time was drawing near and that he should now betake himself to
prayer, he left her and turned toward his sleeping
place to do her bidding. Before entering his little
recess, he looked back once toward that part of the
cave where Mary knelt upon her couch in prayer,
her back to him, her face toward the east. He saw
the cave filled with the light that streamed from
Mary, for she was entirely enveloped as if by flames.
It was as if he were, like Moses, looking into the
burning bush. He sank prostrate to the ground in
prayer, and looked not back again. The glory around
Mary became brighter and brighter, the lamps that
Joseph had lit were no longer to be seen. Mary knelt,
her flowing white robe spread out before her. At the
twelfth hour, her prayer became ecstatic, and I saw
her raised so far above the ground that one could
see it beneath her. Her hands were crossed upon her
breast, and the light around her grew even more
resplendent. I no longer saw the roof of the cave.
Above Mary stretched a pathway of light up to
Heaven, in which pathway it seemed as if one light
came forth from another, as if one figure dissolved

into another, and from these different spheres of light other heavenly figures issued. Mary continued in prayer, her eyes bent low upon the ground. At that moment she gave birth to the Infant Jesus. I saw Him like a tiny, shining Child, lying on the rug at her knees, and brighter far than all the other brilliancy. He seemed to grow before my eyes. But dazzled by the glittering and flashing of light, I know not whether I really saw that, or how I saw it. Even inanimate nature seemed stirred. The stones of the rocky floor and the walls of the cave were glimmering and sparkling, as if instinct with life.

Mary's ecstasy lasted some moments longer. Then I saw her spread a cover over the Child, but she did not yet take It up, nor even touch It. After a long time, I saw the Child stirring and heard It crying, and then only did Mary seem to recover full consciousness. She lifted the Child, along with the cover that she had thrown over It, to her breast and sat veiled, herself and Child quite enveloped. I think she was suckling It. I saw angels around her in human form prostrate on their faces. It may, perhaps, have been an hour after the birth when Mary called St. Joseph, who still lay prostrate in prayer. When he approached, he fell on his knees, his face to the ground, in a transport of joy, devotion, and humility. Mary again urged him to look upon the Sacred Gift from Heaven, and then did Joseph take the Child into his arms. And now the Blessed Virgin swathed the Child in red and over that in a white veil up as far as under the little arms, and the upper part of the body from the armpits to the head, she wrapped up in another piece of linen. She had only four swaddling cloths with her. She laid the Child in the Crib, which had been filled with rushes and fine moss over which was spread a cover that hung down at the sides. The Crib stood over the stone trough, and at this spot the ground stretched straight and level as far as the passage, where it made a broader flexure toward the

south. The floor of this part of the cave lay somewhat deeper than where the Child was born, and
down to it steps had been formed in the earth. When
Mary laid the Child in the Crib, both she and Joseph
stood by It in tears, singing the praises of God.
The seat and the couch of the Blessed Virgin were
near the Crib. I saw her on the first day sitting
upright and also resting on her side, though I noticed
in her no special signs of weakness or sickness. Both
before and after the birth, she was robed in white.
When visitors came, she generally sat near the Crib
more closely veiled.

On the night of the Birth there gushed forth a
beautiful spring in the other cave that lay to the
right. The water ran out, and the next day Joseph
dug a course for it and formed a spring.

In those visions to which the event itself, and not
the feast of the Church, gave rise, I saw, indeed, no
such sparkling joy in nature as I sometimes see at
holy Christmastide. Then the joy has an interior signification. But yet, I saw extraordinary gladness, and
in many places, even in the most distant regions of
the world, something marvelous on that midnight.
By it the good were filled with joyful longings, and
the bad with dread. I saw also many of the lower
animals joyfully agitated. I saw fountains gushing
forth and swelling, flowers springing up in many
places, trees and plants budding with new life, and
all sending forth their fragrance. In Bethlehem it
was misty, and the sky above shone with a murky,
reddish glare. But over the valley of the shepherds,
around the Crib, and in the vale of the Suckling
Cave floated bright clouds of refreshing dew.

I saw the herds of the three oldest shepherds near
the hill under sheds; but those further on near the
shepherds' tower, were partly in the open air. The
three eldest shepherds, roused by the wonders of the
night, I saw standing together before their huts, gazing around and pointing out the magnificent light

that shone over the Crib. The shepherds at the distant tower were also in full movement. They had climbed up the tower and were looking toward the Crib over which they, too, saw the light. I saw something like a cloud of glory descend upon the three shepherds. I saw in it figures moving to and fro, and heard the approach of sweet, clear voices singing softly. At first, the shepherds were frightened. Soon there stood before them five or seven lovely, radiant figures holding in their hands a long strip like a scroll upon which were written words in letters a hand in length. The angels were singing the *Gloria*. The angels appeared also to the shepherds on the tower and where else, I do not now recall. I did not see them hurrying off at once to the cave. The first three were indeed an hour and a half distant from it, and those on the tower as far again. But I saw that they began at once to reflect upon what gifts they should take to the newborn Saviour, and to get them together as quickly as possible. The three shepherds went to the Crib early next morning.

I saw that Anne at Nazareth, Elizabeth in Juttah, Noemi, Anna, and Simeon in the Temple—all had on this night visions from which they learned the birth of the Saviour. The child John was unspeakably joyous. But only Anne knew where the newborn Child was; the others, and even Elizabeth, knew indeed of Mary and saw her in vision, but they knew nothing of Bethlehem.

I saw something very wonderful taking place in the Temple. The writings of the Sadducees were more than once hurled by an invisible force from the places in which they were kept, which circumstance gave rise to unaccountable dread. The fact was ascribed to sorcery, and large sums of money were paid to hush the matter up.

I saw that in Rome, across the river where numbers of Jews dwelt, a well of oil gushed forth spontaneously, to the wonder of all the witnesses. And when Jesus was born, a magnificent statue of the god Jupiter fell with violence from its place. All were struck with fear. Sacrifices were offered and another idol, I think Venus, was interrogated as to the cause. The devil was forced to speak by its mouth, and he proclaimed that it had happened because a virgin unmarried had conceived and brought forth a son. He told them also of the miracle of the oil well. Where this took place now stands a church in honor of the Mother of God. I saw that the pagan priests were deeply perplexed at the whole affair. They searched their writings, and discovered the following history. About seventy years previously, this idol (Jupiter) had been greatly venerated. It was magnificently ornamented with gold and precious stones, grand ceremonies were held in its honor, and numerous sacrifices offered to it. But there was in Rome at that time an extraordinarily pious woman who lived on her own means. I know not for certain whether she was a Jewess or not; but she had visions, uttered prophecies, and informed many persons as to the cause of their sterility. This woman had thrown out words to this effect that they should not honor the idol at so great a cost, for that they would one day behold it burst asunder in their midst. This speech proved so offensive that she was imprisoned and tormented until by her prayers she obtained from God the information as to when that misfortune would happen. The pagan priests demanded what had been revealed to her, and when at last she replied: "The idol will be shattered when an Immaculate Virgin shall bring forth a son," they hooted at her, and released her as a fool. And now the people recalled the fact and declared that the woman had spoken truly. I saw also that the Roman consuls, of whom one was named Lentulus and who was a friend of St. Peter and an ancestor of the martyr-priest Moses, made notes of this occurrence, as well as that of the bursting forth of the oil well.

On this night, I saw the Emperor Augustus at the Capitol where he had an apparition of a rainbow upon which sat the Virgin and Child. From the oracle that he caused to be interrogated upon what he had seen, he received the answer: "A Child is born, and before Him we must all flee!" The emperor at once erected an altar and offered sacrifice to the Son of the Virgin, as to the "Firstborn of God."

I had also a vision of Egypt far beyond Matarea, Heliopolis, and Memphis. There was in that region a large idol that used to give answers to all kinds of questions. Suddenly it became mute. The king ordered immense sacrifices to be offered throughout his whole dominions. Then was the devil, upon the command of God, forced to say: "I have become silent, I must give place to another. The Son of the Virgin is born, and a temple will be here erected to His honor." Upon hearing this, the king wanted to raise a temple to the newborn Child next to that of the god, but I do not clearly recall the story. I know, however, that the idol was put aside and that a temple was erected to the Virgin and Child whom it had proclaimed, and who were afterward honored with pagan rites.

I beheld a great wonder in the country of the Three Kings. There was a tower on a mountain to which the Kings retired in turn with a retinue of priests, in order to observe the stars. What they saw they committed to writing and communicated to one another. On this night there were two of them there, Mensor and Seir. The third, who dwelt toward the east side of the Caspian Sea, was called Theokeno. He was not present. There was a certain constellation at which they always gazed, and whose variations they noted. In it they saw visions and pictures. Upon this night also, they had several visions of various kinds. It was not in one star alone that they saw those visions, but in several that formed a figure, and there seemed to be a movement in them. They saw the vision of the moon over which arose a beautiful rainbow-colored arch on which was seated a Virgin. The left limb was drawn up in a sitting posture, the right hung a little lower and rested on the moon. To the left of the Virgin and rising above the arch, was a grapevine, and on her right a sheaf of wheat. In front of the Virgin was a chalice like that used at the Last Supper. It appeared to issue, but with greater clearness and brightness, from the brilliancy that emanated from her. Out of the chalice arose a Child, and over the Child shone a bright disk like an empty ostensorium. It was surrounded by radiating beams. It reminded me of the Blessed Sacrament. On the Virgin's right was an octangular church with a golden door and two small side-doors. With the right hand, the Virgin put the Child and the host into the church which, meanwhile, grew larger and larger, and in which I saw the Most Holy Trinity. Above the church arose a tower. Theokeno, the third king, had similar visions in his own home.

Over the head of the Virgin sitting on the arch shone a star, which suddenly shot from its place and skimmed along the heavens before the Kings. It was for them a voice announcing as never before that the Child, so long awaited by them and by their ancestors, was at last born in Judea, and that they were to follow that star. For some nights immediately preceding that blessed one, they had from their tower seen all kinds of visions in the heavens, kings journeying to the Child and offering their homage to It. So now they hurriedly gathered together their treasures and with gifts and presents began the journey, for they did not want to be the last. I saw all three after a few days meeting on the way.

9. Adoration of the Shepherds.
Devout Visits to the Crib

In the early dawn after the birth of Jesus, the three oldest of the shepherds came to the Crib Cave with the gifts they had gathered together. These consisted of little animals bearing some resemblance to deer. They were very lightly built and nimble, had long necks and clear, beautiful eyes. They followed or ran along beside the shepherds who led them with fine, guiding cords. The shepherds carried also large, live birds under their arms, and dead ones slung over their shoulders.

They told Joseph at the entrance of the cave what the angel had announced to them, and that they had come to do homage to the Child of Promise and to offer Him gifts. Joseph accepted their presents and allowed them to lead the animals into the space that formed a kind of cellar near the side entrance of the cave. Then he conducted them to the Blessed Virgin, who was sitting on the ground near the Crib, a rug under her, the Infant Jesus on her lap. The shepherds, their staves resting on their arms, fell on their knees and wept with joy. They knelt long, tasting great interior sweetness, and then entoned the angelic canticle of praise, and a Psalm that I have forgotten. When they were about to take leave, Mary placed the Child in their arms.

Some of the other shepherds came in the evening, accompanied by women and children, and bringing gifts. They sang most sweetly before the Crib the *Gloria,* some Psalms, and short refrains of which I remember the words: "O Child, blooming as a rose art Thou! As a herald Thou comest forth!" They brought gifts of birds, eggs, honey, woven stuffs of various colors, bundles of raw silk, and ears of corn, also several bundles of a corn with heavy grains growing on a stalk with large leaves like those of rushes.

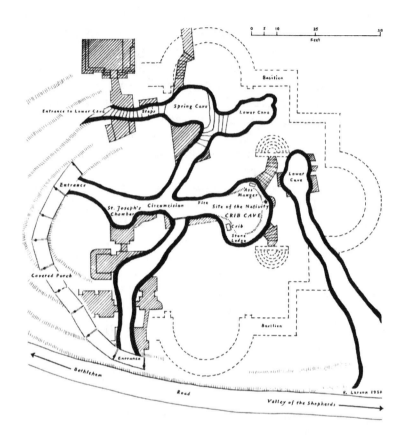

Cave of the Nativity, Bethlehem

The site of the Nativity is attested to by an unbroken tradition dating back to the 2nd Century. This plan is a suggested reconstruction of the original arrangement based on the description in the *"Life of Mary"* and the present form of the caves (shaded areas). During the centuries there have been many additions and enlargements. Sister Emmerich stated that new grottoes were cut in the rock even during the lifetime of Our Lord. The basilica, erected by Constantine over the cave in the 4th Century, and still in use, is one of the oldest Christian churches in the world.

R.L.

The three oldest shepherds came back in turn and helped Joseph to make the Crib Cave and its surroundings more comfortable. I saw also several pious women with the Blessed Virgin, performing some services for her. They were Essenians, and lived in the valley, not far from the Crib Cave, in little rocky cells adjoining one another. They owned little gardens near their cells, and they taught the children of their community. St. Joseph had invited them to come, for he was acquainted with them even in early youth. When he was hiding in the Crib Cave, from his brethren, he visited these pious women who dwelt in the side of the rock. They now came in turn to the Blessed Virgin, bringing little necessaries and bundles of wood. They cooked and washed for the Holy Family.

Some days after the birth of Jesus, I saw a touching scene in the Crib Cave. Joseph and Mary were standing by the Crib and gazing with emotion upon the Infant Jesus, when suddenly the ass fell upon its knees and lowered its head to the ground. Mary and Joseph shed tears. I saw Mary at another time standing by the Crib. As she gazed upon the Child, the deep conviction stole upon her that It had come upon earth to suffer. That reminded me of a vision I had had at an earlier period in which I had been shown how Jesus, while still in His Mother's womb and from the moment of His birth, had suffered. I saw under the heart of Mary a glory and in it a bright shining Child. As I gazed upon It, it seemed as if Mary were hovering over It and surrounding It. I beheld the Child growing and all the torments of the Crucifixion inflicted upon It. It was a sad, a fearful sight! I wept and sobbed aloud. I saw other forms around It beating and pushing, scourging and crowning It. Then they laid the Cross upon It, next nailed It to the same, and pierced It in the side. I saw the whole Passion of Christ in the Child. It was a frightful sight! As the Child hung on the Cross, It said to me: "All this did I suffer from My conception until My thirty-fourth year, when My Passion was outwardly consummated." (The Lord died when He was thirty-three years and three months old.) "Go and announce it to men!" But how can I announce it to men?

I saw Jesus also as the newborn Child, and I saw how many of the children that went to the Crib illtreated the Infant Jesus. The Mother of God was not there to protect the Child, and the children went with all kinds of switches and rods, and struck It in the face until the Blood flowed. The Child meekly extended Its little hands before Its face, in order to ward off the blows. The smallest children were they that struck the most maliciously. The parents of some even twisted and wrapped the rods for them. They brought thorns, nettles, whips, little rods of all kinds, each having its own signification. One came with a very slender rod, like a reed. But when it was about to strike the Child, the rod snapped, and fell back upon itself. I knew several of the children. Some went about boasting in their fine clothes, but I stripped them, and whipped some of them well.

While Mary was still standing by the Crib in deep meditation, some shepherds drew near with their wives, in all about five persons. To give them room to approach the Crib, the Blessed Virgin withdrew a little to the spot upon which she had given birth to the Child. The people did not actually adore, but they gazed down upon the Child deeply moved, and before leaving they bowed low over It as if kissing It.

It was day. Mary sat in her usual place with the Infant Jesus on her lap. He was swathed, the hands and face alone free, Mary had something like a piece of linen in her hands with which she was busied. Joseph was at the fireplace near the entrance of the cave, and appeared to be making a shelf to hold some vessels. I was standing next the ass. And now came in three aged female Essenians, who were cordially

welcomed, though Mary did not rise. They brought
quite a number of presents: small fruits, birds with
red, awl-shaped beaks as large as ducks, which they
carried by the wings, oval rolls about an inch in
thickness, some linen, and other stuff. All were
received with rare humility and gratitude. The women
were very silent and recollected. Deeply moved, they
gazed down upon the Child, but they did not touch
It. When they withdrew, it was without farewells or
ceremony. Meanwhile, I was taking a good look at
the ass. It had a very broad back, and I thought to
myself: "You good beast! You have carried a great
burden!"[1] and I wanted to feel it, to see if it were
real. I ran my hand over its hair, and it felt as smooth
as silk.

Now came two married women with three little
girls about eight years old. They appeared to be
strangers and people of distinction, who had come
in obedience to a call more miraculous than that
received by any previous visitor. Joseph welcomed
them very humbly. They brought presents less in size
than the others, but of greater value: grain in a bowl,
small fruits, and a cluster of thick, triangular, gold
leaves on which was a stamp like a seal. I thought:
"Strange! That looks like the representation of the
eye of God! But no! How can I compare the eye of
God with red earth!" Mary arose and placed the Child
in the ladies' arms. Both held Him a little while,
praying silently with uplifted heart, and then kissed
Him. The three little girls were silent and deeply
impressed. Joseph and Mary conversed with their
visitors and when they left, Joseph accompanied them
part of the way. Ah! Could we, like these women,
behold the beauty, the purity, the innocent wisdom
of Mary! She knew all things! But in her humility,
she appears unconscious of her gifts. Like a child,
she casts down her eyes; and when she raises them,

---

1. The Creator.

her glance, like a flash of lightning, like the truth, like a ray of unsullied light, pierces one through and through. That is because she is perfectly pure, perfectly innocent, full of the Holy Ghost, and without any reflection on self. No one can resist her glance.

These people appeared to have come at least some miles and that secretly, for they avoided being seen in the city. Joseph behaved with great humility during such visits, retiring and looking on from some distant corner.

I saw also Anne's maid and an old man servant coming from Nazareth to the Crib. The maid was a widow and related to the Holy Family. She brought all sorts of necessaries from Anne to Mary, with whom she took up her abode. The old man shed tears of joy, and returned with news to Anne.

The day after, I saw the Blessed Virgin and the Infant Jesus leave the Crib Cave with the maid for some hours. Stepping from the door of the cave, Mary turned toward the shed on the right, went some steps forward, and concealed herself in that side cave in which, at the birth of Jesus, a spring had welled up. She remained there four hours, because some men, spies of Herod, had come from Bethlehem, in consequence of the rumor set afloat by the words of the shepherds, that a miracle had there taken place in connection with a child. These men met St. Joseph in front of the Crib Cave. After exchanging a few words with him, they left him with a contemptuous smile at his humility and simplicity.

The Crib Cave was retired, and very pleasantly situated. No one from Bethlehem went there, only the shepherds whose duties called them thither. No one in Bethlehem took any interest in what was going on outside for, in consequence of the influx of strangers, the city was all alive, and much buying and selling going on. Cattle was being bought and slaughtered, for many people paid their taxes in cattle. There were numbers of pagans in the city in the capacity of servants.

The wonderful apparition of the angels was soon noised among the dwellers of the mountain valleys far and near, and with it the birth of the Child in the cave. The innkeepers from whom the Holy Family on their journey had received hospitality now came, one after another, to do homage to Him whom unknown they had entertained. I saw that hospitable keeper of the last inn, first sending presents by a servant, and then coming himself to honor the Child. I saw also the good wife of that man who had been so cross to Joseph, and other shepherds and good people coming to the Crib. They were very much affected by what they saw. All were in holiday attire, and were going up to Bethlehem for the Sabbath. The good wife might have gone to Jerusalem which was nearer, but she preferred coming here to Bethlehem.

A relative of Joseph, and father of that Jonadab who, at the Crucifixion of Jesus presented a strip of linen to Him, had also come to the Crib Cave on his way to Bethlehem for the Sabbath. Joseph was very kind to him. This relative had heard from people of his place of Joseph's wonderful situation; he came therefore to bring him gifts and to visit the Infant Jesus and Mary. But Joseph would not accept anything, although he pawned the little she-ass to this relative with the understanding that she might be redeemed for the same amount of money received. After that, Mary, Joseph, the maid, and two of the shepherds who were standing in front of the entrance, celebrated the Sabbath in the Crib Cave. A lamp with seven wicks was lighted, and upon a small table covered with white and red, lay the prayer rolls.

The numerous eatables presented by the shepherds were either given to the poor or handed around for the entertainment of others. The birds were hung on a spit before the fire, turned from time to time, and sprinkled with the flour of a reed-like plant which was very plentiful around the area of Bethlehem and

Hebron. From its grain a shining, white jelly was prepared and cakes baked. I saw under the fireplace very
hot and clean holes in which birds could be roasted.

After the Sabbath, the Essenian women got a meal
ready under the arbors which Joseph, with the help
of the shepherds, had put up at the entrance of the
cave. Joseph went into the city to engage priests for
the circumcision of the Child. The cave was cleared
and put in order. The partition that Joseph had put
up in the passage was removed, and the ground spread
with carpets, for in this passage near the Crib Cave,
the place for the ceremony was prepared.

10. The Circumcision

Joseph returned from Bethlehem with five priests
and a woman whose services were necessary on such
occasions. They brought with them the circumcision
stool and an octangular slab with all that was needed
for the ceremony. All this was placed in order in the
passage. The stool was hollow and formed a chest,
which could be taken apart, thus affording a kind of
low seat with a support on the side. It was covered
with red. The circumcision stone was, perhaps, over
two feet in diameter. In the center was a metal plate
under which, in a hollow of the stone, were all kinds
of little boxes containing fluids. These boxes were in
separate compartments, and at one side lay the
circumcision knife. The stone was laid upon the little stool which, covered with a cloth, always stood on
the spot upon which Jesus was born, and the circumcision stool was placed next to it. That evening
a repast was spread under the arbor at the entrance
to the cave. A crowd of poor people had followed the
priests, as is usual on such occasions, and during the
meal they were continually receiving something both
from the priests and from Joseph. The priests went
to Mary and the Child, spoke with the mother, and
took the Child in their arms. They also spoke to Joseph

about the name the Child was to receive. They prayed and sang the greater part of the night, and circumcised the Child at daybreak. Mary was very much troubled, very anxious about It. After the ceremony, the Infant Jesus was swathed in red and white as far as under the little arms, which also were bound and the head wrapped in a cloth. The Child was again laid on the octangular stone, and prayers recited over It. If I remember rightly, the angel had already told Joseph that the Child should be called Jesus, and I have a faint recollection that one of the priests did not at first approve the name, consequently, they still continued in prayer. Then I saw a radiant angel standing in front of the priest and holding before him a tablet like that above the Cross, upon which was inscribed the name of Jesus. I saw the priest writing the name upon a scrap of parchment. I know not whether he or any of the others saw the angel, but deeply moved, he wrote the name under divine inspiration. After that, Joseph received the Child back and handed It to the Blessed Virgin who, with two other women, was standing back in the Crib Cave. Mary took the weeping Child into her arms and quieted It. Some shepherds were standing at the entrance of the cave. Lamps were burning, and the dawn was breaking. There was some more praying and singing and, before the priests departed, they took a little breakfast. I saw that all present at the circumcision were good people. The priests were enlightened and later attained salvation. Alms were distributed the whole morning to many poor people who presented themselves. Afterward followed a crowd of beggars, filthy, black creatures, very repulsive to me. They carried bundles and, coming up from the valley of the shepherds, passed the Crib as if going to Jerusalem for the celebration of a feast. They were very boisterous, cursing and scolding horribly, because they did not receive by way of alms, as much as they wanted. I do not know exactly what was the matter with them. During the ceremony of circumcision, the ass was tied further back than usual; at other times, it stood in the Crib Cave.

During the day, I saw the nurse again with Mary attending to the Child. That night, the Child was very restless from pain. It cried, and Mary and Joseph tried to soothe It by carrying It up and down the cave.

While reflecting upon the mystery of the circumcision, I had a vision. I saw two angels with little tablets in their hands, standing under a palm tree. Upon one tablet were pictured various instruments of martyrdom, of which I remember one, a pillar which stood in the middle. On it was a mortar, which had two rings. On the other tablet were letters denoting the seasons and years of the Church. On the palm tree and as if growing out of it, was kneeling a Virgin, her flowing mantle, or veil, for it was fastened over her head, floating around her. In her hands was a heart upon which I saw a tiny, shining Child. I saw an apparition of God the Father draw near to the palm tree, break off a heavy branch that formed a cross, and lay it on the Child. Then I saw the Child raised, as it were, on the cross, and the Virgin reaching the palm branch with the crucified Child on it to God the Father, the heart alone remaining in her hand.

On the evening of the following day, I saw Elizabeth on an ass and accompanied by an old servant, coming from Juta to the cave. Joseph received her most cordially. The joy of Mary and Elizabeth was extremely great as they embraced each other. Elizabeth pressed the Child to her heart. She slept in Mary's cave next the place in which Jesus was born. Before the sacred spot stood a stool upon which they often laid the Child.

Mary told Elizabeth all that had happened to her, and when Elizabeth heard of their difficulty in getting a lodging on their arrival in Bethlehem, she wept heartily. Mary gave her all the details of the

Infant Jesus' birth. I remember hearing her say that she had been in ecstasy ten minutes at the time of the Annunciation, that it appeared to her as if her heart had grown double its size and that she was filled with unspeakable happiness. But at the Child's birth she had experienced an intense longing. She felt while kneeling that she was upheld by angels, and as if her heart was broken asunder and one-half taken from her. She had also been ten minutes in ecstasy at the time of the birth. She had been conscious of an emptiness within her, a longing after something outside of herself. Suddenly a light shone before her, and the figure of the Child seemed to grow before her eyes. Then she saw It moving and heard It crying and, coming to herself, she raised It from the rug to her breast, for at first seeing It environed with glory, she had hesitated to take It up.

Elizabeth said: "Thou hast not given birth in the same way as other mothers. The birth of John was sweet also, but it was not like that of thy Child."

Once I saw Elizabeth with Mary and the Child concealing themselves toward evening in the side cave. They remained there the whole night, for visitors from Bethlehem were approaching by whom they did not want to be seen.

The Jewish women do not leave their children long without other nourishment than the breast; and so the Infant Jesus was fed in those first days on pap made of the sweet, light, nutritious pith of a certain rush-like plant.

As in the Temple at Jerusalem, the holy Feast of the Maccabees began at this time, it was also celebrated by Joseph in the Crib Cave. He fastened three lamps with seven little lights on the walls of the cave and, during a whole week, lighted them morning and evening. Once I saw in the cave one of the priests who had been present at the Child's circumcision. He had a roll of writings from which he prayed with St. Joseph. It seemed to me that he wanted to find out whether Joseph kept that feast or not. I think, too, that he announced to him another, for a fast-day was near at hand. I saw the preparations for it in Jerusalem. Food was prepared the day before the feast, the fire was covered, servile work was put aside, the doors and windows were hung with tapestry.

Anne often sent servants with gifts of provisions and utensils, all of which Mary soon distributed to the poor. Once Anne sent a beautiful little basket of fruit with large, newly-blown roses stuck in among it. The pink roses were paler than ours, almost flesh-colored, and there were some yellow, and some white. Mary was very much pleased, and placed it beside her.

And now came Anne herself, accompanied by her second husband and a servant. The Infant Jesus stretched out His little arms to her, and great was her joyful emotion. Mary gave her a full account of all as she had done to Elizabeth. They mingled their tears together, pausing at times to fondle the Infant Jesus.

Anne had brought with her many things for Mary and the Child, coverlets, swathing-bands, etc. Although Mary had already received so many things from her, yet the Crib Cave was still quite poor in appearance, since whatever was at all unnecessary was given away at once. Mary told Anne that the Kings from the East were approaching with rich gifts, and that their coming would attract much attention. Anne, therefore, resolved to go and stay with her sister, who dwelt at some hours' distance, and to return after the departure of the royal visitors. Then I saw Joseph set to work to clear out the Crib Cave as well as those in its vicinity, in order to prepare for the arrival of the Kings whom Mary in spirit had seen coming. He went also to Bethlehem to make the second payment of taxes and to look around for a dwelling, for he intended to settle in Bethlehem after Mary's Purification.

11. Journey of the Three Kings To Bethlehem

Some days after their departure from home, I saw the caravan of Theokeno come up with those of Mensor and Seir at a ruined city. Rows of tall pillars were still standing here and in many places large beautiful statues. A band of wild robbers had taken up their quarters among the ruins. They were clothed in the skins of beasts and armed with spears; they were of a brownish color, short and stout, but very agile. The three caravans left this city together at daybreak and, after journeying half a day, rested in a very fertile district where there was a spring around which were many roomy sheds. This was an ordinary halting place for caravans. Each of the Kings had in his train, as companions, four nobles of his own race; but he himself was like a patriarch over all. He took care of all, commanded all, dispensed to all. In each caravan were to be found people of different color. Mensor's race was of a pleasing brownish color; Seir's was brown; and Theokeno's of a bright yellow. I saw no shining black, saving the slaves, of whom each king possessed some.

The nobles holding staves in their hands, sat upon their dromedaries high among the piled-up packages, which were covered with hangings. These were followed by other animals almost as large as horses, on which servants and slaves rode among the baggage. On their arrival, they unloaded the animals and watered them at the spring. This spring was surrounded by a little mound upon which was a wall with three open entrances. In this enclosed space was a cistern, somewhat lower than the surrounding surface. It had a pump with three pipes furnished with faucets. Over the cistern was a cover usually kept locked. But a man from the ruined city had accompanied the travellers, and he on payment of a tax, unlocked the reservoir. The travellers had leathern vessels, which could be folded perfectly flat. They were divided into four compartments, which when filled afforded drink to four of the camels at once. These people were extremely careful of the water; not a drop was suffered to go to waste. Then the beasts were put up in an enclosed, but uncovered space close to the spring, the stall of each animal being separated from its neighbor's by a partition. There were some troughs before them, into which was poured the feed which had been brought with them. It consisted of corn, the grains of which were as large as acorns. Among the baggage were bird baskets, high and narrow, which hung on the sides of the animals among the broad packages. In the separate compartments of these baskets, either singly or in pairs, according to their different sizes, were birds like doves or hens. They served for food on the way. In leathern chests, they had loaves, all of the same size, like single plates, closely packed together. Only as many as were needed were taken out at once. They had with them very costly vessels of yellow metal set with precious stones. They were almost exactly of the shape of our sacred vessels, some like chalices, some like little boats and dishes, out of which they drank and upon which they handed around the food. The rims of most of these vessels were set with precious stones.

The three races were somewhat different in costume. Theokeno and his followers, as well as Mensor, wore high caps embroidered in colors, and white bands wound thickly around their heads. Their short coats reached to the calf of the leg, and were very simple with only a few buttons and ornaments on the breast. They were enveloped in light, wide, and very long mantles which trailed behind. Seir and his followers wore caps with little white pads and round cowls embroidered in colors. They had shorter mantles, which were, however, longer behind than in front. Under their mantles were short tunics buttoning down to the knee and ornamented on the breast with laces, spangles, and innumerable glittering buttons, button on button. On one side of the breast was a little sparkling shield like a star. All had bare feet bound with laces to which soles were fastened. The nobles wore short swords or large knives in their girdles, and they had many bags and boxes hanging about them. Among the kings and their relatives were men about fifty, forty, thirty, and twenty years old. Some wore their beard long, others short. The servants and camel drivers were much more simply clothed; indeed, some had only a strip of stuff or an old garment around them.

When the beasts had been fed, watered, and stalled, and the attendants themselves had drunk, a fire was made in the middle of the enclosure in which they had encamped. The wood used for that purpose consisted of sticks about two and a half feet long which the poor people of the surrounding country had brought hither in well-arranged bundles, as if prepared expressly for travellers. The Kings constructed a three-cornered log pile and laid the sticks around the top, leaving an opening on one side to admit air. The pile was very skillfully put together. But I cannot say for certain how they lit the fire. I saw one of them put one piece of wood into another, as if into a box, swing it round and round a little while, and then draw it forth burning. And so they kindled a fire, and then I saw them killing some birds and roasting them.

The Three Kings and the ancients acted, each one in his own family, like the father of the house, cutting up the food and helping it around. The carved birds and little loaves were laid on small dishes, or plates, which stood upon little feet, and passed around; and in the same way, the cups were filled and handed to each one to drink. The lowest among the servants, of whom some were Moors, reclined on the bare earth. They appeared to be slaves. The simplicity, the kindness, the good nature of the Kings and nobles, were unspeakably touching. They gave to the people who gathered around them something of all that they had; they even held out to them the golden vessels and let them drink like children. Mensor, the brownish, was a Chaldaean. His city, whose name sounded to me something like Acajaja, was surrounded by a river, and appeared to be built on an island. Mensor spent most of his time in the fields with his herds. After the death of Christ, he was baptized by St. Thomas, and named Leander. Seir, the brown, on that very Christmas night stood prepared at Mensor's for the expedition. He and his race were the only ones so brown, but they had red lips. The other people in the neighborhood were white. Seir had the baptism of desire. He was not living at the time of Jesus' journey to the country of the Kings. Theokeno was from Media, a country more to the north. It lay like a strip of land further toward the interior and between two seas. Theokeno dwelt in his own city; its name I have forgotten. It consisted of tents erected on stone foundations. He was the wealthiest of the three. He might, I think, have taken a more direct route to Bethlehem, but in order to join the others he made a circuitous one. I think that he had even to pass near Babylon in order to come up with them. He also was baptized by St. Thomas and named Leo. The names Caspar, Melchior, and Balthasar were given to the kings, because they so well suited them, for Caspar means "He is won by love"; Melchior, "He is so coaxing, so insinuating, he uses so much address, he approaches one so gently"; Balthasar, "With his whole will, he accomplishes the will of God."

From Mensor's city, Seir dwelt at the distance of a three days' journey, each day counting twelve hours; and Theokeno further on, at a distance of five such days. Mensor and Seir were together when they saw in the stars the vision of the birth of Jesus, and both set out on the following day with their respective caravans. Theokeno, also, had the same vision in his own home, and he hurried to join the other two. Their journey to Bethlehem was about seven hundred and some odd hours. In the odd number, six occurs. It was a journey of about sixty days, each day twelve hours long; but they accomplished it in thirty-three days, on account of the great speed of their camels, and because they often travelled day and night.

The star that guided them was like a ball from whose lower surface light streamed as from an open mouth. It always appeared to me as if guided by an apparition that held it by a thread of light. By day I saw walking before the caravan a figure more brilliant than the light of the sun. When I reflect upon the length of the journey, the rapidity with which they made it appears to me astonishing. But those beasts have so light and even a step that their march looks to me as orderly and as swift, their movements as uniform, as the flight of birds of passage. The homes of the Three Kings formed a triangle with one another. Mensor and Seir dwelt nearest to each other; Theokeno was the most distant.

When the caravan had rested till evening, the people that had followed helped to load the beasts again, and then carried off home all that the travellers left behind them. When the caravan set out, the star was visible, shining with a reddish light, like the moon in windy weather. Its train of light was pale and long. The Kings and their followers went part of the way on foot beside their animals, praying with heads uncovered. The road here was such as to prevent their travelling quickly; but when it became level, they mounted and pushed on at a swift rate. Sometimes they slackened their pace and all sang together, the sound of their voices on the night air producing a most touching effect. When I gazed upon them riding forward in such order, their hearts filled with joy and devotion, I could not help thinking: "Ah, if our processions

could only pattern after this!" Once I saw them passing the night in a field near a spring. A man from
one of the huts in the neighborhood unlocked it for
them. They watered their beasts and, without unpack-
ing, refreshed themselves by a short rest.

Again I saw the caravan upon a high plateau. On
their right extended a mountain chain, and it seemed
to me that they were drawing near to a point in the
road where it again made a descent to a thickly settled district whose houses lay among trees and fountains. The inhabitants of this place wove covers out
of threads stretched from tree to tree, and adored
images of oxen. They bountifully supplied food to the
crowd that followed the caravan, but the dishes out
of which they ate were used no more. I was surprised
at that.

The next day I saw the Kings near a city whose
name sounded like Causur, and which was built of
tents on stone foundations. They stopped to rest with
the king to whom the city belonged, and whose tent
palace lay at a little distance. The Three Kings had
since their meeting travelled fifty-three or sixty-three
hours. They told the king of Causur all that they had
seen in the stars. He was very greatly astonished.
He looked through a tube at the star that was guiding them, and in it he saw a little Child with a Cross.

He begged them, in consequence, to inform him
on their return of all that they discovered, that he
might erect altars and offer sacrifice to the Child.
On the Kings' departure from Causur, they were
joined by a considerable train of nobles, who were
going to travel the same way. Later they rested at
a spring and made a fire, but they did not unload
their camels. When again on their way, I heard them
softly and sweetly singing together short strophes,
such as: "Over the mountains we shall go. And before
the new King kneel!"

One of them began and the others took up and
sang with him the strophes, which they in turn com-

posed and entoned. In the center of the star was plainly visible a little Child with a Cross.

Mary had a vision of the Kings' approach when they were resting a day in Causur, and she told it to Joseph and Elizabeth.

At last I saw the Kings arrive at the first Jewish city, a small, straggling place where many of the houses were surrounded by high hedges. They were here in a straight line from Bethlehem, notwithstanding which they proceeded along toward the right as the streets ran in that direction. As they entered this place, they sang more sweetly than ever and were full of joy, for the star was here shining upon them with unusual brilliancy, although the moonlight was so bright that one could see shadows distinctly. The inhabitants of the city, however, either did not see the star, or they took no special notice of it. They were exceedingly obliging. When some of the cavalcade dismounted, they assisted them greatly in watering their camels. It reminded me of Abraham's time, for then people were all so good and ready to assist one another. Many of them, bearing branches in their hands, led the caravan through the city and even went a part of the way with them. The star was not constantly shining before them; sometimes it was quite dull. It appeared to shine out more clearly wherever good people lived; and when the travellers beheld it more brilliant than usual, their hearts were filled with emotion thinking that there, perhaps, they would find the Messiah. The Kings were not without apprehension lest their large caravan would create notice and comment.

The next day they went without halting around a dark, foggy city and, at a short distance from it, crossed a river which empties into the Dead Sea. That evening, I saw them enter a city whose name sounded like Manathea, or Madian. Their caravan was now perhaps two hundred strong, so great was the crowd their generosity drew after them. A street ran through this last place, the inhabitants of which consisted partly of Jews, partly of heathens. The caravan was led into the space between the city and its surrounding wall, and there the Kings pitched their tents. I saw here, as in the former city, how anxious they became when they discovered that no one knew anything of the newborn King, and I heard them telling how long the star had been looked for among them.

12. Genealogy of the Kings

I heard that the Three Kings traced their genealogy back to Job, who had dwelt on the Caucasus and had jurisdiction over other districts far and wide. Long before Balaam, and before Abraham's sojourn in Egypt, they had the prophecy of the star and the hope of its fulfillment. The leaders of a race from the land of Job had upon an expedition to Egypt, in the region of Heliopolis, received from an angel the revelation that from a virgin the Saviour would be born whom their descendants would honor. They were also instructed to go no farther, but to return to their homes and watch the stars. They celebrated festivals in memory of the event, erected altars and triumphal arches which they adorned with flowers, and then turned back home. There may, perhaps, have been three thousand of these people collected together at this time. They were dwellers in Media and star worshippers, of a beautiful, yellowish-brown color and of tall and noble stature. They roamed from place to place with their herds, ruling wherever they pleased by their irresistible power. They had, as the Kings now related, been the first to announce the prophecy to their people, and the first to introduce among them the observation of the stars. When both the prophecy and the study had fallen into general oblivion, they were received first by one of Balaam's scholars, and long after him by three prophetesses, the daughters of the Three Kings' forefathers. And now at last, five hundred years since the time of those prophetesses, the star had appeared which they were to follow. Those three prophetesses were contemporary. They were deeply versed in the stars; they had visions and the spirit of prophecy. They foresaw that a star would arise out of Jacob and that an inviolate Virgin would bring forth the Saviour. Clothed in long garments, they went about the country announcing this prophecy, exhorting to good, foretelling the future down to the most remote ages, and promising that messengers from the Saviour would come to their people and lead them to the worship of the true God. The fathers of these virgins built a temple to the promised Mother of God on the spot where their lands joined, and in its vicinity a tower from which to observe the constellations and their various changes. From these three princes, about five hundred years after and through a lineal descent of fifteen generations, sprang the Holy Kings. It was by their intermingling with other races that they became so different in color. For a length of time, some of their ancestors were constantly on the tower observing the stars. What they saw was noted down and taught orally; and, in consequence of these observations, many changes gradually crept into their temple and worship.

All periods remarkable on account of their reference to the coming of the Messiah were pointed out to them by visions in the stars. During the last year since Mary's Conception, these visions were more and more significant, and the coming of salvation more explicitly shown. At the time of the Blessed Virgin's Conception, they saw the Virgin with the scepter and the scales in whose evenly balanced plates lay wheat and grapes. They saw, too, a prefiguration of the bitter Passion itself, for they beheld the newborn King involved in a war from which He came out victorious over all His enemies.

This observing of the stars was accompanied by religious ceremonies, fasting, prayer, purification, and self-denial. They watched not one star alone, but a whole constellation; by certain coincidences among the different stars as they gazed, were formed the visions and pictures that they saw. The wicked, engaging in this star worship, were affected by evil influences and thrown into convulsions by their demoniacal visions. It was by the agency of such people that the practice arose of sacrificing the aged and little children. But such cruelties gradually fell into disuse. The Kings saw the visions clearly and from them tasted sweet, interior consolation, without feeling the effects of any malign influence. They became, on the contrary, better and more pious. With great simplicity and candor, they described what they saw to their inquisitive auditors; but when they perceived that what their forefathers had so patiently awaited for two thousand years was not received with implicit belief, they became sad. The star was hidden by a cloud; but when it again appeared, looking so large among the drifting clouds and so near to the earth, the Kings arose from their couches, called the people of the city together, and pointed it out to them. The people gazed awestruck; some were deeply impressed, others were vexed at the Kings for disturbing their rest, while the majority sought but to profit by the princely bounty.

I heard the royal travellers saying how far they had journeyed up to this time. They reckoned the day's journey on foot as one of twelve hours. Before reaching their place of meeting, one had made a journey of three such days, the other five of twelve hours. But on their beasts, which were dromedaries, subtracting the night and the hours of rest, they could treble that distance; therefore the three days' journey on foot up to the place of meeting were equivalent to only one, and the five days counted but for two. From that place to where they were at present they had made a fifty-six days' journey of twelve hours, or six hundred and seventy-two hours. They had, therefore, from Christ's birth up to the present, counting the days that passed until they met and those devoted to resting, consumed about twenty-five days. At this place also, they took a day to rest. The people here were singularly importunate and shameless; they pressed around the Kings like swarms of wasps. The royal travellers dealt out to them freely small triangular yellow pieces like tin and also darker grains. They must have possessed unnumbered treasures. When the caravan was departing, it wound around the city, in which I saw idols standing in the temple. On the opposite side they crossed a bridge and went through a little Jewish place that contained a synagogue. And now they were on a good road, hastening toward the Jordan. About one hundred persons had joined their caravan. They had still a journey of about twenty-four hours to Jerusalem. But I saw them passing through no more cities, and they were met but by few people, as it was the Sabbath. The nearer they drew to Jerusalem, the more disheartened they became; for the star no longer shone with its usual brightness and, since their entrance into Judea, they saw it but seldom. They had hoped also to find the people on their route exulting with joy and celebrating with magnificence the birth of the newborn Saviour, to honor whom they themselves had come so far. But beholding no sign of excitement, they grew anxious and perplexed, thinking that, perhaps, after all they had made a mistake.

It may have been midday when they crossed the Jordan. They paid the ferrymen, though only two of them lent a helping hand. They held back[1] and let them attend to their transportation themselves. The Jordan was not broad at that time and it was full

---

1. As it was the Sabbath.

of sandbanks. Boards were laid over crossbeams, and the dromedaries stood upon them. The passage across the river was made expeditiously. The Kings first appeared to be going toward Bethlehem, but soon they turned and went on to Jerusalem. I saw the city towering up high against the sky. The Sabbath was over before the caravan arrived outside the city.

13. The Kings Before Herod

The caravan of the Kings took about a quarter of an hour to pass any given point. When it halted before Jerusalem, the star had become invisible; consequently, the travellers were very much troubled. The Kings rode upon dromedaries, and three other dromedaries were laden with the baggage. The rest of the cavalcade were mounted upon nimble animals of a yellowish color with small heads, I know not whether they were horses or asses, but they were very different in appearance from our horses. The animals upon which the nobles rode were very handsomely caparisoned and hung with golden stars and little chains. Some of the followers went to the gate of the city, and returned with officers and soldiers. The arrival of the Kings at that time when no feast was being celebrated, when no special commercial interest seemed to bring them, and also by that particular road, was something remarkable. They explained to the officials why they had come, and spoke of the star and the Child. But their hearers were ignorant on the subject, and so the Kings began again to think that they had surely erred, since they could not find one person who looked as if he knew anything connected with the Redemption of the world. The people gazed at them in wonder, unable to conceive what they wanted. The Kings explained that they were ready to pay for whatever they got from them, and that they wished to confer with their King. And now arose great hurrying to and fro, the travellers meantime interchanging questions and answers with the crowd gathered around them. Some had indeed heard of a child that was to be born at Bethlehem; but they were poor, ignorant people, and their words had no weight. Others laughed derisively and the Kings grew troubled and disheartened; and then they perceived by the expressions of the people that Herod knew nothing of what they sought and that he was by no means beloved by his subjects. They became anxious as to how they should address him. They had recourse to prayer, their courage revived, and they said to one another: "He who has brought us so quickly here by means of the star, will also lead us home in safety." They now led the caravan around the city and brought it in at the side nearer Mount Calvary. Not far from the fish market, they and their animals were conducted into a circular court, which was surrounded by halls and dwellings, and before whose gates guards were standing. In the middle of the court was a well, at which they watered the beasts, and all found quarters in the stalls and places under the arches. On one side of the court arose the mountain on which it lay; on the other, it was free and shaded by trees. I saw people coming with torches and examining the baggage.

Herod's palace stood higher up the mountain not far from this court. I saw the road leading to it lighted up by torches and lanterns hung on poles. I saw officials going down from the palace and conducting thither Theokeno, the eldest of the Kings. He was received under an archway and ushered into a hall. There he made known his errand to a courtier, who reported it to Herod. Herod became almost insane at the news, and gave orders for the Kings to present themselves before him on the following morning. He also sent word to them to rest while he made inquiries, and he would inform them of the result.

When Theokeno returned, he and his two royal companions became still more uneasy, and ordered the baggage that had been unpacked to be packed again. They slept none that night. I saw some of them going around the city with guides. It seemed to me that they suspected Herod of knowing all, but of being unwilling to disclose the truth to them. They still sought the star. In Jerusalem itself all was quiet, but there was much running to and fro and questioning among the sentinels at the court.

It may have been about eleven o'clock at night when Theokeno was sent for by Herod. There appeared to be some kind of festivity going on, for the palace was ablaze with lights, and I saw females in it. The news brought by Theokeno threw Herod into the greatest terror. He dispatched servants to the Temple and also into the city, and I saw priests and scribes and aged Jews going to him with rolls of writings under their arms. They wore their priestly garments, also their breastplates, and their girdles on which letters were inscribed. There were about twenty around him, expounding the writings. I saw them also mounting with him to the roof of the palace and gazing at the stars. Herod was very uneasy and perplexed. But the scribes tried to divert him, by endeavoring to prove that there was nothing in the talk of the Kings; that those Eastern people were always superstitiously raving about the stars; and that, if there was any truth in what they said, surely the priests of the Temple and the dwellers in the Holy City would have known it long ago.

Next morning at daybreak, I saw one of the courtiers going down to the caravan and bringing up all three of the Kings to Herod's palace. They were ushered into an apartment around which were pots of foliage and bushes. Refreshments were spread at the entrance. But the Kings declined the proffered food, and remained standing until Herod entered. They approached him with an obeisance, and without preamble put to him the question as to where they should find the newborn King of the Jews, for they had seen

His star and they were come to do Him homage.
Herod was very much troubled, but he concealed his
fears. Some of the scribes were still with him. He
questioned the Kings closely concerning the star, and
told them that of Bethlehem Ephrata ran the Promise.
But Mensor related to him the last vision they had
seen in the star, whereupon Herod's anxiety became
almost too great for concealment. Mensor said that
they had seen a Virgin with a Child lying before her.
From the right side of the Child issued a branch
formed of light, upon which stood a tower with many
gates, which tower increased in size until it became
a city. The Child appeared standing above it with
sword and scepter; and they had seen not only themselves, but all the kings of the earth, coming to bow
down before and adore that Child, for Its kingdom
was to vanquish all other kingdoms. Herod advised
them to go quietly and without delay to Bethlehem,
and when they had found the Child to return and
inform him that he too might go and adore Him. I
saw the Kings going down from the palace, and leaving Jerusalem at once. The day was dawning, and
the lights on the way leading up to the palace were
still burning. The crowd that had followed the royal
caravan had passed the night in the city.

Herod who, about the time of Christ's birth, had
gone to his palace at Jericho, had been even before
the coming of the Kings very restless and uneasy.
Two of his illegitimate sons had been raised by him
to high positions in the Temple. They were Saducees,
and by them he was kept informed of all that tran-
spired, as well as of all who were opposed to his
designs. Among these he was told of one, a man good
and upright, a distinguished functionary of the Temple. Herod sent him a courteous and friendly invitation to come to him in Jericho. When the good man
was on his way to comply with the invitation, Herod's
creatures fell upon him and murdered him in the
desert, making it appear as if robbers had perpe-

trated the awful deed. Some days later, Herod returned to Jerusalem, in order to take part in the Feast of the Consecration of the Temple. Then he thought he would, in his own way, give pleasure to the Jews and show them honor. He caused to be made a golden figure something like a lamb, though still more like a goat, for it had horns. This figure was to be erected above the gate leading from the outer court of the women into the court of sacrifice. Herod insisted upon this and, moreover, expected to be thanked for what he had done. But the priests resisted. Herod threatened them with a fine. They replied that the fine indeed they would pay; but that the figure, according to their Law, they could never accept. Herod fell into a rage, and ordered it to be set up secretly. Thereupon, one of the officers of the Temple, fired with zeal, seized it as it was being brought in, cleft it in twain, and hurled it to the ground. This gave rise to a tumult, and Herod ordered the offender to be imprisoned. Herod was, on account of this affair, extremely displeased, and regretted having come to the feast; but his courtiers sought by all kinds of diversions to remove the impression from his mind.

There was among some pious people in Judea the expectation of the near advent of the Messiah, and the circumstances attendant on the birth of Jesus had been noised abroad by the shepherds. Herod had heard all and had at Bethlehem made secret inquiries into it. His spies, however, having found only poor Joseph, and having besides orders not to attract attention, reported that it was nothing, that they had found only a poor family buried in a cave, and the whole affair not worth talking about. But now, all of a sudden, appeared the great caravan of the Kings. Their questioning after the King of Judah was marked by such confidence and precision, they spoke with such certainty of the star, that Herod could scarcely hide his anxious perplexity. He hoped to learn the particulars of the affair from the Kings themselves, and then take measures accordingly. But when the Kings, warned by God, did not return, he explained their flight as a consequence of their falsehood and disappointment; they were, he thought, ashamed to come back and be looked upon as fools. He therefore caused to be proclaimed in Bethlehem and in a general way, that the people should have nothing to do with the strangers. When he thought to make away with Jesus, he found that He was no longer in Nazareth. He caused search to be made after Him for a long time. When he had to give up all hope of finding Him and his anxiety was, in consequence, so much the more increased, he took the desperate resolution to murder all the children. He was so cautious in executing his measures that he transported his troops beforehand, in order to avoid any insurrection.

14. The Kings Arrive at Bethlehem

I saw the Kings leaving Jerusalem in the same order in which they had come. They left by a gate to the south: first, Mensor, the youngest; then Seir, and lastly, Theokeno. They were followed by a crowd as far as a brook outside the city, and here the rabble left them and turned back home. On the opposite side of the brook, the Kings halted and looked for their star. To their great joy, they saw it, and on again they went, singing sweetly. But what I wondered at was, that the star did not guide them by a direct route from Jerusalem to Bethlehem; they went more to the west and passed a little city that is well known to me. Beyond the same, I saw them halting at a beautiful place to pray. A well sprang up before them; they dismounted and dug a basin for the water, surrounding it with sand and sods. They remained here several hours and watered their beasts; for in Jerusalem, on account of their anxiety and trouble, they had had no rest.

The star, which by night looked like a globe of light, now had the appearance of the moon when seen by day; but still it did not appear exactly round, but somewhat pointed. I saw that it was often hidden behind the clouds.

The highroad between Bethlehem and Jerusalem swarmed with people, travellers with their baggage on asses. They were, perhaps, on account of the census, returning from Bethlehem to distant homes, or going up to Jerusalem to the Temple or the markets. But on the route taken by the Kings, it was very quiet. Perhaps the star guided them that way, that they might escape notice, and arrive in Bethlehem in the evening.

It was twilight when the caravan drew up before Bethlehem at the same gate at which Mary and Joseph had stopped. When the star had disappeared, the Kings went to the house, the former abode of Joseph's parents, and in which Joseph and Mary had recently been inscribed. Here they thought they were to find the newborn King. It was a spacious mansion with numerous small buildings around it, an enclosed courtyard in front, and stretching beyond that a lawn with trees and a fountain. I saw on the lawn Roman soldiers, because of the tax offices in the house. Crowds of people thronged around the newcomers whose beasts were being watered under the trees near the fountain. The Kings and their followers dismounted. The people showed them every mark of respect; they were not rude to them as they had been to Joseph. They presented green branches, and supplied them with food and drink; but I could see that that was principally in consideration of the gold pieces which the Kings were freely disbursing.

I saw the travellers tarrying long in doubt and anxiety. At last, I saw a light rising in the heavens on the opposite side of Bethlehem over the region of the Crib. The light was like that of the rising moon. I saw the caravan again set out and wind around the south side of Bethlehem toward the east, thus bringing on one hand the field in which Christ's birth had been announced to the shepherds. They had to go around a ditch and some ruined walls. They had made choice of this route, because they had while in Bethlehem been directed to the valley of the shepherds as a good place for encamping. Some of the Bethlehemites followed the cavalcade, but the Kings said nothing to them of the object of their search.

St. Joseph appeared to know of their arrival. Whether he had learned it through someone from Jerusalem, or in vision, I know not; but I saw him during the day bringing all kinds of things from Bethlehem, fruit, honey, and vegetables. I saw him also clearing out the cave, making more room, taking away the partitions that cut off his own little sleeping place from the passage, and stowing away the wood and the cooking utensils under the shed before the door. When the caravan had filed down into the valley of the Crib Cave, all dismounted and began to set up their tents while the people that had crowded after them from Bethlehem returned to the city. The encampment was partly pitched when over the cave shone out the star and in it a Child plainly visible. It stood directly above the Crib, its stream of light falling straight down upon it. The Kings and their followers uncovered their heads and watched it sinking lower and lower, increasing in size as it approached the earth. It looked to me as large as a sheet, I think. All were at first amazed. It was already dark; no dwelling was to be seen around, only the hill of the Crib Cave, looking like a rampart on the plain. But soon their amazement turned to joy, and they sought the entrance of the cave. Mensor pushed back the door and there, in the upper end of the cave, which was resplendent with light, he beheld Mary sitting with the Child, and looking just like the Virgin they had so often seen in the star pictures. Mensor stepped back and told his companions what he had seen, then all three entered the passage. I saw Joseph coming out to them with an old shepherd, and speaking to them in quite a friendly way. The Kings told him in a few words that they had come to adore the newborn King of the Jews whose star they had seen, and bring Him gifts. Joseph humbly bade them welcome, and they went back to their tents, in order to prepare themselves for the ceremony of their presentation. The old shepherd accompanied the Kings' servants to the little valley behind the hill, where there were sheds and shepherd stalls, in order to care for the beasts. The caravan filled the whole of the little valley.

And now I saw the Kings taking down from the camels and putting on their wide, flowing mantles of yellow silk. They fastened around their girdles with little chains, bags, and golden boxes with knobs, that looked to me like sugar bowls. They, along with the flowing mantles, made them look quite broad. They took also a little table with low feet that could be opened and folded at pleasure. It served as a salver. A cloth with tasselled fringe was thrown over it, and on it placed the boxes and dishes containing the gifts.

Each King was accompanied by his four relatives. All followed St. Joseph with some of their servants to the shed before the entrance to the cave. Here they spread the cloth over the table and stood on it several of the boxes they had hanging at their girdles, to be presented as their gifts in common. Then two youths of Mensor's train went in at the door, laid down strips of carpet all the way up to the Crib, and withdrew to a distance. And now Mensor and his four companions entered, having previously laid aside their sandals. Two servants bore the table with the gifts through the passage up to the Crib Cave; but at the entrance, Mensor took it from them, carried it in himself, and on bended knee placed it at Mary's feet. The other Kings and their companions remained standing at the entrance. I saw the cave filled with supernatural light. Opposite the entrance and on the spot where Jesus was born, was Mary leaning on one arm in a posture more reclining than sitting; by her side was Joseph, and on her right, in a raised trough with a cover thrown over it, lay the Infant Jesus. At Mensor's entrance, Mary rose to a sitting posture, drew her veil around her, and took the Child, which she enveloped in its folds, upon her lap. But she drew the veil aside sufficiently to allow the Child to be seen as far as below the little arms. She held It upright leaning against her breast, Its little head supported by her hand. The Infant folded Its little hands upon Its breast as if in prayer. It was shining with light, was very gracious, and at times extended Its little hands, as if grasping something. Mensor fell on his knees before Mary, bowed his head, crossed his hands on his breast, and offered the gifts with some reverent words. Then he took from the bag at his girdle a handful of little metal bars, about a finger in length, thick and heavy. They were pointed at the upper end, granular in the middle, and shone like gold. He laid them humbly on Mary's lap by the Child, as his gift to her. Mary accepted them graciously and humbly, and covered them with the end of her mantle. Mensor's companions stood behind him with heads lowly bowed. Mensor gave gold, because he was full of love and confidence, and had always with unshaken devotion and untiring efforts, sought after salvation.

When Mensor and his companions withdrew, Seir with his four relatives entered and knelt. He carried in his hand a golden censer, in shape like a boat, filled with small, greenish grains like resin. He gave incense, for he was the one that clung to God, voluntarily, reverently, and lovingly following His Will. He placed his gift upon the little table, and knelt long in adoration.

After Seir, came Theokeno, the eldest of the Kings. He could not kneel, because he was too old and stout. He stood bowing low, and laid upon the table a little golden ship in which was a fine, green herb. It was fresh and living, stood erect like a delicate green bush, and had small white flowers. Theokeno offered myrrh, for myrrh is typical of mortification and vanquished passions. This good man had had to struggle against severe temptations to idolatry and polygamy. He remained very long before the Infant Jesus, so long that I felt anxious for the good people, the Kings' followers, who at the entrance were so patiently awaiting their turn to see the Child.

The words of the Kings and their followers were extraordinarily simple and childlike; they were as if inebriated with love. They always began: "We have seen His star and that He is King over all kings. We have come to adore Him and to bring Him gifts." With the tenderest tears and most fervent prayers, they commended to the Child Jesus themselves, their goods, and property, all that they valued on earth. They begged Him to take their hearts, their souls, their actions, their thoughts; they entreated Him to enlighten them, to bestow upon them all the virtues, and to the whole earth to grant peace, happiness, and love. They were glowing with love. No words could depict their ardor and humility, nor the tears of joy that bathed their cheeks and flowed down the beard of the eldest. They were perfectly happy; they believed that, at last, they had entered into the star after which their forefathers had so long legitimately sighed, and at which they themselves had so longingly gazed. All the joy of the promise of many hundreds of years now fulfilled, welled up in their hearts.

Joseph and Mary also wept. I never before had seen them so full of joy. The honor paid their Child and Saviour and the recognition of Him by the Kings, of that Child for whom their poverty could afford so poor a couch, of that Child the knowledge of whose high dignity lay hidden in the silent humility of their own hearts—all that comforted them immeasurably. They saw brought to Him from so great a distance by God's almighty power, and in spite of the machinations of man, what they themselves could not procure for Him, viz., the adoration of the great, and magnificent gifts offered with holy profusion. Ah! They adored with those great ones, and the honor their Child received inundated their heart with exceedingly great joy.

The Mother of God accepted everything most humbly and thankfully. She spoke not, but the movement of her veiled head told all. The Infant Jesus lay on her mantle and covered by her veil, through which His little form shone brightly. It was only at the close of their visit that the Blessed Virgin addressed some kind words to each, throwing her veil back a little as she spoke.

The Kings now returned to their tents, which were lighted up and looked very beautiful.

At last, the good servants arrived at the Crib. During the adoration of the Kings, they had with Joseph's help erected a white tent on the hill toward the shepherd field to the left of the Crib Cave. They had brought with them on their beasts of burden the tent with all its covers and poles, the latter of which fitted into one another. At first I thought that Joseph had put it up, and I began to wonder where he had got it so quickly and opportunely; but when the caravan was about to leave, I saw that tent taken down and packed up with the rest. There was a kind of shed of straw matting put up in it, under which the chests were placed. After the servants had pitched the tent and arranged all things in it, they took their stand at the door of the Crib Cave, humbly awaiting admittance.

And now they began to enter, five at a time, accompanied by one of the nobles to whom they belonged. They knelt before Mary, and silently adored the Child.

Lastly, came the boys in their little mantles, and then there may have been in all about thirty persons present. When all had withdrawn, the Kings again came in together. They had changed their mantles for others of raw silk, white and flowing, and they carried censers and incense. Two servants had previously laid down over the floor of the cave, a carpet of a deep red color, on which Mary sat with the Child while the Kings offered incense. This carpet Mary kept ever afterward. She walked on it, and took it with her on the ass to Jerusalem when she went there for her Purification. The Kings incensed the Child, Mary, Joseph, and the whole cave. This was with them a ceremony expressive of veneration.

I saw the Kings afterward in the tent reclining on a carpet around a little low table. Joseph brought in little plates of fruit, rolls, honeycomb, and small dishes of vegetables. Then he sat down and ate with them. He was so delighted, and not at all shamefaced; he wept for joy almost the whole time. When I saw that, I thought of my own father, and how, at my profession in the convent, he had to sit among so many fine people. In his humility and simplicity, he had indeed felt intimidated, but it did not prevent his giving vent to his feelings in tears of joy.

When Joseph returned to the Crib Cave, he removed all the rich gifts to a recess at the right of the Crib, where he had screened a little corner from sight. Anne's maid who had remained to wait upon Mary, retired to the little cellarlike cave on the left of the Crib Cave, and did not come forth until all the visitors had departed. She was a quiet, modest person. I saw neither Mary nor Joseph nor the maid examining the gifts or showing any worldly pleasure on their account. They were accepted with thanks, and with liberality were again distributed to the needy. That maid was a relative of Anne, and a robust and very serious person.

On this evening and during the night, I saw in Bethlehem only at Joseph's paternal house a noisy bustling to and fro and, when the Kings entered the city, there was some little excitement; around the Crib Cave all was, at first, very quiet. After awhile, I saw here and there in the distance Jews lurking and whispering together, and giving notice in the city of what they saw. I saw also in Jerusalem on this day many old Jews and priests hurrying to and fro with writings to Herod, and then all became quiet as if they wished the subject dropped.

At last, the Kings with their people held, under the cedar over the Suckling Cave, a religious service. The singing was most touching, the boys' sweet voices mingling with those of the elders. After the service, the Kings went with a part of their followers to a large inn at Bethlehem. The others slept in the tents between the Crib and the Suckling Cave, which latter they had also taken possession of for the storing of part of their treasures. The white tent before the Crib was occupied by some of the most distinguished of the nobles.

15. The Second Day of the Kings At the Crib. Their Departure

On the next day, the Kings again visited the Crib Cave separately. During the whole day, I saw much given away by them, especially to the shepherds out in the field where the beasts had been sheltered. I saw poor old women bent with age going around with mantles over their shoulders given them by the Kings' generosity. I saw crowds of Jews from Bethlehem thronging around the good people, trying by every means in their power to extort presents from them, and looking through all that they had with a design to cheat. I saw the Kings freeing several of their people who wanted to remain among the shepherds. They gave them some of the beasts of burden with all kinds of covers and vessels packed on them, also golden grains, or gold dust, and they parted from them most cordially. I know not why their number was so diminished; perhaps many went away, or were sent home the preceding night. There was also a quantity of bread given away. I do not know where they got so much, but true it is that they had it. They were accustomed to bake wherever they encamped. I think they must already have received a warning to diminish their luggage as much as possible on their return journey.

That evening I saw the Kings in the Crib Cave, taking leave. Mensor entered first alone, and the Blessed Virgin gave him the Child in his arms. He shed abundant tears, and his face was beaming with joy. Then followed the others and took leave with many tears. They again offered numerous gifts: a great roll of precious stuff; pieces of silk, some whitish, others red; also flowered stuffs, and many very fine covers. They left their large mantles also with the Holy Family. They were fine wool of a pale delicate color, and so light that they floated on the breeze. They brought also numerous dishes piled one above the other, boxes of grain, and a basket full of pots containing delicate green plants bearing tiny leaves and white blossoms. About three of these small pots stood in the middle of a larger one; still another could have found room between them and the rim of the large pot. They were arranged in the basket, one above the other. There were also long, narrow baskets containing birds, such as I had seen hanging on the dromedaries, and which they used for food. They all wept much when parting from the Child and Mary. I saw the Blessed Virgin standing by them when they took their leave. The Kings' gifts were received by Mary and Joseph with touching humility and sincere thanks to the donors, but without any manifestations of pleasure. During the whole of this wonderful visit, I never saw in Mary the least shadow of self-interest. In her love for the Child Jesus and compassion for St. Joseph, she thought that the possession of these treasures would, perhaps, prevent their being treated in Bethlehem with such contempt as had been shown them upon their arrival, for Joseph's trouble and mortification on that account had been to her a source of suffering.

Lamps were already lighted in the Crib Cave, when the Kings took leave. They went out behind the hill toward the east, to the field in which were their people and beasts. In it stood a high tree whose spreading boughs shaded a wide circumference. The tree was very old and had a legend of its own, for Abraham and Melchisedech had met under its branches. The shepherds and the people around regarded it as sacred. A spring gushed up before it, the waters of which the shepherds used at certain seasons on account of their healing qualities. There was near the tree a furnace which could be covered, and at both sides huts affording shelter at night. A hedge surrounded the whole tract. Thither went the Kings, and found all the followers still remaining to them gathered together. A light was suspended from the tree, and under it they prayed, and sang with indescribable sweetness.

Joseph entertained the Kings again in the tent by the Crib, and then they and their nobles returned to their inn at Bethlehem. Meanwhile, the governor of the city, (acting on a secret order from Herod or moved by a spirit of officiousness, I know not) had resolved to arrest the Kings then in Bethlehem, and accuse them to Herod as disturbers of the peace. I know not when he was going to execute his resolve, but to the Kings that night in Bethlehem and to their followers in their tents near the Crib, an angel appeared in sleep, warning them to depart forthwith and to hasten home by another way. Those in the tents immediately awakened Joseph, and told him the order just received. While they proceeded to arouse the whole encampment and order the tents to be taken down, which was done with incredible speed, Joseph hurried off to Bethlehem to announce it to the Kings. But they, leaving most of their baggage behind them, had already started from the city. Joseph met them on the way and told them his errand. They informed him that they, too, had received similar instructions from an angel. Their hurried departure was unnoticed in Bethlehem. Issuing forth quietly and without their baggage, an observer might have concluded that they were going to their people, perhaps for prayer. While they were still in the Cave, weeping and taking leave, their followers were already starting in separate bands in order to be able to travel more quickly, and were hurrying to the south, by a route different from that by which they had come, through the desert of Engaddi along the Dead Sea.

The Kings implored the Holy Family to flee with them. On their refusal, they begged Mary at least to conceal herself with Jesus in the Suckling Cave, that she might not on their account be molested.

They left many things to St. Joseph to give away. The Blessed Virgin, taking the veil from her head, bestowed it upon them. She had been accustomed to envelope the Infant Jesus in its folds when holding Him in her arms. The Kings still held the Child in their arms. They were shedding tears and uttering most touching words. At last they gave their light silk mantles to Mary, mounted their dromedaries, and hurried away. I saw the angel by them in the field, pointing out the way they should take. The caravan was now much smaller, and the beasts but lightly burdened. Each King rode at about a quarter of an hour's distance from the others. They seemed to have vanished all on a sudden. They met again in a little city, and then rode forward less rapidly than they had done on leaving Bethlehem. I always saw the angel going on before them, and sometimes speaking with them.

Mary, wrapping the Child Jesus in her mantle, at once withdrew to the Suckling Cave. The gifts of the Kings and all that they had left, were also taken thither by the shepherds who had tarried around the encampment in the valley. The Kings' people who had preferred to remain behind their masters lent a helping hand.

The three oldest of the shepherds, who had been the first to do homage to Jesus, received very rich presents from the Kings. When it was discovered in Bethlehem that the caravan had departed, the travellers were already near Engaddi, and the valley in which they had encamped was, with the exception of some tentpoles left standing and the footprints in the grass, lonely and still as before.

The appearance of the royal caravan had caused great excitement in Bethlehem. Many now regretted that they had refused lodgings to Joseph; some spoke of the Kings and their followers as of a swarm of adventurers, while others connected their advent with the accounts they had heard of the wonderful apparitions to the shepherds. I saw from the city hall a proclamation made to the assembled citizens; viz., that they should beware of all preposterous opinions and superstitious reports, and go no more to the abode of those people outside the city.

When the crowd had dispersed, I saw Joseph at two different times conducted to the city hall. The second time, he took with him some of the gifts of the Kings, which he presented to the old Jews who had taken him to task, and he was set at liberty. There was another way leading from the city to the neighborhood of the Crib Cave, not by the city gate, but from that place where Mary, on the evening of her arrival with Joseph in Bethlehem, had rested under the tree while waiting for Joseph to find a lodging. This point of egress I saw the Jews blocking up with a fallen tree. They also erected a watch-house with a bell from which was a rope stretched across the road. Thus anyone trying to go that way would soon be discovered.

I saw also about sixteen soldiers with Joseph at the Crib Cave. But when they found besides himself only Mary and the Child, they returned to the city to report.

Joseph had carefully concealed the royal gifts. There were other caves in the hill under that of the Crib. No one knew of them but Joseph, who had discovered them long ago in his boyhood. They had existed from the time of Jacob who, when Bethlehem counted only a couple of huts, had there a tent with his followers.

The gifts of the Kings, the woven stuffs, the mantles, the golden vessels—all after the Resurrection were consecrated to religious uses. Each King had three light mantles and one, thick and heavy, for bad weather. The thin ones were of very fine wool, yellow and red mixed, and so light that they floated on the breeze as the wearers moved along. On festive occasions, they were exchanged for mantles of silk; they were not dyed, but of the original, lustrous shade. The train was embroidered around the edge with gold, and it was so long that it had to be carried. I had also a vision of the raising of silkworms. In a region between the country of Seir and Theokeno, I saw trees full of silkworms. Every tree was surrounded by a little ditch of water, in order to prevent the worms from crawling away. Fodder was scattered under the trees, and from their branches hung little boxes. Out of these boxes the weavers took chrysalides, about a finger in length, from which they wound off a web like that of a spider. They fastened a number of these chrysalides before the breast, and spun from them a fine thread which they rolled on a piece of wood provided with a hook. I saw the silk weavers among the trees at their looms, which were very simple. The strips of stuff woven were as wide, perhaps, as my bed.

16. The Return of St. Anne

After the departure of the Kings, the Holy Family went over into the other cave, and I saw the Crib Cave quite empty, the ass alone still standing there. Everything, even the hearth, had been cleared away. I saw Mary peaceful and happy in her new abode which had been arranged somewhat comfortably. Her couch was near the wall and by her rested the Child Jesus in an oval basket made of broad strips of bark. The upper end of the basket, where the head of the Infant Jesus lay, was arched over with a cover. The basket itself stood on a woven partition, before which Mary sometimes sat with the Child beside her. Joseph had a separate space at a little distance. Above the movable partition, there projected from the wall a pole to which a lamp was suspended. I saw Joseph bringing in a pitcher of water and something in a dish. But he did not go any more to Bethlehem for necessaries; the shepherds brought him all that he needed.

And now I saw Zachary coming for the first time from Hebron to visit the Holy Family. He wept for joy as he held the Child in his arms, and recited, with some little changes, the canticle of thanksgiving that he had uttered at John's circumcision. He spent the following day with Joseph, and then took his departure.

Many persons going up to Bethlehem for the Sabbath called also at the Crib Cave; but when they no longer found Mary there, they went on to the city.

Anne now came back to the Mother of God. She had been eight days with her youngest sister, who had married into the tribe of Benjamin. She lived about three hour's distance from Bethlehem, and had several sons who later became disciples of Jesus; among them was the bridegroom of Cana. Anne's eldest daughter was with her. She was taller than Anne and looked almost as old. Anne's second hus-

band also was with her. He was older and taller than
Joachim, was named Eliud, and was engaged at the
Temple where he had something to do with the cattle intended for sacrifice. Anne had a daughter by
this marriage, and she, too, was called Mary. At the
time of Christ's birth, the child may have been from
six to eight years old. By her third husband, Anne
had a son, who was known as the brother of Christ.
There is a mystery connected with Anne's repeated
marriages. She entered into them in obedience to the
divine command. The grace by which she had become
fruitful with Mary had not yet been exhausted. It
was as if a blessing had to be consumed.

Mary told Anne all about the Kings, and she was
very much touched at God's bringing those men so
far to adore the Child. She was filled with emotion
on seeing their gifts, upon which she looked as expressions of their adoration. She helped to arrange and
pack them, and she also gave many of them away.
Anne's maid was still with Mary. When in the Crib
Cave, she stayed in the little cellar-like cave to the
left, and now she slept under a shed that Joseph
had put up for her just in front of their present
abode. Anne and her daughters slept in the Crib
Cave. I saw that Mary let Anne take care of the
Child Jesus, a favor she had not granted to anyone
else. I saw something that very much affected me.
The hair of the Infant Jesus, which was yellow and
crisp, ended in very fine rays of light which glistened and sparkled through one another. I think they
curled the Child's hair, for they twisted it over the
little head when they washed it. Then they put a little cloak around Him. I always saw Mary, Joseph,
and Anne full of devout emotion for the Child Jesus;
but their expression of it was quite unaffected and
simple, as is always the case among holy, chosen
souls. The Child displayed a love in turning toward
Its Mother such as is by no means usual in young
children. Anne was so happy when she was nursing

the Child. Mary always laid It in her arms. The King's gifts were now hidden in the cave in which Mary had taken up her abode. They were in a wicker chest placed in a recess of the wall and perfectly concealed from sight. Anne's husband with her daughters and maid soon returned home, taking with them many of the royal gifts. Anne was now all alone with Mary and Joseph, and she remained until Eliud and the maid came back. I saw her and Mary weaving or embroidering covers. She slept in the cave with Mary, but separate.

There were again in Bethlehem, soldiers seeking in many houses after the king's son newly-born. They especially importuned with their questions a noble Jewish lady who was in childbed, but they went no more to the Crib Cave. It was now reported that only a poor, Jewish family had been there, but of them nothing more could be learned. Two of the old shepherds went to Joseph (two of those that had first gone to the Crib) and warned him of what was going on in Bethlehem. Then I saw Joseph, Mary, and Anne with the Child Jesus making their way from the cave to the tomb under that large cedar tree beneath which I had heard the Kings singing one evening. It was distant from the cave about seven and a half minutes. The tree stood upon a hill at the foot of which was an obliquely lying door opening into a passage that led to a perpendicular door which closed the entrance to the tomb. The shepherds often stayed in the forepart of it. In front of the tomb was a spring. The tomb cave itself was not square, but rather rounded in form. At the upper end, which was somewhat broader, something like a scalloped stone coffin stood on heavy supports upon a foundation of stone; one could see between it and the coffin. The interior of the cave was of soft, white stone. I saw the Holy Family entering it by night with a covered light. In the cave that they had vacated nothing now

was to be seen which could attract notice. The beds
had been rolled up and taken away, as well as all
their household effects. It looked like an abandoned
dwelling place. Anne carried the Child in her arms,
Joseph and Mary at her side, while the shepherds
led the way as guides. And now I had a vision, but
I do not know whether it was seen by the Holy Family or not. I saw around the Child Jesus in the arms
of Anne a glory made up of seven angelic figures
entwined together and leaning one upon the other.
There were, besides, many other figures in this aure-
ola, and on either side of Anne, of Joseph, and of
Mary, I saw figures of light supported by them, held
up, as it were, under the arms.[1] Passing through the
first entrance, they shut it and went on into the interior of the tomb cave.

A couple of days before Anne's return home, I saw
some shepherds entering the tomb cave and speaking to Mary; they told her that government officials
were coming to seek her Child. Joseph hurried off
with the Child Jesus wrapped in his mantle, and I
saw Mary, for half a day perhaps, sitting in the cave
very anxious and without the Child.

When Eliud with Anne's maid came again from
Nazareth to take Anne home, I saw a very beautiful ceremony celebrated in the Crib Cave. Joseph
had taken advantage of Mary's withdrawal to the
tomb cave, and with the help of the shepherds had
adorned the whole interior of the Crib Cave. It was
festooned with flower garlands, both walls and roof,
and in the center stood a table. All the beautiful carpets and stuffs of the Kings that had not yet been
removed, were spread over the floor and hung in festoons from the walls. A cover was spread on the table,
and on it was placed a pyramid of flowers and foliage
that reached to the opening in the roof. On top of
the pyramid hovered a dove. The whole cave was full

---

1. This signifies the numerous disciples that proceeded from Anne.

of light and splendor. The Child Jesus in His little basket cradle was placed upon a stool on the table. He sat upright as He had done on the lap of His Mother at the adoration of the Kings. Joseph and Mary were standing on either side of Him. They were adorned with wreaths, and they drank something out of a glass. I saw choirs of angels in the cave. All were very happy and full of emotion. It was the anniversary of Joseph and Mary's espousals.

When the celebration was over, I saw Anne and Eliud going away and taking with them on two asses what still remained of the Kings' gifts.

The Holy Family immediately set about preparing for their own departure. Their household effects had steadily diminished. The portable partitions and other pieces of furniture made by Joseph were now bestowed upon the shepherds, who removed them at once.

I saw the Blessed Virgin going twice by night to the Crib Cave with the Child Jesus, and laying It on a carpet on the spot upon which It was born. Then she knelt down at Its side and prayed. I saw the whole cave filled with light as at the moment of the Birth. It was now entirely cleared out, for Anne on reaching home had dispatched two of her servants to get whatever the Holy Family would not need on their journey. I saw them returning with the two asses on which they rode laden with goods. The cave to which the Holy Family had removed, as well as the Crib Cave, were now quite empty; they had also been swept out, for Joseph wanted to leave everything perfectly clean.

On the night preceding their departure for the Temple, I saw Mary and Joseph taking formal leave of the Crib Cave. They spread the deep red cover of the Kings first over that spot upon which the Child Jesus was born, laid the Child on it, and kneeling beside It prayed. Then they laid the Child in the Crib and again prayed beside It; and, lastly, on the place where It had been circumcised where, too, they knelt in prayer. Joseph had caused the young she-ass to be pawned among his relatives, for he was still resolved to return to Bethlehem and build himself a house in the valley of the shepherds. He had mentioned his intention to the shepherds, saying that he would take Mary for awhile to her mother, that she might recover from the hardships undergone in her late abode. He left all kinds of things with them.

17. Mary's Purification

Before the break of day, Mary seated herself on the ass, the Child Jesus on her lap. She had only a couple of covers and one bundle. She sat upon a side seat that had a little footboard. They started to the left around the Crib hill and off by the east side of Bethlehem unperceived by anyone.

I saw them at midday resting at a spring that was roofed in and surrounded by seats. A couple of women came out here to Mary, bringing to her little mugs and rolls.

The offering that the Holy Family had with them was hanging in a basket on the ass. The basket had three compartments; two contained fruit, and in the third, which was of open wickerwork, were doves. Toward evening, when about a quarter of an hour's distance from Jerusalem, they turned and entered a small house that lay next a large inn. The owners were a married couple without children, and by them the holy travellers were welcomed with extraordinary joy. The house lay between the brook Cedron and the city. I saw Anne's man servant and the maid stopping with these people on their journey home, at which time also they engaged quarters for the Holy Family. The husband was a gardener; he clipped the hedges and kept the road in order. The wife was a relative of Johanna Chusa. They appeared to me to be Essenians.

The whole of the next day, I still saw the Holy Family with the old people outside Jerusalem. The Blessed Virgin was almost all the time alone in her room with the Child which lay upon a low, covered projection of the wall. She was always in prayer, and appeared to be preparing herself for the sacrifice. I received at that moment an interior instruction as to how we should prepare for the Holy Sacrifice. I saw in her room myriads of angels adoring the Child Jesus. Mary was wholly absorbed in her own interior. The old people did out of pure love all they could for the Mother of God. They must have had some presentiment of the Child's holiness.

I had a vision also of the priest Simeon. He was a very aged, emaciated man with a short beard. He had a wife and three grown sons, the youngest of whom was already twenty years old. Simeon dwelt at the Temple. I saw him going through a narrow, dark passage in the wall of the Temple to a little cell which was built in the thick walls. It had only one opening, from which he could look down into the Temple. Here I saw the old man kneeling and praying in ecstasy. The apparition of an angel appeared before him, telling him to notice particularly the first Child that would, early the next morning, be brought for presentation, for that It was the Messiah whom he had now awaited so long. The angel added that, after seeing the Child, he would die. Oh, what a beautiful sight that was to me! The little cell was so bright, and the old man radiant with joy! He went home full of gladness, announced to his wife the good tidings of the angel, and then returned to his prayer. I have seen that the pious priests and Israelites of those times did not sway to and fro so much when at prayer as the Jews of our days; but I saw them scourging themselves. Anna in her Temple cell was also rapt in prayer; and she, too, had a vision.

Early in the morning while it was still quite dark,

I saw the Holy Family accompanied by the two old people going into the city and to the Temple. The ass was laden as if for a journey, and they had with them the basket of offerings. They first entered a court that was surrounded by a wall, and there the ass was tied under a shed. The Blessed Virgin and Child were received by an old woman and conducted along a covered walk up to the Temple. The old woman carried a light, for it was still dark. Here in this passage came Simeon full of expectation to meet Mary. He spoke a few joyous words with her, took the Child Jesus, pressed Him to his heart, and then hurried to another side of the Temple. Since the preceding evening, when he had received the announcement of the angel, he had been consumed by desire. He had taken his stand in the women's passage to the Temple, hardly able to await the coming of Mary and her Child.

Mary was now led by the woman to a porch in that part of the Temple in which the ceremony of presentation was to take place. Anna and another woman (Noemi, Mary's former directress) received her. Simeon came out to the porch and conducted Mary with the Child in her arms into the hall to the right of the women's porch. It was in this porch that the treasure box stood by which Jesus was sitting when the widow cast in her mite. Old Anna, to whom Joseph had handed over the basket of fruit and doves, followed with Noemi, and Joseph retired to the standing place of the men.

It was understood at the Temple that several women were coming today to offer sacrifice, and preparations had been made accordingly. Numerous pyramidal lamps were burning round the walls, the little flames rising out of a disk supported upon an arm in the form of an arch, which shone almost as brightly as the light itself. On the disk hung extinguishers which, when struck together above the flame, put it out. Before the altar, from whose corners projected horns, was placed a chest, the doors of which opened outward and afforded supports for a tolerably large slab, the whole forming a table. This surface was covered first with a red cloth and over that a white transparent one, both of which fell to the floor. On the four corners burned lamps with several branches; in the center of the table was a cradle-shaped basket, and near it two oval dishes and two small baskets. All these objects, as also the priests' vestments, which were lying on the horned altar, were kept in the chest whose open doors formed the table. A railing enclosed the whole. On both sides of this hall were rows of seats in tiers where priests were sitting in prayer.

Simeon conducted Mary through the altar rail and up to the table of sacrifice. The Infant Jesus, wrapped in His sky-blue dress, was laid in the basket cradle. Mary wore a sky-blue dress, a white veil, and a long, yellowish mantle. When the Child had been placed in the cradle, Simeon led Mary out again to the standing place of the women. He then proceeded to the altar proper, whereon lay the priestly vestments and at which, besides himself, three other priests were vesting. And now one of them went behind, one before, and two on either side of the table, and prayed over the Child, while Anna approached Mary, gave her the doves and fruit in two little baskets, one on top of the other, and went with her to the altar rail. Anna remained there while Mary, led again by Simeon, passed on through the railing and up to the altar. There upon one of the dishes she deposited the fruit, and into the other laid some coins; the doves she placed upon the table in the basket. Simeon stood before the table near Mary while the priest behind it took the Child from the cradle, raised It on high and toward the different parts of the Temple, praying all the while. Simeon next received the Child from him, laid It in Mary's arms, and, from a roll of parchment that lay near him on a desk, prayed over her and the Child.

After that Simeon again led Mary to the railing, whence Anna accompanied her to the place set apart for the women. In the meantime, about twenty mothers with their firstborn had arrived. Joseph and several others were standing back in the place assigned to the men.

Then two priests at the altar proper began a religious service accompanied by incense and prayers, while those in the rows of seats swayed to and fro a little, but not like the Jews of the present day.

When these ceremonies were ended, Simeon went to where Mary was standing, took the Child into his arms and, entranced with joy, spoke long and loud. When he ceased, Anna also filled with the Spirit, spoke a long time. I saw that the people around heard them indeed, but it caused no interruption to the other ceremonies. Such praying aloud appeared not to be unusual. But all were deeply impressed, and regarded Mary and the Child with great reverence. Mary shone like a rose. Her public offerings were indeed the poorest; but Joseph in private gave to Simeon and to Anna many little, yellow, triangular pieces to be employed for the use of the Temple, and chiefly for the maidens belonging to it who were too poor to meet their own expenses. It was not everyone that could have his children reared in the Temple. Once I saw a boy in Anna's care. I think he was the son of a prince, or king, but I have forgotten his name.

I did not witness the purification ceremonies of the other mothers; but I had an interior conviction that all the children offered on that day would receive special grace, and that some of the martyred innocents were among them. When the Most Holy Child Jesus was laid upon the altar in the basket cradle, an indescribable light filled the Temple. I saw that God was in that light, and I saw the heavens open up as far as the Most Holy Trinity.

Mary was now led back into the court by Anna and Noemi. Here she took leave of them, and was joined by Joseph and the old people with whom she and Joseph had lodged. They went with the ass straight out of Jerusalem, and the good, old people accompanied them a part of the way. They reached Bethoron the same day, and stayed overnight in the house which had been Mary's last stopping place on her journey to the Temple thirteen years before. Here some of Anne's people were waiting to conduct them home.

18. Feast Picture

I saw the festival of the Purification celebrated also in the spiritual church. It was filled with angelic choirs and in the center above them, I saw the Most Holy Trinity and in It something like a void. In the middle of the church stood an altar and on it a tree with broad, pendent leaves, similar to the trees in Paradise by which Adam fell.

I saw the Blessed Virgin with the Child Jesus in her arms floating up from the earth to the altar, while the tree on the same inclined low before her and began to wither. A magnificent angel in priestly garments, a halo round his head, approached Mary. She gave him the Child, and he laid It upon the altar. At that instant I saw the Most Holy Trinity as ever before in Its fullness. I saw the angel give to Mary a little shining ball whereon was the figure of a swathed Child, and I saw her with this gift hovering over the altar. From all sides, I saw crowds of poor people approaching Mary with lights. She reached those lights to the Child on the ball into which they seemed to pass, and then to reappear. I saw that all these lights united into one, which spread over Mary and the Child, and illumined all things. Mary had extended her wide mantle over the whole earth. And now there was a festival.

I think that the withering of the Tree of Knowledge at Mary's appearance and the offering of the Child to the Most Holy Trinity signified the reuniting of the human race with God, and through Mary those scattered lights became one light in the light of Jesus, and illumined all things.

19. Death of Holy Simeon

I saw that Simeon, after prophesying in the Temple, returned home and fell sick. I saw him on his couch giving his last advice to his wife and sons, and imparting to them his joy. Then I saw him die. There were several old Jews and priests praying around him.

When he had breathed his last, they carried the body into another room where, without stripping it, it was washed. The body was laid on a board pierced with holes, under which was a copper basin to receive the water as it fell. A large sheet was thrown over the corpse, and under that the washing was performed. Green leaves and herbs were then strewn plentifully over it and a wide cloth bound firmly around it, as is done in the swathing of a child. The corpse was so stiff and straight that I was tempted to think it was bound to a board. The burial took place in the evening. Six men with lights carried the corpse on a board with low, curved sides to the sepulcher hewn in a hill not far from the Temple. It was entered through an oblique door; the interior walls were ornamented with stars and various figures like the Blessed Virgin's cell at the Temple. I noticed the same kind of ornamentation in St. Benedict's first cloister. The corpse was deposited in the center of the little cave, the passage around it being left free; then some religious rites were solemnized. They laid all kinds of things around the corpse: coins and little stones and leaves, I think. I do not now remember all distinctly. Simeon was related to Veronica and, through his father, with Zachary also. His sons served in the Temple, and were always, though in secret, on terms of friendship with Jesus and His relatives. Some of them before and some after the Ascension of Our Lord, joined the disciples. At the time of the first persecution they did much for the Community.[1]

20. Return of the Holy Family to Nazareth

I saw the Holy Family returning to Nazareth by a much more direct route than that by which they had gone to Bethlehem. On their first journey, they had shunned the inhabited districts and seldom put up at an inn; but now they took the straight route, which was much shorter.

Joseph had in his cloak pocket some little rolls of thin, yellow, shining leaves on which were letters. He had received them from the Holy Kings. The shekels of Judas were thicker, and in the form of a tongue.

I saw the Holy Family arrive at Anne's, in Nazareth. The eldest sister of Mary, Mary Heli, with her daughter Mary Cleophas, a woman from Elizabeth's place, and that one of Anne's maids who had been with Mary in Bethlehem were there. A feast was held such as had been celebrated at the departure of the child Mary for the Temple. Lamps burned above the table, and there were some old priests present. Things went on quietly. Though there was great joy over the Child Jesus, yet it was a calm, inward joy. I have never seen much excitement among those holy souls. They partook of a slight repast, the women as usual eating apart from the men. I can remember no more of this vision, although I must have been present in a very real way, for I had to accomplish in it a work of prayer.

---

1. The early Christians.

In Anne's garden, notwithstanding the season, I saw numbers of pears, plums, and other fruits still on the trees, although the leaves had already fallen. I have always forgotten to say a word about the weather in Palestine during the winter season, because being so accustomed to it myself, I think that everyone else knows it, too. I often see rain and fog, and sometimes snow, but it soon melts away, and I see many trees upon which fruit is still hanging. There are in the year several harvests, the first in what corresponds to our spring. In the present season, winter, I see the people on the roads wrapped up in mantles which are thrown over the head also. On the sacred night of Christmas, I always see everything green, blossoming, and full of flowers, the animals frolicsome, the vineyards laden with luscious grapes, and I hear the sweet caroling of birds; but immediately after, it is again quiet and just as it usually is there at this season. The tree outside of Bethlehem and under which Mary stood while Joseph was seeking an inn was, as long as she remained under it, quite green. It afforded ample shelter. But when she left it, it resumed its wintry nakedness. This was perhaps only a mark of reverence; but the Blessed Virgin was fully conscious of it. The shepherd field was, however, already green at this season, for they watered it.

The road from Anne's house to Joseph's in Nazareth was about one half-hour's distance, and ran between gardens and hills. I saw Joseph at Anne's loading two asses with many different things, and going on before with Anne's maid to Nazareth. Mary followed with Anne, who carried the Child Jesus.

Mary and Joseph had no care of the housekeeping. They were provided with all things by Anne, who often went to see them. I saw her maid carrying provisions to them in two baskets, one on her head, the other in her hand.

I saw the Blessed Virgin knitting, or crocheting

little robes. To her right side was fastened a ball of wool and she had in her hands two short needles of bone, I think, with little hooks at the end; one was about half an ell long, the other shorter. The stitches were arranged on the needles above the hooks, over which in doing the work the thread was thrown, and the stitch thus formed. The finished web hung between the two needles. I saw Mary thus working, either standing or sitting by the Child Jesus, who lay in His little basket cradle.

I saw St. Joseph, out of long strips of bark—yellow, brown, and green—platting screens, large surfaces, and covers for ceilings. He had a stock of this woven board-like work piled under a shed near the house. He wove into them all kinds of patterns, stars, hearts, etc. I thought as I looked at them that he had no idea how soon he would have to leave all.

I saw the Holy Family while at Nazareth visited also by Mary Heli. She came with St. Anne, bringing with her her grandson, a boy of about four years, the child of her daughter Mary Cleophas. I saw the holy women sitting together, caressing the Child Jesus, and laying It in the little boy's arms; they acted just as people do nowadays. Mary Heli lived in a little town about three hours east of Nazareth. She had a house almost as large as her mother's. It had a courtyard surrounded by a wall, and in it a well with a pump. On pressing with the foot at the base of the pump, the water flowed out into a stone basin before it. Mary Heli's husband was named Cleophas. Their daughter Mary Cleophas, who had married Alpheus, lived at the other end of the town.

That evening I saw the holy women praying together. They were standing in front of a little table, which was fastened to the wall and covered with red and white. On it lay a roll which Mary unfolded and hung up on the wall. A figure was embroidered on it in pale colors; it was like a corpse entirely enveloped in a long, white mantle. It had something in its arms.

I saw a picture like it at Anne's during the festival before Mary's departure for her Presentation in the Temple. A lamp was burning during their prayer. Mary stood a little in front of the table with Anne and Mary Heli on either side. At certain times, they crossed their hands upon their breast, folded them together, or stretched them forth. Mary read out of a roll that lay before her. They prayed in measured and steady tones; it reminded me of choir chanting.

21. The Flight into Egypt

When Herod saw that the Kings did not return, he thought they had failed to find Jesus, and the whole affair seemed to be dying out. But after Mary's return to Nazareth, Herod heard of Simeon's and Anna's prophecies at the Presentation of the Child in the Temple, and his fears were reawakened. I saw him in as great disquietude as at the time of the Kings' stay in Jerusalem. He was conferring with some aged Jews who read to him from long rolls of writings mounted on rods. He had given orders for a number of men to be gathered together in a large court, and there provided with weapons and uniforms. Things went on as they do with us when soldiers are recruited. I saw that he sent these troops to various places around Jerusalem, from which the mothers were to be summoned to the Holy City. He caused their numbers to be everywhere ascertained. He took these precautions in order to prevent the tumult that would necessarily follow if the news of the projected slaughter of the children was spread. I saw those soldiers in three different places, in Bethlehem, in Gilgal, and in Hebron. The inhabitants were in great consternation, because not able to divine why a garrison was placed in their towns. The soldiers remained about nine months in those places, and the murder of the little ones began when John was about two years old.

Anne and Mary Heli were still at the home of the Holy Family in Nazareth. Mary, with her Child, slept in the apartment to the right behind the fireplace; Anne, to the left; and between hers and that of St. Joseph, Mary Heli. These rooms were not so high as the house itself, and were cut off from one another only by wicker partitions. The ceiling also was of wickerwork. Mary's couch was surrounded by a curtain, or screen. At her feet, in His own little bed, lay the Infant Jesus within Mary's reach when she sat upright. I saw a radiant youth standing at the side of Joseph's couch and speaking to him. Joseph sat up, but overcome by sleep, again lay down. Then the youth caught him by the hand and raised him up. Joseph, now thoroughly aroused, stood up and the youth vanished. Then I saw Joseph going to the lamp that burned in the center of the house, and getting a light. He proceeded to Mary's chamber, knocked, and asked permission to enter. I saw him going in and speaking to Mary who, however, did not open her screen. After this he went out to the stable for the ass, and returning, went into a room wherein were stored all kinds of household goods. He was getting things ready for a journey. Mary arose, quickly clothed herself for travelling, and went to arouse Anne, who got up at once along with Mary Heli and the little boy. I cannot express how touching was the trouble of Anne and the sister. Anne embraced Mary over and over again with many tears, clasping her to her heart as if she were never again to see her. The sister threw herself flat on the floor, and wept. Only just before setting out, did they take the Infant Jesus from His little bed. They all pressed the Child to their heart, and It was given to the little boy to embrace. Mary then took the Child upon her breast, resting It in a strip of stuff that fastened over her shoulders. A long mantle enveloped both Mother and Child, and Mary wore over her head a large veil, which hung down on both sides of her face. She made but few preparations for the journey, and all she did was done quietly and quickly. I did not see her even swathing the Child afresh. The holy travellers took only a few things with them, far fewer than they had brought from Bethlehem, only a little bundle and some coverings. Joseph had a leathern bottle filled with water and a basket with compartments in it, in which were loaves, little jugs, and live birds. There was a cross seat for Mary and the Child on the ass, also a little footboard. They went forward a short distance with Anne, for they took the road in the direction to her house, only somewhat more to the left. When Joseph approached with the ass, Anne again embraced and blessed Mary, who then mounted and rode off. It was not yet midnight when they left the house. The Child Jesus was twelve weeks old. I had seen three times four weeks.

I saw Mary Heli going to her mother's house in order to send Eliud with a servant to Nazareth, after which she returned with the boy to her own home. I next saw Anne in Joseph's house packing everything up for Eliud and the servant to remove to her own house.

The Holy Family passed by many places that night, and not till morning did I see them resting under a shed and taking a little refreshment.

I saw them taking their first night's lodgings in the little village of Nazara, between Legio and Massaloth. The poor, oppressed people of this place who lodged the Holy Family were not, properly speaking, Jews. They had to go far over a mountainous road to Samaria to worship, for their temple was on Mt. Garizim, and they always had to work like slaves on the Temple of Jerusalem and other public buildings. The Holy Family could go no further. They were well received by these outcasts with whom they remained the whole of the following day. On their return from Egypt, they again visited those poor people. They did the same both going and returning from the Temple the first time that the Child Jesus made the journey to it. The whole family at a later period was baptized by John, and they afterward joined the disciples of Jesus.

The Holy Family on their flight met only three inns at which to spend the night: here, at Nazara; again at Anim, or Engannim, among the camel dealers; and lastly, among the robbers. At other times, they rested during their tiresome wanderings in valleys and caves and the most out-of-the-way places. Further on from Nazara, I saw them hidden under the great pine tree near which Mary, on her journey to Bethlehem, had been so cold. The persecution of Herod was known in these parts and it was, consequently, unsafe for them. The Ark of the Covenant had once rested under this tree, when Joshua assembled the people and made them renounce their idols.

Later, I saw the Holy Family by a well and balsam bush resting and refreshing themselves. The branches of the bush were notched, and out of them oozed the balsam in drops. The Child Jesus lay on Mary's lap, His little feet bare. To the left behind them, lay Jerusalem far up above the level of the country in which they then were.

When the Holy Family had passed the walls of Gaza, I saw them in the wilderness. No words can depict the difficulties of this journey. They always travelled a mile eastward of the ordinary highway and, as they shunned the public inns, they suffered the want of all necessaries. I saw them quite exhausted with not a drop of water (the little jug was empty) drawing near to a low bush some distance from the road. The Blessed Virgin alighted from the ass and sat down upon the dry grass. Suddenly there jetted high before them a spring of water, which spread over the plain. I witnessed their joy. Joseph dug a hole at a little distance, and led the ass to it. The poor beast gladly drank from it as it filled. Mary bathed the Child in the spring, and refreshed herself. The sun shone out beautifully for a short time, and the weary travellers were strengthened and full of grateful emotion. They tarried here for two or three hours. On the sixth night, I saw them in a cave near the mount and city of Ephraim. The cave was in a wild ravine, about one hour's distance from the grove of Mambre. I saw the Holy Family arrive, worn-out and dejected. Mary was very sad; she wept, for they were in want of everything. They rested here a whole day and many wonders were vouchsafed them for their refreshment. A spring gushed forth in the cave, a wild goat came running to them and allowed itself to be milked, and they were visibly consoled by an angel. One of the Prophets had often prayed in this cave. Samuel had once sojourned in it, David had guarded his father's sheep around it, and to it had often retired to pray. He had in this cave, received through angels, the divine commands, among them that to slay Goliath.

The last stopping place of the Holy Family in Herod's dominion was near its confines. The innkeepers appeared to be camel dealers, for I saw a number of camels in an enclosed pasture ground. The people were rude and wild, and they enriched themselves by thieving; still they received the Holy Family most graciously. This place was distant a couple of hours from the Dead Sea.

Once I saw Mary sending a messenger to Elizabeth, who then brought her child to a very concealed place in the desert. Zachary accompanied her only a part of the way. When they reached a certain body of water, Elizabeth and the child crossed over on a raft, while Zachary went on to Nazareth by the same route taken by Mary on her visit to Elizabeth. I saw him on his journey. Perhaps he was going to make some inquiries, for there were some friends at Nazareth distressed at Mary's departure.

On a starry night, I saw the Holy Family going through a sandy wilderness covered with low thickets. The scene was as vivid before me, as if I were really crossing the desert with them. Here and there under the copsewood, venomous snakes lay coiled. With loud hissing, they approached the path and darted their heads angrily toward the Holy Family. But they, shielded by the light that environed them, stepped securely along. I saw other animals with immense fins like wings on their blackish body, with short feet, and a head like that of a fish. They darted along, flying over the ground. At last, the Holy Family came behind the bushes to a deep fissure in the ground, like the walls of a narrow defile, and here they rested.

The last place in Judea by which they passed, had a name that sounded like Mara. I thought of Anne's ancestral place, but it was not it. The people were very rude and uncivilized, and the Holy Family could get nothing from them by way of refreshment.

Leaving this last place and scarcely knowing how to proceed, they pressed on through a desolate region. They could find no road, and a dark, pathless mountain-height stretched out before them. Mary was exhausted and very sad. She knelt with Joseph, the Child in her arms, and cried to God. And behold! Several large, wild beasts, like lions, came running around them, exhibiting friendly dispositions. I understood that they had been sent to show the way. They looked toward the mountain, ran thither and then turned back again, just like a dog that wants someone to follow it. At last the Holy Family followed them and, after crossing the mountain, arrived at a very dismal region.

22. The Holy Family Among Robbers

At some distance from the road by which they were travelling, a light glimmered through the darkness. It proceeded from a hut belonging to a gang of robbers, who had hung a light on a neighboring tree, thus to allure travellers. The road too, here and there, was broken by pits over which cords with little bells were stretched. The ringing of these bells gave notice to the robbers of the presence of luckless wayfarers. All on a sudden, I saw a man with about five comrades surrounding the Holy Family. All were actuated by wicked intentions. But when they looked at the Child, I saw a glittering ray like an arrow penetrating the heart of the leader, who straightaway commanded his comrades to offer no injury to the strangers. Mary also saw the ray. The robber now took the Holy Family to his home, and told his wife how strangely his heart had been moved. The people were at first shy and shamefaced, something very unusual for them; still they approached, little by little, and gathered around the Holy Family, who had seated themselves in a corner on the ground. Some of the men went in and out, while the woman brought to Mary little rolls, fruits, honeycomb, and cups containing something to drink. The ass also was placed under shelter. The woman cleared out a small room for Mary and brought her a little tub of water in which to bathe the Child. She also dried the swathing bands for her at the fire. The husband was deeply impressed by the demeanor of the Holy Family, and especially the appearance of the Child. He said to his wife, "This Hebrew Child is no ordinary child. Beg the Lady to allow us to wash our leprous child in His bathing water. It may, perhaps, do it some good." The wife went to request the favor of the Blessed Virgin; but before she had time to speak, Mary bade her take the water she had used for Jesus' bath, wash the sick child in it, and it would become cleaner than it was before attacked by the disease. The boy was about three years old and stiff from leprosy. His mother carried him in and put him into the bath. Wherever the water touched him, the leprosy fell like scales to the bottom of the tub; the boy became clean and well. The mother was out of herself with joy; she wanted to embrace Mary and the Child Jesus. But Mary, stretching out her hand, warded her off; she would allow neither the Child nor herself to be touched by her. She told her to dig a hole deep down to a rock, and pour the water just used into it, that she might always have it for similar purposes. Mary spoke with her long, and exacted from her a promise to embrace the first opportunity of escape from her present abode. The people were all delighted; they stood around the Holy Family gazing at them in wonder. During the night, other members of their band came to the hut, and to them the boy's cure was related. The robbers' reverential bearing toward the Holy Family was so much the more remarkable, since I saw that night many travellers, attracted to their hut by the light, immediately taken prisoner and carried deep into the forest to an immense cave that served for their special storehouse. It lay under a thicket, the entrance closely concealed. In it were clothes, carpets, meat, goats, sheep, and innumerable other stolen things, all in profusion. I saw also boys about seven or eight years old whom the robbers had kidnapped. They were cared for by an old woman who lived in the cave.

Mary slept none that night; she sat upon her couch on the floor perfectly still. At early dawn the Holy Family started again on their journey in spite of the robber and his wife, who wanted them to stay longer. They took with them a supply of provisions put up by their grateful host and hostess who also accompanied them a part of the way, that they might escape the snares.

The robber and his wife took leave of the Holy Family with expressions of deep feeling, uttering these remarkable words: "Remember us wherever you go!" Upon hearing them, I had a vision in which I saw that the cured boy afterward turned out to be the Good Thief who on the cross said to Jesus: "Remember me when Thou comest into Thy Kingdom." The robber's wife, after some time, joined those that dwelt around the balsam garden.

The Holy Family went from here further on into the desert. When they had again lost all trace of anything like a path, they were a second time surrounded by all kinds of animals, among them huge winged lizards and even serpents, which pointed out the way to them.

At a later period, when unable to advance through the sandy plain in which they were, I saw a very lovely miracle. On either side of the road sprouted up the plant Rose of Jericho, with its crisped branches, its tiny flowers in the center, and its straight root. On they went now right joyously, watching as far as the eye could see these plants springing up, and so across the whole plain. I saw that it was revealed to the Blessed Virgin that, at some future day the people of the country would gather these roses and sell them to travellers in exchange for bread. The name of this region sounded like Gaza, or Goze.

I saw the Holy Family arrive at a town and district called Lepe or Lape, in which were numerous canals and ditches with high dams. I saw them crossing the water on a raft. Mary sat on a log, and the ass was standing in something like a trough, or tub. Two ugly, brown-complexioned, half-naked men with flat noses and protruding lips, ferried them over. Our holy travellers came now to the house on the outskirts of the town; but the occupants were so rough and pitiless that, without saying a word, Mary and Joseph moved further on. I think this was the first pagan Egyptian city they had yet reached. They had made, up to this time, ten days' journey in the Jewish country and then in the wilderness.

I next saw the Holy Family on Egyptian territory, in a level, green country full of pasture grounds. In the trees were stationed idols like swathed dolls, or like fishes wrapped in broad bands upon which were figures or letters. Occasionally, I saw people fat, but short in stature, approaching these idols and venerating them. The Holy Family sought a little rest under the cattle shed, the cattle going out of their own accord to make room for them. They were in want of food, having neither bread nor water. Mary no longer had nourishment for her Child, and no one gave them anything. Every species of human misery was experienced by them during this flight.

At last, some shepherds drew near to water their cattle. They, too, would have gone away without giving them anything, had not Joseph's entreaties moved them to unlock the well and allow them to have a little water.

Again, I saw the Holy Family weary and exhausted in a forest, at whose egress stood a slender date tree, the fruit all clustered on top. Mary approached the tree, the Child Jesus on her arm, prayed and raised the Child up to it. Instantly the tree bowed down its top as if kneeling, so that Mary could gather all its fruit. It afterward remained in that position. I saw Mary dividing a quantity of the fruit among the naked children who had run after them from the last village.

At a quarter of an hour's distance from this tree, stood another unusually large one of the same kind, very high, and hollow like an old oak. In it the Holy Family lay concealed from the people that followed them. That evening I saw them taking shelter within the walls of a ruined place, where they stayed overnight.

23. The Balsam Garden

On the next day, the Holy Family continued their journey through a sandy, desolate wilderness. Famishing for water and exhausted by weariness, they sat down on one of the sandhills, and the Blessed Virgin sent up a cry to God. Suddenly, a stream of pure water gushed forth at her side. Joseph removed the sandhill that was over it, and a clear, beautiful, little fountain jetted up. He made a channel for it, and it flowed over quite a large space, disappearing again near its source. Here they refreshed themselves, and Mary bathed the Child Jesus, while Joseph gave drink to the ass and filled the water bottles. I saw all kinds of animals like turtles drinking at the gushing waters. They did not appear at all afraid of the Holy Family.

The soil over which the water had flowed soon began to clothe itself with verdure, and numbers of balsam trees afterward grew there. When the Holy Family returned from Egypt, those trees were large enough to furnish balsam for their refreshment. The place soon grew into a little settlement. Wherever the heathens planted these trees they withered. They thrived only when the Jews whom the Holy Family had known in this country went to live there. I think the wife of that robber whose boy had been cured of leprosy by the bath of the Child Jesus went there, too, for she soon escaped from the robbers. Her boy, however, remained with them some time longer.

A balsam hedge surrounded the garden, and in its center were several large fruit trees. At a subsequent period, another large well was dug, out of which quantities of water were raised by means of a wheel turned by oxen. This water mingled with that of Mary's spring and watered the whole garden; unmixed, it would have proved injurious. I have seen that the oxen employed in turning the wheel could not by any means be forced to work from Saturday noon till early on Monday morning.[1]

24. The Holy Family Reach Heliopolis

I saw the Holy Family on their way to Heliopolis. From their last night lodgings they were accompanied thither by a good man who, I think, was one of the workmen on that canal over which they had been ferried. They now crossed a long and very high bridge over a wide river (the Nile), which appeared to have several branches, and came to a place before the city gate which was surrounded by a kind of promenade. Here on a tapering pedestal, stood a great idol with the head of an ox, and in its arms something like the figure of a swathed child. The idol was encompassed by a circle of benches, or tables of stone upon which the worshippers laid their sacrifices. Not far off was a very large tree, under which the Holy Family sat down to rest.

They had scarcely seated themselves when the earth began to quake, the idol tottered, and tilted over. A hue and cry instantly arose from the people, and many of the workmen on the canal in the neighborhood came rushing up. But the good man who had accompanied the Holy Family started with them for the city. They were already at the opposite side of the idol place when the terrified crowd, with menacing and abusive words, angrily surrounded them. Suddenly the earth heaved, the huge tree fell, its roots breaking up out of the ground, and there arose a lake of muddy water into which the idol splashed. It sank so deep that one could scarcely see its horns, and some of the most wicked of the bystanders sank with it. The Holy Family now entered the city unmolested, and put up near an idolatrous temple, a large stone building containing many rooms. Some

---

1. Compare *Catholic Missions,* an account of the Balsam Garden, by an eyewitness. 1883, p. 234, etc.

of the idols in the temples of the city were likewise overturned.

Heliopolis is also called On. Aseneth, wife of the Egyptian Joseph, resided here with the pagan priest Putiphar, and here also Dionysius the Areopagite studied. The city extends to a great distance around the many-branched river. One sees it from afar lying high above the general level. The river flows through it under the arches that support some of the buildings. Great logs lie in some parts of the river branches, placed there to enable the inhabitants to cross. I saw the ruins of enormous buildings, huge masses of heavy masonry, towers half standing, and even temples almost entire. I saw, too, pillars like towers, around the outside of which one could mount to the top.

The Holy Family dwelt under a low colonnade, in which there were other dwellings besides their own. The supporting pillars were rather low, some round, some square, and above ran a highway for the accommodation of vehicles and pedestrians. Opposite this colonnade was a pagan temple with two courts. Joseph put up before their little abode a screen of light woodwork. There was room for the ass, also. The screen, or light wall that Joseph put up, was of the same kind as he was accustomed to make. I remarked behind a similar screen and set up against the wall, an altar consisting of a small table covered with red and over that a white, transparent cloth; on it stood a lamp.

I saw St. Joseph working at home, and often also abroad. He made long rods with round knobs at the ends, little three-legged stools with a handle by which to grasp them, and a certain kind of basket. He made, also, a great many light, wicker partitions, and little, light towers, some hexagonal, others octagonal. They were formed of long, thin boards, tapering toward the top and ending in a knob. They had an entrance, and were large enough to allow a man to sit inside as in a sentry box; they had steps outside, up which one could mount. I saw little towers like these standing here and there before the pagan temples, also on the flat roofs of the houses. People used to sit in them; perhaps they were watch houses, or maybe they were intended as screens from the sun. I saw the Blessed Virgin weaving tapestry and doing another kind of work. For the latter she used a staff on the top of which a knot was fastened. I cannot say whether she was spinning or not. I often saw people visiting her and the little Infant Jesus. The Child lay on the ground by Mary's side, in a kind of cradle like a little boat. Sometimes I saw it raised on a frame like a sawing-jack. There were not many Jews in Heliopolis, and I saw them going about with a downcast look as if they had no right to live there.

North of Heliopolis, between it and the Nile, which there divides into several branches, lay the little territory of Goshen, and in it a little place cut up by canals, among which dwelt numbers of Jews whose religious ideas were very much confused. Several of them became acquainted with the Holy Family, and Mary did all kinds of feminine work for them, receiving as payment bread and other provisions. The Jews in the Land of Goshen had a temple, which they compared with the Temple of Solomon; but it was very different.

Not far from his dwelling, Joseph built an oratory where the resident Jews, who possessed no such place of their own, used to assemble with the Holy Family for prayer. It was surmounted by a light cupola which could be thrown open, thus enabling the worshippers to stand under the open sky. In the center of the hall stood an altar, or table of sacrifice, covered, as usual, with red and white; on it lay rolls of parchment. The priest, or teacher, was a very old man. The men and women were not so separated from one another at prayer as in Palestine; the men stood on one side, the women on the other.

The Holy Family dwelt a little more than a year at Heliopolis. They had much to suffer from the Egyptians who hated and persecuted them, on account of their overturned idols; and as the houses were all solidly built, Joseph could not find work at his trade. They left Heliopolis, therefore, but not before they had learned from an angel of the slaughter of the Bethlehemite babes. Both Mary and Joseph were deeply grieved, and the Child Jesus, who was now able to walk, being a year-and-a-half old, shed tears the whole day.

25. The Murder of The Innocent Children

I saw the mothers with their boys, from infants in the arms up to the age of two years, going to Jerusalem. They were from those different places around the Holy City, in which Herod had placed garrisons and in which, by means of officials, he had issued a proclamation to that effect; viz. from Bethlehem, Gilgal, and Hebron. I saw many women even from the Arabian frontiers taking their children to Jerusalem, and these had more than a day's journey to make. The mothers went in bands, some with two children and riding on asses. On their arrival in the city, they were all conducted to a large building, and the husbands who accompanied some of them dismissed. The mandate was joyously obeyed, for the poor people imagined they were going to receive a reward.

The building into which the mothers and their children were ushered, was not far from the house occupied by Pilate at a later period. It stood alone, and so encompassed by walls that no one outside could hear anything going on within. A gateway through double walls led into a large court enclosed on all sides by buildings. Those to the right and left were of one story; that in the middle, which looked like an old, deserted synagogue, was two stories in height. From all three, doors opened into the court. The middle building was a hall of justice, for I saw in the court before it a stone block, pillars with chains, and such trees as could be bound together by their branches and then suddenly snapped asunder, in order to tear people to pieces.

The mothers were led through the court and into the two side buildings, where they were shut up. It looked to me at first as if they were in a sort of hospital, or lazarhouse. When they saw themselves thus unexpectedly deprived of liberty, they began to fear, to cry, and to lament.

The lower story of the court of justice was a great hall like a prison, or guardroom; the upper one was also a large hall from which windows opened upon the court. The officers of justice were assembled in the latter, rolls of writing lying before them on tables. Herod himself was there. He wore his crown and a purple mantle bordered with black and lined with white fur. He stood at the windows with many others, looking down upon the slaughter of the Innocents.

The mothers, one by one, with their boys, were summoned from the side buildings into the great hall under the judgment hall. On their entrance, the children were taken from them by the soldiers and carried out into the court where about twenty others were actively at work with swords and lances, piercing the little creatures through throat and heart. Some of the children were still in swaddling clothes, infants in the mother's arms; while others, able to run around, wore little woven dresses. The soldiers did not remove the children's clothing but, having pierced them through the heart and throat, they grasped them by one arm or leg and slung them together in a heap. It was a terrible sight!

The mothers were, one after another, pushed back into the large hall by the soldiers. When the fate of

their little ones dawned upon them, they raised a
frightful cry, tore their hair, and clung to one another.
There were so many of them and, toward the last,
they were so crowded together that they could scarcely
stir. I think the slaughter lasted till near evening.
The bodies of the murdered children were buried
together in a great pit in the court. I saw the mothers that night fettered, and taken back to their homes
by the soldiers. Similar scenes were enacted in other
places, for the massacre was carried on during several days.

The number of the Holy Innocents was indicated
to me by another number which sounded like *ducen,*
and which I had to repeat until, I think, the whole
amounted to seven hundred and seven, or seven hundred and seventeen.

The place of the children's massacre in Jerusalem
was the subsequent hall of justice, and not far from
that of Pilate; but it was at his time very greatly
changed. At Christ's death, I saw the pit in which
the murdered children were buried, fall in. Their
souls appeared and left the place.

Elizabeth had fled with John into the desert. After
a long search, she found a cave, and there she
remained with him for forty days. After that, I saw
that an Essenian belonging to the community on
Mount Horeb and a relative of Anna the Prophetess,
brought food to John, at first every eight, afterward
every fourteen days, and otherwise provided for him.
Before Herod's persecution, John could have been
hidden in the neighborhood of his parents' house;
but he had made his escape into the desert impelled
by divine inspiration. He was destined to grow up
in solitude, apart from intercourse with his fellow
beings, and destitute of the customary nourishment
of man. I saw that that wilderness produced certain
fruits, berries, and herbs.

26. The Holy Family Go to Matarea

The Holy Family left Heliopolis on account of the persecution they there endured and because Joseph could not obtain work. They took byroads and went still further into the country, journeying southward toward Memphis. Passing through a little town not far from Heliopolis, they halted in the forecourt of an open, pagan temple, and sat down to rest; when, all on a sudden, down tumbled the idol and fell to pieces. It had the head of an ox with triple horns, and several cavities in the body to receive the sacrifices that were to be consumed. At once arose a tumult among the pagan priests; they seized the Holy Family and threatened them with punishment. But one of them represented to his companions, as they were consulting what measures to take, that the best thing for them to do would be to commend themselves to the God of these strangers; for he remembered, he said, what plagues had come upon their forefathers when they had persecuted those people, and that upon the night of their departure from Egypt the firstborn in every house had died. These words were effectual, and the Holy Family was left in peace. The pagan priest who had spoken for them went soon after to Matarea with several of his people, and there joined the Holy Family and the Jewish community.

Mary and Joseph next went to Troja, a place on the eastern side of the Nile, opposite Memphis. It was large and very dirty. They had some idea of remaining there, but they were not well received; indeed, they could get not even a drink of water, much less a few dates for which they begged. Memphis lay west of the Nile, which was at that point very broad and contained some islands. A part of the city lay also on this side of the river and, in Pharao's time, a large palace with gardens and high towers, from which Pharao's daughter often looked out on the country around. I saw the spot upon which, among the tall bulrushes, the child Moses was found. Memphis was like three cities in one, for it was built on both sides of the Nile, and appeared also to be connected with Babylon, a city lying eastward of the river and nearer to its mouth. In Pharao's time, the country in general around the Nile between Heliopolis, Babylon, and Memphis, was so covered with high stone dams and buildings, and so linked together by canals, that those three cities presented the appearance of one large city. But at the time of the Holy Family, all were separate, immense wastes intervening between them.

The holy travellers proceeded northward from Troja along the river toward Babylon, a dirty, low-lying city. Between the Nile and Babylon, they took the route by which they had come and returned a distance of about two hours. Buildings in ruins were scattered here and there along the whole road. After crossing a small branch of the river, or a canal, they reached Matarea, which was built upon a tongue of land jutting out into the Nile. The river bathed the city on two sides. It was, in general, a wretched enough place, built only of date-wood and solid mud covered with rushes. Joseph found plenty of work here. He built more substantial houses of wickerwork with galleries around them, to which the occupants could go for air and recreation.

Here the Holy Family dwelt in a dark, vaulted cave that lay in a retired spot on the land side, not far from the gate by which they had entered. Joseph, as at Heliopolis, built a light screen before it. One of the idols in a little temple fell at their arrival and later all the others did the same. The people were in consternation, but one of the priests quieted them by recalling to their remembrance the plagues of Egypt. After some time, as a little community of Jews and converted pagans gathered around the Holy Family, the priests gave over to them the little temple whose idol had fallen at their coming, and Joseph turned it into a synagogue. Joseph was like the patriarch of the community. He taught them how to sing the Psalms correctly, for Judaism in those parts had greatly deteriorated. Only the poorest Jews dwelt here in Babylon, and that in the most wretched dens and caves. But in the Jewish settlement between On and the Nile, they were numerous and better off. They had a regular temple, for they had lapsed into frightful idolatry. They had a golden calf, a figure with an ox's head, around which were ranged other representations of animals like polecats, or ferrets. These last mentioned animals defend people against the crocodile. *(Ichneumon)*. They had, too, an imitation of the Ark of the Covenant and horrible things in it. The idolatry they practiced was of the most shameful kind and, in a subterranean hall, they carried on the most infamous wickedness, deluded by the hope that from it their messiah should come forth. They were exceedingly stiff-necked, and would not be converted. Later on, however, many of them left that settlement and went to Babylon, about two hours distant. In doing so, they could not, on account of the numerous dykes and canals, travel by a straight road; they had to make a detour around On.

These Jews of the Land of Goshen had already made the acquaintance of the Holy Family, while the latter abode in On. Mary while there had done various kinds of work for them, such as knitting and embroidering covers and bands. She would never undertake works for vanity or extravagance, but only useful things and religious vestments. I saw women bringing work to her, which they wanted done in accordance with the requirements of vanity and fashion, and Mary returning it although so much in need of the pay she would have received for it. The women mocked and scornfully derided her.

The Holy Family at first suffered greatly from

want. Good water could not be had and wood failed;
the inhabitants used only dried grass and reeds for
their cooking. The Holy Family generally ate cold
food. Joseph had plenty to do. He improved the poor
huts for the people; but they treated him almost
like a slave, giving him for his labor only what they
themselves thought proper. Sometimes he brought
home something as a remuneration for his work,
and sometimes he brought nothing. The people were
very unskillful in building their huts. They had no
wood, excepting here and there a log or two; and
even if they had had wood, they had no tools to
shape it, for they had only knives of bone or stone.
Joseph had brought the most necessary tools with
him.

The Holy Family were soon settled somewhat
comfortably. They had little stools and tables, wicker
screens, and a well-ordered fireplace also. The Egyptians ate sitting flat on the ground. In the wall of
Mary's sleeping place I saw a recess that Joseph
had hollowed out, and in it was Jesus' little bed.
Mary's couch was beside it, and I have often seen
her by night kneeling in prayer to God before that
little bed. Joseph slept in another enclosed corner.

The oratory of the Holy Family was in a passage
outside. Joseph and the Blessed Virgin had separate places in it and Jesus, too, had His little corner, where He prayed sitting, standing, or kneeling.
There was a kind of little altar before the Blessed
Virgin's place, a small table covered with red and
white. This table was like a leaf on hinges that could
be let down from or put up against the wall. When
let down, it disclosed a shelf in the wall itself and
on the shelf were various objects, among them something that was held as sacred. I saw little bushes
in pots formed like chalices; a withered, though still
whole branch, on top of which was the lily that had
blossomed in Joseph's hand when he had been chosen by lot in the Temple for Mary's spouse; and

something like fine, thin, white sticks that were placed crosswise in the rounded part of the recess. The blossoming lily branch was the top of Joseph's staff; it was stuck in a box about one-and-a-half inches in diameter. The little sticks that were arranged crosswise, were also in a box, a transparent one. There were about five of those little white sticks of the thickness of a coarse straw. They were crossed and bound in the middle to a kind of little sheaf. But one pays very little attention to such things when in vision; one's thoughts are chiefly intent upon the holy personages there presented.

I saw that the Holy Family had to subsist on fruits and bad water. They had been so long without good water that Joseph resolved to saddle the ass, take his leathern bottle, and start for the balsam spring in the desert in order to get some. But the Blessed Virgin was told in prayer by an angelic apparition that she should seek and find a spring at the back of their present abode. I saw her going over the hill in which they dwelt, to a deep vacant lot that lay at some distance between ruined walls. A large, old tree stood on that ground. Mary had in her hand a rod provided with a little scoop, such as the people of that country commonly carry on journeys. She stuck it into the ground near the tree, and a beautiful, clear stream of water instantly gushed forth. She hurried back joyfully to call Joseph, who soon removed the upper crust of earth and disclosed a well which had long ago been dug out and lined with masonry, but which for some time had been choked up and dry. He soon restored it and paved it around very beautifully with stones. At the side of the well toward which Mary had approached, lay a great stone almost like an altar. I think it was used for that purpose in former times.

The Blessed Virgin after that often washed Jesus' clothes and bands here, and dried them in the sun. The well remained unknown and was used only by the Holy Family until Jesus had grown large enough to go on little errands and even to bring water for His Mother. Once I saw Him taking other children to the well and giving them a drink of the water which He scooped up in a hollow, crooked leaf. The little ones told this to their parents, and so the well became known. Others now began to go to it, though it remained principally in the use of the Jews. Even in the time of the Holy Family, it possessed healing properties for the leprous. Later, when a little chapel had been built over the dwelling of the Holy Family, there was near the high altar a flight of steps leading down to their first abode. There I saw the spring. It was surrounded by dwellings, and its waters used for the cure of leprosy and similar diseases. Even the Turks kept a light burning in the little chapel, and dreaded being overtaken by some misfortune if they neglected it. But the last I saw of the spring, it was lying solitary, surrounded only by trees.

I saw the Boy Jesus bringing water from the well for His Mother for the first time. Mary was in prayer when the Boy slipped to the well with a bottle, and brought it back full of water. Mary was unspeakably affected when she saw Him coming back with the water. She knelt down and implored Him never to do that again, for He might fall into the well. But Jesus replied that He would take care, and that He wanted to render her that service whenever she needed it. If Joseph happened to be working at a little distance from home, and did he leave a tool lying behind him, I used to see the Boy Jesus running after it and bringing it to him. The Boy noticed everything. I think the joy that Mary and Joseph experienced on His account, must have outweighed all their sufferings. Though perfectly childlike, He was very wise, skilled in everything; He knew and understood everything. I often saw Mary and Joseph filled with unspeakable admiration.

When the Boy Jesus took to their owners the covers embroidered or woven by His Mother, who hoped to receive bread in return for her work, I often saw Him teased at first, and consequently sad. But after awhile, the Holy Family was very much loved by the people. I saw other children giving Jesus figs and dates, while many of their elders sought the Holy Family for help and consolation. All in trouble said, "Let us go to the Jewish Child." I saw the Boy going on all kinds of errands, even to a Jewish town a mile distant, to get bread in exchange for His Mother's work. The wild animals, numerous on His route, did Him no harm; on the contrary, they and even the serpents showed Him affection. Once I saw Him going with other children to the Jewish town; He was weeping bitterly over the degradation of the Jews.

When He went for the first time alone to that Jewish town, He wore, also for the first time, the brown robe woven by Mary. It was trimmed around the border with yellowish flowers. I saw Him kneeling and praying on the way. Two angels appeared to Him and spoke of Herod's death, but He said nothing of it to His parents.

27. The Return of the Holy Family from Egypt

I saw the Holy Family's departure from Egypt. Herod was long since dead, but danger still threatened and they could not return. I saw St. Joseph, who was always busy at his trade, very much troubled one evening. The people for whom he had been working had given him nothing; consequently, he had nothing to take home where there was so much need. He knelt down in the open air and prayed. He was greatly afflicted; his sojourn among these people was becoming intolerable. They practiced infamous idolatry, even sacrificing deformed children.

The parent that sacrificed a healthy, well-formed child, was thought to be very pious. They had, besides, still more shameful rites that they carried on in secret. Even the Jews in the Jewish towns were to Joseph objects of horror.

While in his trouble he prayed to God for help, I saw an angel appear to him. He bade him arise, and on the following morning depart from Egypt by the public high road. He told him also not to fear, for that he would accompany him. I saw Joseph hastening with the news to the Blessed Virgin and Jesus, and all setting to work to get their few movables packed together on the ass.

Next morning their intention to depart having become known, crowds of sorrowing neighbors came to them, bringing with them all kinds of gifts in little vessels of bark. Several mothers brought their children. There was among them a noble lady with a little boy of several years. She called him Mary's son, because having long abandoned the hope of having a boy, this child had been vouchsafed to her at Mary's prayer. She gave to the Boy Jesus triangular coins, yellow, white, and brown. Jesus first looked at them and then at His Mother. This lady's little son was later on admitted by Jesus into the number of His disciples, and was named Deodatus. The mother's name was Mira.

The people of the place, of whom there were more pagans than Jews, were sincerely grieved at the Holy Family's departure, though a few were glad. These last looked upon them as sorcerers who obtained all they desired through the help of Lucifer, the prince of devils. The Jews could no longer be recognized as Jews, so deeply were they sunk in idolatry.

The Holy Family started, accompanied by all their friends. They took the direction between On and the Jewish town, turning away from On a little to the south, in order to reach the balsam garden. They wanted to rest there awhile and replenish their water supply. The garden was already flourishing. The balsam trees were as tall as moderately large grapevines and in four rows surrounded the garden, which had an entrance. There were sycamores and all kinds of fruit trees, some like dates. The spring sent a stream around the whole garden. The friends that had accompanied them here took leave, but the Holy Family remained for some hours. Joseph had made some little vessels out of bark; they were covered with pitch, very smooth and nice. He snapped from the reddish balsam twigs the clover-like leaves, and hung the flasks underneath, in order to gather the balsam drops for the journey. When they stopped to rest, he often made, for their ordinary use, vessels and flasks of that kind out of bark. The Blessed Virgin washed and dried some things here. After having rested and refreshed themselves, they proceeded on their way by the common high road.

I had many visions of their journey, which was made without any special danger to them. Mary was often very much distressed, because walking through the hot sand was so painful for the Boy Jesus. Joseph had made for Him, out of bark, shoes that reached above the ankle where they were firmly fastened; still I saw the holy travellers frequently pausing while Mary shook the sand out of the Child's shoes. She herself wore only sandals. Jesus was dressed in His little brown robe, and they often had to seat Him on the ass. For protection against the scorching rays of the sun, all three wore very broad hats made of bark and fastened under the chin with a string.

I saw them passing by many cities, but I now recall only the name Rameses. At last, I saw them in Gaza, where they stopped for three months. There were many pagans in that city. Joseph did not want to return to Nazareth, but to go to Bethlehem; still he was undecided, because he heard that Archelaus was now reigning over Judea, and he, too, was very cruel. But an angel appeared and put an end to his doubts by telling him that he should return to Nazareth. Anne was still living. She and some of her relatives were the only ones that knew where the Holy Family were during all those years.

I had a glimpse of the Boy Jesus, now seven years old, as He walked between Mary and Joseph on their journey back to Judea from Egypt. I did not see the ass with them then, and they were carrying their bundles themselves. Joseph was about thirty years older than Mary. I saw them on a road in the desert, about two hours' distance from John's cave. The Boy Jesus, as He walked, gazed in that direction, and I saw that His soul was turning to John. At the same time, I saw John at prayer in his cave. An angel in the form of a boy appeared to him, telling him that the Saviour was passing by. John ran out of the cave and, with outstretched arms, flew toward the point that his Saviour was passing. He hopped about and danced with joy. This vision was most touching. John's cave lay deeply buried in a hill. It was not much wider than his own little bed, though it extended some distance in length. The entrance was only a little opening, through which he used to swing himself out. In the top was an oblique aperture that admitted light. I saw in it a reed stand, upon which lay some honeycomb and dried locusts. The latter were yellow and speckled, as large, perhaps, as crabs. The desert in which Jesus fasted is four hours' distance from here. John was clothed in his camel's skin. The angel that appeared to him was like a boy of his own age. I saw him at different periods, small at first and then larger, just as if he were growing up with John. He was not always with him; he used to appear and disappear.

28. John as a Child Growing Up In the Desert

John had already been long in the desert before the Holy Family's return from Egypt. That he had retired there at so young an age was due principally to divine inspiration and partly to his own inclinations, for he was of a meditative nature and loved solitude. He was never in a school; the Holy Ghost Himself taught him in the desert. He was much talked of even from his childhood, for the wonders attendant on his birth were known and a light was often seen around the child. Herod soon laid snares for him, and even before the children's massacre, Elizabeth was obliged to flee with him into the desert. He could walk and help himself at the time. He took refuge not far from the first cave of Magdalen, and Elizabeth visited him sometimes.

When in his sixth or seventh year, I saw him again led into the desert by his mother. When Elizabeth left the house with the boy, Zachary was not home. He loved John so much and his grief at losing him was so great that he was obliged to absent himself in order not to witness his departure. He had, however, given him his blessing; for he was in the habit of blessing both mother and child whenever he left home. John wore a garment of skin. It passed from left to right over the shoulder and breast, was fastened under the right arm, and hung down behind. This was his only garment. His hair was brownish and darker than that of Jesus. He bore in his hand a white staff which he had brought with him from home, and which he always kept in the desert.

I saw him as just described hastening across the country by the hand of his mother. Elizabeth was a tall, active, old woman with a small, delicate face, and she was completely enveloped in a large mantle. John often ran on before her, hopping and jumping, perfectly unrestrained and childlike in action, though not distracted in soul. I saw them crossing a river. There was no bridge at that point, and so they crossed on a raft that was floating on the water. Elizabeth was a very resolute person, no difficulty daunted her; she herself rowed the raft across, using for that purpose the branch of a tree. They now turned eastward and entered a ravine, rocky and desolate above, but lower down covered with bushes and overgrown with strawberries. John now and then ate one. After going some distance into the ravine, Elizabeth took leave of John. She blessed him, pressed him to her heart, kissed him on the cheeks and forehead, and turned away, looking back at him as she retraced her steps, weeping. But the boy appeared wholly unconcerned, and quietly walked on deeper into the ravine. I followed the child with a feeling of uneasiness at his going so far from his mother, and fearing that he would not be able to find his way home again. But just then, a voice said to me, "Be not uneasy. The child knows well what he is about." I went with him and, in several visions, saw his whole after life in the desert. He often told me himself how he denied himself in every way and mortified his senses, his understanding becoming clearer and clearer, learning in an unexplainable way something from everything around him. I saw him when a child playing with flowers and animals. The birds were particularly familiar with him. They lighted upon his head when he was walking or praying, and perched upon his staff when he laid it across the branches. There they sat in numbers, while he watched them and played with them. I saw him also going after other animals, following them into their dens, feeding them, playing with them, or earnestly watching them.

At the opposite extremity of this rocky ravine, the country was somewhat more open, and John pressed on until he reached a little lake with a low shore covered with white sand. I saw him there wading far out into the water. The fish swam up and gathered around him; he seemed quite at home with them. He lived in this region a long time, and I saw that he wove for himself out of branches a sleeping hut among the bushes. It was very low and only large enough to allow him to lie in it. Both here and afterward in other places, I often saw by him radiant figures, angels, with whom he treated fearlessly and confidently, though most reverently. They appeared to be teaching him, directing his attention to different things. He had fastened a piece of wood to his staff, thus giving it the form of a cross, also a strip of broad grass, or bark, or leaves like a little flag. He often played with it, waving it here and there. While he lived in this part of the desert, I saw his mother visiting him twice, but they did not meet at this spot. He must have known when she was coming, for he always went some distance to meet her. Elizabeth brought him a tablet with a slender reed for writing.

After his father's death, John went secretly to Juttah, to console Elizabeth. He remained concealed with her for some time. She told him many things of Jesus and the Holy Family, some of which he noted down with strokes on his tablet. Elizabeth wanted him to go with her to Nazareth, but he would not. He returned again to the desert.

Once when Zachary had gone with a herd to the Temple, he was set upon by Herod's soldiers and rudely maltreated in a narrow pass on the side of Jerusalem nearest to Bethlehem, at a spot whence the city could not be seen. The soldiers dragged him into a prison on that side of Mount Zion by which, at a later period, the disciples used to ascend. Zachary was frightfully maltreated, tortured, and at last pierced with a sword, because he would not disclose John's retreat. Elizabeth was at the time in the desert with John. When she returned to Juttah, he accompanied her part of the way, and then went back to the desert. On reaching Juttah, Elizabeth learned of the murder of her husband and great were her lamentations.

Zachary was buried by his friends in the vicinity of the Temple. He is not that Zachary who was slain between the altar and the Temple and whom I saw at the time of the Crucifixion with the other risen dead. He issued from that part of the wall in which the aged Simeon once had his cell for prayer, and walked about the Temple. The last Zachary was murdered in a struggle that had taken place among many at the Temple, concerning the genealogy of the Messiah and certain privileges and places of individual families.

Elizabeth's sorrow was so great that she could no longer bear to remain in Juttah, without John; consequently, she returned to him in the desert. She soon after died there and was buried by an Essenian, a relative of Anna the Prophetess. The house in Juttah, a very handsomely ordered one, was occupied by her sister's daughter. John secretly returned to it once after his mother's death, after which he buried himself still deeper in the desert and thenceforth was altogether alone. I saw him journeying to the south around the Dead Sea, then up the eastern side of the Jordan, from wilderness to wilderness toward Kedar and even toward Gessur. When he passed from one wilderness to another, I saw him running through broad fields by night. He went to that region where long after I saw John the Evangelist sitting and writing under the high trees. Under those trees grew bushes with berries, of which he sometimes ate. I saw him also eating a certain herb that bears a white flower and has five round leaves like clover. We have at home herbs like them, only smaller. They grow under the hedges, and the leaves have a sourish taste. When I was a child I used to love to chew them while minding the cattle off in the solitary fields, because I had seen John eating them. I also saw him drawing forth from holes in the trees and picking out of moss on the ground lumps of some brownish-looking stuff, which he ate. I think it was wild honey, for it was very plentiful there. The skin that he had brought with him from home, he now wore around his loins, and over his shoulders hung a brown, shaggy cover which he had woven himself. There were in the desert wool-bearing animals which ran tamely around John, and camels with long hair on their neck. They stood most patiently and allowed him to pull it out. I saw him twisting the hair into cords and weaving from them that covering which he wore hanging around him when he appeared among men and baptized.

I saw him in continual and familiar communication with angels, by whom he was instructed. He slept upon the hard rock and under the open sky, ran over rough stones through thorns and briers, disciplined himself with thistles, wore himself out working on trees and stones, and lay prostrate in prayer and contemplation. He levelled roads, made little bridges, and changed the course of well springs. I often saw him writing in the sand with a reed, kneeling and standing motionless in ecstasy, or praying with outstretched arms. His penance and mortification became more and more severe, his prayer longer and more fervent. He saw the Saviour only three times face to face with his bodily eyes. But Jesus was with him in spirit; and John, who was constantly in the prophetic state, saw in spirit the actions of Jesus.

I saw John when full grown. He was a powerful, earnest man. He was standing by a dry well in the desert, and appeared to be in prayer. A light hovered over him like a cloud, and it seemed to me as if it came from on high, from the water above the earth. Then a light, shining stream fell over him into the basin below. While gazing on this torrent,

I saw John no longer at the edge of the basin; he was in it, the shining water flowing over him, and the basin filled by the sparkling stream. Then again, I saw him, as at first, standing on the basin's edge; but I did not see him out of it, nor coming out. I think that the whole was perhaps a vision which John himself had had, and by which he was instructed to begin to baptize; or it may have been a spiritual baptism bestowed upon him in vision.

29. Feast Picture of John the Baptist

I saw in the desert in which John dwelt a spiritual church rising up out of the waters that flowed in streams from on high, from Paradise, that floated in clouds, and welled up in fountains. The church was immeasurably vast; it seemed to be symbolical of Baptism, and it grew with the baptized. It was perfectly transparent like crystal. An octagonal tower arose from the interior and reached up far out of sight. Under it was a great fountain like the baptism fountain of John which he had formed in the desert after a model shown him in vision. In the tower grew a genealogical tree upon which appeared John and his ancestors. There was also an altar, and a wonderful representation of John's conception, birth, circumcision, and life in the desert, of the baptism of Jesus and John's beheading. Far up in the tower, as if on a ladder reaching to Heaven, were seen in admirable order the whole host of Saints, the entire history of the Promise and the Redemption, and the abodes of the Blessed, endless in number. High above all the rest hovered the Blessed Virgin in a mantle so wide as to cover all. All these representations were white and transparent. And now came immense crowds from all sides, kings and peoples in all kinds of costumes; they looked like nations that were migrating. Many passed by the baptism church and went into the desert, where there is no water of life. Many others entered the church and knelt down by the baptism fountain, by the side of which stood John under the appearance that he presented as a child in the desert. He struck the water with his little staff and sprinkled it over them. And, no matter how tall they were on entering the church, all that were thus sprinkled became small. But many only passed in and out of the church. They who had become little ones, like unto those that enter the Heavenly Kingdom, ascended the high, wonderful tower on the ladder that reached to Heaven. There were at the baptism holy godparents. The whole church, which appeared to be a building and still was formed of water, floated on high as if supported by a cord let down from Heaven.

30. The Holy Family at Nazareth.
Jesus at the Age of Twelve in The Temple of Jerusalem

There were three separate rooms in the house at Nazareth, that of the Mother of God being the largest and most pleasant; in it Jesus, Mary, and Joseph met to pray. I very seldom saw them together at other times. They stood at prayer, their hands crossed upon their breast, and they appeared to speak aloud. I often saw them praying by a light. They stood under a lamp that had several wicks, or near a kind of branched candlestick fastened to the wall, and upon which the flame burned. They were most of the time alone in their respective rooms, Joseph working in his. I saw him cutting sticks and laths, planing wood, and carrying up a beam, Jesus helping him. Mary was generally engaged sewing or knitting with little needles, at which she sat on the ground, her feet crossed under her, and a little basket at her side. They slept alone, each in a separate room. The bed consisted of a cover which in the morning was rolled up.

I saw Jesus assisting His parents in every possible way, and also on the street and wherever opportunity offered, cheerfully, eagerly, and obligingly helping everyone. He assisted His foster-father in his trade, or devoted Himself to prayer and contemplation. He was a model for all the children of Nazareth; they loved Him and feared to displease Him. When they were naughty and committed faults, their parents used to say to them: "What will Joseph's Son say when I tell Him this? How sorry He will be!" Sometimes they gently complained to Him before the little ones, saying, "Tell them not to do such or such a thing anymore." And Jesus took it playfully and like a little child. He would beg the children affectionately to do so and so, would pray with them to His Heavenly Father for strength to become better, and would persuade them to acknowledge their faults and ask pardon on the spot.

About an hour's journey from Nazareth toward Sephoris, is a little place called Ophna. There, during the boyhood of Jesus, dwelt the parents of James the Greater and of John. In those early years, they associated with Jesus, until their parents removed to Bethsaida and they themselves went to the fishery.

There lived in Nazareth an Essenian family related to Joachim. They had four sons, a few years older or younger than Jesus, named respectively, Cleophas, James, Judas, and Japhet. They, too, were playmates of Jesus, and with their parents were in the habit of making the journey to the Temple along with the Holy Family. These four brothers became, at the time of Jesus' baptism, disciples of John, and after his murder, disciples of Jesus. When Andrew and Saturnin crossed the Jordan to Jesus, they followed them and spent the whole day with Him. They were among those disciples of John whom Jesus took with Him to the marriage feast at Cana. Cleophas is the same to whom, in company with Luke, Jesus appeared at Emmaus. He was married and dwelt at Emmaus. His wife afterward joined the women of the Community.

Jesus was tall and slender with a delicate face and a beaming countenance and though pale, He was healthy-looking. His perfectly straight, golden hair was parted over His high, open forehead and fell upon His shoulders. He wore a long, light-brownish gray tunic, which reached to His feet, the sleeves rather wide around the hand.

At the age of eight years, Jesus went for the first time with His parents to Jerusalem for the Pasch, and every succeeding year He did the same.

In those first visits, Jesus had already excited attention in Jerusalem among the friends with whom He and His parents stayed, also among the priests and doctors. They spoke of the pious, intelligent Child, of Joseph's extraordinary Son, just as amongst us one might, at the annual pilgrimages, notice in particular this or that modest, holy-looking person, this or that clever peasant child, and recognize him again the next year. So Jesus had already some acquaintances in the city when, in His twelfth year, with their friends and their sons, He accompanied His parents to Jerusalem. His parents were accustomed to walk with the people from their own part of the country, and they knew that Jesus, who now made the journey for the fifth time, always went with the other youths from Nazareth.

But this time Jesus had, on the return journey not far from the Mount of Olives, separated from His companions, who all thought that He had joined His parents who were following. Jesus had, however, gone to that side of Jerusalem nearest to Bethlehem, to the inn at which the Holy Family before Mary's Purification had put up. Mary and Joseph thought Him on ahead with the other Nazarenes, while these latter thought that He was following with His parents.

When at last they all met at Gophna, the anxiety of
Mary and Joseph at His absence was very great.
They returned at once to Jerusalem, making inquiries
after Him on the way and everywhere in the city
itself. But they could not find Him, since He had not
been where they usually stayed. Jesus had slept at
the inn before the Bethlehem gate, where the people knew Him and His parents.

There He had joined several youths and gone with
them to two schools of the city, the first day to one,
the second to another. On the morning of the third
day, He had gone to a third school at the Temple,
and in the afternoon into the Temple itself where
His parents found Him. These schools were all different, and not all exactly schools of the Law. Other
branches were taught in them. The last mentioned
was in the neighborhood of the Temple and from it
the Levites and priests were chosen.

Jesus by His questions and answers so astonished
and embarrassed the doctors and rabbis of all these
schools that they resolved, on the afternoon of the
third day, in the public lecture hall of the Temple
and in presence of the rabbis most deeply versed in
the various sciences "to humble the Boy Jesus." The
scribes and doctors had concerted the plan together;
for, although pleased at first, they had in the end
become vexed at Him. They met in the public lecture hall in the middle of the Temple porch in front
of the Sanctuary, in the round place where later
Jesus also taught. There I saw Jesus sitting in a
large chair which He did not, by a great deal, fill.
Around Him was a crowd of aged Jews in priestly
robes. They were listening attentively, and appeared
to be perfectly furious. I feared they would lay hands
upon Him. On the top of the chair in which Jesus
was sitting, were brown heads like those of dogs.
They were greenish brown, the upper parts glisten-
ing and sparkling with a yellow light. There were
similar heads and figures upon several long tables,

or benches, that stood in the Temple sideways from this place, covered with offerings. The place was very large and so crowded that one could scarcely imagine himself in a church.

As Jesus had in the schools illustrated His answers and explanations by all kinds of examples from nature, art, and science, the scribes and doctors had diligently gathered together masters in all these branches. They now began, one by one, to dispute with Him. He remarked that although, properly speaking, such subjects did not appear appropriate to the Temple, yet He would discuss them since such was His Father's will. But they understood not that He referred to His Heavenly Father; they imagined that Joseph had commanded Him to show off His learning.

Jesus now answered and taught upon medicine. He described the whole human body in a way far beyond the reach of even the most learned. He discoursed with the same facility upon astronomy, architecture, agriculture, geometry, arithmetic, jurisprudence and, in fine, upon every subject proposed to Him. He applied all so skillfully to the Law and the Promise, to the Prophecies, to the Temple, to the mysteries of worship and sacrifice that His hearers, surprised and confounded, passed successively from astonishment and admiration to fury and shame. They were enraged at hearing some things that they never before knew, and at hearing others that they had never before understood.

Jesus had been teaching two hours, when Joseph and Mary entered the Temple. They inquired after their Child of the Levites whom they knew, and received for answer that He was with the doctors in the lecture hall. But as they were not at liberty to enter that hall, they sent one of the Levites in to call Jesus. Jesus sent them word that He must first finish what He was then about. Mary was very much troubled at His not obeying at once, for this was the

first time He had given His parents to understand
that He had other commands than theirs to fulfill.
He continued to teach for another hour, and then He
left the hall and joined His parents in the porch of
Israel, the women's porch, leaving His hearers confounded, confused, and enraged. Joseph was quite
awed and astonished, but he kept a humble silence.
Mary, however, drawing near to Jesus, said, "Child,
why hast Thou done this to us? Behold, Thy father
and I have sought Thee sorrowing!" But Jesus
answered gravely, "Why have you sought Me? Do you
not know that I must be about My Father's business?" But they did not understand. They at once
began with Him their journey home. The bystanders
gazed at them in astonishment, and I was in dread
lest they should lay hands upon the Boy, for I saw
that some of them were full of rage. I wondered at
their allowing the Holy Family to depart so peaceably. Although the crowd was dense, yet a wide path
was made to permit the Holy Family to pass. I saw
all the details and heard almost the whole of Jesus'
teaching, but I cannot remember all. It made a great
impression upon the scribes. Some recorded the affair
as a notable event, while here and there it was whispered around, giving rise to all kinds of remarks and
false reports. But the true statement, the scribes
kept to themselves. They spoke of Jesus as of a very
forward boy, possessed indeed of fine talents, but
said those talents required to be cultivated.

I saw the Holy Family again leaving the city, outside of which they joined a party of about three men,
two women, and some children. I did not know them,
but they appeared to be from Nazareth. They went
together to different places around Jerusalem, also
to Mount Olivet. They wandered around the beautiful pleasure grounds there found, occasionally standing to pray, their hands crossed on their breast. I
saw them also going over a bridge that spanned a
brook. This walking around and praying of the lit-

tle party reminded me forcibly of a pilgrimage. When Jesus had returned to Nazareth, I saw a feast in Anne's house, at which were gathered all the youths and maidens among their friends and relatives. I know not whether it was a feast of rejoicing at Jesus' having been found, a feast solemnized upon the return from the Paschal journey, or a feast customary upon the completion of a son's twelfth year. Whatever it may have been, Jesus appeared to be the object of it.

Beautiful bowers were erected over the table, from which hung garlands of vine leaves and ears of corn. The children were served with grapes and little rolls. There were present at this feast thirty-three boys, all future disciples of Jesus, and I received an instruction upon the years of Jesus' life. During the whole feast, Jesus instructed the other boys, and explained to them a very wonderful parable which, however, was only imperfectly understood. It was of a marriage feast at which water could be turned into wine and the lukewarm guests into zealous friends; and again, of a marriage feast where the wine could be changed into Blood and the bread into Flesh, which Blood and Flesh would abide with the guests until the end of the world as strength and consolation, as a living bond of union. He said also to one of the youths, a relative of His own named Nathanael: "I shall be present at thy marriage."

From His twelfth year, Jesus was always like a teacher among His companions. He often sat among them instructing them or walked about the country with them.

31. Death of St. Joseph.
Jesus and Mary in Capharnaum

As the time drew near for Jesus to begin His mission of teaching, I saw Him ever more solitary and meditative; and toward the same time, the thirtieth year of Jesus, Joseph began to decline. I saw Jesus and Mary often with him. Mary sometimes sat on the ground by his couch, or upon a low, round three-legged stool, which served also for a table. I seldom saw them eating; but when they did, or brought some refreshment to Joseph's bedside, it consisted of three, white, rather long, four-cornered pieces, about two fingers in breadth, that lay side by side on a little plate, and I saw also some little fruits in a dish. They gave him something to drink out of a mug.

When Joseph was dying, Mary sat at the head of his bed, holding him in her arms. Jesus stood just below her near Joseph's breast. The whole room was brilliant with light and full of angels. After his death, his hands were crossed on his breast, he was wrapped from head to foot in a white winding sheet, laid in a narrow casket, and placed in a very beautiful tomb, the gift of a good man. Only a few men followed the coffin with Jesus and Mary; but I saw it accompanied by angels and environed with light. Joseph's remains were afterward removed by the Christians to Bethlehem, and interred. I think I can still see him lying there incorrupt.

Joseph had of necessity to die before the Lord, for he could not have endured His Crucifixion; he was too gentle, too loving. He had already suffered much from the persecution Jesus had had to support from the malice of the Jews from His twentieth to His thirtieth year; for they could not bear the sight of Him. Their jealousy often made them exclaim that the carpenter's Son thought He knew everything better than others, that He was frequently at variance with the teachings of the Pharisees, and that He always had around Him a crowd of young followers. Mary never ceased to suffer from these persecutions. Such pains always seem to me sharper than those of martyrdom. Unspeakable was the love with which Jesus in His youth bore the jealous persecution of the Jews.

After Joseph's death, Jesus and Mary removed to a little village of only a few houses between Capharnaum and Bethsaida. A man named Levi, who was very much attached to the Holy Family, had given Jesus a house there in which to dwell. It stood alone surrounded by a ditch of standing water. A couple of Levi's people also were in the house in the capacity of servants, and Levi himself supplied all necessaries from Capharnaum. It was to this little place that Peter's father retired when he gave over to him the fishery at Bethsaida.

Jesus had already many followers among the young people of Nazareth, but they were not faithful to Him. He walked with them in the country around the lake and went up to Jerusalem with them for the feasts. The Lazarus family in Bethania were already acquainted with the Holy Family. The Pharisees of Nazareth were against Jesus; they called Him a vagrant. Levi gave Him that house that He might, without fear of disturbance, live in it and gather His followers around Him.

There was on the lake around Capharnaum, a region of extraordinarily fertile and charming valleys. There were several harvests during the year, and uncommonly beautiful leaves, blossoms, and fruits—all at the same time. Many distinguished Jews had gardens and castles there, Herod among the number. The Jews of Jesus' time were no longer like their fathers; through commerce and their intercourse with heathens, they had become very corrupt. One never saw the women in public nor at work in the fields, excepting the very poorest gleaning some ears of corn. They were to be seen only on pilgrimages to

Jerusalem and other holy places. Husbandry and all kinds of traffic were carried on mostly through slaves. I have seen all the cities of Galilee. Where now scarcely three villages are in existence, there were then almost a hundred and an innumerable crowd of people.

Mary Cleophas, who with her third husband, the father of Simeon of Jerusalem, dwelt in Anne's house near Nazareth, afterward removed with her boy Simeon to Mary's in Nazareth. The rest of her family and her servants remained at Anne's.

When Jesus, a short time after, went from Capharnaum by way of Nazareth to the region of Hebron, He was accompanied by Mary as far as Nazareth, where she awaited His return. She was always so solicitous about Him. There came also to comfort the Holy Family on the death of St. Joseph and to see Jesus again, Joses Barsabas, the son of Mary Cleophas by her second marriage with Sabas, and the three sons of her first marriage with Alpheus: Simon, James the Less, and Thaddeus, all three of whom already carried on business away from home. They had had no close communication with Jesus since His childhood. They knew in general of Simeon's and Anne's prophecies on the occasion of His Presentation in the Temple, but they attached no importance to them. They preferred to follow John the Baptist, who soon after passed through these parts.

JESUS BEGINS HIS
PUBLIC TEACHING

1. Jesus on His Way to Hebron

Jesus went through Nazareth in going from Capharnaum to Hebron, passing through the indescribably beautiful country of Genesareth and by the hotbaths of Emmaus. These baths were on the declivity of a mountain, about an hour's distance further on from Magdalum in the direction of Tiberias. The meadows were covered with very high, thick grass, and on the declivity stood the houses and tents between rows of fig trees, date palms, and orange trees. The road was crowded, for a kind of national feast was going on. Men and women in separate groups were playing for wagers, the prize consisting of fruit. There Jesus saw Nathanael, called also Chased, standing among the men under a fig tree. Just at the moment when Nathanael was struggling aganst a sensual temptation that had seized him and was glancing over at the women's game, Jesus passed and cast upon him a warning look. Without knowing Jesus, Nathanael was deeply moved by His glance, and thought: "That man has a sharp eye." He felt that Jesus was more than an ordinary man. He became conscious of his guilt, entered into himself, overcame the temptation, and from that time kept a stricter guard over his senses. I think I saw there, also, Nephtali, known as Bartholomew, and that a glance from Jesus touched him also.

Jesus journeyed with two of His young friends to Hebron in Judea. They did not remain faithful to Him. They separated from Him, but after His Resurrection, converted by His apparition on Mount Thebez in Galilee, they once again joined His followers. In Bethania Jesus visited Lazarus, who looked much older than Jesus; he appeared to me to be fully eight years his senior. Lazarus had large possessions, landed property, gardens, and many servants. Martha had her own house, and another sister named Mary, who lived entirely alone, had also her separate dwelling. Magdalen lived in her castle at Magdalum. Lazarus was already long acquainted with the Holy Family. He had at an early period aided Joseph and Mary with large alms and, from first to last, did much for the Community. The purse that Judas carried and all the early expenses, he supplied out of his own wealth.

From Bethania Jesus went to the Temple in Jerusalem.

2. The Family of Lazarus

The father of Lazarus was named Zarah, or Zerah, and was of very noble Egyptian descent. He had dwelt in Syria, on the confines of Arabia, where he held a position under the Syrian king; but for services rendered in war, he received from the Roman emperor property near Jerusalem and in Galilee. He was like a prince, and was very rich. He had acquired still greater wealth by his wife Jezabel, a Jewess of the sect of the Pharisees. He became a Jew, and was pious and strict according to the Pharisaical laws. He owned part of the city on Mount Zion, on the side upon which the brook near the height on which the Temple stands, flows through the ravine. But the greater part of this property, he had bequeathed to the Temple, retaining, however, in his family some ancient privilege on its account. This property was on the road by which the Apostles went up to the Cenacle, but the Cenacle itself formed no longer a part of it. Zarah's castle in Bethania was very large. It had numerous gardens, terraces, and fountains, and was surrounded by double ditches. The prophecies of Anna and Simeon were known to the family of Zarah, who were waiting for the Messiah. Even in Jesus' youth, they were acquainted with the Holy Family, just as pious, noble people are wont to be with their humble, devout neighbors.

The parents of Lazarus had in all fifteen children, of whom six died young. Of the nine that survived, only four were living at the time of Christ's teaching. These four were: Lazarus; Martha, about two years younger; Mary, looked upon as a simpleton, two years younger than Martha; and Mary Magdalen, five years younger than the simpleton. The simpleton is not named in Scripture, not reckoned among the Lazarus family; but she is known to God. She was always put aside in her family, and lived altogether unknown.

Magdalen, the youngest child, was very beautiful and, even in her early years, tall and well-developed like a girl of more advanced age. She was full of frivolity and seductive art. Her parents died when she was only seven years old. She had no great love for them even from her earliest age, on account of their severe fasts. Even as a child, she was vain beyond expression, given to petty thefts, proud, self-willed, and a lover of pleasure. She was never faithful, but clung to whatever flattered her the most. She was, therefore, extravagant in her pity when her sensitive compassion was aroused, and kind and condescending to all that appealed to her senses by some external show. Her mother had had some share in Magdalen's faulty education, and that sympathetic softness the child had inherited from her.

Magdalen was spoiled by her mother and her nurse. They showed her off everywhere, caused her cleverness and pretty little ways to be admired, and sat much with her dressed up at the window. That window-sitting was the chief cause of her ruin. I saw her at the window and on the terraces of the house upon a magnificent seat of carpets and cushions, where she could be seen in all her splendor from the street. She used to steal sweetmeats, and take them to other children in the garden of the castle. Even in her ninth year she was engaged in love affairs.

With her developing talents and beauty, increased also the talk and admiration they excited. She had crowds of companions. She was taught, and she wrote love verses on little rolls of parchment. I saw her while so engaged counting on her fingers. She sent these verses around, and exchanged them with her lovers. Her fame spread on all sides, and she was exceedingly admired.

But I never saw that she either really loved or was loved. It was all, on her part at least, vanity, frivolity, self-adoration, and confidence in her own beauty. I saw her a scandal to her brother and sisters whom she despised and of whom she was ashamed on account of their simple life.

When the patrimony was divided, the castle of Magdalum fell by lot to Magdalen. It was a very beautiful building. Magdalen had often gone there with her family when she was a very young child, and she had always entertained a special preference for it. She was only about eleven years old when, with a large household of servants, men and maids, she retired thither and set up a splendid establishment for herself.

Magdalum was a fortified place, consisting of several castles, public buildings, and large squares of groves and gardens. It was eight hours east of Nazareth, about three from Capharnaum, one and a half from Bethsaida toward the south, and about a mile from the Lake of Genesareth. It was built on a slope of the mountain and extended down into the valley which stretches off toward the lake and around its shores. One of those castles belonged to Herod. He possessed a still larger one in the fertile region of Genesareth. Some of his soldiers were stationed in Magdalum, and they contributed their share to the general demoralization. The officers were on intimate terms with Magdalen. There were, besides the troops, about two hundred people in Magdalum, chiefly officials, master builders, and servants. There was no synagogue in the place; the people went to the one at Bethsaida.

The castle of Magdalum was the highest and most magnificent of all; from its roof one could see across the Sea of Galilee to the opposite shore. Five roads led to Magdalum, and on every one at one half-hour's distance from the well-fortified place, stood a tower built over an arch. It was like a watchtower whence could be seen far into the distance. These towers had no connection with one another; they rose out of a country covered with gardens, fields, and meadows. Magdalen had men servants and maids, fields and herds, but a very disorderly household; all went to rack and ruin.

Through the wild ravine at the head of which Magdalum lay far up on the height, flowed a little stream to the lake. Around its banks was a quantity of game, for from the three deserts contiguous to the valley the wild beasts came down to drink. Herod used to hunt here. He had also near his castle in the country of Genesareth a park filled with game.

The country of Genesareth began between Tiberias and Tarichea, about four hours' distance from Capharnaum; it extended from the sea three hours inland and to the south around Tarichea to the mouth of the Jordan. The rising valley with the baths near Bethulia, artificially formed from a brook nearby, lay contiguous to this region, and was watered by streams flowing to the sea. This brook formed in its course several artificial lakes and waterfalls in different parts of the beautiful district which consisted entirely of gardens, villas, castles, parks, walks, orchards, and vineyards. The whole year round found it teeming with blossoms and fruits. The rich ones of the land, and especially of Jerusalem, had here their villas and gardens. Every portion was under cultivation, or laid off in pleasure grounds, groves, and verdant labyrinths, and adorned with walks winding around pyramidal hillocks. There were no large villages in this part of the country. The permanent residents were mostly gardeners and custodians of the property, also shepherds whose herds consisted of fine sheep and goats. There were besides all kinds of rare animals and birds under their care. No street ran through Magdalum, but two roads from the sea and from the Jordan met here.

3. Jesus in Hebron, Dothain, and Nazareth

When Jesus arrived at Hebron, He left there His companions, saying that He was desirous of visiting a friend. Zachary and Elizabeth were no more. Jesus then went to the wilderness which lay to the south of Hebron, between it and the Dead Sea, whither Elizabeth had taken the boy John. To reach it, one had to climb a mountain covered with white pebbles, and then cross a lovely valley of palm trees. I saw Jesus entering the wilderness, and going into the cave to which John was first taken by Elizabeth. Then He crossed a little brook over which John also had passed. I saw Him alone and in prayer, as if preparing for His teaching mission. When He left the desert, He went again to Hebron. I saw Him as He journeyed lending a helping hand everywhere along the road. At the Dead Sea, He helped some people who were on a kind of raft formed of beams and covered by an awning. On it were men, cattle, and merchandise. Jesus called to them and shoved a plank out to them from the shore. He helped them to land, and stood by while they repaired their raft. They were at a loss as to who He was; for though there was nothing remarkable in His dress, yet His charming graciousness and dignity of bearing greatly impressed them. At first they thought it must be John the Baptist, who had already made his appearance at the Jordan; but they soon discovered their mistake, for John's complexion was brown, much darker than that of Jesus, and his whole appearance rough. Jesus celebrated the Sabbath in Hebron, and there dismissed His travelling companions. He visited the sick in their homes, consoling and assisting them in every way. He raised them in His arms, carried them, and made their beds; but I did not see Him curing anyone. To all He appeared to be a benevolent, a wonderful person. He visited the possessed and they grew calm in His presence, though as yet He drove no devil out. Wherever He went, He rendered aid when aid was needed. He raised the fallen, He refreshed the thirsty, He guided the traveller, over bridge and brook—and all looked in astonishment upon the kind-hearted wayfarer. From Hebron He went to the spot where the Jordan flows into the Dead Sea. Here He crossed the river in a boat, and journeyed along its eastern bank to Galilee. I saw Him travelling on between Pella and the country of Gergesa, making short journeys and helping all in need. He went to all the sick, even to the lepers, consoling them, raising them in His arms, making their beds, exhorting them to prayer, and pointing out, to the admiration of all, what treatment was necessary, what remedies to use in the different cases. At one place, some people knew of the prophecies of Simeon and Anna and they questioned Him as to whether He was the one to whom they referred. It was a common thing for people to follow Him from one place to another out of the love He inspired. The possessed were calm when near Him.

He went also to the rapid little stream that flows into the Jordan below the Sea of Galilee (the Hieromax), not far from that steep mountain from which He subsequently cast the swine into the sea. Near the river stood a row of little mud huts like shepherds' huts, which were occupied by the men who were at that moment on the shore laboring at their barks. They could not succeed in their work. I saw Jesus go up to them, make some suggestions in a friendly way, drag a beam to the spot, and put His hand to the work. He pointed out various expedients and, as He worked, exhorted them to patience and charity.

After that I saw Jesus in Dothain, a scattered little place northeast of Sephoris, and in which there was a synagogue. The inhabitants were not bad, though very much neglected. Abraham had once owned fields there for his cattle intended for offerings. Joseph and his brethren used to guard their flocks in this same region, and it was here that the former was sold. Dothain, at the time of Our Lord, was but a sparsely settled place, but its soil was good and its meadows extended down to the Sea of Galilee. It contained a large building like a madhouse, in which many possessed lived. On Jesus' arrival, they became perfectly furious and dashed themselves almost to death. The keepers could not bind them. Jesus entered and spoke to them, and they became quite calm. He addressed to them a few more words, after which they quietly left the house and repaired to their several homes. The people were amazed at what they saw. They were unwilling for Jesus to depart, and one of them invited Him to a marriage feast. I saw all the wedding ceremonies as at Cana. Jesus was like an honored stranger at the feast. He spoke wisely and graciously, giving the bride and groom good advice. They afterward joined the disciples when Jesus appeared upon Thebez.

When Jesus returned to Nazareth, He went around among His parents' acquaintances, but He was everywhere coldly received. When He sought to enter the synagogue in order to teach, they turned Him away. Then He repaired to the public marketplace and spoke of the Messiah to the crowd, of whom some were Sadducees, others Pharisees. He told them that the Messiah would be different from what each one's ideas pictured. John the Baptist, He called "The voice in the wilderness." Two youths, clothed in long garments and wearing girdles like priests, had followed Jesus from the country of Hebron; but they went not always with Him. Jesus kept the Sabbath in Nazareth.

After that I saw Jesus and Mary, Mary Cleophas, the parents of Parmenas, in all about twenty persons, leave Nazareth and go to Capharnaum. They had with them asses laden with baggage. The house in Nazareth had been cleaned and adorned. It was so well arranged that, with its rich hangings, it reminded me of a church. It was left unoccupied. The third husband of Mary Cleophas and some of her sons still carried on business in Anne's abode, and they took care of that house of the Holy Family. Mary Cleophas with her youngest sons, Joses Barsabas and Simeon, dwelt at this time quite near to the small house not far from Capharnaum which Levi had fitted up for the Lord, and the parents of Parmenas lived at no great distance.

Jesus journeyed again from place to place, and appeared chiefly where John had been when he left the desert. He entered the synagogue and instructed, He consoled and relieved the sick. When He taught in the synagogue of a certain little town and spoke of John's baptism, of the coming of the Messiah, and of penance, the people murmured. They mocked Him, and I heard some of them say: "Three months ago, His father, the carpenter, was still alive. Then He worked with him. Now He has travelled a little and back He comes to impart to us His wisdom."

Jesus went also to Cana and taught. He had relatives there whom He visited. At this time He was not yet accompanied by any of His future disciples. It looked as if He were studying men, and building up upon the foundation that John had laid. Sometimes a good man accompanied Him from place to place.

Once I saw four men, among them some of His future disciples, on the high road between Samaria and Nazareth. They were in a shady place waiting for Jesus who, with one companion, was coming that way. When He arrived in sight, they set forward to meet Him. They told Him that they had been baptized by John, and that he had spoken of the near coming of the Messiah. They told Him also of John's severe language toward the soldiers, only a few of whom he had baptized. Among other things, he had said that it would be better to take the stones out of the Jordan and baptize them rather than such as they. I saw these disciples of John walking on with Jesus.

Jesus then went along the Sea of Galilee toward the north. He spoke very plainly of the Messiah. In many places, the possessed cried after Him. Out of one man He drove a devil, and He taught in the schools.

Six men who were coming from the baptism of John met Jesus. Among them were Levi, known later as Matthew, and two sons of the widowed relatives of Elizabeth. They all knew Jesus, some through relationship, others by hearsay; and they strongly suspected, though they had had no assurance of it, that He was the One of whom John had spoken. They spoke of John, of Lazarus and his sisters, especially of Magdalen. They supposed she had a devil, for she was already living apart from her family in the castle of Magdalum. These men accompanied Jesus, and were filled with astonishment at His discourse. The aspirants to baptism going from Galilee to John used to tell him all that they knew and heard of Jesus, while they that came from Ainon, where John baptized, used to tell Jesus all they knew of John.

Jesus went alone to the sea, passing through a

fence into an enclosed fishery where lay five ships. On the shore were several huts for the accommodation of the fishermen. Peter, the owner of this fishery, was in one of the huts with Andrew. John and James, with their father Zebedee and several others, were on the boats. In the middle one was Peter's father-in-law with his three sons. I once knew all their names, but now I have forgotten them. The father was surnamed Zelotes, because he had gained his point in a dispute with the Romans concerning the right of navigation on the lake. There were about thirty men on the boats.

Jesus went along the shore by the fenced-off way between the huts and the boats, speaking with Andrew and the others. I know not whether he spoke to Peter. They did not know Him as yet. He spoke of John and of the near coming of the Messiah. Andrew was already a baptized disciple of John. Jesus told them that He would come to them again.

4. Jesus Journeys Over Libanus To Sidon and Sarepta

Jesus turned off from the lake, and went further on toward Libanus. This He was led to do chiefly by the numerous reports current throughout the country and the great excitement to which they gave rise. Many looked upon John as the Messiah, but others spoke of another whom John's words seemed to designate.

The companions of Jesus on this journey numbered from six to twelve. Some turned off at different points on the road, while others joined Him. His instructions pleased them, and they began to think that He must be the One of whom John spoke. Jesus attached Himself particularly to none. He was properly speaking alone, but He was sowing and preparing. In all that He did I saw many relations to the actions of the Prophets and to their fulfillment, especially to those of Elias.

Jesus went with His companions over a spur of Libanus toward the great city Sidon lying along the sea. From the mountain height, the view was indescribably beautiful. The city was apparently quite close to the sea; but viewed from its own plane, one could see that it was fully forty-five minutes distant from the shore. It was a large, busy place. Gazing down upon it from on high, one might fancy that he was looking upon an innumerable fleet of ships; for from the numerous flat roofs arose a forest of high poles and flagstaffs, with long streamers of red and other colors, while white canvas was stretched from pole to pole, or floated in the breeze. These booths were swarming with people at their different avocations. Between the houses, I saw all kinds of shining vessels being prepared. The country around was dotted with exceedingly fertile spots, all teeming with fruit. In and around these gardens were numbers of immense trees, some surrounded by seats. Steps led up into others, so that quite a company could sit in their branches as in a summer house. The plain in which the city lay between the mountain and the sea was not very broad.

There were both Jews and pagans in the city. They carried on business with one another, and idolatry was general. The Lord on His way taught and preached in the shady places under the great trees, speaking of John, of his baptism, and of penance.

Jesus was well received in the city. He had been there once before. In the school He taught of the coming of the Messiah and of the downfall of idolatry. Queen Jezabel who so persecuted Elias was from this city.

Jesus left His companions in Sidon, and went to a little place more to the south and away from the sea. He wanted to be alone to pray. On one side it was entirely flanked by a wood. It had thick walls, and was surrounded by vineyards. It was Sarepta, the place in which Elias was fed by the widow. The

Jews, as also the pagans, had a superstition connected with that fact. They always allowed pious widows to live in the city walls. They thought by so doing they secured themselves from every danger, and could practice every species of vice in the city. Old men dwelt in the walls at the time of which I am now speaking.

Jesus lodged with an old man in the city wall, in the house once occupied by that widow who fed Elias. The old men who then dwelt in the walls were something like hermits. They lived there in accordance with an ancient custom honoring Elias, meditating and explaining the Prophecies, and chiefly engaged in prayer for the coming of the Messiah. Jesus taught them concerning the Messiah and the baptism of John. They were pious, but entertained many erroneous ideas, of which one was that the Messiah was to come in worldly splendor. Jesus often retired to the wood near Sarepta and there prayed alone. He taught in the synagogue, and occupied Himself also in instructing the children. In the villages around, in which there were numbers of heathens, He exhorted the people not to mix with them. There were some good people here, and some very bad ones. Jesus had no companions, excepting occasionally some resident of the place. I saw Him teaching men and women in the open air, often on hillocks and under trees.

The climate here is such that it always seems to me we are in May, because in Palestine the grain for the second harvest is as far advanced as it is with us in that month. They do not cut the grain so close to the ground as we do. They grasp the stalk below the ear, and cut it off about an ell long. They do not thrash it. They stand the little sheaves upright and pass over them a roller fastened between two oxen. The grain is much drier than ours, and falls out readily. They separate it in the open air, or in a kind of circular barn with a thatched roof, but open on all sides.

From Sarepta Jesus went to a place lying to the northeast, not far from the plain upon which Ezechiel, caught up in spirit, had the vision of the dry bones coming together. Sinews and flesh took possession of them, the winds passed over them, spirit and life entered into them. I was told that the coming together of the bones and their clothing with flesh were fulfilled by the teaching and baptism of John. But the spirit and life breathed into them was accomplished by Jesus through Redemption and by the descent of the Holy Ghost. Jesus consoled the people, who were very poor and oppressed, and explained to them the vision of Ezechiel.

When He left this place, He went northward to the country which John had first visited on leaving the desert. It was a little sheep rearing place. Noemi and her daughter Ruth dwelt there a long time. Noemi had so good a name among the people that she is still spoken of in those parts. Later she removed to Bethlehem. The Lord taught very zealously here. The time approached for Him to retrace His steps southward and thence to Samaria for His baptism. Jacob also owned fields up here. Through this place ran a little river, back of which far up in the desert lay John's spring. From this spring the road became very steep, reminding me of that which Adam and Eve took when driven from Paradise. It led down to the battlefield of Ezechiel. On Adam and Eve's route, the trees became smaller and smaller and quite misshapen until at last they reached a desolate region where grew some miserable bushes. Paradise was as high above the earth as is the sun. After the Fall it disappeared behind a mountain which seemed to rise before it.

The Saviour, on His return from the shepherds' country to Sarepta, followed the route trodden by the Prophet Elias when going from the brook Carith to Sarepta. Jesus taught here and there as He journeyed on, passing by Sidon. From Sarepta He was soon to go southward for His baptism. He kept the Sabbath in Sarepta.

After the Sabbath Jesus started for Nazareth, teaching at various points on the road. He was sometimes attended by companions, and sometimes alone. He went barefoot, putting His sandals on only when about to enter any town or village. He passed through the valleys toward Mount Carmel, and once He was near the road leading down into Egypt, but He turned off to the east.

The Mother of God, Mary Cleophas, the mother of Parmenas, and two other women, I saw going to Nazareth, while Seraphia (afterward *Veronica),* Johanna Chusa, and the son of Veronica, who later on joined the disciples, were on their way to the same place from Jerusalem. They were going to visit Mary, with whom they had become acquainted on their yearly journeys to the Holy City.

Mary and Joseph, as also other pious families, were in the habit of visiting through devotion three places during the year; viz., the Temple of Jerusalem, the pine tree near Bethlehem, and Mount Carmel. Anne's family and other pious people usually went to the last named place in May when returning from Jerusalem. There were on the mountain a well and a cave of Elias, the latter like a chapel. Devout Jews were constantly visiting these hallowed places. They came, not at fixed times; but whenever it best suited them, and prayed for the coming of the Messiah. Jewish hermits dwelt on the mountain, and later on Christian cenobites had there their cells.

In a little town on the west side of Mount Tabor, Jesus taught in the school, and spoke of John's baptism. There were five followers around Him, among them some future disciples. The Sanhedrin of Jerusalem dispatched couriers with letters to all the principal places of Palestine in which were Jewish schools and rabbis, telling them to be on their guard against a certain Man, of whom the Baptist said that He was the One that was to come and that He would soon present Himself for baptism. They should have an eye upon the Man and give information of His actions; for if He were indeed the Messiah, He needed not the baptism of John. The members of the Sanhedrin also were very much annoyed when they learned that Jesus was He who as a Boy had taught in the Temple. The couriers went likewise to a city on the road near Hebron, four hours from the sea, in that country wherein the spies of Aaron and Moses found the huge bunches of grapes. The city is called Gaza. There was a very long row of tents reaching from the city to the sea, and under them different kinds of woollen and silk stuffs exposed for sale.

Jesus with five followers taught, here and there, down to the country around Jacob's Well, where He celebrated the Sabbath. When He and His companions were returning to Nazareth, the Blessed Virgin went out to meet her Son. But when she saw that He was not alone, she paused at a distance and went back without saluting Him. I wondered at her self-denial. Jesus taught in the school at Nazareth, the holy women being present.

The next day, when Jesus taught in the synagogue before a large audience, the holy women were not present. He was attended by five disciples and about twenty of the young Nazarenes, companions of His boyhood. His hearers murmured at His teaching. They whispered among themselves that He would now, perhaps, take possession of the place of baptism that John had abandoned and there baptizing give Himself out for one like unto John. But, they continued, He was very different from John. John had dwelt in the desert preparing for his mission, but this Jesus they knew well, and they declared that they would not allow Him to deceive them.

5. Jesus in Bethsaida and Capharnaum

Jesus left Nazareth to go to Bethsaida where He aimed at rousing some of the people by His teaching. The Blessed Virgin and His followers remained behind. During His stay in Nazareth, Jesus had stopped with His friends in His Mother's house. But so much discontent and murmuring arose in the little town on His account that He resolved to go to Bethsaida for awhile, and return to Nazareth at some future time. He was accompanied by Amendor, the son of Veronica; a son of one of the three widowed relatives of Jesus, whose name sounds like Sirach; and one of Peter's relatives known later as one of the disciples.

At Bethsaida, Jesus taught very forcibly in the synagogue on the Sabbath. He told His hearers that they should now enter into themselves, repair to the baptism of John, and purify themselves by penance; otherwise a time would come when they would cry *woe! woe!* There were many people in the synagogue, but none of the future Apostles, excepting, I think, Philip. The others, belonging to Bethsaida and the country around, were celebrating the Sabbath elsewhere. They were in a house near the fishery in the neighborhood of Capharnaum. During this preaching of Jesus, I prayed that the people would go to the baptism of John and be truly converted. Thereupon I had a vision in which I saw that John was the *preparer,* who washed from the people their rawness, their coarseness. I saw him working so actively, so vigorously, preaching so vehemently that his camel skin slipped from shoulder to shoulder. This, I think, was merely symbolical, for at the same time I saw something like scales falling from some of the newly baptized, black vapors issuing from others, and light, shining clouds descending upon others.

In Capharnaum also Jesus taught in the school. Crowds came from all sides to hear Him, among them Peter, Andrew, and many others who had already been baptized by John.

When Jesus left Capharnaum, I saw Him teaching two hours distant from the city toward the south.

His hearers were numerous. He had with Him only the three disciples, for the future Apostles who had heard Him in Capharnaum had, without exchanging words with Him, gone again to the sea. Jesus spoke here also of John's baptism and the fulfilled Promise. He then went on toward the south, teaching here and there, down to Lower Galilee in the direction of Samaria, and kept the Sabbath in a school between Nazareth and Sephoris. The holy women from Nazareth were present, also Peter's wife and the wives of some others of the future Apostles.

The place consisted of only a few houses and a school. It was separated from Anne's former residence by a field. Of the future Apostles, Peter, Andrew, James the Less, and Philip, all disciples of John, came to hear Jesus. Philip belonged to Bethsaida; he was tolerably well educated, and was much engaged in writing. Jesus did not tarry long here. He took no meal, but only taught. The Apostles had, probably, celebrated the Sabbath in the neighborhood, for the Jews often visited other places on the Sabbath. Being informed of Jesus' presence, they had come to hear Him. He had not yet spoken to any of them in particular.

6. Jesus in Sephoris, Bethulia, Cedes, and Jezrael

From the last place, Jesus crossed a mountain with the three disciples and went to Sephoris, four hours' distance from Nazareth. He stopped at His great-aunt's. She was Anne's youngest sister Maraha, and the mother of a daughter and two sons. These sons were habited in long, white garments. They were named respectively Arastaria and Cocharia, and later on they joined the disciples.

The Blessed Virgin, Mary Cleophas, and other women had also come hither. The feet of Jesus were washed, and a repast prepared in His honor. He

passed the night in Maraha's house, which had been
the home of Anne's parents. Sephoris was a large
city, and in it were three different sects: the Pharisees, the Sadducees, and the Essenians, each with
its own school. This city often suffered severely from
war. At the present day, it is scarcely in existence.
Jesus stayed some days here, preaching and exhorting His hearers to go to the baptism of John. He
taught in two synagogues on the same day, in a large,
high one, and in a small one. The large one belonged
to the Pharisees. They listened indignantly to His
words, and murmured against Him. The women were
present at this instruction; but in the other synagogue, the small one that belonged to the Essenians,
there was no place for women. Jesus was kindly
received by the Essenians.

As Jesus was teaching in the school of the Sadducees, something very wonderful took place. There
were in Sephoris numbers of demoniacs, simpletons,
lunatics and possessed. They were instructed in a
school near the synagogue, which latter place they
were obliged to attend when prayer and teaching
were going on. They had a hall in the rear reserved
for themselves, and they were made to listen attentively. Custodians armed with whips stood among
them, each with few or more under his charge, according as they were more or less troublesome. Before
Jesus entered, I saw these poor creatures during the
teaching of the Sadducees distorting their countenance and falling into convulsions. Their keepers had
to bring them to order with the lash. When Jesus
made His appearance, they were at first quite still;
but after a little while one began and then another
to cry out: "That is Jesus of Nazareth, born in Bethlehem, and visited by Wise Men from the East. His
Mother is now with Maraha. He is preaching new
doctrine, which we must not tolerate." And so they
went on recounting aloud the whole life of Jesus and
all that had happened to Him up to the present time.

Now this one began, then that one took it up. The
lashes of the custodians availed naught, for soon all
began to cry out together and the confusion became
general. Then Jesus commanded them to be brought
to Him outside the synagogue, and He sent two disciples to collect all the other insane from the different quarters of the city and bring them also. Soon
there was a crowd, fully fifty such unfortunates
around Him, and multitudes of others, all eager to
see what would happen. The insane kept up their
cries. Then Jesus spoke, saying: "The spirit that
speaks through these, is from below. Let it again go
below!" And at the same instant, all became quiet.
They were cured, and I saw several fall to the ground.

And now a great tumult, excited by the cure, broke
out in the city, and Jesus and His followers were in
great danger. The excitement became so great that
Jesus escaped into a house and left the city that night.
The Blessed Virgin, the three disciples, with Cocharia
and Aristaria, the sons of Anne's sister, left the city
also. The Mother of Jesus was in great trouble and
anxiety, for this was the first time she had seen her
Son so violently persecuted. Jesus had appointed some
trees outside the city as a meeting place, and from
there all went on together to Bethulia.

The majority of those cured by Jesus in Sephoris,
went to John's baptism. Later on they were the principal ones of the city who followed Jesus.

Bethulia is that city at whose siege Judith slew
Holofernes. It was built on a mountain southeast of
Sephoris. The view from it extended far around into
the distance. Magdalen's castle in Magdalum was
not far off, and Magdalen herself was at this time
at the height of her glory. Bethulia, too, possessed a
castle and the place was rich in springs.

Jesus and His disciples entered an inn outside
Bethulia, and thither came Mary and the holy women
again to meet Him. I heard Mary talking to Him,
begging Him not to teach here again, for she was

afraid there might be another insurrection. But Jesus replied that He knew what He had to accomplish. Mary asked: "Shall we not now go to John's baptism?" To which Jesus answered gravely: "Why shall we now go to John's baptism? Have we need of it? I shall journey and reap still a while longer, and I shall say when it is time to go to the baptism." As afterward at Cana, Mary kept silence. I have seen that the holy women received baptism not till after Pentecost, and then in the Pool of Bethsaida. The holy women went on into the city. Jesus taught on the Sabbath in the synagogue, and many from the country around came to hear Him. Here in Bethulia, also, I saw numbers of insane and possessed on the highroad outside the city and, here and there, on the streets through which Jesus passed. They were quieted and freed from their paroxysms. The people said among themselves: "This man must possess a power like unto that of the ancient prophets, since those unfortunates grow calm on His appearance." They felt benefitted by His presence, even though apparently He did nothing special for them; and so they sought Him in the inn to thank Him. He taught and exhorted to John's baptism, and spoke with as much vehemence as did John himself.

The people of Bethulia gave to Jesus and His followers a most honorable reception. They would not allow Him to put up at the inn outside the city, but strove among themselves as to who should have the honor of entertaining Him in their houses. They that had not Jesus, at least wanted one of the five disciples who were with Him. But they, the disciples, would not leave their Master. At last, Jesus promised to make the inn and the houses of the good people His headquarters alternately. Their great enthusiasm and love for Him were not altogether disinterested, and Jesus charged them with it during His instruction in the synagogue. They had a secondary design. They wanted, by entertaining the new Prophet, to attract to their city that esteem which they had lost by their trade and intercourse with heathens. They were also destitute of a pure love of truth. When Jesus left Bethulia, I saw Him in a valley teaching under the trees. Besides the five disciples, there were now about twenty others following Him. The holy women had already returned to Nazareth. Jesus had left Bethulia because He was so much besieged by the people. Numbers of sick and possessed from the country around had gathered in the city, hoping to be cured; but Jesus did not as yet wish to heal so openly. As He journeyed away from Bethulia, He left the Sea of Galilee behind. The place in which He next taught was an old place of instruction formerly used by the Essenians, or Prophets. It consisted of an elevated, grassy mound, surrounded by little parapets against which the audience could rest comfortably. There were about thirty people around Jesus in this place.

That evening I saw Him with His followers arrive at the little village with its synagogue, about one hour's distance from Nazareth, whence not long before He had set out to go to Sephoris. The inhabitants received Him with every mark of kindness. They conducted Him to a large house in front of which was a courtyard, washed His feet, as also those of the disciples, cleaned and brushed His travelling garments, and prepared for Him and His followers a repast. Jesus taught here in the synagogue. The holy women were in Nazareth.

Next day He went about two miles further on toward the Levitical city, Cedes, or Cesion. He was followed by about seven possessed, who still more plainly than those of Sephoris, proclaimed His mission and history. Aged priests and youths in long, white garments came forth from the city to meet Him, for some of His followers had already gone before Him into the city.

Jesus did not free the possessed here. They were

confined in a house by the priests, that they might not create disorder. But He freed them later after His baptism. He was quite well received and entertained in this place, but when He proposed to teach, they questioned Him: What call had He? What mission? Was He merely Joseph and Mary's Son? Jesus answered evasively that He who had sent Him and to whom He belonged, would make all that known at His baptism. He taught many other things on this point and also of the baptism of John. His instructions were given on a hill in the center of the place where, as at Thebez, a stand had been prepared for the purpose, not exactly in the open air, but under a rush-covered tent or shed.

Jesus went from here through the pastoral region where later, after the second Pasch, He healed a leper. He taught in the different little villages around. But for the Sabbath, He went with His companions to Jezrael, a scattered place, the houses, which were built in groups, being separated from one another by ruins, towers, and gardens. A high road ran through the city, called King's street. Jesus had with Him only three of His companions, several having gone on before.

Jezrael was the home of strict observers of the Jewish Law. They were not Essenians, however, but Nazarites. They made vows for a time, longer or shorter, and practiced various kinds of mortification. They had a large institution, comprising different sections. The unmarried men occupied one part exclusively, the unmarried women another. The married also made vows of continency for a certain period, during which the husbands lived in a house next to that of the unmarried men, while the wives retired to that of the single women. They were all habited in gray and white. Their Superior wore a long, gray garment edged with fringe and little white ornaments like fruit, and bound by a gray girdle on which were inscribed white letters. Around one arm was a

band of coarse, gray and white woven stuff as thick
as a twisted napkin, one end of which—ornamented
with tufted fringe—hung down a little. He wore a
collar, or little mantle, almost like that of Argos, the
Essenian, excepting that it was gray and open behind
instead of in front. A blank shield was fastened on
it in front, while behind it was tied or laced. On the
shoulders hung slit lappets. All wore black, shining,
puffed caps, with some words stamped on the front;
three bands met on top forming a ball, which, like
the rim, was white and gray. The Nazarites had long,
thick curly hair and beards. I tried to think which
of the Apostles looked like them and, at last, I remembered that it was Paul. His hair and garments, when
he persecuted the Christians, were in the style of
the Nazarites. I saw him afterward, also, with the
Nazarites, for he was one of them. They used to let
their hair grow until their vow was accomplished,
when they cut it off and burned it in sacrifice. They
sacrificed pigeons, also. One could assume and fulfill the unfulfilled vows of another. Jesus celebrated
the Sabbath with them. Jezrael is separated from
Nazareth by a mountain range. Not far from it is a
well near which Saul once encamped with his army.

Jesus taught on the Sabbath of the baptism of
John. He said that, although their piety was praise-
worthy, yet excess was dangerous; that there are different ways to salvation; that splits in the community
would easily give rise to sects; that, in their pride,
they looked down upon their weaker brethren who
could not do so much as they themselves, but who
should be succored by the stronger. Such teaching
as His was very necessary here, for in the suburbs
there were people who had mixed with the heathens,
and who were destitute of rule or direction, because
the Nazarites had separated from them. Jesus visited these people in their homes, and invited them
to His instruction on baptism.

Next day Jesus was present at a repast given Him

by the Nazarites, at which circumcision was spoken of in connection with baptism. For the first time, I heard Jesus speaking of circumcision, but I cannot exactly recall His words. He said something to this effect, that the law of circumcision had a reason for its existence which would soon be taken away, when the people of God would come forth no longer according to the flesh from the family of Abraham, but spiritually from the Baptism of the Holy Ghost. Great numbers of the Nazarites became Christians; but they clung so tenaciously to Judaism that many of them, seeking to combine Christianity with it, fell into heresy.

7. Jesus Among the Publicans

When Jesus left Jezrael, He journeyed awhile toward the east, then went around the mountain which lay between Jezrael and Nazareth and, about two hours from the former place, reached a number of houses standing in rows on either side of the highroad. They were occupied by publicans. Some poor Jews dwelt under tents at a little distance from the road. That road, along which the dwellings of the publicans stood, was fenced in by wickerwork, the entrance at either end being closed. Rich publicans lived here who rented many tolls in the country and again leased the same to under-collectors. Matthew was one of these latter taxgatherers, but belonging to another place. Mary, the niece of Elizabeth, once dwelt here, I think. Having become a widow, she went to Nazareth and afterward to Capharnaum. She was the same that was present at the Blessed Virgin's death. The commercial highroad to Egypt from Syria, Arabia, and Sidon passed through this place. Great bales of white silk in bundles like flax were brought this way on camels and asses; also fine woollen stuffs both white and colored; great, heavy, woven strips of carpet; and lastly spices. When the camels arrived in this district, the gates were closed and the merchants had to unpack their goods, which were carefully examined. They had to pay a tax, partly in merchandise, and partly in money. The latter was mostly three-or four-cornered yellow, white, or reddish pieces, on which was stamped a figure, raised on one side and hollow on the other. They gave also coins different from these. I saw on those coins little towers, a virgin, also an infant in a little ship. Little bars of gold, such as were offered by the Kings at the Crib, I never saw again excepting with some strangers who came to John the Baptist.

The publicans were all leagued together. When one received more than his fellows, he divided with the rest. They were wealthy and lived well. Their homes were surrounded by courtyards, gardens, and walls, reminding me of those of our well-to-do peasants. They lived entirely among themselves, for others would not associate with them. They had a school of their own and a teacher.

Jesus was well received by them, His followers also. I saw several women arrive here; I think Peter's wife was among them. One of them spoke with Jesus, and they soon went away. Perhaps they were either coming from or going to Nazareth, and were executing some commission for the Mother of God. Jesus stayed first with one, then with another of the publicans, and taught in their school. He especially pointed out to them the fact that they often extorted from travellers more toll than was just. They became very much confused, and could not divine how He knew that. They were more humble than the other Jews, and took His words better. Jesus urged them to receive baptism.

8. Jesus in Kisloth-Thabor

Jesus left the publicans after having taught among them the whole night. Many of them desired to make

Him presents, but He would accept nothing. Several followed Him, for they wanted to go with Him to baptism. On this day, He journeyed through the country by Dothain and passed the madhouse where, on His first journey from Nazareth, He had calmed the raving and the possessed. As He was passing it, they called Him by name and clamored violently to be released. Jesus commanded their custodians to free them, promising that He would answer for the consequences. They were all set at liberty. Jesus cured them all, and they followed Him. Toward evening, He arrived at Kisloth, a city on Mount Thabor, inhabited mainly by Pharisees. They had heard of Jesus; but they were displeased at seeing Him followed by publicans (whom they looked upon as malefactors), possessed known to be such, and a motley crowd of others. He entered their school and taught of the baptism of John; then, addressing His followers, He exhorted them before attaching themselves to Him to think seriously whether they would be able to persevere or not, for they must not think His path an easy one. He expounded to them also several parables on building. If a man desired to build himself a house, he should consider first whether the owner of the ground would allow him to use it for that purpose; in like manner, they that would follow Him should first expiate their offences and do penance. Again, if a man would erect a tower, he must first estimate the cost. And many other things Jesus taught that were not well received by the Pharisees. They listened only to catch Him in His words. I saw them concerting together to give Him an entertainment at which they hoped to ensnare Him in His speech.

They prepared a great feast in a public hall, down which stood three tables, side by side, and right and left burned lamps. Over the middle table, at which Jesus, some of the disciples, and the Pharisees sat, the aperture, customary in the roofs of that country, stood open. The followers of Jesus were seated at the side tables. In this city there must have been an ancient custom commanding the poor, of whom there were numbers dwelling in the greatest abandonment, to be invited; for as soon as Jesus sat down at table, He turned to the Pharisees asking where were the poor, and whether it was not their right to take part in the feast. The Pharisees were embarrassed, and they answered that the custom had long fallen into disuse.

Then Jesus commanded His disciples Arastaria and Cocharia, the sons of Maraha, and Kolaiah, the son of the widow Seba, to go gather together the poor of the city and bring them to the feast. The Pharisees were highly displeased at the command, for it gave rise to much comment throughout the city. Many of the poor were already in bed and asleep. I saw the disciples rousing them. Numerous and varied were the joyous scenes I then witnessed in the huts and haunts of the poor. At last they arrived and were received and welcomed by Jesus and His disciples. The latter served them while Jesus addressed to them a very beautiful instruction. The Pharisees, though greatly irritated, had not a word to say, for Jesus was in the right, and at this the people rejoiced. Great excitement prevailed in the city. After partaking plentifully of the various good things, the poor people departed, taking with them a supply for their friends at home. Jesus had blessed the food for them, prayed with them, and exhorted them to go to John's baptism. He would not tarry longer in the city, and left that night with His followers. Many of the latter, however, discouraged partly by His exhortations, left Him for their homes while others went to prepare for John's baptism.

9. Jesus in the Shepherd Village of Chimki

Jesus journeyed during the night between two valleys. I saw Him sometimes conversing with His followers, then again falling behind and praying on His knees to His Father, after which He again rejoined them. On the following afternoon I saw Him arrive at a shepherd village whose houses lay scattered here and there. It possessed a school, but no resident priest; the people were attended by one from a distance. When Jesus arrived, the school was closed. He assembled the shepherds in an apartment of the inn and there instructed them. As the Sabbath was approaching, there came that evening several priests of the sect of the Pharisees, some of them from Nazareth. Jesus spoke of baptism and the near advent of the Messiah. The Pharisees were very hostile toward Him; they spoke of His humble origin, and tried to make little of Him. Jesus slept here that night.

Jesus, in His instructions on the Sabbath, expounded many parables. He called for a grain of mustard seed and, when they brought it to Him, He spoke for some time of it, saying that if they had faith equal only to a grain of that seed, they would be able to transport the pear tree before them into the sea. A large pear tree laden with fruit stood nearby. The Pharisees mocked at His teaching, which they considered childish. Jesus explained at length, but I have forgotten. He also recounted the parable of the unjust steward.

The people of this place and of the whole country around were in admiration of Jesus. They related what they had heard from their fathers of the teaching and works of the last Prophets, and they compared this new Teacher to them with this exception, however, that He was much milder. The shepherd settlement was named Chimki. The hills of Nazareth could be discerned in the distance, for they were only about two hours off. It was a scattered little place, a few houses only around the synagogue. Jesus took up His abode with a poor family, the mistress of which lay sick of the dropsy. He had compassion upon her and cured her, laying His hand upon her head and stomach. She was perfectly restored, and served her Guest at table. Jesus forbade her to speak of what had happened until He should have returned from the baptism. Whereupon she asked why she might not tell it everywhere. Jesus answered: "If thou wilt publish it everywhere, thou shalt become dumb," and she did become dumb, and remained so until His return from baptism. At this time it may have been about fourteen days until then, for at Bethulia or Jezrael He had spoken of three weeks.

Jesus taught three days in the synagogue of this place. The Pharisees were greatly incensed against Him. He spoke of the coming of the Messiah, saying, "Ye are expecting Him to appear surrounded by worldly glory. But He is already come, and He will make His appearance as a poor Man. He will teach truth. He will get more blame than praise, for He wills justice. But separate not from Him, that ye may not be lost. Be ye not like those children of Noe who mocked him when he so laboriously built the ark that was to save them from the flood. All they that derided not went into the ark and were saved." Then turning to His disciples, He addressed them, saying, "Separate not from Me like Lot from Abraham when, seeking more fertile regions, he went to Sodom and Gomorrha. And look not around after the glory of the world which fire from Heaven shall destroy, that ye may not be turned into pillars of salt! Remain with Me under every trial. I will always help you," etc. The Pharisees, still more irritated, exclaimed: "What is this that He promises them, seeing that He has nothing Himself?" Then turning to Him, they asked: "Art Thou not from Nazareth? The son of Joseph and Mary?" But Jesus answered evasively that He whose Son He was, would manifest it. Then they continued: "Why dost Thou speak here as elsewhere of the Messiah? We have heard of Thy teaching. Thinkest Thou indeed that we shall imagine that Thou meanest Thyself?" Jesus answered: "Upon that question I have nothing to say, excepting these words, yes, ye do think it." The excitement in the synagogue became great, the Pharisees extinguished the lights, while Jesus and the disciples, although it was night, left the place and journeyed some distance along the highroad. I saw them sleeping under a tree.

10. Jesus in a Shepherd Village Near Nazareth

On the following morning I saw crowds of people on the road waiting for Jesus. They had not been with Him in that last place, but had gone on ahead of Him. I saw Him turning aside from the road with them and, about three o'clock in the afternoon, coming up to another shepherd field. In it were only some light huts occupied by the shepherds in grazing time. There were no women here. The shepherds went forward to meet Jesus; they must have been informed of His coming by those that had gone on before. While some of their number went to meet Him, the others busied themselves killing birds and lighting a fire in order to prepare a meal. This took place in an open hall, something like an inn, the fireplace being separated from the guest room by a wall. All around the hall ran a mossy bank with a platted support for the back overgrown by green foliage. The hosts led the Lord and His followers in, about twenty in number, equal to that of the shepherds themselves. All washed their feet, a separate basin being assigned to Jesus. He asked for more water and, after using it, commanded it not to be thrown out. When all were ready for table, Jesus questioned the shepherds, who appeared anxious about something, as to the cause of their trouble, and asked if there were not some of their number absent. In answer to His questions, they acknowledged that they were sad on account of two of their companions who were lying sick of leprosy. Fearing that it might be the unclean leprosy, and dreading lest Jesus might not come to them on that account,

they had taken care to conceal them. Then Jesus
ordered them to be brought before Him, and He sent
some of His disciples after them. At last, they appeared
so closely enveloped from head to foot in sheets that
it was with great difficulty they could walk, though
each was supported on either side. Jesus addressed
them, telling them that their leprosy had come not
from within, but from an outward infection. While He
spoke, I was spiritually enlightened that, not through
malice, but through temptation they had sinned. Jesus
commanded them to wash in the water which He had
used for His feet. They obeyed, and I saw the crusts
falling from them leaving the scars behind. The water
was then poured into a hole in the ground and covered with earth. Jesus strictly commanded the good
people to say not a word of their cure until He should
have returned from the baptism.

He afterward gave an instruction upon John, the
baptism, and the coming of the Messiah. His hearers questioned Him very simply as to which they
should follow, Himself or John, and they desired to
know which was the greater. Jesus answered: "The
greatest is he who serves as the least and last of
all. He who for the love of God humbles himself as
the least—he is the greatest." He exhorted them also
to go to the baptism, spoke of the difficulties to be
encountered in following Him, and sent away all that
had done so excepting the five disciples. He appointed
a meeting place in the desert, not far from Jericho,
I think in the region of Ophra. Joachim had owned
a pasture ground in those parts. Some of Jesus' hearers left Him entirely, some went straight to John,
while others returned home to prepare for their journey to the baptism.

Jesus and the five disciples afterward went on to
Nazareth, which at most was only about a short
hour's distance. They approached by the side whose
gate opens to the east on the road leading to the
Sea of Galilee, but they went not into the city.

Nazareth had five gates. A little less than a quarter of an hour's distance from the city, rose the mountain from whose steep summit they often hurled people, and whence, at a later period, they wanted to cast Jesus. At the foot of this mountain lay some huts. Jesus directed the five disciples to seek lodgings in them, as He did Himself. They were supplied with water to wash their feet, a piece of bread, and a place in which to sleep. Anne's property lay to the east of Nazareth. The shepherds had bread baked in the ashes, also a well dug in the earth, but without masonry.

11. Jesus with Eliud, the Essenian

The valley through which Jesus went by night from Kisloth-Thabor is called Edron, and the shepherd village in whose synagogue the Pharisees of Nazareth had so derided Him was named Chimki. The people with whom Jesus and the five disciples put up outside of Nazareth were Essenians and friends of the Holy Family. The Essenians, both men and women, dwelt around here in the ruins of old stone vaults, solitary and unmarried. The former wore long white garments, the latter mantles, and both cultivated little gardens. They had once dwelt near Herod's castle in the valley of Zabulon but out of friendship for the Holy Family had come hither.

He with whom Jesus stayed was named Eliud. He was a very venerable, gray-haired old man with a long beard. He was a widower, and his daughter took care of him. He was the son of a brother of Zacharias. The Essenians lived very retired around here, attended the synagogue at Nazareth, and were very devoted to the Holy Family. The care of Mary's house during her absence had been entrusted to them.

Next morning the five disciples of Jesus went into Nazareth to visit their relatives and acquaintances, also the school. Jesus, however, stayed with Eliud,

with whom He prayed and very confidentially conversed, for to that simple-hearted, pious man many
mysteries had been revealed.

There were four women in Mary's house besides
herself: her niece, Mary Cleophas; Johanna Chusa,
a cousin of Anna the Prophetess; the relative of
Simeon, Mary, mother of John Marc; and the widow
Lea. Veronica was no longer there, nor was Peter's
wife, whom I had lately seen at the place where the
publicans lived.

The Blessed Virgin and Mary Cleophas came to
Jesus in the morning. Jesus stretched out His hand
to His Mother, His manner to her being affectionate, though very earnest and grave. Mary was anxious about Him. She begged Him not to go to
Nazareth, for the feeling against Him there was very
bitter. The Pharisees belonging to Nazareth, who had
heard Him in the synagogue of Chimki, had again
roused indignation against Him. Jesus replied to His
Mother's entreaties that He would await where He
was the multitude that were to go with Him to the
baptism of John, and then pass through Nazareth.
Jesus conversed much with His Mother on this day,
for she came to Him two or three times. He told her
that He would go up to Jerusalem three times for
the Pasch, but that the last time would be one of
great affliction for her. He revealed to her many other
mysteries, but I have forgotten them.

Mary Cleophas was a handsome, distinguished-
looking woman. She spoke with Jesus that morning
of her five sons, and entreated Him to take them
into His own service. One was a clerk, or a kind of
magistrate, named Simon; two were fishermen, James
the Less and Jude Thaddeus, and these three were
the sons of her first marriage. Alpheus, her first husband, was a widower with one son when she married him. This stepson was named Matthew. She wept
bitterly when she spoke of him, for he was a publican. Joses Barsabas, who also was at the fishery, was

her son by her second husband Sabas; and, by her third marriage with the fisherman Jonas, she had another son, the young Simeon still a boy. Jesus consoled her, promising that all her sons would one day follow Him. Of Matthew, whom He had already seen when on His way to Sidon, He spoke words of comfort, foretelling that he would one day be one of His best disciples.

The Blessed Virgin returned from Nazareth with some of her female relatives to her abode near Capharnaum. Servants had come with asses from the latter place to conduct them home. They took several pieces of furniture with them which, after their last journey, had been left behind in Nazareth, various kinds of tapestry and woven stuffs, packages of other things, and some vessels. All were packed in chests formed of broad strips of inner or outer bark, and fastened to the sides of the asses. Mary's house in Nazareth was so ornamented that it had, during her absence, the appearance of a chapel. The fireplace looked like an altar. A chest was placed over it on which stood a flowerpot with a plant growing in it. After Mary's departure this time, the Essenians occupied the house.

12. Jesus Discourses with Eliud, the Essenian, Upon the Mysteries of the Old Testament and the Most Holy Incarnation

Jesus passed the whole day in most confidential intercourse with Eliud, who asked Him various questions about His mission. Jesus explained all to the old man, telling him that He was the Messiah, speaking of the lineage of His human genealogy and the Mystery of the Ark of the Covenant. I learned then that that Mystery had, before the flood, been taken into the ark of Noe, that It had descended from generation to generation, disappearing from time to time, but again coming to light. Jesus said that Mary at her birth had become the Ark of the Covenant of the Mystery. Then Eluid who, during the discourse frequently produced various rolls of writing and pointed out different passages of the Prophets which Jesus explained to him, asked why He, Jesus, had not come sooner upon earth. Jesus answered that He could have been born only of a woman who had been conceived in the same way that, were it not for the Fall, all mankind would have been conceived; and that, since the first parents, no married couple had been so pure both in themselves and in their ancestors as Anne and Joachim. Then Jesus unfolded the past generations to Eliud, and pointed out to him the obstacles that had delayed Redemption.

I learned from this conference many details concerning the Ark of the Covenant. Whenever it was in any danger, or whenever there was fear of its falling into enemies' hands, the Mystery was removed by the priests; yet still was it, the Ark, so holy that its profaners were punished and forced to restore it. I saw that the family to whom Moses entrusted the special guardianship of the Ark existed until Herod's time. At the Babylonian Captivity, Jeremias hid the Ark and other sacred things on Mount Sinai. They were never afterward found, but the Mystery had been removed. A second Ark was, at a later period, constructed on the first model, but it did not contain the sacred objects that had been preserved in the first. Aaron's rod, also a portion of the Mystery were in the keeping of the Essenians on Horeb. The Sacrament of the Blessing was, however, but I know not by what priest, again replaced in the Ark. In the pit, which was afterward the Pool of Bethsaida, the sacred fire had been preserved. I saw in pictures very many things, which Jesus explained to Eliud, and I heard part of the words, but I cannot recall all.

He related the fact of His having taken Flesh of the blessed germ of which God had deprived Adam before his fall. That blessed germ, by means of which all Israel should have become worthy of Him, had descended through many generations. He explained how His coming had been so often retarded, how some of the chosen vessels had become unworthy. I saw all this as a reality. I saw all the ancestors of Jesus, and how the ancient Patriarchs at their death gave over the Blessing sacramentally to the first-born. I saw that the morsel and the drink out of the holy cup, which Abraham had received from the angel along with the promise of a son, Isaac, were a symbol of the Most Holy Sacrament of the New Covenant, and that their invigorating power was due to the Flesh and Blood of the future Messiah. I saw the ancestors of Jesus receiving this Sacrament, in order to contribute to the Incarnation of God; and I saw that Jesus, of the Flesh and Blood received from His forefathers, instituted a most august Sacrament for the uniting of man with God.

Jesus spoke much to Eliud also of the sanctity of Anne and Joachim, and of the supernatural Conception of Mary under the Golden Gate. He told him that not by Joseph had He been conceived, but from Mary according to the flesh; that she had been conceived, of that pure Blessing which had been taken from Adam before the Fall, which through Abraham had descended until it was possessed by Joseph in Egypt, after whose death it had been deposited in the Ark of the Covenant, and thence withdrawn to be handed over to Joachim and Anne.

Jesus said that to free man He had been sent in the weakness of humanity; that He received and felt everything like a man; that, like the serpent of Moses in the desert, He would one day be raised up on Mount Calvary where the body of the first man lay buried. He referred also to the sad future that awaited Him and to the ingratitude of man.

Eliud simply and confidently asked question after question. Although he understood all that Jesus said better than did the Apostles, although looking upon

things in a more spiritual sense than they, yet all
was not clear to him; he could not rightly comprehend how the mission of Jesus was to be accomplished. He asked Jesus where His Kingdom was to
be, in Jerusalem, in Jericho, or in Engaddi. Jesus
answered that where He Himself was, there would
His Kingdom be, and that He would have no external Kingdom.

The old man spoke to Jesus so naturally and simply. He related to Him many things of His Mother,
as if He knew them not, and Jesus listened to him
so kindly. He told Him of Joachim and Anne, and
spoke of the life and death of the latter. Jesus
remarked that no woman had ever been more chaste
than Anne; that she had married twice after Joachim's
death in accordance with the command of God, for
it was proper that the number of fruits destined to
be produced by this branch should be filled up.

As Eliud recounted the circumstances of Anne's
death, I had a vision of the same. I saw her lying
on a rather high couch in a back room (something
like Mary's) of her own large house. She was unusually animated and talkative, and not at all like a
dying person. I saw her blessing her little daughters, also her other relatives, who were in the
antechamber. Mary was standing at the head, Jesus
at the foot of her bed. Jesus was, at this time, a
young man, His beard just beginning to appear. Anne
blessed Mary, begged the blessing of Jesus, and continued speaking in a joyous strain. Suddenly she
glanced upward, became white as snow, and I saw
drops like pearls starting out on her forehead. I cried
out: "Ah, she is dying! she is dying!" and, in my eager-
ness, I wanted to clasp her in my arms. Then it
seemed to me that she came and rested in them. On
awaking I still thought that I held her.

Eliud related also many things connected with the
virtues of Mary in the Temple. As he spoke, I saw
it all in vision. I saw that her teacher Noemi was

one of Lazarus's relatives. She was about fifty years old and, like all the other women who served in the Temple, she was an Essenian. I saw that Mary learned from her how to knit. Even as a child, she used to go with Noemi when the latter went to cleanse the different vessels and utensils that had been soiled with the blood of sacrifice. Certain parts of the animal sacrificed were received by them, then cut up and prepared as food for the priests and others who served in the Temple; for they depended in part upon that for support. I saw the Blessed Virgin at a later period helping in these duties. I saw Zachary, when it was his turn to serve in the sanctuary, visiting the child Mary. Simeon, also, knew her. And so, as Eliud was recounting it to the Lord, I saw all her pious and lowly serving in the Temple.

They spoke, also, of Christ's conception, and Eliud told of Mary's visit to Elizabeth. Eliud mentioned also a spring that Mary had found there; and that, too, I saw.

I saw the Blessed Virgin going with Elizabeth, Zachary, and Joseph from Zachary's house to another little property belonging to him, and on which there was no water. The Blessed Virgin went alone into the garden, a little rod in her hand, and prayed. She pierced the earth with the rod, and a tiny stream gushed out and flowed around a little knoll. When Zachary and Joseph removed the earth with a spade, an abundant supply rushed forth, and soon formed a most beautiful spring. Zachary dwelt about five hours southward from Jerusalem, and a little to the west.

In confidential discourse like the above, interrupted only by prayer, Eliud treated with Jesus. He honored Him, but quite simply and joyously, looking upon Him as a chosen human being. Eliud's daughter did not dwell in the same house with her father, but at some distance in a rocky cavern.

There were about twenty Essenians living on the mountain. The women dwelt apart from the men, about five or six together. All honored Eliud as their Superior and daily assembled around him for prayer. Jesus ate with him alone, but very sparingly, their repast consisting of bread, fruit, honey, and fish. Weaving and agriculture formed the chief occupation of these people.

The mountain at whose base the Essenians dwelt, was the highest peak of a ridge on one of whose plateaus Nazareth was built. A valley lay between it and the city. On the other side the descent was steep and overgrown with verdure and grapevines. The abyss at its base, the one into which the Pharisees at a later period wanted to precipitate Jesus, was full of all kinds of rubbish, ordure, and bones. Mary's house stood on a hill outside the city, part of it extending into the hill like a cave. The top of the house, however, arose above the hill, on the opposite side of which lay other dwellings.

Mary and the other women accompanied by Colaya, Lea's son, arrived at her house in the valley of Capharnaum. Her female friends in the neighborhood came out to meet her. Mary's dwelling at Capharnaum belonged to a man named Levi, who lived in a large house not very far from it. It had been rented from Levi by Peter's family and given over to the Holy Family; for Peter and Andrew knew the Holy Family in a general way, also through John the Baptist, whose disciples they were. The house had several buildings attached to it in which relatives of the family and the disciples could stay when visiting the Holy Family. It appeared to have been chosen on that account. Mary Cleophas had with her her little boy Simeon, about two years old, the son of her third marriage.

Toward evening Jesus accompanied Eliud from his house to Nazareth. Outside the city walls, where Joseph had had his carpenter shop, lived several people, poor but good, who had been known to Joseph, and among whose sons were some of the playmates of Jesus' childhood. Eliud took Jesus to visit these people. They offered their guests a morsel of bread and a little fresh water. The water was especially good in Nazareth. I saw Jesus sitting on the ground among them and exhorting them to go to the baptism of John. They acted somewhat shyly in Jesus' regard. They had in the past looked upon Him as one of themselves. But now that He was so gravely introduced to them by Eliud, whom they all so highly honored, whose advice they often asked, from whom they were accustomed to seek consolation, and who, moreover, united in persuading them to go to the baptism, they could scarcely reconcile themselves to the position He now held toward them. They had indeed heard of the Messiah, but they could hardly think that Jesus was He.

13. Jesus and Eliud
Walking and Conversing Together

The next day Jesus went with Eliud southward from Nazareth through the valley of Esdrelon on the road to Jerusalem. When about two hours beyond the brook Kison, they arrived at a village consisting of a synagogue, an inn, and only a few houses. It was one of the environs of the not far distant Endor, and nearby was a celebrated spring. Jesus put up at the inn. The people of the place behaved rather coldly, though not inimically toward Him. Eliud was not held in special esteem by them, for they were rather pharisaical. Jesus notified their head men that He intended to teach in the synagogue, but they replied that that was not usual for strangers. Jesus told them that He had a special call to do so and, entering the school, He taught of the Messiah whose Kingdom was not of this world, whose coming would not be attended by outward splendor, also of John's baptism. The priests of the synagogue were not favorably inclined toward Jesus. Jesus bade them give Him the Scriptures. He unrolled them and explained many passages from the Prophets. Eliud's confident communications with Jesus were to me singularly touching. He knew of and believed in His mission and supernatural advent, still without appearing to have a suspicion that He was God Himself. He told Jesus quite naturally, as they walked together, many things connected with His youth, what the Prophetess Anna had related to him, also what she had heard from Mary after the return from Egypt, for Mary had sometimes visited her in Jerusalem. Jesus, in turn, related to Eliud some things that he did not know, each accompanied with significant interpretation. But all was so natural, so simple, like a dear old man speaking with a beloved young friend.

While Eliud was rehearsing what Anna had heard from Mary and told to him, I saw all in pictures. I rejoiced to find them exactly similar to what I had long before seen and partly forgotten.

Jesus spoke to Eliud also of His journey to the baptism. He had gathered together many people and sent them to the desert near Ophra; but He said that He would go alone by the road past Bethania, where He wanted to speak with Lazarus. He spoke of Lazarus by another general name, which I have forgotten. He mentioned also his father, saying that he had been in war. He said that Lazarus and his sisters were rich, and that they would devote all they had to the advancement of Redemption.

Lazarus had three sisters: the eldest Martha, the youngest Mary Magdalen, and one between them also called Mary. This last lived altogether secluded, her silence causing her to be looked upon as a simpleton. She went by no other name than Silent Mary. Jesus, speaking to Eliud of this family, said, "Martha is good and pious. She will, with her brother, follow Me." Of Mary the Silent, He said, "She is possessed of great mind and understanding; but, for the good of her soul, they have been withdrawn from her. She is not for this world, therefore is she now altogether secluded from it. But she has never committed sin. If I should speak to her, she would perfectly comprehend the greatest mysteries. She will not live much longer. After her death, Lazarus and his sister Martha will follow me and devote all that they possess to the use of the Community. The youngest sister Mary has strayed from the right path, but she will return and rise to higher sanctity than Martha."

Eliud spoke also of John the Baptist, but he had not yet seen him and was not yet baptized. Jesus and Eliud spent the night at the inn near the synagogue, and early on the following morning, they journeyed along Mount Hermon toward the somewhat dilapidated city of Endor. Around the inns lay masses of broken walls all the way along the mountain, so broad that a wagon could pass over them. Endor was full of ruins interspersed with gardens. On one side were large, magnificent buildings like palaces, while in other quarters of the city the desolation of war was visible. It seemed to me that the inhabitants were a race apart from the Jews. There was no synagogue in Endor, so Jesus went with Eliud to a large square in which three side buildings containing small chambers were built around a pond. The pond was in the center of a green lawn, and on its waters little barks were sailing. There was a pump nearby, and the place bore the appearance of a health-giving resort. The little chambers around the pond were occupied by invalids. Jesus, accompanied by Eliud, entered one of the buildings. He was hospitably received, and His feet washed. A high seat was erected for Him on the lawn, and there He taught the people. The women who occupied one of the wings, took back seats in the audience. These people were not orthodox Jews. They were more like slaves, cast out and oppressed, who had to pay tribute of all that they earned. After a certain war, they remained behind in the city. I think their leader, Sisara, was defeated not far off, and was then murdered by a woman.[1] His army had been scattered throughout the whole country and reduced to servitude. There were still about four hundred in these parts. Their forefathers had, under David and Solomon, been forced to quarry stones for the building of the Temple. They were long accustomed to such work. The deceased King Herod had employed them in building an aqueduct to Mount Sion of several hours in length. They were very compassionate and stood by one another under all circumstances. They wore long coats and girdles. Their pointed caps covered their ears like those of the ancient hermits. They had no communication with the Jews, although they were allowed to send their children to the Jewish schools. But the poor little creatures were so badly treated and so despised that the parents preferred keeping them home.

Jesus felt great compassion for them. He had the sick brought to Him. They sat in a kind of bed like my reclining chair (I can still see them), under the movable back of which were supports. When the back was let down, the chair formed a bed.

As Jesus instructed them about the Messiah and baptism and exhorted them to the latter, they answered timidly that they could not lay claim to such a privilege, for that they were only poor outcasts. Then He taught them by the parable of the unjust steward. The clear interpretation He gave of it, I perfectly understood. It haunted me the whole day, but now I have forgotten it. Perhaps I shall recall it again. Jesus also related the parable of the son sent by his father to take possession of his vineyard. He always related that when instructing the poor, neglected heathens. The people prepared a repast for Jesus out in the open air. He invited to it the poor and the sick, and He and Eliud served them at table. This action greatly impressed His entertainers. That evening Jesus returned with Eliud to the place out-

---

1. *Judges* 4:2.

side of Nazareth, where He stayed overnight and celebrated the Sabbath in the synagogue.

The following day, Jesus and Eliud returned to Endor, which was only a Sabbath distance from the inn, and there He taught. The inhabitants were Canaanites and, I think, from Sichem; for I heard that day, at least once, the name Sichemite. They had an idol hidden away in a subterranean cavern. By some kind of mechanism on springs, it could be made to rise suddenly out of the earth and seat itself on an altar beautifully ornamented and prepared to receive it. They had procured this idol from Egypt, and it was named Astarte, which I understood yesterday to be the same as Esther. The idol had a face round like the moon. On its outstretched arms it held something long and swathed, like the chrysalis of a butterfly, large in the middle and tapering at either end. It may have been a fish. On the back of the idol was a pedestal upon which stood a high pail, or a small half-tub, which extended over the head. In it was something like ears in green husks, also fruits and green leaves. The idol stood in a cask that reached up to the lower part of the body, and all around it were pots of growing plants. These people worshipped their idol in secret, and Jesus in His instructions to them reprehended them for it. They had been accustomed to sacrifice deformed children to the goddess. There was a companion idol belonging to this goddess, the god Adonis, who I think was Astarte's husband.

This nation, as has been said, had been defeated in three parts under their general Sisara, and scattered as slaves throughout the country. They were at this time greatly oppressed and despised. Not very long before Christ, they had excited some disturbance around Herod's castle in Galilee, after which they were still more oppressed.

In the afternoon, Jesus and Eliud returned to the synagogue and there ended the Sabbath.

The Jews, meanwhile, were very much displeased at Jesus' visit to Endor. But He reprehended them very severely for their hardheartedness toward their abandoned fellow beings. He exhorted them to a spirit of kindness and urged them to take them to the baptism, which they themselves had, at His recommendation, resolved to receive. The Jews of this place became more favorably inclined toward Jesus after they had heard His instructions. Toward evening He returned to Nazareth with Eliud. I saw them conversing together the whole way, sometimes even pausing to stand and talk. Eliud was again recalling many of the incidents of the flight into Egypt, and I saw them again in vision. He began by asking whether Jesus was not going to extend His Kingdom over the good people in Egypt who had been impressed by His presence among them in His childhood.

Here I saw again that the journey of Jesus after the raising of Lazarus through pagan Asia down to Egypt, and which I had seen before, was no dream of mine, for Jesus told Eliud that wherever the seed had been sown, would He before His end reap the harvest.

Eliud knew of the sacrifice of bread and wine, also of Melchisedech; but he knew not what idea to form of Jesus. He questioned Him as to whether He was not another Melchisedech. Jesus answered: "No. Melchisedech had to pave the way for My sacrifice. But I shall be the Sacrifice itself."

I learned also from that conversation that Noemi, Mary's teacher in the Temple, was the aunt of Lazarus, his mother's sister. Lazarus' father was the son of a Syrian king who had, for services in war, received some property as a reward. His wife was a Jewess of distinction. She belonged to the priestly race of Aaron (although Manasses allied with Anna), and dwelt in Jerusalem. They owned three castles: one in Bethania; one near Herodium; and one at Magdalum, on the Sea of Galilee, not far from

Tiberias and Gabara. Herod also had a castle in the country near Magdalum. Jesus and Eliud spoke also of the scandal Magdalen gave her family. Jesus went home with Eliud. There they found assembled the five disciples, the Essenians, and many others who were desirous of going to the baptism. Some publicans, also, had come to Nazareth for the same purpose, and several bands had already started for the place of baptism.

14. Jesus in Nazareth

Next morning Jesus resumed His instructions. Two of the Pharisees from Nazareth came to Him and, in a friendly manner, invited Him to go back with them to the school. They had, as they said, heard so much of His teaching in the country around that they were eager to hear Him explain the Prophets. Jesus went with them. They conducted Him to the house of a Pharisee, in which many others were assembled. The five disciples were with their Master. The Pharisees listened very politely to Jesus while He spoke to them in beautiful parables. His teaching appeared to please them greatly, and they led Him to the synagogue, where a numerous audience awaited Him. Jesus spoke of Moses and explained the Prophecies concerning the Messiah. But whenever He dropped any words from which they might infer that He alluded to Himself, they showed displeasure. One of the Pharisees spread for Him a repast, and He spent the night with His five disciples at an inn near the school.

Next day Jesus addressed a crowd of publicans who were journeying just then to receive the baptism. He afterward taught in the synagogue, making use of the similitude of the grain of wheat which must die in the earth before producing its fruit. His words displeased the Pharisees, and they repeated their remarks about the son of the carpenter Joseph.

They reproached Him also for His communications with publicans and sinners, to which Jesus replied with great firmness. Then they took up the Essenians whom they denominated hypocrites who lived not according to the Law. But Jesus showed them clearly that the Essenians were stricter followers of the Law than the Pharisees, and so the reproach of hypocrisy fell back upon themselves. It was the question of benedictions that had led to the Essenians. Blessings were in common use among them, and the Pharisees were annoyed at seeing Jesus blessing little children. When, for instance, He was entering or leaving the synagogue, He was stopped by many mothers with their children, and His blessing craved for the little ones.

While Jesus dwelt at Nazareth, He had always much to do with the children, who became still and quiet near Him. No matter how passionately they cried, His blessing had power to calm them. The mothers, remembering this, now brought their little ones to Him to see whether He had become too proud to notice them. There were some among them who kicked violently, rolling over and over on the floor, as if they had cramps, screaming loudly all the while. But Jesus' blessing stilled them instantly. I saw something like a dark vapor going out from some of them. Jesus laid His hand on the heads of the boys and gave them the Patriarchs' blessing in three lines, one from the head and one from either shoulder down to the heart where all three united. He blessed the girls in the same way, but without laying His hand on them, though He made a sign on their lips. I thought as I saw Him do it that it meant that they should not prattle so much; still, however, it was significant of something else. Jesus passed the night with His disciples in the house of a Pharisee.

15. Jesus Rejects Three Rich Youths.
He Confounds Many Learned Men
In the Synagogue of Nazareth

To the five followers of Jesus, four others were now added, relatives and friends of the Holy Family. I think there was a son of one of the three widows among them, and one from Bethlehem, who had found out that He was a descendant of Ruth who had married Booz in that city. Jesus formally received them to the number of His disciples. There were in Nazareth a couple of rich families who had three sons. In childhood these latter had associated with Jesus. They were now quite cultured and well educated. The parents, who had heard much of Jesus' wisdom and teaching, agreed together that their sons should today hear a specimen of it. They would then offer Him money to let the young men travel with Him that they might profit by His knowledge. The good people had so high an opinion of their sons that they thought Jesus would gladly become their tutor. So the young men went to the synagogue whither, by the connivance of their wealthy parents and the Pharisees, all the learned men of the city had flocked. They were determined to put Jesus to the test in every way. Among these men were a lawyer and a physician, the latter a tall, portly man with a long beard. He wore a girdle and had some kind of a badge upon one shoulder of his mantle. I saw Jesus, on entering the school, again blessing many children whom their mothers brought to Him, among them some afflicted with leprosy whom He healed. During His discourse, He was interrupted in various ways by the literati who proposed to Him all kinds of subtle questions. But His wisdom silenced them.

To the lawyer's speech, Jesus answered most wonderfully from the Law of Moses, and when divorce was spoken of, He rejected it entirely. Divorced, husband and wife could never be; but if the former could not in any way live with the latter, he might leave her. Still were they one body, and could not again marry. These words of the Lord greatly displeased the Jews.

The physician asked whether He could tell whether a man was of a dry, matter-of-fact nature or of a phlegmatic disposition, under what planets such a one was born, what simples were good for this or that temperament, and how the human body is formed. Jesus answered him with great wisdom. He spoke of the complexion of some of those present, their diseases and the remedies, and of the human body, with a depth of knowledge quite unknown to the physician. He spoke of life, of the spirit, and how it influences the body, of sicknesses that could be cured only by prayer and amendment, of such as needed medicine for their cure—and that in language so profound, and yet so beautiful, that the physician in astonishment declared himself vanquished and that he had never before heard such things. I think he afterward became one of Jesus' disciples. Jesus described to him the human body with all its members, muscles, veins, nerves, and intestines, their special functions and their various relations one with another, in general terms and yet with such accuracy that His questioner was humbled and silenced.

There was an astrologer present who spoke of the course of the stars. He explained how one constellation ruled another, how different stars possess different influences, and he discoursed upon comets and the signs of the Zodiac. Jesus in most appropriate language treated with another upon architecture; with others of trade and commerce with foreign nations, taking occasion at the same time to censure severely the various fashions and frivolities lately introduced from Athens. He condemned likewise the games and juggling now in use among them, and which were also spreading throughout Nazareth and other places. These games were likewise a product of their intercourse with Athens. Jesus stigmatized them as unpardonable since they that indulge in them look upon them as no sin; consequently, they do no penance for them, and therefore they cannot be pardoned.

His hearers were ravished at His wisdom. They begged Him to take up His residence among them, offering to give Him a house and all that He needed, questioning Him also as to why He and His Mother had removed to Capharnaum. Jesus replied that He could not remain with them, and He spoke of His mission and the duties it imposed. In answer to their question as to why He had gone from among them, He said that it was because of His desire to dwell in a more central locality, etc. But they did not understand His reasons, and they were offended at His rejection of their offer, which they thought a very fine one. They looked upon His words, *"mission,"* and *"duties"* as the offspring of pride. And so they left the school that evening.

The three youths, who were about the age of twenty, greatly desired to speak with Jesus. But He would not allow them to do so until His nine disciples were present. That annoyed them. Jesus told them that He insisted upon having witnesses to what He might say to them. When at last they were admitted to an audience, they very modestly and humbly laid before Him their own and their parent's wishes that He would receive them as His pupils. Their parents, they said, would remunerate Him, and as for themselves, they would bear Him company in all His labors, they would serve and help Him. I saw that Jesus was troubled at having to refuse their request, partly for their own sake, and partly on account of His disciples, for He was obliged to assign reasons for His refusal which they could not as yet comprehend. He replied to the youths that he who gave money to obtain something, aimed at gaining some temporal advantage; but that whoever would follow Him, must abandon all earthly possessions, must leave parents and friends, and that His disciples must neither woo nor marry. He laid down many other hard conditions, so that the young men became very much discouraged. They argued that many of the Essenians were married. Jesus replied that they, the Essenians, acted rightly and in accordance with their laws, but that His doctrine was to accomplish fully that for which theirs only paved the way, etc. With this remark and bidding them take time to reflect, He left them.

The disciples were intimidated by His words. His teaching was so severe that they could not understand it, and they grew fainthearted. But on the way from Nazareth to Eliud's, He bade them not despond, that He had good reasons for talking as He had done, that those youths would only at some distant day, and perhaps never, come to Him; but as for themselves, the disciples, they should follow Him calmly and be without anxiety, etc. And so they arrived at Eliud's. I do not think He will again go to Eliud's, for great talk and excitement had arisen in Nazareth on His account. The inhabitants were vexed at His not remaining among them. They thought that He had acquired all His knowledge during His travels. "True," they said, "He is a very clever and extraordinary man; but, for a carpenter's son, He is rather conceited." I saw the three young men returning to their homes. Their parents were very much displeased at the objections Jesus made to receiving them. The sons chimed in with the parents, and all talked at random in their indignation against Him.

On the following day, the three youths went again to Jesus and begged once more to be accepted. They promised Him perfect obedience and faithful service. But Jesus again dismissed them, and I saw that their inability to seize the meaning of His refusal troubled Him. He spoke then with His nine disciples who, by His directions, were to go first to a certain place and afterward to John. On the subject of those whom He had dismissed, Jesus said that they desired to follow Him for the sake of what they might gain, that they were not willing to give all for love. But that they, the disciples, sought for nothing, consequently they had been received. He spoke again in significant and beautiful terms of the baptism, telling them to go over to Capharnaum and say to His Mother that He was going to the baptism. He charged them likewise to speak to the disciples, John, Peter, and Andrew about John (the Baptist) and say to the last named that He (Jesus) was coming.

16. Jesus with Eliud
In the Leper Settlement

I saw Jesus journeying with Eliud in a southwesterly direction from Nazareth, but not exactly on the highroad. He wanted to go to Chim, a leper settlement. They reached it at daybreak, and I saw that Eliud tried to restrain Jesus from entering it, that He might not be defiled; for, as Eliud urged, if it were discovered that He had been there, He would not be allowed to go to the baptism. But Jesus replied that He knew His mission, that He would enter, for there was in it a good man who was sighing for His coming. They had to cross the Kishon. The leper settlement lay near a brook formed by the waters of the Kishon which flowed into a little pond in which the lepers bathed. The water thus used did not return into the Kishon. This settlement was perfectly isolated; no one ever approached it. The lepers dwelt in scattered huts. There were no others in the place, excepting those that attended the infected. Eliud remained at a distance and waited for the Lord. Jesus entered one of the most remote huts wherein lay stretched on the ground a miserable creature entirely

enveloped in sheets. He was a good man. I have forgotten how he contracted leprosy. Jesus addressed
him. He raised himself, and appeared to be deeply
touched at the Lord's deigning to visit him. Jesus
commanded him to rise and stretch himself in a
trough of water that stood near the hut. He obeyed,
while Jesus held His hands extended over the water.
The rigid limbs of the leper relaxed, and he was
made clean. He then resumed his ordinary dress,
and Jesus commanded him not to speak of his cure
until He should have returned from the baptism. He
accompanied Jesus and Eliud along the road till Jesus
ordered him to go back.

I saw Jesus and Eliud the whole day journeying
toward the south through the valley of Esdrelon.
Sometimes they conversed together, and at others
walked apart as if in prayer and meditation.

The weather was not very pleasant at that time,
the sky dark, and fog in the valley. Jesus had no
stick. He never carried one. But Eliud had one with
a little shovel on it like those of the shepherds. Jesus
wore only sandals, though a kind of perfect shoe,
consisting of a thick, woven upper of coarse cotton,
was in use at the time. Once I saw Jesus and Eliud
at noon resting by a well and eating bread.

17. Jesus Transfigured Before Eliud

During the night, I saw them again walking, sometimes together, sometimes separate. And then I witnessed something extraordinary, an unspeakably
lovely vision. While Jesus was walking on ahead,
Eliud passed some remarks upon the symmetry and
beauty of His person. Jesus replied: "If thou shouldst
behold this Body two years hence, thou wouldst find
in it neither beauty nor symmetry, so greatly will
they abuse and maltreat Me." But Eliud understood
not His words. Above all he could not comprehend
why Jesus always spoke of His Kingdom as existing

so short a time; for he thought ten, or even twenty years must elapse before it would be founded. He could not bring himself to think otherwise, since his thoughts were all of an earthly kingdom.

When they had gone on a short distance, Jesus paused and bade Eliud, who was following lost in thought, to approach and He would show him who He was, of what nature was His Body, and of what kind His Kingdom. Eliud drew near to within several steps of Jesus. Then Jesus raised His eyes to Heaven and prayed. A cloud, like those seen in a thunderstorm, descended and enveloped both. From without they could not be seen, but over them opened a Heaven of light which seemed to descend toward them. Above I saw a city of shining walls, I saw the Heavenly Jerusalem! The whole interior was lit up with a rainbow colored light. I saw a figure like God the Father, and Jesus, His form perfectly luminous and transparent, connected with Him by beams of light. Eliud stood awhile gazing upward as if entranced, and then sank prostrate on his face, in which position he remained until the apparition and the light had melted away. Then Jesus resumed His way, and Eliud followed speechless and frightened by what he had seen. It was a vision like the Transfiguration, but I did not see Jesus lifted up.

I think Eliud did not live to see the Crucifixion of Christ. Jesus was more confidential toward him than toward the Apostles, for Eliud was very enlightened and very familiar with many of the mysteries connected with the family of Jesus. Jesus took him as a friend and companion, and clothed him with authority, so that he did much for His community. He was one of the best instructed of the Essenians. In Jesus' time, the Essenians did not dwell all together on the mountains as formerly; they were more scattered throughout the cities. I had that wonderful vision about twelve o'clock at night.

In the morning, I saw Jesus and Eliud arrive at

a shepherd field. It was daybreak, and the shepherds were already out of their huts and with the cattle. They came forward to meet Jesus, who was known to them. They cast themselves down before Him, and then led Him and His companion under a shed where they had their cooking utensils. Here they washed their feet, prepared for them a couch, and set before them bread and little drinking cups. They roasted some turtledoves for their guests. The birds had their nests in the roofs of the huts, and were hopping around in great numbers like hens. And now I saw Jesus dismissing Eliud, who knelt to receive His blessing. The shepherds were present. Jesus told him that he would end his days in peace, that the path which He Himself had to walk would be too difficult for him, that He had admitted him to His Community, that he had already done his part in the vineyard, and that he should receive his reward in His Kingdom. Jesus explained this by the parable of the laborers in the vineyards. Eliud was very grave since the vision of the preceding night, very silent, and deeply impressed. I think he was afterward baptized by the disciples. He accompanied Jesus a part of the way from the shepherd field. The Lord embraced him, and he departed with signs of manly emotion.

The place to which Jesus was going for the Sabbath could be seen from here. Some of His relatives once dwelt there. The place to which He now went alone was called Gur. It was built on a mountain. Joseph's brother, who afterward removed to Zabulon and who had had frequent communication with the Holy Family, once dwelt there. Jesus went unnoticed to an inn, where they washed His feet and presented Him food. He had a chamber to Himself. He caused a roll of the Scriptures to be brought to Him from the synagogue, and out of it He read and prayed sometimes standing, sometimes kneeling, often raising His eyes toward Heaven. He did not go to the school. Once I saw some people going to the inn and asking to speak to Jesus, but He would not see them.

18. A Glance at the Disciples Going to the Baptism

I saw the disciples whom Jesus had dispatched with messages arrive in Capharnaum. They were about five of the best-known. They had an interview with Mary, and then two of them went to Bethsaida for Peter and Andrew. James the Less, Simon, Thaddeus, John, and James the Greater were present. The disciples spoke of the mildness, meekness, and wisdom of Jesus, while the followers of John the Baptist proclaimed with enthusiasm the austere life of their master, and declared that they had never before heard such an interpreter of the law and the Prophets. Even John spoke enthusiastically of the Baptist, although he already knew Jesus. His parents had once lived only a couple of hours from Nazareth, and Jesus loved him even as a child. The disciples celebrated the Sabbath here.

The next day I saw the nine disciples along with those named above on the road to Tiberias, whence they were to go to John, passing near Ephron and then through the desert toward Jericho. Peter and Andrew particularly distinguished themselves by the zeal with which they spoke of the Baptist. He was, they said, of a noble, priestly race; he had been educated by the Essenians in the wilderness, he would suffer no irregularity around him, he was as rigorous as he was wise. Then Jesus' disciples put forward the mildness and wisdom of their Master, to which the others retorted that many disorders arose from such condescension, and they cited instances in proof of what they said. Jesus' disciples replied that their Master, too, had been educated by the Essenians and that, moreover, He had but lately returned from travelling. But John entered not into this discussion. I did not hear him saying anything more in that strain. They started together for the place of baptism, but after a few hours took different directions. As I listened to their conversation, I thought, "Men were then as they now are."

19. Jesus in Gophna

Gur, where Jesus prayed alone in the inn, lay not very far from a city, Mageddo, and a field of the same name. I have clearly seen that, toward the end of the world, there will be fought in that field a battle with Antichrist. Jesus arose with the dawn, rolled up His couch, laid a coin on it, girded Himself, and went forth. His way led Him around many towns and villages, but He met no one, put up at no inn. He passed Mount Garizim near Samaria, which lay to the left, as He journeyed southward. Occasionally He ate a few berries and some other fruit, and in the hollow of His hand or with a concave leaf scooped up some water to quench His thirst.

Toward evening, Jesus entered Gophna, a city on Mount Ephraim. It was built upon very jagged foundations, some high, some low, numerous gardens and pleasure grounds scattered between the houses. Some relatives of Joachim dwelt here, but they had not maintained intimate communications with the Holy Family. Jesus put up at an inn where they washed His feet and gave Him some little refreshment. But soon there came to the inn some of His relatives accompanied by a couple of Pharisees of the better sort, and escorted Him to their own home, one of the handsomest houses in the city. The city itself was of some importance, and possessed at this time jurisdiction over a portion of the country around. Jesus' relative was an official, and was much employed in writing. I think the city belonged to Samaria. Jesus was received with respect. There were several guests at His relative's house and all, stand-

ing or walking, took refreshments in a pleasure garden. Jesus slept here overnight.

It was a day's journey from Gophna to Jerusalem.
There was a little river in this region. During the
loss of the Boy Jesus in the Temple, the Holy Family went to Gophna in search of Him; for when they
missed Him at Michmas, they thought He might perhaps have gone to His relatives there. Mary feared
that He had fallen into the little river.

Jesus, having gone to the synagogue, asked for the
writings of one of the Prophets, and taught of baptism and the Messiah. He proved to His hearers from
the Prophets, that the time must have arrived for
His appearance. He cited events which were to precede His coming, and which had actually been accomplished, alluding especially to one that had happened
three years before. I do not now remember whether
that particular event was a war, or whether it was
that the scepter had passed from Juda. And so He
went on enumerating proofs of accomplished signs
which were to precede the coming of the Messiah.
He mentioned also the multiplication of sects and
the irreligious nature of so many of their ceremonies.
He told them that the Messiah would be in their
midst, and they would not know Him. He alluded,
in words something like the following, to the connection existing between Himself and John: "There
will be one who will point Him out (the Messiah),
but ye will not acknowledge Him. Ye wish to see a
conqueror, an illustrious personage, a man surrounded by magnificence and eminently learned companions. Ye will not recognize as the Messiah one
that comes among you destitute of wealth and authority, unattended by the pomp of worldly splendor and
magnificence, one whose companions are unlettered
peasants and laborers, whose followers are made up
of beggars, cripples, lepers, and sinners."

In this way Jesus spoke at length, interpreting
the Prophecies, and putting forth clearly the con-

nection between Himself and John. Still, He never once said, *"I"*, but spoke of Himself in the third person. His instruction occupied the greater part of the day. His relatives concluded that He must be an envoy, a forerunner of the expected Messiah. On His return to their house, they referred to a book in His presence wherein they had recorded all that had happened in the Temple to Jesus, the Son of Mary, in His twelfth year. They were struck by the similarity between what He had then said and His teaching of today, and on perusal of that record they were still more astonished.

The father of the house was an aged widower. His two daughters, both widows, lived with him. I heard the two daughters talking together of the marriage of Joseph and Mary in Jerusalem, at which they had been present. They recalled the magnificence of that wedding, how well-off Anne had been, but how changed the circumstances of the family had become. They spoke just as people of the world are accustomed to do, a vein of blame and reproach running through their words, as if they of whom they were speaking had greatly degenerated. While thus conversing and, womanlike, recounting the particulars of the wedding and Mary's bridal dress, I saw a circumstantial vision of the whole ceremony and especially of the Blessed Virgin's ornaments. Meanwhile the men were hunting up what had been written years before about Jesus and His teaching as a Boy in the Temple. The parents of Jesus had anxiously sought Him here, and it was thus that the news of where and how He was found had reached them. The affair had attracted much attention, especially as He was a relative of theirs.

While His relatives were still expressing surprise at the connection between His former and His present teaching, by which they were even more prejudiced in His favor, Jesus informed them that He must take leave and, in spite of their remonstrances, set out accompanied by several of the men. They had to cross a little river over a bridge of masonry on which trees were growing. They journeyed some hours to a plain covered with meadows. It was here the Patriarch Joseph was when Jacob sent him to his brethren in Sichem. The regions from which Jesus had lately come had also been much frequented by Jacob. Late in the evening Jesus entered a shepherd village this side of a small river, and His companions left Him. The village lay on both sides of the river, the part on the opposite bank being the larger. The synagogue was on this side. The Lord went to an inn where were assembled two sets of candidates for baptism. They were on their way through the desert to the appointed place. They had spread the news here of Jesus' coming. He conversed with them that evening, and they departed next morning. The servants washed the Lord's feet. He partook of a light repast, and then retired for prayer and rest.

20. Jesus Condemns Herod's Adultery.
The Journey of the Holy Women

Next morning Jesus went to the school, where many were assembled. He spoke, as usual, of the baptism and of the nearness of the Messiah whom they would not acknowledge. He reproached them for their obstinate adherence to old, meaningless customs, on which point these people had a special failing. They were, on the whole, tolerably simple-minded and received His remonstrances well. Jesus requested the High Priest of the synagogue to conduct Him to the sick. He visited about ten, but cured none; for, in the neighborhood of Jerusalem, He had told Eliud and His five disciples that He would perform no more cures until He had been to the baptism. The sick in this place were mostly dropsical, gouty, and infirm women. Jesus exhorted them and told them separately what religious acts they should perform,

according as their infirmities were a part punishment of sin. Some He ordered to purify themselves
and go to the baptism.

There was a meal prepared for Him at the inn, at
which many men of the place were present. Before
the hour for it these men spoke of Herod, of his
unlawful connection with his brother's wife, blaming
him severely and inquiring into Jesus' opinion on
the point in question. Jesus warmly censured Herod's
conduct and denounced the sin of adultery, but He
told them likewise that if they judged others, they
would themselves be judged.

Now there were in this place many sinners. Jesus
spoke with them privately and earnestly reproved
them for living in adultery. He told many all their
secret sins. Trembling with fear, they promised to do
penance. Jesus went from here to Bethania, a distance of perhaps six miles, and again entered a mountainous region. It was the winter season, foggy and
cloudy by day, and sometimes white frost by night.
Jesus enveloped His head in a scarf, and journeyed
straight on toward the east.

I saw Mary and four holy women leaving the house
and wending their way through a field near Tiberias.
They had with them two servants from the fishery.
One went on ahead, the other followed, both laden
with baggage which they carried on a pole across
the shoulder, a pack in front and another behind.
The four women were Johanna Chusa, Mary Cleophas,
Mary Salome, and one of the three widows. They,
too, were going to Bethania by the usual route which
ran by Sichem to the right. When Jesus passed it,
it was on His left. The holy women walked generally in single file, a couple of steps apart. They went
in this way probably because most of the roads,
excepting the broad highways, were narrow, intended
for foot passengers, and led through the mountains.
They walked quickly with a firm step, not swaying
from side to side, as the country people do here. Very

probably this is because from early youth the inhabitants of that country are accustomed to making long journeys on foot. They had their gowns tucked up to about the middle of the calf, their lower limbs bandaged tightly down to the ankle, and bound to the soles of their feet were thick, padded sandals. Over the head was a veil, the ends of which were fastened into the scarf wound round the neck. This scarf was crossed on the breast, thence carried behind and caught in the girdle; sometimes the wearers ran their hands into its folds and there let them rest. The man, going on before the travellers, prepared the way for them. He opened the hedges, removed stones from the path, laid bridges, gave orders at the inns and, in fine, saw to everything. The one who followed put everything again into its first order.

21. Jesus in Bethania

About six miles from Bethania, the road upon which Jesus was travelling again led through a mountainous country. That evening He entered a little village consisting of only one street, about half an hour in length, which ran across a mountain. Bethania was probably still three hours further on. One could see in the distance the region in which it lay, for it was a low plain. From this mountain stretched north and east a desert of about three hours in breadth toward the desert of Ephron. It was between these two deserts that I saw Mary and her companions tonight putting up at an inn.

The mountain is that one upon which Joab and Abisai, in the persecution of Abner, stopped when the latter addressed them. It is called Amma, and lies to the north of Jerusalem. The place where Jesus was faced both north and east. I think it was called Giah. It was opposite the desert Gibeon, which began at the foot of the mountain and stretched off to the desert Ephron. It was about three hours long. Jesus arrived in the evening and entered a house to procure some refreshment. They washed His feet, and set before Him a drink and little rolls. Several persons soon gathered around Him. As He had just come from Galilee, they questioned Him about the Teacher from Nazareth, of whom they had heard so much from John and other sources. They asked also whether John's baptism was of any value. Jesus instructed them in His usual style, exhorted them to baptism and penance, and spoke of the Prophet from Nazareth and of the Messiah. He said that the latter would appear among them, but they would not acknowledge Him, yea, they would even persecute and illtreat Him. They must indeed remark that the time was come for His advent. He would not appear in splendor and triumph. He would be poor and would walk among the simple. The people of this place did not know Jesus, but they received Him well and expressed veneration for Him. Aspirants to baptism had passed through the place and had spoken of Him. After resting about two hours, He continued His journey accompanied by some of the good people.

He arrived in Bethania at night. Lazarus had been perhaps for some days at his house in Jerusalem on the west side of Mount Sion, the same side as Mount Calvary. But he must have heard from the disciples of Jesus' intended visit to Bethania, for he had come thither in time to receive Him. The castle in Bethania belonged in reality to Martha; but Lazarus loved to be there, so he and his sister kept house together. They were expecting Jesus, and a repast was in readiness. Martha dwelt in a house on the other side of the courtyard. There were guests assembled in both houses. With Martha were Seraphia (Veronica), Mary Marcus, and an aged woman of Jerusalem who had been in the Temple when Mary entered and had left soon after. She had desired to remain, but God had other designs for her, and she married. With Lazarus were Nicodemus, John Marc, the only son of Simeon, and an old man named Obed, a brother or brother's son of the Prophetess Anna. All were, in secret, friends of Jesus, partly through John the Baptist, partly through the Holy Family, and again through the prophecies of Simeon and Anna in the Temple. Nicodemus was a thoughtful, inquiring man, who was anxiously awaiting Jesus' coming. All had received the baptism of John, and all were secretly assembled here at Lazarus's invitation. Nicodemus afterward served Jesus and His cause, but in secret. Lazarus had sent some of his servants to meet Jesus on the way. About thirty minutes from Bethania, Jesus came up with a trusty old servant who afterward joined the disciples. The old man prostrated on his face before Him, saying, "I am the servant of Lazarus. If I have found favor before Thee, my Lord, follow me to his house." Jesus bade him rise, and followed him. He was kind to the old man, but at the same time He conducted Himself in accordance with His dignity. It was just that way of acting that gave Him such power to attract. People loved the Man, but felt the God. The servant led Jesus to a porch near a fountain at the entrance of the castle, where all had been prepared for washing His feet and changing His sandals. He wore thick, green, padded soles which He now exchanged for a pair of stout ones with low, leather uppers. From that time He continued to wear these latter. The servant dusted and aired His garments. When the washing of His feet was over, Lazarus and his friends appeared, bringing to Jesus a light refreshment and something in a drinking cup. Jesus embraced Lazarus and greeted the others, extending to them His hand. They served Him hospitably and escorted Him to the house. Sometime after, Lazarus conducted Him across the courtyard to Martha's dwelling. The women there knelt veiled before Him. Jesus raised them by the hand, and told Martha that His Mother was coming to await there His return from the baptism.

They all went back to Lazarus' where a meal was awaiting them. It consisted of roasted lamb, doves, vegetables, little rolls, honey, and fruits. On the table were cups, and the guests reclined on leaning stools, two and two. The women ate in an antechamber. Jesus prayed before the meal began and blessed the food. He was very grave, even a little sad. During the repast, He said that a time of trial was approaching, that He was about to begin a toilsome journey, which would come to a bitter end. He exhorted them, if they were His friends, to stand firm, for like Himself they would have much to suffer. He spoke so feelingly that they all wept, though they did not perfectly understand Him and knew not that He was God.

That want of understanding on the part of those around Jesus is always a subject of wonder to me, since I have seen innumerable testimonies of His Godhead and mission; and I cannot help asking why was not that, which I perceive so clearly, shown to those people. I have seen man created by God, Eve taken from his side and bestowed upon him as a wife, and both fallen from their first innocence. I have seen the Promise of the Messiah, the dispersion of mankind, the wonderful providence of God and His mysteries preparing the way for the coming of the Blessed Virgin. I saw the descent of the Blessing from which the Word became Flesh running like a path of light through all the generations of Mary's ancestors. At last I saw the angel's message to Mary and the ray of light from the Godhead which penetrated her at the instant the Saviour became Man. And after all this, how wonderful did it not seem to me, miserable, unworthy sinner, to see those holy contemporaries and friends of Jesus in His presence—though loving and honoring Him—yet possessed by the thought that His Kingdom was to be an earthly one; to see them regarding Him, indeed, as the promised Messiah, and yet never dreaming

that He was God Himself. He was to them only the
son of Joseph and Mary, His Mother. None guessed
that Mary was a virgin, for they knew not of her
supernatural Immaculate Conception; indeed, they
did not even know of the Mystery of the Ark of the
Covenant. It was already a great deal, and a sign of
special grace, that they loved Him and acknowledged
Him. The Pharisees, although they knew of the
prophecies of Simeon and Anna at the time of His
Presentation in the Temple, and who had listened to
His wonderful teaching in the Temple when still only
a child, were perfectly obdurate. They had indeed
made some inquiries at the time concerning the family of the Child and later on concerning His in-
structors; but they esteemed Him and His relatives
too poor, too insignificant, too despicable. They wanted
a Messiah in every way magnificent. Lazarus, Nicodemus, and many of the followers of Jesus entertained
the secret belief that He was called with His disciples to take possession of Jerusalem, to free the Jews
from the Roman yoke, and to establish them in a
kingdom of their own. Truly, it was then as now,
when each man might look upon him as a Saviour
who would restore his fatherland to freedom and
once again establish the beloved old government.
Neither was it known at that time that the Kingdom which alone can help us, is not of this world of
penance. Yes, they indeed rejoiced for the moment
in the thought, "Now it will soon be all over with
the glory of such or such a tyrant." They did not,
however, venture to mention their thoughts to Jesus.
They stood in great awe of Him; besides, they could
read a fulfillment of their hopes in no trace of His
behavior, in no word that He uttered.

After the meal, all retired to an oratory where
Jesus offered a prayer of thanksgiving that His time,
His mission was now to begin. It was extremely affecting, and all shed tears. The women were present,
but standing back. They recited together the usual

prayers, after which Jesus gave them His blessing, and was conducted by Lazarus to His chamber for the night. This was a large room divided off into alcoves where the men slept; but these alcoves were more beautiful than those of ordinary houses. The beds were not rolled up, as they were in general; they were placed on a kind of stationary platform with a cornice in front ornamented with hangings and fringes. A fine mat was rolled up on the wall by the bed. It could, by means of a pulley, be drawn up or let down before the bed, thus concealing it when not in use, and forming a kind of slanting roof. Beside the bed was a small table, and in a niche of the wall stood a tall water vessel, along with a smaller one for drawing and pouring. A lamp projected from the wall, and on the arm of the same hung a toilet towel. Lazarus lighted the lamp, cast himself on his knees before Jesus, who again blessed him, and departed.

Silent Mary, the simple sister of Lazarus, did not make her appearance. Before others she never uttered a word; but when alone in her room or the garden, she talked aloud to herself and to all the objects around her, as if they had life. It was only before others that she was perfectly mute and still; her eyes cast down, she looked like a statue. On being saluted, however, she inclined and was very polite in all her bearing. When alone, she busied herself in various occupations, attending to her own wardrobe, and keeping all things in order. She was very pious, though she never appeared in the school. She prayed in her own chamber. I think she had visions and conversed with apparitions. Her love for her brother and sisters was unspeakable, especially for Magdalen. From her earliest years she had been what she now was. She had a female attendant, but she was perfectly neat in her person and surroundings with no trace of insanity to be found about her.

No word had as yet been spoken in Jesus' presence in reference to Magdalen, who was then living at Magdalum in the height of her grandeur.

On the night that Jesus went to Lazarus', I saw the Blessed Virgin, Johanna Chusa, Mary Cleophas, the widow Lea, and Mary Salome passing the night at an inn between the desert Gibea and the desert Ephraim, about five hours from Bethania. They slept under a shed enclosed on all sides by light walls. It contained two apartments. The front one was divided off into two rows of alcoves, of which the holy women took possession; the back served as a kitchen. Before the inn was an open hut in which a fire was burning. Here the male attendants slept or kept watch. The innkeeper's dwelling was not far distant.

On the following day, Jesus taught walking about the courtyards and gardens of the castle. He spoke earnestly, feelingly, and lovingly, though His manner was full of dignity and He uttered no unnecessary word. All loved Him and followed Him, though not without a sentiment of awe. Lazarus approached Him the most confidently. The other men were more reserved; they gazed on in admiration.

22. Jesus' Interview with Silent Mary. His Conversation with His Mother

Accompanied by Lazarus, Jesus went also to the abode of the women, and Martha took Him to her silent sister Mary, with whom He wished to speak. A wall separated the large courtyard from a smaller one, which latter, however, was still quite spacious. In it was an enclosed garden adjoining Mary's dwelling. They passed through a gate, and Jesus remained in the little garden while Martha went to call her silent sister. The garden was highly ornamental. In the center stood a large date tree, and all around were aromatic herbs and shrubs. On one side was a fountain or rather a kind of tiny lake with a stone seat in the center. From the opposite edge to the seat was laid a plank, upon which silent

Mary could cross and there sit under an awning and surrounded by the water. Martha went to her and bade her come down into the garden, for there someone was waiting to speak to her. Silent Mary was very obedient. Without a word, she threw her veil around her and followed her sister into the garden. Then Martha retired. Mary was tall and very beautiful. She was about thirty years old. She generally kept her eyes fixed on Heaven. If occasionally she glanced to one side where Jesus was, it was only a side glance and vaguely, as if she were gazing into the distance. Even when speaking of herself, she never used the pronoun, *"I,"* but always *"thou,"* as if she saw herself as a second person and spoke accordingly. She did not address Jesus nor cast herself at His feet. Jesus was the first to salute, and they walked together around the garden. Properly speaking, they did not converse together. Silent Mary kept her gaze fixed on high and recounted heavenly things, as if passing before her eyes. Jesus spoke in the same manner of His Father and to His Father. Mary never looked at Jesus, though while speaking she sometimes half turned to the side upon which He was walking. There was more a prayer, a song of praise, a contemplation, a revealing of mysteries than a conversation. Mary appeared as if ignorant of her own existence. Her soul was in another world while her body lived on earth.

Of their speech during that interview, I can remember that, glancing intuitively upon the Incarnation of Christ, they spoke as if gazing upon the Most Holy Trinity acting in that mystery. Their simple, and yet profoundly significant words I cannot recall. Mary gazing upon it, said, "The Father commissioned the Son to go down to mankind, among whom a Virgin should conceive Him." Then she described the rejoicings of the angels, and how Gabriel was sent to the Virgin. And so she ran through the nine angelic choirs, who all came down with the bearer of the glad tidings, just as a child would joyously describe a procession moving before its eyes, praising the devotion and zeal of all that composed it. Then she seemed to glance into the chamber of the Virgin, to whom she spoke words expressive of her hope that she might receive the Angel's message. She saw the Angel arrive and announce the coming of the Saviour. She saw all and repeated all, as if uttering her thoughts aloud, gazing the while into the distance. Suddenly she paused, her eyes fixed on the Virgin who appeared to be recollecting herself before replying to the Angel, and said very simply, "Then, thou hast made a vow of virginity? Ah, if thou hadst refused to be the Lord's Mother, what would have happened? Would there have been found another virgin?" Then addressing her nation, she exclaimed: "Had the Virgin refused, long wouldst thou, O orphaned Israel, still have groaned!" And now, filled with joy by the Virgin's consent, she burst forth into words of praise and thanksgiving, rehearsed the wonders of Jesus' birth and, addressing the Divine Child, said, "Butter and honey shalt Thou eat." She again repeated the Prophecies, recalled those of Simeon and Anna, etc., spoke with the different personages connected with them, and all this as if gazing upon those scenes, contemporary with them. At last, descending to the present, she said, speaking as if alone: "Now goest Thou on the painful, bitter way," etc. Although she knew that the Lord was at her side, yet she acted and spoke as if He were no nearer to her than all the other visions just recounted. Jesus interrupted her from time to time with prayer and thanksgiving, praising His Father and interceding for mankind. The whole interview was inexpressibly touching and wonderful.

Jesus left her. Relapsing into her usual silence and exterior apathy, she returned to the house. When Jesus went back to Lazarus and Martha, He said to them something like the following: "She is not without understanding, but her soul is not of this world.

She sees not this world, and this world comprehends her not. She is happy. She knows no sin."

Silent Mary, in her altogether spiritual state of contemplation, was really and truly oblivious to all that happened to her or around her. She was always thus abstracted. She had never before spoken in the presence of others as she had just done in that of Jesus. Before all others she kept silence, though not from pride or reserve. No; it was because she saw not those people interiorly, saw not what they saw, but gazed upon Redemption and the things of Heaven alone. When at times accosted by a learned and pious friend of the family, she would indeed utter some words audibly, though without understanding a single word of what had been said to her. Not having reference to or connection with the vision upon which she was interiorly gazing at the time, she heard without hearing; consequently her reply, bearing upon what was then engrossing her own attention, mystified her hearers. It was for this reason that she was regarded by the family as a simpleton. Her state necessitated her dwelling alone, for her soul lived not in time. She cultivated her little garden and embroidered for the Temple. Martha brought her her work. She was skillful with her needle, which she plied in uninterrupted musing and meditation. She prayed most piously and devoutly, and endured a kind of expiatory suffering for the sins of others, for her soul was often oppressed as if the weight of the whole world was upon her. Her dwelling was comfortably fitted up with sofas and different kinds of furniture. She ate little and always alone. She died of grief at the immensity of Jesus' Passion, which in spirit she foresaw.

Martha spoke to Jesus of Magdalen and her own great anxiety on her account. Jesus comforted her, telling her that Magdalen would certainly be converted, but that she must on no account weary of praying for her and exhorting her to change her life.

At about half-past one the Blessed Virgin arrived with Mary Chusa, Lea, Mary Salome, and Mary Cleophas. The servant had in advance announced their approach. Martha, Seraphia, Mary Marcus, and Susanna proceeded to that hall at the entrance of the castle where Jesus the day before had been received by Lazarus. They took with them refreshments and the vessels necessary for washing their guests' feet. After welcoming the newly-arrived and performing for them that duty of hospitality, the latter changed their dress, lowered their skirts, and put on fresh veils. All were clothed in undyed wool, yellowish-white or brownish. They partook of a light refreshment, and then accompanied Martha to her house.

Jesus and the men now presented themselves to salute the holy women, after which Jesus retired for an interview with the Blessed Virgin. He told her most earnestly and lovingly that He was about to begin His career, that He was now going to John's baptism whence He would return and once more be with her for a short time in the region of Samaria, but that then He would retire to the desert for forty days. When Mary heard Him speak of the desert, she became very uneasy. She besought Him not to go to so frightful a place where He would die of hunger and thirst. Jesus replied that henceforth she should not seek to deter Him by human considerations, for He must accomplish what was marked out for Him; a very different life was now about to commence for Him, and they who would adhere to Him must suffer with Him; that He must now fulfill His mission, and she must sacrifice all purely personal claims upon Him. He added that although He would love her as ever, yet He was now for all mankind. She should do as He said and His Heavenly Father would reward her, for what Simeon had foretold was about to be fulfilled—a sword should pierce her soul. The Blessed Virgin listened gravely. She was very much troubled, though at the same time strong in her resignation to God, for Jesus was very tender and loving.

That evening Lazarus gave a feast to which Simon the Pharisee, and some others of the sect were invited. The women ate in an adjacent room, which was separated by a grating from the men's dining hall, but within hearing of all that Jesus said. He taught of faith, hope, charity, and obedience. He said that they who desired to follow Him must not look back. They should practice what He taught and suffer the trials that might befall them, but that He would never abandon them. He again alluded to the thorny path before Him, to the buffetings and persecutions He would have to undergo, and impressed upon them the fact, that whoever called themselves His friends, would have to suffer with Him. His hearers, deeply touched, listened in wonder to His words, but what He said in allusion to His bitter Passion they did not rightly understand. They did not take His words in their simple and literal meaning, but looked upon them as the figurative expressions of prophecy. The Pharisees present, though less favorably disposed than the others, found nothing to carp at in Jesus' speech. This time, however, He spoke very moderately.

23. Jesus Journeys with Lazarus to the Place of Baptism

The entertainment over, Jesus rested awhile and then started with Lazarus toward Jericho to the place of baptism. One of Lazarus' servants went on ahead with a lighted torch, for it was night. After walking for about half an hour, they reached an inn belonging to Lazarus where at a later period the disciples often stopped. This inn must not be confounded with that other of which I have often made mention, and at which also the disciples frequently put up. That one was farther on in an opposite direction. The hall in which Jesus and Mary were received by Lazarus on their arrival at his house, was the same in which Jesus was stopping and teaching before the resurrection of Lazarus when Magdalen went to meet Him. On arriving at the inn, Jesus removed His sandals and went barefoot. Lazarus, touched with compassion, begged Him in consideration of the rough, stony roads not to do so. But Jesus gravely replied: "Let it be thus! I know what it behooveth Me to do," and so they entered into the wilderness. The desert, broken up by narrow chasms, stretched out before them a distance of five hours toward Jericho. Then came the fruitful vale of Jericho, also interspersed by wild tracts, about two hours' in breadth, whence to John's place of baptism was a journey of another two hours. Jesus walked more quickly than Lazarus, and was often an hour ahead of him. A multitude, among them some publicans whom Jesus had sent from Galilee to the baptism, were now on their return journey. They passed Jesus in the desert, though at some distance, on their way back to Bethania. Jesus stopped nowhere. He passed Jericho on His left and a couple of other places on the way, but paused at none.

Lazarus' friends, Nicodemus, Simeon's son, and John Marc, had spoken but little with Jesus. But to one another they were constantly interchanging words of admiration at His behavior, His wisdom, His human, yes, even His personal attractions. In His absence or when walking behind Him, they said to one another: "What a man! There never before was such a one, there never again will be another like Him! How earnest, how mild, how wise, how discerning, and yet how simple! But I cannot perfectly comprehend His words, though I accept them with the thought, 'He said it!' One cannot look Him in the face, for He seems to read one's thoughts. Look at His figure— how majestic in bearing! How swiftly He moves, and yet no undignified haste! Whoever walked like Him! How quickly He journeys from place to place, and yet shows no signs of weariness! He is always ready to start again for hours. What a man He has turned out to be!" Then they went on to speak of His childhood, His teaching in the Temple, and referred to the dangers attendant on His first voyage when He had aided the sailors. But not one of them dreamed that he was speaking of the Son of God. They saw that He was greater than all other men, they honored Him, and stood in awe of Him; still He was to them only a man, though, indeed, a man full of prodigies. Obed of Jerusalem was an aged man, the fraternal nephew of the husband of old Anna the Prophetess. He was a pious man, one of the so-called Elders at the Temple, a member of the Sanhedrin. He was one of the secret disciples of Jesus and, as long as he lived, lent assistance to the Community.

JOHN PREACHING PENANCE AND BAPTIZING

1. John Leaves the Desert

John received from On High a revelation concerning the baptism, in consequence of which shortly before leaving the desert he dug a well within reach of the inhabited districts. I saw him on the western side of a steep precipice. On his left ran a brook, perhaps one of the sources of the Jordan which rises on Libanus in a cave between two ridges. It cannot be seen from a distance. To the right lay a level space in the midst of the wilderness, and there he dug a well. I saw him kneeling on one knee and supporting on the other a long roll of bark upon which he was writing with a reed. The sun was darting hot beams upon him as he knelt facing Libanus toward the west. While thus engaged, he became like one entranced. I saw him as if in ecstasy, and standing by him was a man who drew plans and wrote upon the roll. When John returned to consciousness, he read what had been written, and at once set vigorously to work at the well. The bark roll lay beside him on the ground, weighted by a stone at either end to prevent it from rolling together. John often examined it. It seemed as if all he had to do was there marked down.

Side by side with his vision of the well, I beheld a scene in the life of Elias. I saw him sitting in the desert, sad and dejected, on account of some fault he had committed. At last he fell asleep, and had a dream, in which it seemed to him that a little boy approached and pushed him with a stick, and that he feared falling into a well nearby. The thrusts he received from the child were so violent as to send him rolling forward some steps. At this stage of the dream an angel awoke him and gave him to drink. This took place on the same spot upon which John now dug the well.

I recognized the signification of every layer of earth through which John dug and of every step in the work until its completion. All had some relation to human obduracy and its other characteristics, which he had to overcome before the grace of the Lord could take effect upon mankind. This work of John's was, like all his actions and his whole life, a symbol, a prefiguration. By it the Holy Spirit not only instructed him what he was to do, but *he really accomplished in its performance all that the work itself signified, God accepting the good intention which he had thereto associated.* The Holy Ghost urged John on in his work, as formerly the inspired Prophets.

He removed the sod from a wide circumference and dug out of the hard marl a large circular basin, which he very carefully and beautifully lined with stones, excepting in the center where it was dug to a little water. With the excavated earth, he formed around the basin a rim which he divided into five sections. Opposite the openings between four of these sections and at equal distances around the basin, he planted four slender saplings whose tops were covered with luxuriant foliage. These four trees were of different kinds, each bearing its own signification. But in the center of the basin, he set a very choice tree with narrow leaves; its blossoms hung in pyramidal clusters surrounded by a prickly calyx. This tree had long lain partially withered before John's cave. The four little trees were more like slender berry bushes. John protected their roots by little mounds of earth.

When the basin had been excavated down to the well, in which later on the central tree was planted, John hollowed out a channel from the brook near his cave to the basin. Then I saw him gathering reeds in the wilderness, inserting one into the other and, through this conduit (which he covered with earth) conducting the waters of the brook to the basin. The reed pipe could be closed at pleasure. He had made a path through the bushes down to one of the openings in the basin's rim. It ran all around the basin between it and the four trees I have just described. Before the opening at the entrance there was no tree, and on this side alone was access to the basin free; on all the others the path was hemmed in by bushes and rocks. John planted on the mounds at the foot of the four trees an herb well known to me. I was fond of it when a child and, whenever I found it, I used to transplant it to the neighborhood of my home. It has a tall, succulent stalk and bears brownish-red, globular blossoms. It is a very efficacious remedy for ulcers and such sore throats as that from which I am today suffering. John set around also various other plants and young trees. During his labor, he consulted from time to time the bark roll before him, and measured all off with a stick, for it seemed to me that every step of the work, even to the trees that he had planted, was therein sketched. I remember having seen in it a drawing of the middle tree.

John labored thus for several weeks and when he had finished, there was only a small quantity of water in the bottom of the basin. The middle tree, whose leaves had lately been brown and withered, had now become fresh and green. In a vessel formed of the bark of a large tree and whose sides had been smeared with pitch, John now brought water from another well and poured it into the basin. This water was from a well near one of the caves in which John had first dwelt. It had gushed from a rock upon which he struck with the end of his standard. I heard that he could not have built the fountain at that earlier dwelling place of his because it was too rocky there, and that, too, had its own signification. After that he let as much water into the basin from the brook as was necessary. If the reservoir became too full, the water could flow off by the channels in the rim and refresh the vegetation of the surrounding surface. I saw John stepping into the water up to the waist. With one hand he clasped the tree in the center while he struck the water with a little staff to the end of which he had fastened a cross and pennant. Every stroke sent the water in a spray above his head. At the same time, I saw descending upon him from above a cloud of light and, as it were, an effusion from the Holy Spirit, while angels appeared upon the rim of the basin and addressed to him some words. I saw that this was John's last labor in the desert.

That well was in use even after Jesus' death. When the Christians were obliged to flee, the sick and travellers were baptized there; it was frequented also as a place of devotion. It was at that time, that is during Peter's time, protected by a surrounding wall.

Soon after the completion of the baptismal well, John left the desert for the haunts of men. Wherever he went, he made a wonderful impression. Tall of stature, strong and muscular, though emaciated by fasting and corporal mortification, he presented an extraordinarily pure and noble appearance, his manner simple, straightforward, and commanding. His face was thin and haggard; his expression, grave and austere; his auburn hair in curls over his head, and his beard short. Around his waist was a tunic that reached to the knee, and his rough brown mantle appeared to be of three pieces. The back part was fastened around the waist by a strap, but in front it was open, leaving the breast uncovered and the arms free. His breast was rough with hair almost the color of his mantle, and in his hand he carried a staff bent like a shepherd's crook.

Coming down from the desert, he built first a little bridge over a brook. He took no notice of the crossing that lay at some distance, for he never turned out of his way, but worked straight on wherever he went. There was an old highway in those regions. He was near Cidessa here, and he instructed the people in the neighborhood. They were the first pagans that afterward went to his baptism. They lived in mud huts entirely neglected. They were the descendants of a mixed multitude who, after the destruction of the Temple, the last one before Jesus' coming, had settled here. One of the latest of the Prophets had foretold to them that they should remain in these parts until a man should come to them, a man like John, who would tell them what they should do. Later on they removed toward Nazareth.

John allowed nothing to prove an obstacle in his way. He walked boldly up to all he met, and spoke of one thing only, penance and the near coming of the Lord. His presence everywhere excited wonder and made the lightest grave. His voice pierced like a sword. It was loud and strong, though tempered with a tone of kindness. He treated all kinds of people as children. The most remarkable thing about him was the way in which he hurried on straight ahead, deterred by nothing, looking around at nothing, wanting nothing. It was thus I saw him hastening on his way through desert and forest, digging here, rolling away stones there, removing fallen trees, preparing resting places, calling together the people who stood staring at him in amazement, yes, even bringing them out of their huts to help him. I saw their looks of astonishment. He tarried long nowhere, but was soon in another place. He went along the Sea of Galilee, around Tarichea, down to the valley of the Jordan, then past Salem, and on through the desert toward Bethel. He passed by Jerusalem. He had never been in the Holy City; he gazed sadly upon it, and uttered lamentations over it. Entirely possessed by the thought of his mission, on he went, earnest, grave, simple, full of the Holy Spirit, crying aloud the selfsame words: "Penance! Prepare! The Lord is nigh!" He entered the shepherd valley, and journeyed on to the place of his birth. His parents were dead, but some youths, his relatives on Zachary's side, resided there. They were among the first to join him as disciples. When he passed through Bethsaida, Capharnaum, and Nazareth, the Blessed Virgin did not see him, for since Joseph's death, she seldom went out of the house. But several male relatives of her family were present at his exhortations, and accompanied him some distance on his way.

During the three months immediately preceding the baptism, John twice made the circuit of the country announcing Him who was to come. His progress was made with extraordinary vehemence. He marched on vigorously, his movements quick though unaccompanied by haste. His was no leisurely travelling like that of the Saviour. Where he had nothing to do, I saw him literally running from field to field. He entered houses and schools to teach, and gathered the people around him in the streets and public places. I saw the priests and elders here and there stopping him and questioning his right to teach, but soon, astonished and full of wonder, they allowed him to proceed on his way.

The expression, "To prepare the way for the Lord," was not wholly figurative, for I saw John begin his mission by actually preparing the way and traversing the roads and different places over which Jesus and His disciples afterward travelled. He cleared them of stones and briars, made paths, laid planks across brooks, cleaned the channels, dug wells and reservoirs, put up seats, resting places, and sheds to afford shade in the various places where later on the Lord rested, taught, and acted. While thus engaged, the earnest, simple-hearted, solitary man—by his rough garments and conspicuous figure—attracted the attention of the people, and excited wonder when he entered the huts sometimes to borrow a tool, sometimes even to claim assistance from the inmates. Everywhere he was soon surrounded by a crowd whom he boldly and earnestly exhorted to penance, and to follow the Messiah of whom he announced himself the precursor. I often saw him pointing in the direction in which Jesus was passing at that moment. But yet I never saw Jesus with him, although they were sometimes scarcely one hour apart. Once I saw him at the most only a short hour's distance from Jesus, crying out to the people that he himself was not the looked-for Redeemer, but only His poor precursor; but that there went the Saviour, and he pointed to Him. John saw the Saviour face to face only three times in his whole life. The first time that he did so, was in the desert when the Holy Family were journeying from Egypt. He had then been hurried by the Spirit to greet his Master whom, years before while still in his mother's womb, he had saluted. He felt the nearness of his Saviour, and he knew that He thirsted. The boy prayed and thrust his little staff into the ground, whereupon a plentiful stream sprang forth. He then hurried further on the road and took his stand by the running water, to watch Jesus, Mary, and Joseph as they passed by. When they appeared and as long as they remained in sight, he danced about with joy, waving his little standard.

The second time that John saw Jesus was at the baptism; and third was when, at the Jordan, he rendered testimony to Him as He was passing at a distance. I heard the Saviour speaking to His Apostles of John's great self-command; for even at the baptism he had restrained himself within the bounds of solemn contemplation, although his heart was almost bursting with love and desire. After the ceremony, he was more anxious to abase and humble himself than to yield to his love and seek for Jesus.

But John saw the Lord always in spirit, for he
was generally in the prophetic state. He saw Jesus
as the accomplishment of his own mission, as the
realization of his own prophetic vocation. Jesus was
not to John a contemporary, not a man like unto
himself. He was to him the Redeemer of the world,
the Son of God made man, the Eternal appearing in
time, therefore he could in no way dream of associ-
ating with Him. John felt also that he himself was
not like his fellow men, existing in time, living in
the world and connected with it; for even in his
mother's womb had the Hand of the Eternal touched
him, and by the Holy Spirit had he in a way superior to the relations of time, been brought into communication with his Redeemer. As a little boy he had
been snatched from the world and, knowing nothing
but what appertained to his Redeemer, had remained
in the deepest solitude of the wilderness until, like
one born anew, earnest, inspired, ardent, he went
forth to begin his wonderful mission, unconcerned
about aught else. Judea is now to him the desert;
and as formerly he had had for companions the fountains, rocks, trees, and animals, as with them he had
lived and communed, so now did he treat with men,
with sinners, no thought of self arising in his mind.
He sees, he knows, he *speaks* only Jesus. His word
is: "He comes! Prepare ye the ways! Do penance!
Receive the baptism! Behold the Lamb of God who
beareth the sins of the world!" In the desert, blame-
less and pure as a babe in the mother's womb, he
comes forth from his solitude innocent and spotless
as a child at the mother's breast. "He is pure as an
angel," I heard the Lord say to the Apostles. "Never
has impurity entered into his mouth, still less has
an untruth or any other sin issued from it."

John baptized in different places: first, at Ainon
in the neighborhood of Salem; then at On opposite
Beth-Araba on the west side of the Jordan, and not
far from Jericho. That third place was on the east

side of the Jordan, a couple of hours further north than the second. The last time he baptized was at Ainon, whither he had returned. It was there that he was taken prisoner.

The water in which John baptized was an arm of the Jordan formed by a bend of the river to the east, and of about an hour in length. At some places it was so narrow that one could leap over it; at others it was broader. Its course must have changed here and there, for in many places I saw it dry. This bend of the river encircled pools and wells which were fed by its waters. One of these pools, separated by a dam from the arm of the river, formed the baptism place of John at Ainon. Under the dam ran pipes, by means of which the pool could be emptied or filled at pleasure. John himself had so arranged it. On one side of the pool, its waters flowed inland like a creek, and into this extended tongues of land. The aspirants for baptism stood in the water up to the waist between two of these tongues, supporting themselves by a railing that ran along before them. On one tongue stood John. He scooped up water in a shell and poured it on the head of the neophyte, while on the opposite tongue stood one of the baptized with his hand resting on the shoulder of the latter. John himself had laid his hand upon the first. The upper part of the body of the neophytes was not entirely nude; a kind of white scarf was thrown around them, leaving only the shoulders bare. Near the pool was a hut into which they retired for unrobing and dressing. I never saw women baptized here. The Baptist wore a long, white garment during the ceremony.

The region in which John baptized was an exceedingly charming and well-watered district called Salem. It lay on both sides of an arm of the Jordan, but Ainon was on the opposite side of the river. It was larger than Salem, further north and nearer the river. Around the numerous creeks and pools of this region were pasture grounds for cattle, and droves of asses grazed in the verdant meadows. The country around Salem and Ainon was, as it were, free, possessing a kind of privilege established by custom, by virtue of which the inhabitants dared not drive anyone from its borders.

John had built his hut at Ainon on the old foundations of what was once a large building, but which had fallen to ruins, and was now covered with moss and overgrown by weeds. Here and there arose a hut. These ruins were the foundations of the tent castle of Melchisedech. Of this place in particular, I have had visions, all kinds of scenes belonging to early times, but I can now recall only this, that Abraham once had a vision here. He pulled two stones in position, one as an altar, and upon the other he knelt. I saw the vision that was shown to him—a City of God like the Heavenly Jerusalem, and streams of water falling from the same. He was commanded to pray more for the coming of the City of God. The water streaming from the City spread around on all sides. Abraham had this vision about five years before Melchisedech built his tent castle on the same spot. This castle was more properly a tent surrounded by galleries and flights of steps similar to Mensor's castle in Arabia. The foundation alone was solid; it was of stone. I think that even in John's time, the four corners where the principal stakes once stood were still to be seen. On this foundation, which now looked like a mount overgrown with vegetation, John had built a little reed hut. The tent castle in Melchisedech's time was a public halting place for travellers, a kind of charming resting place by the pleasant waters. Perhaps Melchisedech, whom I have always seen as the leader and counsellor of the wandering races and nations, built his castle here in order to be able to instruct and entertain them. But even in his time, it had some reference to baptism. It was also the place from which he set out to his building near Jerusalem, to Abraham, and elsewhere. Here it was, also, that he assembled the various races and peoples whom he afterward separated and settled in different districts. Jacob, too, had once lived at Ainon a long time with his herds. The cistern of the baptism pool was in existence at that early time, and I saw that Jacob repaired it. The ruins of Melchisedech's castle were near the water and the place of baptism; and I saw that in the early days of Christian Jerusalem a church stood on the spot where John had baptized. I saw this church still standing when Mary of Egypt passed that way when retiring into the desert.

Salem was a beautiful city, but it was ruined during a war, I think at the destruction of the Temple before the time of Jesus. The last Prophet, also, dwelt there awhile.

John, perhaps for about two weeks, had been attracting public attention by his teaching and baptizing, when some messengers sent by Herod from Callirrhoe came to him. Herod was at that time living in his castle at Callirrhoe, on the eastern side of the Dead Sea. There were numerous baths and warm springs in the vicinity. Herod wanted John to come to him. But John replied to the messengers: "I have much to occupy me. If Herod wishes to confer with me, let him come himself." After that I saw Herod going to a little city about five miles south of Ainon. He was riding in a low-wheeled chariot, and surrounded by a guard. From its raised seat he could command a view upon all sides as from a canopied throne. He invited John to meet him in the little city. John went to a man's hut outside the city, and thither Herod repaired alone to meet him. Of their interview, I remember only that Herod asked John why he dwelt in so miserable an abode at Ainon, adding that he would have a house built for him there. But to this John replied that he needed no house, that he had all he wanted and that he was accomplishing the will of One greater than he. He spoke earnestly and severely, though briefly, standing the while with his face turned away from Herod.

I saw that Simon, James the Less, and Thaddeus, the sons of Mary Cleophas by her deceased husband Alpheus, and Joses Barsabas, her son by her second marriage with Sabas, were baptized by John at Ainon. Andrew and Philip also were baptized by him, after which they returned to their occupations. The other Apostles and many of the disciples had already been baptized.

One day many priests and doctors of the Law came to John from the towns around Jerusalem intending to call him to account. They questioned him as to who he was, who had sent him, what he taught, etc. John answered with extraordinary boldness and energy, announced to them the coming of the Messiah and charged them with impenitence and hypocrisy.

Not long after, multitudes were sent from Nazareth, Jerusalem, and Hebron by the Elders and Pharisees to question John upon his mission. They made his having taken possession of the place chosen for baptism a subject of complaint.

Many publicans had come to John. He had baptized them and spoken to them upon the state of their conscience. Among them was the publican Levi, later called Matthew, the son of Alpheus by his first marriage, for he was a widower when he married Mary Cleophas. Levi was deeply touched by John's exhortations, and he amended his life. He was held in low esteem by his relatives. John refused baptism to many of these publicans.

2. Herod's Soldiers.
Deputies From the Sanhedrin.
Crowds of Neophytes Come to John

In Dothain, where Jesus had calmed the raving possessed, Jews and pagans had, since the Babylonian Captivity, dwelt together indiscriminately. On a hill in the vicinity, the heathens had their idols and a place of sacrifice. The Jews, roused by the rumor of the advent of the Messiah who was to come from Galilee, would no longer suffer the heathens to dwell among them. The report had been spread both by John himself when journeying through those parts, and by those whom he had there baptized. A neighboring prince of Sidon had dispatched soldiers to the defense of the idols and Herod also sent troops thither to bring the people to order.

These troops were made up of the rabble. I saw them with Herod at Callirrhoe. They told him that they would first be baptized by John, but this was mere policy. They thought by so doing they would have more success among the people. Herod replied that it was not at all necessary to be baptized by John, especially as he wrought no miracles, and neither were they obliged to recognize his mission, but that they might make inquiries at Jerusalem. Then I saw them going to Jerusalem. They had among them chief men of three different ranks, whose office it was to propose the questions to John, and by that I saw they were of three different sects. They had an interview with the priests in the judgment hall in which Peter afterward denied the Lord. In it sat many judges, and it was full of people. The priests derided the soldiers' question, as to whether they should receive John's baptism or not. Their answer was that they might or they might not, it was all the same. About thirty of the soldiers went to John, who reproved them sharply as if to imply that he had little cause to hope for their amendment. He administered baptism to only a few of them in whom he perceived still a little good. These last also he sternly reproached for their dissimulation.

The multitude gathered at Ainon was very great. John baptized none for several days, being engaged in vehement and zealous preaching. Crowds of Jews, Samaritans, and heathens occupied the hills and ramparts around, separate from one another, some under shelter, some under sheds, and some in the open air. John's pulpit was in the center of the encampment, and all listened to him as he preached. Their number amounted to many hundreds. They came to hear his teaching and receive baptism, after which they departed. Once, in particular, I saw many heathens, also people from Arabia and others from a land still farther east. They brought large asses and sheep with them. They had relatives around the country whom they visited here and there, and at last came to John.

In Jerusalem, the Sanhedrin held a great consultation about John, the result of which was that nine messengers were dispatched to him from three different authorities. Annas sent Joseph of Arimathea, also Simeon's eldest son, and a priest whose office it was to inspect the sacrifices; three members of the council, and three private citizens were also chosen for the mission. Their instructions were to question John as to who he was, and to summon him to appear in Jerusalem; for if his mission was authorized, he should first have presented himself at the Temple. They likewise found fault with his unseemly raiment and, moreover, with his administering baptism to the Jews when it was customary to do so only to heathens! Some believed that he was Elias returned from the other world.

Andrew and John the Evangelist were with the Baptist. Many of the disciples and most of the future Apostles excepting Peter, who had already been baptized, and Judas the Traitor (who, however, had been at the fishery around Bethsaida making inquiries concerning Jesus and John) were with John at this time.

For three days, John had not baptized; but he had just resumed that work as the messengers from Jerusalem arrived. They wanted an audience with him right away, but John replied roughly and shortly that they must wait until he was ready. When at last they gained a hearing, they represented to him that he acted entirely too independently, that he should present himself at Jerusalem, and should adopt a less unsightly garb. When the envoys departed, Joseph of Arimathea and the son of Simeon remained with John and received from him baptism. There were many present whom John would not baptize; consequently they went to the envoys and charged John with partiality.

The future Apostles, returning to their own part of the country, told what they knew of John, and in consequence of his teaching, listened favorably to Jesus.

As Joseph of Arimathea was journeying back to Jerusalem, he met Obed, a relative of Seraphia (Veronica). He was a server in the Temple. Joseph, in answer to his questions, told him much about John. Obed then went and received the baptism. As a Temple server, he belonged to the number of the secret disciples. It was only at a later period that he followed Jesus openly.

3. John Receives an Admonition To Go to Jericho

I saw John crossing the Jordan to baptize the sick. He had only his linen scarf thrown around him and his mantle hanging from his shoulders. At one side hung a leathern bottle of baptismal water; on the other, the shell he used in baptizing. On the shore of the river opposite John's place of baptism, were many sick persons who had been brought thither, some in litters and some on a kind of wheelbarrow. They could not be taken across the river on the raft, and so they implored John to come to them. He did so attended by two of his disciples. He prepared a beautiful basin separated from the river by a dyke. This he did himself, for he always had a spade with him. Through a channel, which he could close at pleasure, he let in the water from the river and then poured into it the bottle of baptismal water that he had brought with him. He instructed the sick and then baptized them, pouring water out of a shell over them as they lay on the edge of the basin. When he had finished, he returned to Ainon by the east bank of the Jordan. Here I beheld an angel appear to him and tell him to go to the other side of the Jordan near Jericho, for the time was drawing nigh. *One* would soon arrive there, and he should announce His coming. At this command, John and his disciples took down their tents at the place of baptism near Ainon. They journeyed for some hours along the east side of the Jordan, then crossed the river, pursued their course along the western bank for a short distance, and again pitched their tents. There was a bathing place here, consisting of pits lined with white masonry and connected with the Jordan by canals that could be opened or closed as needed. There were no islands in this part of the river.

This second baptism place lay between Jericho and Bethagla on the western side of the Jordan and opposite Beth-Araba, which was situated somewhat further down on the east side of the river. From this place of baptism to Jericho, the distance was about five miles. The direct road led through Bethania and a desert. There was an inn on the route, but built a short distance off from the road. This region was a pleasure resort. The water of the Jordan is beautiful, becoming so clear when allowed to stand. In many places also it is highly odoriferous owing to the blossoms that fall into it from the bushes in full bloom upon its banks. At times it is very shallow, one can see almost to the bottom, and I saw along the shore deep caves hollowed out of the rocks. I like so much to be in the Holy Land, though I never exactly understand the seasons there. When it is winter with us everything there is in full bloom, and in our summer they already have their second harvest. There is also a season of thick mists and heavy rains. There were about one hundred people with John, among them his disciples and numerous pagans. They all set to work preparing the place and building the tent. All sorts of things were brought over from the baptism place at Ainon. All was now better arranged, and the sick were carried thither in beds. It was in this part of the Jordan that Elias divided the waters with his mantle and passed over with Eliseus, who did the same on his return. Eliseus also rested here, and over this same spot the Children of Israel crossed.

From the Temple of Jerusalem messengers, both Pharisees and Sadducees, were now dispatched to John. He knew through the angel of their coming. When they reached the neighborhood of the Jordan, they sent a courier on before, to summon John to meet them at a place nearby. But he replied by their messenger that, if they wanted to speak with him, they might come to him. They did so, but John paid no attention to them. He went on teaching and baptizing. They listened for awhile and then withdrew. When John had finished, he ordered them to meet him under the shelter or tent that the disciples had erected.

And now, accompanied by his disciples and many others, he went to them. They put all kinds of questions to him, asking whether he was this one or that one, and I saw that he invariably answered in the negative. Then they asked who that *One* was of whom he spoke so much, for the old Prophecies were still remembered, and the rumor was current among the people that the Messiah had come. John answered that among them had arisen One whom they knew not, that he himself had never seen Him, and yet before his birth, he had been commanded by Him to prepare His ways and to baptize Him. If they would return at a certain time, he continued, they would behold Him there, for He was coming to receive baptism. Then he chided them severely, telling them that they had not come to the baptism, but merely for the purpose of seeing what was going on. They retorted that they now knew who he was, that he was baptizing without a mission, that he was a hypocrite clothed in rough garments, etc., and thus abusing him, they went their way. Not long after, about twenty other messengers from the Sanhedrin arrived in Jerusalem. They were men of all conditions, among them some priests wearing caps and broad girdles and long scarfs hanging from the arm. The ends of these scarfs were rough as if trimmed with fur. They addressed John very earnestly, telling him that they had been sent to him by the whole Sanhedrin, to summon him to appear before the Council in order to prove his calling and mission. They urged as a proof of his having none, his want of obedience to the Sanhedrin. I heard John replying in plain terms, bidding them tarry a little while and they should see coming to him the One from whom he had his mission. He told them undisguisedly that the One to whom he so plainly referred had been born in Bethlehem and reared in Nazareth, that He had fled into Egypt, etc., but that he himself had never seen Him. The deputies of the Sanhedrin reproached John with maintaining a secret understanding with Jesus, asserting that their communications were carried on by means of trusty messengers. To this John replied that he could not show to their blind eyes the messengers between Jesus and himself, they could not be seen by them. Indignant at his words, the deputies departed.

Multitudes from all sides, heathens as well as Jews, came to John. Herod very often sent people to hear him, and they carried back to their master an account of his teaching.

All things were very beautifully arranged at this place of baptism. John, with the help of his disciples, had put up an immense tent in which the sick and weary found refreshment, and in which also instructions were given. They sang hymns. I heard them singing a Psalm that treated of the passage of the Children of Israel through the Red Sea. By degrees there sprang up at this place a little village of huts and tents covered partly with skins, partly with rushes. The concourse of strangers was very great. They came from the most distant countries, even from the land of the Three Kings. They brought with them numbers of camels, asses, and beautiful, little frolicsome horses. They always journey this way into Egypt. All encamped around John's baptism place to hear his teaching concerning the Messiah and to receive baptism.

From this place they proceeded in crowds to Bethlehem. Not far from the Crib Cave, off toward the shepherd field was a well of Abraham. He and Sara had dwelt for a period in this region, and during an illness he had had an eager craving after some water from this well. But when it was brought to him in a bottle, he mortified himself, denied himself the cooling draught for the love of God. In reward he was cured. The water of this well was hard to raise on account of its great depth. A large tree stood by it, and the well itself was near the spot upon which lay buried Maraha, Abraham's nurse. When he came to these parts, he brought her with him on a camel. This spot had, like Mount Carmel and Horeb, become a place of pilgrimage for devout Jews. The three Holy Kings had once prayed there.

There were not as yet many Galileans among John's followers, only a few of the subsequent disciples of Jesus. Many went from the region of Hebron, among them numbers of heathens. Therefore did Jesus in His discourses on His way through Galilee, so zealously exhort His hearers to go to John's baptism.

4. Herod's Interview with John.
The Celebration of a Festival at the Place of Baptism

The place at which John taught was about a short

hour further on from where he was accustomed to baptize. It was one of the holy memorial places of the Jews, and was surrounded by walls like a garden inside and around which were rush-covered huts. In the center of this enclosure lay a stone upon the spot where the Children of Israel, when crossing the Jordan, had first rested the Ark of the Covenant and celebrated a festival of thanksgiving. John had erected his tent for teaching, a large canopy of latticework covered with rushes, over this stone at whose base was the chair from which he taught. Here John was holding forth to his disciples when Herod came marching by, but he continued his discourse undisturbed by his presence.

Herod had gone to Jerusalem to meet his brother's wife, who had repaired thither with her daughter Salome, then about sixteen years old. He desired to marry the mother, and had in vain laid the question of the lawfulness of such a union before the Sanhedrin. The refusal of the Council to sanction his desires excited his wrath and, as he feared the public voice, he determined to silence it by the decision of the Prophet John. He doubted not that John, in order to win his favor, would approve the step he wished to take.

I saw Herod's cavalcade consisting of himself, Salome, the daughter of Herodias, her female attendants, and about thirty followers marching toward the Jordan. Herod and the women rode in a chariot. He had sent a courier on to John, but the latter would not suffer Herod to come to the place of baptism. He regarded him as a man who, with his women and followers, would defile the sacred ceremonies. He suspended the baptism therefore, and, followed by his disciples, went to the place destined for preaching. Here he spoke boldly on the question which Herod intended to propose. He said that Herod should wait for the One who was to come after him, that he himself would not baptize there much longer, for he must make way for Him whose precursor he was.

John's words were so pointedly directed against Herod, that the latter could not fail to see that his design was known. However, he caused a large roll of writings on the subject of his suit to be presented to John. The latter would not pollute the hand so often raised in baptism by contact with them, and so they were laid before him. Then I saw Herod and his train indignantly leaving the place. He was still residing at the baths of Callirrhoe, some hours distant from John's place of baptism. He left behind him some of his followers with the writings in order to compel John to give his sanction to what they contained, but in vain. After Herod's departure, John returned to the place of baptism. The women in Herod's retinue were arrayed magnificently, though with tolerable modesty. Magdalen was more fantastic in her attire.

A three days' festival was now celebrated at the stone of the Ark of the Covenant where John's teaching tent had been erected. I cannot now say for certain whether it was to commemorate the passage of Israel through the Jordan, or some other event. John's disciples adorned the place with branches of trees, garlands, and flowers. Peter, Andrew, Philip, James the Less, Simon, and Thaddeus were there, and many of the subsequent disciples of Jesus. This spot was always regarded as sacred by the devout among the Jews, but at this time it was rather dilapidated. John had it repaired. He, as well as some of his disciples, were in priestly robes. Over a gray undergarment, the Baptist wore a white robe, long and wide, girded at the waist by a sash woven in yellow and white, the ends fringed. On either shoulder was a setting as if of two curved precious stones, upon which were engraven the names of the Twelve Tribes of Israel, six on each. On his breast was a square shield, yellow and white, fastened at the corners by fine golden chains. In this shield were set twelve precious stones each bearing the name of one of the twelve tribes.

Around his shoulders hung a long linen scarf like a handtowel. It was a white and yellow stole fringed at the ends. His robe also was fringed with white and yellow silk balls like fruit. His head was uncovered, but under the neck of his robe he wore a narrow strip of woven stuff which could be drawn over the head like a cowl, and which then hung over the forehead in a point.

Before the stone upon which the Ark of the Covenant had rested stood a small altar. It was not exactly square. In the center of the surface was a cavity covered by a grating, and below it a hole for ashes; on the sides were pipes, which looked like horns. There were present many disciples in white garments and broad girdles such as the Apostles used to wear in the early assemblies for divine worship. They served at the incense sacrifice. John burned several kinds of herbs, also spices, and I think some wheat on the portable altar of incense. All was decorated with green branches, garlands, and flowers. Crowds of aspirants to baptism were present.

The priestly garments and ornaments of the Baptist had all been prepared at this place of baptism. In those days there dwelt near the Jordan some holy women recluses, who worked at all kinds of necessary things and prepared the sacred robes of the Baptist. They were not baptized.

The ceremonies performed by John at this time reminded one of the opening of a new church. He wore a long, white garment when baptizing. He performed no manual labor, with the exception of completing the place for Jesus' baptism. He did all with his own hands, the disciples carrying to him the materials.

I saw John at this place holding forth in a long and vehement discourse. Arrayed in his priestly vestments, he stood above the tent, which was surrounded by galleries like the tents of the kings in Arabia. Tiers of seats were erected within the walls of the enclosure, and on them stood an innumerable crowd of listeners. John spoke of the Saviour, who had sent him and whom he had never seen, also of the passage through the Jordan. Incense was again offered in the tent, and fragrant spices.

From Maspha down into Galilee the news had spread that John was to hold this great meeting for instruction, consequently multitudes of men were present. Almost all the Essenians had come. Most of the people were clad in long, white garments. I saw married couples arriving, the wives sitting between panniers of doves on asses which the husbands led. The men offered bread; the women, doves. John stood during the ceremony behind a grating and received the loaves, which were laid on a grated table and the flour still clinging to them removed. They were then piled in pyramids on dishes, blessed by John, and raised on high as if for an offering. It was afterward cut into pieces and distributed among the people, they that came from the greatest distance receiving the largest portions, since they had the most need of it. The flour scraped from the loaves, and the crumbs of the cutting, fell through the grated table on a tray and were burned on the altar. The doves brought by the women were divided also. The ceremony occupied almost half a day. The whole festival lasted during the Sabbath and three days inclusively. At its conclusions, I saw John busied again at the place of baptism.

5. The Island Upon Which Jesus Received Baptism Rises Out of The Jordan

John delivered to his disciples at the Jordan a discourse upon the nearness of the Messiah's baptism. He told them that he had never seen Him, "But," said he, "I shall, as a proof of what I say, show unto you the place at which He will receive baptism. Behold, the waters of the Jordan will divide and from their midst an island will arise." At the same moment

I beheld the waters of the river dividing and, on a level with its surface appeared a small, white island circular in shape. This happened at the spot over which the Children of Israel had crossed the Jordan with the Ark of the Covenant and at which also Elias had divided the waters with his mantle. Wonder seized upon the beholders. They prayed and sang praises. John and his disciples laid great stones in the water. Upon them they placed branches and trees, over which they scattered fine, white gravel, thus forming from the shore to the island a bridge beneath which the water could flow. Then they planted twelve small trees around the island, connecting their upper branches in such a way as to form a kind of latticed arbor. Between the trees they set hedges of low bushes, of which numbers were found here and there along the Jordan. They had red and white blossoms, the fruit was yellow with a little crown like the medlar. These hedges looked very beautiful, for some were covered with blossoms, others full of fruit.

The new island, the spot upon which the Ark at the passage through the Jordan rested, appeared to be rocky and the bed of the river deeper than in Joshua's time. But when John called it forth for the place of Jesus' baptism, the water seemed to be much lower, so that I could not determine whether it had sunk or the island had risen.

To the left of the bridge, not in the middle of it, but nearer to the shore of the island, there was a deep hole in which welled up clear water. Some steps led down to it. Nearby rising above the surface of the water lay a smooth, red stone of triangular form, upon which Jesus was to stand, and to the right of it was a slender, fruit-bearing palm tree which He was to clasp with one arm during His baptism. The edge of the well was laid out in ornamental style and very beautifully wrought.

I saw that the Jordan was very much swollen when

Joshua led the Israelites through it. The Ark of the Covenant was borne far ahead of the people. Among the twelve carriers and attendants were Joshua, Caleb, and one whose name sounded something like Enoi. When arrived at the Jordan, the forepart of the Ark, which was usually borne by two, was now taken charge of by one alone, while the others supported the back. As soon as the leader set the foot of the Ark in the river, the rushing waters instantly stood still, rose up like galleries on either side, and continued rising and swelling, until like a mountain they could be seen far away in the region of the city of Zarthan. They flowed toward the Dead Sea leaving the bed of the river such that the carriers bore the Ark over dry-shod. The Israelites crossed in the same way, but at some distance from the Ark and further down the river.

The Ark of the Covenant was borne by the Levites far into the riverbed to a spot upon which were four square, blood-red stones arranged in order. On either side lay two rows of triangular stones, six in number. They were smooth, as if cut with a chisel. Besides these there were twelve others on each side. The twelve Levites set down the Ark of the Covenant on the four central stones and stepped, six to the right, six to the left, on the twelve lying near. These latter were triangular, the sharp end sunk in the earth.

There were twelve others still further off. They, too, were triangular, very large and massive, and were differently variegated, some of them marked with all kinds of figures and flowers. Joshua caused twelve men from the Twelve Tribes to be chosen to bear these stones on their shoulders to the shore, and thence to a place at some distance where they were deposited in a double row for a memorial. At a later period a city rose in the neighborhood of this spot. The names of the Twelve Tribes and of those that bore them were engraved on the stones. Those upon which the Levites stood were still larger than the others and, before the Israelites left the bed of the river, they were turned so that their point stood upward. The stones borne to the shore were no longer to be seen in John's time. Whether they lay buried in the earth or had been destroyed by war, I cannot now say. John, however, had pitched his tent between the sites of the double rows. At a subsequent period, I think through the influence of Helena, a church was built on the spot.

The place upon which the Ark of the Covenant rested in the Jordan was the exact spot upon which, later on, was the baptismal well of Jesus on the island, which otherwise appeared to be destitute of water.

When the Israelites and the Ark of the Covenant had crossed and the twelve stones had been turned upward, the Jordan began again to flow.

The water in the baptismal well on the island was so low down that from the shore only the head and neck of him that was being baptized could be seen. The descent to the well was by a very gentle slope. The octangular basin, about five feet in diameter, was surrounded by a broad ledge in five sections upon which was standing room for several.

The twelve triangular stones, upon which the Levites had stood, extended to both sides of Jesus' baptismal well, their sharp ends rising out of the ground. In the well itself lay those four red ones upon which the Ark had rested. They were now below the surface of the water though in earlier times, when the waters of the Jordan were low, their points were distinctly visible.

Close to the edge of the well was a three-cornered pyramidal stone resting on the sharp end. It was on this that Jesus was standing at His baptism when the Holy Spirit came upon him. On His right, and close to the edge of the well, arose the slender palm tree which He clasped during the baptism; on His left stood the Baptist. This triangular stone upon which Christ stood was not one of the twelve that surrounded the inside of the well. I think John brought it himself from the shore. There was a mystery connected with it also. It was covered with all kinds of veining and flowers. The other stones, the twelve, were of different colors, and they, too, were pierced by innumerable veinings and covered with flowers. They were larger than those carried to the land. It seems to me that they were precious stones that had been placed there by Melchisedech before the waters of the Jordan had begun to flow. But when he placed them there they were small. He had in this way laid the foundations of many subsequent buildings. These foundations had long lain cancelled by mud and earth, but when brought to light, they became holy places wherein something remarkable happened.

I think also that the gems worn by the Baptist in his breastplate at this feast had been taken either from those twelve stones or from those that had been removed to the shore.

6. New Embassy from Jerusalem. Herod Again Seeks an Interview With John

When John was once more busy at the place of baptism, I again saw about twenty deputies from all the authorities of Jerusalem approaching with the intention of calling him to account. They paused on the spot where the festival had been celebrated and sent word to him to appear, but John heeded not. Next day I saw them distant from the baptism place about a short half-hour. But John would not allow them so much as to enter the circle of the numerous dwellings on the outskirts of the enclosure. This was the circle that was hedged off. When he had finished his labors, I saw him speaking to the envoys, though standing at some distance from them. He spoke in his customary style, paying no attention to the questions put to him, but dwelling upon Him who would soon come to be baptized, who was greater then he and whom he had never seen.

Then I saw Herod sitting in a kind of chest upon a mule. He was accompanied by his brother's wife, with whom he was then living. She was magnificently and shamelessly adorned, her hair in curls, her robes wide and flowing. She, too, rode a mule and was attended by a retinue of servants. I saw them coming into the neighborhood of the place of baptism. The wife, without dismounting, halted at some distance; but Herod alighted and approached on foot for a conference with John who, however, would not permit him to come nearer than was absolutely necessary. Herod expostulated with John for having pronounced against him a sentence of excommunication shortly after he laid before him the papers in defense of his unlawful connection. John had excluded him from all share in the baptism and the salvation of the Messiah if he refused to break off his shameful relations with his brother's wife. Herod inquired of John whether he knew a Man by the name of Jesus of Nazareth of whom the whole country was talking, whether or not he kept up communication with Him, and whether that Man was the One whose coming he was constantly announcing. He urged that John need not hesitate to inform him on these points, for that he intended to lay his case before Him. John answered that that Man would give him (Herod) just as little quarter as he himself did, that he (Herod) was and would always be an adulterer, that he might present his case where he would, but it would always remain adultery. When Herod asked John why he did not approach nearer to him and why he would speak to him only from a distance, John answered: "Thou wast blind before, but thy adultery has made thee still blinder. The nearer I approach to thee, the blinder wilt thou become. But when I shall be in thy power, thou wilt do that of which thou wilt have cause to repent." In these words of John lay the prophecy of his own death. Herod and the wife now left, very much irritated.

The time drew near for Jesus to come to the baptism, and I saw that John was greatly troubled in mind. It was as if his time was now short. His manner of acting was no longer so spirited, and he became deeply depressed. By turns from Jericho, from Jerusalem, and from Herod came people deputed to drive John from the place of baptism. John's followers had pitched their encampment to a great distance around the place. The newcomers demanded of John that he should retire to the other side of the Jordan. Herod's soldiers broke down the hedges of the enclosure and drove the people away; but they did not proceed as far as John's tent, which lay between the two rows formed by the twelve stones. John's words to his disciples on this occasion were anxious and dejected. He earnestly longed for Jesus to present Himself at the baptism, for then, as he said, he would retire before Him to the opposite side of the Jordan. He told them that he would not much longer be among them, which words troubled them very much, for they did not want him to leave them.

When John was informed of Jesus' approach, he roused himself and with new courage began to baptize. Crowds came to him, chiefly those whom Jesus had exhorted to receive baptism, among them many publicans, also Parmenas and his parents from Nazareth. When John discoursed of the Messiah, saying that for Him he himself would soon make room, his words breathed so great humility as to cause real trouble to his disciples. The disciples whom Jesus had left in Nazareth also came to John. I saw them with him in his tent conversing about Jesus. John was so inflamed with ardent love for Jesus that he grew almost impatient at His not proclaiming Himself the Messiah openly and in unmistakable terms. When John baptized these disciples, he received the assurance of the nearness of the Messiah. He saw a cloud of light hovering over them, and had a vision of Jesus surrounded by all His disciples. From that moment, John became unspeakably joyous and expectant, constantly glancing into the distance, to see whether or not the Lord was yet in sight. The island with the baptismal well had grown beautifully green, but no one went to it excepting John occasionally. The path over the bridge was usually kept barred.

7. Jesus Baptized by John

Jesus, walking more quickly than Lazarus, reached John's place of baptism two hours before him. It was morning twilight when, on the road near the place, He caught up with a crowd of people who also were going to the baptism, and He walked on with them. They did not know Him, but they could not keep their eyes off Him, for there was something about Him very remarkable. When they reached the end of their journey, it was morning. A crowd more numerous than usual was assembled to whom John was with great animation preaching of the nearness of the Messiah and of penance, proclaiming at the same time that the moment was approaching for him to retire from his office of teacher. Jesus was standing in the throng of listeners. John felt His presence. He saw Him also, and that fired him with zeal and filled his heart with joy. But he did not on that account interrupt his discourse, and when he had finished he began to baptize.

He had already baptized very many and it was drawing on to ten o'clock, when Jesus in His turn came down among the aspirants to the pool of baptism. John bowed low before Him, saying: "I ought to be baptized by Thee, and comest Thou to me?" Jesus answered: "Suffer it to be so now, for so it becometh us to fulfill all justice that thou baptize Me and I by thee be baptized." He said also: "Thou shalt receive the baptism of the Holy Ghost and of blood." Then John begged Him to follow him to the island. Jesus replied that He would do so, provided that some of the water with which all were baptized should be poured into the basin, that all present should be baptized at the same place with Himself, and that the tree by which He was to support Himself should be transplanted to the ordinary place of baptism, that all might share the same conveniences.

The Saviour now went with John and His two disciples, Andrew and Saturnin. Andrew had followed those disciples and adherents of the Lord whose conversation between Capharnaum and this place has been recorded above. They crossed the bridge to the island and into a little tent that, close to the eastern edge of the baptismal well, had been erected for the purpose of robing and disrobing. The disciples followed the Lord to the island, but at the far end of the bridge the people stood on the shore in great crowds. On the bridge itself three could stand abreast. One of the foremost in the latter position was Lazarus.

The baptismal well lay in a gently inclined, octangular basin the bottom of which was encircled by a similarly shaped rim connected with the Jordan by five subterranean canals. The water surrounded the whole basin, filling it through incisions made in the rim, three in the northern side serving as inlets, and two on the southern acting as outlets. The former were visible, the latter covered, for at this point were the place of action and the avenue of entrance. For this reason the water did not here surround the well. From this south side, sodded steps led down into it by an inclination of about three feet in depth.

In the water off the southern shore, was a red triangular, sparkling stone sunk close to the margin of the basin, the flat side toward the center of the well, the point toward the land. This side of the well upon which were the steps leading down into it, was somewhat higher than the opposite one. This latter, viz. the north side, was the one with the three inflowing canals. On the southwestern side was a step leading to the somewhat deeper part of the margin and on this side only was there access to the well. In the well, in front of the triangular stone, there stood a green tree which had a slender trunk. The island was not quite level. It was rather elevated toward the center and in some parts rocky. It was covered with moss and in the middle of it was the wide-spreading tree connected with which were the tops of the twelve trees planted around the edge of the island. Between every two of the trees, was a hedge of several small shrubs.

The nine disciples that were always with Jesus during His last days went down to the well with Him and took their stand on the ledge around it. Jesus entered the tent and there laid off, first, His mantle and girdle; then a yellow, woollen garment which was closed in front by laces; then that narrow, woollen strip which He wore around His neck and crossed over the breast, and which He was accustomed to wind around His head at night and in stormy weather. Retaining His brown, woven undergarment, He stepped forth and descended to the margin of the well, where He drew it off over His head. About His loins was fastened a broad linen band which was also wound around each limb for about half a foot. Saturnin received the garments of the Lord as He disrobed, and handed them to Lazarus, who was standing on the edge of the island.

And now Jesus descended into the well, and stood in the water up to His breast. His left arm encircled the tree, His right hand was laid on His breast, and the loosened ends of the white, linen binder floated out on the water. On the southern side of the well stood John, holding in his hand a shell with a perforated margin through which the water flowed in three streams. He stooped, filled the shell, and then poured the water in three streams over the head of the Lord, one on the back of the head, one in the middle, and the third over the forepart of the head and on the face.

I do not now clearly remember John's words when baptizing Jesus, but they were something like the following: "May Jehovah through the ministry of His cherubim and seraphim, pour out His blessing over Thee with wisdom, understanding, and strength!" I cannot say for certain whether these last three words were really those that I heard; but I know that they were expressive of three gifts, for the mind, the soul, and the body respectively. In them was contained all that was needed to convert every creature, renewed in mind, in soul, and in body, to the Lord.

While Jesus ascended from the depths of the baptismal well, Andrew and Saturnin, who were standing to the right of the Baptist around the triangular stone, threw about Him a large linen cloth with which He dried His Person. They then put on Him a long, white baptismal robe.[1] After this Jesus stepped on the red triangular stone which lay to the right of the descent into the well, Andrew and Saturnin each laid one hand upon His shoulder, while John rested his upon His head.

This part of the ceremony over, they were just about mounting the steps when the Voice of God came over Jesus, who was still standing alone and in prayer upon the stone. There came from Heaven a great, rushing wind like thunder. All trembled and looked up. A cloud of white light descended, and I saw over Jesus a winged figure of light as if flowing over Him like a stream. The heavens opened, I beheld an apparition of the Heavenly Father in the figure in which He is usually depicted and, in a voice of thunder, I heard the words: "This is My beloved Son in whom I am well pleased."

Jesus was perfectly transparent, entirely penetrated by light; one could scarcely look at Him. I saw angels around Him.

But off at some distance on the waters of the Jor-

---

1. Before the baptism of Jesus, only a small white scarf was put upon the newly baptized; but after Jesus' baptism, a larger garment was used.

dan, I saw Satan, a dark, black figure, as if in a cloud, and myriads of horrible black reptiles and vermin swarming around him. It was as if all the wickedness, all the sins, all the poison of the whole region took a visible form at the outpouring of the Holy Ghost, and fled into that dark figure as into their original source. The sight was abominable, but it served to heighten the effect of the indescribable splendor and joy and brilliancy spread over the Lord and the whole island. The sacred baptismal well sparkled and glanced, foundations and margin and waters—a pool of living light. One could see the four stones that had once supported the Ark of the Covenant shining beneath the waters as if in exultation; and on the twelve around the well, those upon which the Levites had stood, appeared angels bending in adoration, for the Spirit of God had before all mankind rendered testimony to the living Foundation, to the precious, chosen Cornerstone of the Church around whom we as so many living stones, must build up a spiritual edifice, a holy priesthood, that thereby we may offer an acceptable, spiritual sacrifice to God through His beloved Son in whom He is well pleased.

Jesus then ascended the steps and entered the tent near the baptismal well. Saturnin brought the garments which Lazarus had been holding all this time, and Jesus put them on. When clothed, He left the tent and, surrounded by His disciples, took His stand on the open space near the central tree. John in joyous tones addressed the crowd and bore witness to Jesus that He was the Son of God and the promised Messiah. He cited the Prophecies of the Patriarchs and prophets now fulfilled, recounted what he had seen, reminded them of the voice of God which they had heard, and informed them that when Jesus returned he himself would retire. John referred also to the sacred memories that embalmed the spot upon which they were standing on account of the Ark of the Covenant's having rested here when Israel was journeying to the

Land of Promise. Now, he continued, had they seen the Realization of the Covenant witnessed to by His Father, the Almighty God Himself. John referred all to Jesus, and called this day that had beheld the fulfillment of the desire of Israel blessed. Meanwhile many newcomers had arrived on the spot, and among them some friends of Jesus. I saw in the crowd Nicodemus, Obed, Joseph of Arimathea, John Marc, and others. John bade Andrew announce the baptism of the Messiah throughout Galilee. Then Jesus spoke, confirming in plain and simple words the truth John had proclaimed. He told them that He would withdraw from them for a short time, after which all the sick and afflicted should come to Him and He would heal and console them. They should in the meantime prepare themselves by penance and good works. He would withdraw for awhile, and then return to lay the foundations of that Kingdom which His Father had given to Him. Jesus made use of a parable when thus addressing the crowd: that of a king's son who, before taking possession of his throne, withdrew into solitude, there to prepare himself and implore the assistance of his father.

Among His numerous listeners were some Pharisees, who received His words with ridicule. "Perhaps, after all," they said, "He is not the carpenter's son, but the supposititious child of some king. Is He now about to return to His kingdom? Will He assemble His subjects and march upon Jerusalem?" The idea appeared to them foolish and absurd.

John recommenced his work, and continued throughout the whole day baptizing at the sacred well of Jesus all that were on the island. They were for the most part people who later on joined the Community of Jesus. They stepped into the water that covered the rim of the pool, the Baptist standing outside on the edge itself baptizing.

8. Jesus Travels Over Luz and Ensemes to Visit the Two Inns at Which the Holy Family Rested on Their Journey to Bethlehem and Their Flight into Egypt

Jesus journeyed that same day with His followers the distance of a couple hours toward Jerusalem to a little, obscure place whose name sounded like Bethel. There was a kind of hospital in the place and in it many sick. Jesus entered, and with His followers partook of some food. Several aged persons approached and saluted Him reverently as a Prophet, for they had heard from the lately baptized what John had proclaimed of Him. Accompanied by His disciples, Jesus visited the sick in their chambers consoling them and telling them that, if they would believe in Him, He would come again and cure them. But on this occasion He healed only one sick man, him of the third chamber. The poor man was greatly emaciated, his head covered with ulcers and white tetter. Jesus blessed him and bade him arise. The man obeyed and fell on his knees at Jesus' feet.

Andrew and Saturnin baptized many of this place. Jesus ordered a tub of water, large enough for a child perhaps, to be set on a stool in one of the rooms. I saw Him blessing the water and sprinkling something into it with a sprig. I think it was some of the baptismal water from the leathern bottle brought hither by the disciples. They that were to be baptized bared their shoulders to the breast, and lowered their head over the tub while Saturnin baptized them. I think the words he used were dictated to him by Jesus and were different from those employed by John; but I do not remember them clearly. Jesus celebrated the Sabbath in this place, after which Andrew and Saturnin went to Galilee.

Jesus proceeded to a city named Luz and, going into the synagogue, held a long discourse during which He explained very many ancient mysterious symbols from the Scriptures. I remember that He spoke of the Children of Israel. After crossing the Red Sea, they had on account of their sins wandered so long in the desert, before being allowed to pass through the Jordan and into the Promised Land. Now was the actual fulfillment of what was then only typical, for the baptism in the Jordan had been symbolized by the passage of the Israelites through its waters. If they now remained true and observed God's commands, they should indeed be put into possession of the Promised Land and the City of God. Jesus spoke in a spiritual sense, signifying thereby the Heavenly Jerusalem. But His hearers dreamed only of an earthly kingdom and of deliverance from the Romans. Jesus then spoke of the Ark of the Covenant and of the severity of the Old Law, for whoever approached so near the Ark as to touch it instantly fell dead; but now was the Law fulfilled and grace poured forth in the Son of Man. Now, too, was being fulfilled that of which the angel's conducting Tobias back into the Promised Land was a figure; for they who, faithful to the commands of God, had so long pined in captivity were now to be introduced into the freedom of the Law of grace. Jesus referred also to Judith, the widow, who had delivered Bethuel from oppression by cutting off the head of Holofernes, the Assyrian, as he lay sunk in the fumes of wine. Now would the Virgin, foreseen from eternity, become great and exalted, while the proud heads that had once oppressed Bethuel would fall. By this Jesus signified the Church and her triumph over the powers of the world.

Still many other similitudes of a like bearing Jesus spoke, all which had now been fulfilled. But He never once said the words: "I am He." He spoke always as of a third person. Then He referred to His followers, saying that they should abandon all things and have no immoderate care for their maintenance, for it was a far greater thing to be regenerated than to find

nourishment for the body. But if they would be born
again of water and the Holy Ghost, He who had
regenerated them would also nourish them. They
that follow Him, He said, must leave their relatives
and live in continence, for it was not now the time
for sowing, but for reaping. He spoke of the manna
also. The people listened in astonishment and reverence, but interpreted all His teaching in an earthly
and material sense.

Lazarus now departed. The other friends of Jesus
had already left Him at the Jordan. The holy women,
too, who had been staying with Susanna in Jerusalem,
had gone away through the desert.

From Luz Jesus travelled southward with His disciples and crossed the desert. After journeying for
some time, they came to a double row of date trees.
As they passed under them, the disciples expressed
a doubt as to whether they might gather and eat
the fruit that had fallen. Jesus told them to eat it
without scruple and henceforth not to be so constrained in acting, that they should cultivate purity
of soul and holiness of speech rather than make so
much account of that which went into the mouth.

I saw Jesus entering some houses that stood in a
row off by themselves on the road. He there visited
about twelve sick persons whom He consoled and
some of whom He cured. Several of these last followed Him.

Jesus next entered a little town called Ensemes,
whither many had come to meet Him. They now presented themselves before Him, for it had already been
announced that the new Prophet was nigh. They came
with their children by the hand, saluted Him solemnly,
and prostrated before Him. Jesus told them kindly
not to do that. He was conducted to their home by
the most distinguished of the place. The Pharisees
escorted Him thence to the synagogue, for they were
well-disposed and rejoiced to have among them a
Prophet. But when they learned from the disciples

that Jesus was the Son of Joseph, a carpenter of Nazareth, there arose in their breast all sorts of prejudices against Him, for they had at first thought that He was another Prophet. When Jesus spoke of the baptism they, in order to ensnare Him, asked which baptism was to be preferred, His own or John's. Jesus answered by repeating what John had said of his own baptism and, also, of that of the Messiah. "But," He added, "whoever despises the baptism of the Precursor will not honor that of the Messiah." Still Jesus never said: "I am He," but always spoke of Himself in the third person, calling Himself "The Son of Man," as the Gospel records. In the house to which He had been conducted, He partook of a meal, and before retiring for rest prayed with His disciples.

From Ensemes Jesus and His followers crossed the brook Cedron into Judah. For the most part He followed the by-ways and valleys, the indirect routes by which the Blessed Virgin and Joseph had journeyed to Bethlehem, and paused at those places where they had put up. The atmosphere was foggy and the season tolerably cool, while in the deep valleys might sometimes be seen snow or frost. On the sunny side, however, all was green and lovely, fruit still hanging on the trees and bushes. The Lord and His disciples ate of it on the way. Jesus avoided the large cities, because there was already much talk everywhere of His baptism, the circumstances attending it, and the testimony of John. The same rumors created a great stir in Jerusalem. Jesus intended to make His public appearance only after His return from the desert of Galilee. He made this little journey into these parts only through affection to certain individuals and with a view to induce them to go to the baptism. He was not always accompanied by all His disciples; sometimes only two were with Him. The others scattered among the houses of the shepherds lying off the road, and tried to rectify the notions of the occupants, for all were so partial to

John that they looked upon Jesus as merely His assistant, and called Him only "The Helper." The disciples related to them the apparition of the Holy Ghost, the words heard at the baptism, and the testimony rendered by John. They explained that the latter was only the preparer of the way of the Lord, and consequently so ardent and vehement, for it was his to break the way.

As a result of the disciples' exhortations, numbers of the shepherds and weavers dwelling around in the valleys came to Jesus to pay Him homage, and to listen under the trees and sheds to His short instructions. Jesus blessed and exhorted them.

Jesus explained to the disciples on the way the meaning of the words they had heard at the baptism, "This is My beloved Son." These words, said Jesus, were spoken by His Eternal Father of all who, free from sin, should receive the Baptism of the Holy Ghost.

This region was that through which Joseph and Mary had journeyed to Bethlehem. Joseph was familiar with it, for his father owned meadows in the country around. Joseph had indeed kept clear of Jerusalem by a day and a half's journey, and had shunned the other cities. As the shepherds' houses were to be met all along the road, he made only a few hours a day, for the Blessed Virgin found both sitting on the cross-saddle and continual walking very painful.

The chief places to which Jesus went were the houses of two shepherds at which during their journey His parents had asked admission. He went first to the one by whom Mary had been badly received. The master of the house was a rough, old man, and he refused hospitality to Jesus also. He looked like some of the peasants of our own day who say: "What more do I want? I pay my tithes, I go to church," and, for the rest, live as they list. And thus spoke the people of this house in Jesus' time. "What more do we want? We have our Law of Moses given to us by God Himself, and more than that we do not need." Then Jesus spoke of the mercy and hospitality exercised by all the holy Patriarchs, for where would the Blessing and the Law then be had Abraham repulsed the angels that brought the former? The Lord spoke to them a parable: "He that had refused shelter when she knocked at his door to the travel-wearied Virgin, so soon to become a Mother, and had scorned the companion of her journey when so meekly seeking admission to the inn, had repulsed the Son also along with the salvation that He brought with Him." Jesus uttered these words so significantly that I saw them fall like a thunderbolt upon the heart of one present, for this was the house from which Mary and Joseph had been contemptuously repulsed when on their journey to Bethlehem. I recognized it at once. The most aged of the occupants became greatly distressed, for without naming Himself, Mary, or Joseph, Jesus had in this parable related what they had done.

Hereupon one of them cast himself at Jesus' feet, begging Him to tarry with them and accept refreshment, for, as he said, Jesus must surely be a Prophet, since He knew all that had happened here thirty years ago. But Jesus would accept nothing from them. He taught the shepherds who had assembled around Him, saying that one action is the type, the kernel of that which follows, that the roots of sin are destroyed by contrition and penance, and that by conversion man would be born anew in the Baptism of the Holy Ghost and bring forth fruits of eternal life.

From this place Jesus journeyed on through the valleys, teaching here and there as He went. The possessed cried after Him, but became silent upon His command.

He arrived at a second shepherd inn which stood on a hill. The Holy Family had been there also. The man of the house owned numerous herds. In rows of houses along the valleys, dwelt shepherds and tent weavers. Stretched in the open air were long strips of stuff upon which the weavers worked one to another. There were many flocks of sheep in this region, and wild animals not a few. The doves went in flocks like hens, and there was another kind of bird, large with a long tail, very numerous here. In the wilderness ran animals with little horns like deer; they were not timid, but mixed up freely with the herds. Jesus was most cordially received. The people of the house with the neighbors and children went out joyously to meet Him, and cast themselves down before Him. The Blessed Virgin and St. Joseph had been most kindly entertained at this house, which was now kept by a couple of young people, children of the old householder. The latter was still alive, a little, stooped old man who carried a small shepherd staff. Jesus accepted food here: fruits, herbs which they dipped in sauce, and small rolls baked in the ashes. The members of this family were very pious and enlightened.

They introduced Jesus into the room wherein the Blessed Virgin had passed the night, and which they had long ago changed into an oratory. It was at first merely a retired corner of the house cut off by only a partition, but later they had so arranged it as to form a separate apartment with an entrance of its own. From a four-cornered, they had changed it into an eight-cornered room; the ceiling running up from the different corners formed a central obtuse point, from which hung a lamp. There was also in the roof an aperture that could be opened at pleasure. In front of the lamp was a narrow table, something like our Communion rail, upon which one could lean when in prayer. The room was very neat and beautiful like a chapel. The venerable old man led Jesus in and pointed out to Him the spot in which His Holy Mother had rested, also where Anne, His grandmother had slept; for she, too, had put up here on her journey to visit the Blessed Virgin in Bethlehem.

These people knew of the birth of Jesus, the adoration of the Three Kings, the prophecies of Simeon and Anna in the Temple, the flight into Egypt, and of the admirable teaching of Jesus in the Temple. Several of these days they commemorated with prayer in their little chapel, for from the very beginning this family had sincerely believed, hoped, and loved. Like the simple peasants that they were, they questioned Jesus as to how things were then in Jerusalem, for they had heard that, among the great ones there, the report was current that the new Messiah would, in quality of King of the Jews, restore to them the scepter and free them from the Roman yoke. They asked Jesus whether, indeed, things would so turn out. Jesus answered their questions by a parable. "A young prince," He said, "had been sent by the king, his father, to take possession of his throne, to restore the Sacred Mystery, and to free his people from bondage. But they to whom he was sent would not recognize him as the king's son, they persecuted and maltreated him. Nevertheless, he would after a time be exalted, he would draw to himself in the kingdom of his father all that faithfully kept his commandments."

Many accompanied Jesus into the little chapel and there listened to His teaching. He also performed some cures here. The old shepherd conducted Him to one of his neighbors who had for long years been confined to bed with the gout. Jesus took her by the hand and commanded her to arise. She obeyed instantly and, casting herself on her knees, thanked the Lord, after which she followed her Benefactor to the door. The poor woman had been as crooked and stooped as Peter's mother-in-law.

Jesus asked to be taken down into a deep valley in which were many sick. He cured several, perhaps about ten, and consoled the rest.

John was still baptizing the crowds that continued to present themselves. The tree from Jesus' baptismal pool had been removed to the center of the

large pool and had become beautifully green. This
latter pool was reached by steps descending from the
shore. Many tongues of land jutted out into it, and
on them the people in turn took their stand, descending on one side and ascending on the other.

When Jesus left the shepherd house, distant from
Jerusalem about five hours, the people followed Him.
They had associated with the shepherds who had
visited Jesus in the Crib and, on that account, were
so upright in intention.

The Lord and His disciples pursued their journey
through byways and retired places. Here and there
assembled around Him crowds of shepherds and
laborers whom He instructed in similitudes borrowed
from their own occupations. He exhorted them repeatedly to baptism and penance, and spoke of Redemption and the near coming of the Messiah.

I saw on Jesus' road a fertile spot on the declivity of the mountain and there, engaged in all kinds
of field and vineyard labor, were many people. I saw
plowing, sowing, planting going on, and heaps of corn
being gathered together. It was very fruitful here
although, as in other places, frost or snow covered
the valleys. The corn was not put up in sheaves. The
ears were cut off about one-half a foot in length and
then bound together in the center, so that they piled
up in heaps. They were not gathered in as had been
done long before in the harvest, but were allowed to
stand outdoors in heaps high and broad like hills.
They were covered with straw when the rainy season came on, and the field was plowed up anew. The
ears were afterward cut off with a curved knife, the
straw pulled out and thrown on the heaps. Then I
saw the gathering in, the ears piled on litters and
borne away by four men. The straw remained lying
in rows; it was afterward rolled into bundles, I think
for burning. In other places they were plowing. The
plow had no wheels, but was drawn by men. The one
that I saw was like a sled on three sharp heavy run-

ners, between two of which was the place for yoking. Usually the plow was not guided from behind, but asses or men pulled it in front. The fields were plowed both in length and breadth. The harrows used by these people were three-cornered, the broad part in front. They seemed to work quite well. Where the soil was rocky, a little earth spread over it afforded sufficient support for vegetation. The sowers carried their sack slung round the neck, the two ends hanging on their breast. The plants that I saw set out were garlic, and a certain large-leaved plant used for seasoning, I think. One species is called dhurra.

The disciples gathered the people together on the way, and Jesus taught them in parables of plowing, sowing, and reaping. He spoke to the disciples of the seed they would scatter by means of Baptism. He appointed two, one of whom was Saturnin, to baptize shortly at the Jordan. He addressed them, saying: "This is the seed. And like unto the people before us, shall ye in two months begin your harvest." Then He spoke of the straw that was to be cast into the fire.

While Jesus was thus teaching, a crowd of laborers from Sichar came in sight along the road, carrying spades, pickaxes, and long poles. They looked like slaves, and appeared to be returning home from work on some public building or road. They halted at some distance and listened with a timid air to the words of Jesus, not daring to approach nearer to the Jews. But Jesus, raising His voice, bade them draw near, telling them that His Heavenly Father called all to Himself through Him; and then He spoke of the equality of all that do penance and receive Baptism. The poor creatures were so affected by Jesus' gentle words that, falling on their knees, they implored Him to come to Samaria and help them also. Jesus replied that He would indeed go to them, but not just yet, for He must now go away for awhile in order to prepare His Kingdom, of which His Father had sent Him to take possession.

And now the shepherds again conducted Jesus over all the roads and byways that His Mother had traversed. But when they found that He was better acquainted with them than even they themselves, they exclaimed in wonder: "Lord, Thou art a Prophet! Thou art a filial Son, thus to know and trace the footsteps of Thy Blessed Mother!"

After Jesus had taught and exhorted the multitude, He went to the little city of Beth-Araba. It was afternoon when He and His disciples arrived. They proceeded to an open square, and Jesus mounted the stone pulpit under the trees. A crowd gathered around Him, and He taught. The people here were men of good will.

9. Jesus in the Valley of Shepherds Near Bethlehem

Jesus leaving Beth-Araba directed His steps, followed by many of His last audience, toward the valley of the shepherds about three and a half hours distant. Once I saw Him with the disciples under an open shed, eating corn and red berries, which they had gathered on the way. Then the disciples separated, each taking a different road, Jesus having appointed the place at which they should again join Him. As they went along, they told all whom they met about Jesus and exhorted them to penance and Baptism, if they had not already been baptized. Many of those whom they thus exhorted followed them to the appointed meeting place, there to listen to the teaching of Jesus. Jesus Himself took very circuitous routes, and I often saw Him passing half the night alone on the hills in prayer, so that the whole time of the journey was entirely filled up. I heard the disciples beseeching Him not to bring on an untimely death by the little care He took of His body, His fasting, His going barefoot, His long night-watches during that cold, damp season. But Jesus reproved them gently and went gravely on His way.

Before daybreak I beheld Him and His disciples descending the mountain side into the valley of the shepherds. The shepherds dwelling around already knew of His coming. All had been baptized by John, and some even had had dreams and visions of the approach of the Lord. Several were on the watch for Him. They gazed uninterruptedly toward the point whence He might be seen coming down the mountain. Suddenly He appeared in sight. They beheld Him shining with glory and surrounded by light, descending into the valley, for many of these simple-hearted people were highly favored with grace. Instantly they sounded a horn, to arouse the more distant dwellers and summon them to the spot. This was their custom at every extraordinary occurrence. All hastened to meet the Lord. They knelt before Him, with head lowly bent, their long staves resting in their arms; many of them prostrated flat on their face. They wore short doublets to the knee, mostly of sheepskin, some open on the breast, others closed, their wallets hung on their shoulder. They greeted Jesus in words from the Psalms that foretold the coming of the Messiah and proclaimed Israel's gratitude for the fulfillment of the Promise. Jesus showed them great affection, and congratulated them on their happy state. Here and there He taught in the huts that lay around the broad meadow valley, His instructions turning upon the pastoral life which He treated in parables.

Then, followed by His hearers, He passed farther on through the valley toward Jerusalem to the shepherd tower. This tower stood on an eminence in the center of a field, its foundation being huge fieldstones. It consisted of a very high superstructure of beams, supported in part by the green trees around it. The walls were hung with mats. There were galleries and outside steps around it, and at various distances little, covered standing places like sentry boxes. From a distance it looked like a ship with high masts and spreading sails; it also bore some resemblance to the towers in the land of the Three Kings from which they watched the stars. The whole country around could be scanned from this tower, even Jerusalem and the mountain upon which Jesus was at a later period tempted by Satan.

The shepherds made use of it to catch their herds and ward off threatening danger. Some of them with their families dwelt around it in a circle of about five hours in circumference, in farmhouses surrounded by gardens and field. But their general rendezvous was in the near neighborhood of the tower. Here they kept their various utensils, and here the herdsmen received their food. All along the base of the tower-hill were huts, and at some distance from it a large enclosed shed wherein the wives of the herdsmen dwelt and prepared the food. These women did not go forth with the rest to meet the Lord and His disciples, but later on they were instructed by Jesus. There were about twenty shepherds living around here. Jesus instructed them, called their attention to the happiness of their state of life, and told them that He had come to visit them because they had greeted Him in His infancy and had lovingly treated both Himself and His parents. He taught especially in parables of shepherds and herds, telling them that He, too, was a Shepherd, that He had under Him other shepherds who till the end of time should gather together, heal, and guide His flocks.

Then the shepherds told Jesus all about the glad tidings brought them by the angels, also about Mary, Joseph, and the Child. They had seen, they said, the image of the Child in the star that had hovered over the Crib Cave. They told of the Kings and how they in their turn had beheld the shepherd tower in the stars, and of the numerous gifts they had left here on their return to their own country. Many of them had been put to use both in the tower and in the surrounding huts, which were formed of coarse can-vas. Some of the old men present had in their youth been at the Crib. They repeated the story all over again to Jesus.

Next day Jesus and the disciples were escorted by the shepherds farther on toward Bethlehem to the dwellings of the sons of the three eldest shepherds to whom the angels at Christ's birth had first appeared, and who first had offered Him their homage of veneration. They were now dead and lay buried not far from the dwellings, which were about one hour's distance from the Crib Cave. Three sons of the old shepherds were still alive and they were themselves old men. They were held in great respect by all the others, their families being something like superiors over the rest, something similar to the Three Kings among their people. They received Jesus very humbly and joyfully, and led Him to the graves of their fathers. The site was an isolated hill covered by a vineyard; the base was surrounded by a kind of covered walk from which opened various caves and cellars. The cave containing the remains of the old shepherds was high up on the hill. The light entering from above disclosed the three graves which lay together in the ground, two parallel, the third lengthwise between them, thus 1 — 1. They were closed by doors. The shepherds opened the graves for Jesus, and I saw the brown faces of the closely enveloped corpses. The space around the coffins was filled with little pebbles. The shepherd crooks lay in the coffins by their owners.

The shepherds also showed Jesus the treasure that they still had from the gifts of the Three Kings and which was concealed here in the cave. It consisted of little solid bars of gold and whole pieces of very costly stuffs embroidered in gold. They asked Jesus whether or not they should give it to the Temple. He answered by telling them to keep it for the Com-munity which was to form the new Temple, and He foretold to them that there would one day be a church erected over this tomb.[1] On this hill began a vineyard that extended toward Gaza. It was the usual burial-place of the shepherds.

From here the Lord was conducted to the place of His birth in the Crib Cave distant about an hour. Their way led through a remarkably beautiful meadow valley. Three paths ran through it between tracts of fruit trees trimmed into shape. The shepherds told on the way of the angelic *Gloria,* and I saw all again in pictures. The angels had appeared in three different places: first, to the three shepherds; then, on the following night, at the shepherd tower; and lastly, at the well near the spot at which Jesus had the day before been welcomed by the shepherds. Around the shepherd tower they appeared in greater numbers, large, wingless figures. The shepherds took Jesus into the tomb cave of Maraha, Abraham's nurse, near the great pine tree.

10. The Crib Cave, A Place of Devotion Among the Shepherds

The path to the Crib Cave ran along the east, from which side Bethlehem was not directly accessible, since no straight road led thither. The city could scarcely be seen from this side, for it was separated from the valley of the shepherds by dilapidated walls, and massive ruins of similar masonry between which ran deep ravines. The nearest direct entrance into the city was by the south gate that led to Hebron. Leaving this gate, one would have to go around toward the east in order to reach the region of the Crib. This region was contiguous to the valley of the shepherds from which one could go to it without entering Bethlehem. Both the Crib Cave and the adjoining caves belonged to the shepherds, who used them for

---

1. This prediction was afterward fulfilled by St. Helena.

storing their utensils and sheltering their cattle. No one from Bethlehem had any communication with this region, neither road nor path leading thither. Joseph, whose father's house stood on the south side of the city, had often when a boy visited the shepherds here, concealed himself in the caves from his brothers, and spent therein much time in prayer.

When Jesus now visited the Crib in company with the shepherds, it was already very much changed, for they had fitted it up as a place of devotion. No one was allowed to step on the sacred ground; consequently a grated passage had been made around the cave, thus enlarging the space covered by it. Into this passage opened cells hewn in the rock. It was like a cloister. The ground and walls of the cave were covered with the tapestry and carpets left by the Kings. They were woven in colors, the principal figure in them being pyramids.[2] Two flights of steps ran from the passage up above the Crib Cave. The roof of the latter, wherein had once been oblique openings to admit light, had been entirely removed and replaced by a domelike cupola through which the light streamed. By one of the flights mentioned above, one could mount from the dome of the cave to the top of the hill and thence proceed toward Bethlehem. All these changes had been made with the means left by the Kings.

The Sabbath was just beginning and the lamps had been lighted in the Crib Cave when the shepherds brought Jesus hither. The Crib itself still occupied the same place. Jesus pointed out to the shepherds something that they did not know; viz., the exact spot upon which He was born. He gave them an instruction and they celebrated the Sabbath in the Cave. He told his hearers that His Heav-

2. Probably many-colored triangles. The triangle was a favorite figure among the Jews for the ornamentation of walls. Sister Emmerich frequently refers to it, as, for instance, in Mary's little chamber at the Temple.

enly Father had chosen this place for His nativity at the time of Mary's Immaculate Conception, and I saw that it had been the theater of several significant events of the Old Testament. Abraham and Jacob had been within its walls, and before them had Seth, the Child of Promise, been born therein of Eve after a penance of seven years. An angel appeared to Eve on that occasion, telling her that this was the seed that God had given her in the place of Abel. Seth was for a long time hidden here and nursed, also in the Suckling Cave of Abraham's nurse Maraha; for, as Jacob's sons pursued Joseph, so did the brothers of Seth pursue him. The Suckling Cave was now Maraha's tomb.

The shepherds led Jesus into the adjacent cave also, where for a time the Holy Family had tarried. The fountain that had sprung up therein on the night of Christ's Nativity, they had beautifully enclosed, and they made use of its waters in sickness. Jesus commanded them to take some of the water away with them. On leaving the cave, He visited the shepherds' huts.

Saturnin baptized several aged men who were unable to go to the baptism of John. Into the water which they had brought from the fountain of the cave near the Crib, they poured some of Christ's baptismal water from the pool on the island in the Jordan. At John's baptism all confessed their sins publicly; but at that of Jesus each acknowledged his sins privately, gave proofs of contrition, and received pardon. The old men whom Saturnin baptized knelt, their shoulders bared to the breast, their head bowed over a large basin. In this manner they were baptized. The form made use of at this baptism was similar to that employed by John at the baptism of Jesus. But to the word Jehovah and the invocation of the three gifts, was added "and in the name of the One that has been sent."

11. Jesus Visits Certain Inns, The Halting Places of the Holy Family on Their Flight into Egypt

Jesus had spent His nights alone and in prayer. Upon leaving the shepherds He addressed His disciples, telling them that He was now going to make another journey to some people who had hospitably sheltered Him and His parents on their flight, that He would cure their sick and convert a sinner, that no footstep of His holy parents should remain unblessed, and that everyone who had shown them compassion and kindness on their flight, He would now seek out and lead to salvation. The mercy and benevolence of all such persons have been to them a pledge and a furtherance of salvation; their effects will continue forever. As now, He said, He was visiting all that had at that time shown charity to Him and His, so would His Heavenly Father be mindful of all that showed mercy and charity to even the most insignificant of His brethren. Jesus then appointed a place near the city and Mount Ephraim, where His disciples were to await His coming.

He now journeyed alone around Herod's dominions toward the desert near Anim, or Enzannim, a few hours from the Dead Sea. His way lay through a wild, though tolerably fertile region where, hedged in by enclosures, were pastured a great many camels divided into droves of forty. There was an inn for the accommodation of travellers through the desert, and to it Jesus went. Several huts and sheds stood nearby, and the proprietors of the inn owned many camels.

This inn was the last in Herod's dominions met by the Holy Family on their flight into Egypt. The people were a bad set who carried on thievery, but notwithstanding they had received the Holy Family kindly. The neighboring city contained many disorderly characters who had settled there after some war.

Jesus went to the inn and asked hospitality. The

proprietor was a man about fifty years old, called Reuben, who had been there at the time of the flight into Egypt. When Jesus glanced at him and addressed him, grace shot like a ray of light into his breast. The words of Jesus and His salutation fell upon him like a blessing, and deeply moved he exclaimed: "Lord, it is as if the Promised Land enters with Thee into my house!" Jesus replied that, if he would believe in the Promise and would not cast away from him its fulfillment, he would indeed share in the Promised Land. Then He spoke of good works and their consequences, telling him that He had now come to announce salvation to him, because he had kindly entertained His Mother and His foster-father so many years before when on their flight to Egypt. In like manner does every action, the good as well as the bad, bear its own fruit. At these words of Jesus, the man cast himself trembling on the ground before Him, saying: "Lord, whence is this to me, a poor, despised, miserable man, that Thou shouldst enter my house?" Jesus answered that He had come to cleanse sinners from their iniquity and lead them back to God. The man still spoke of his own baseness, and said that all the inhabitants of the place belonged to a miserable, lost generation; he also told Jesus of his poor, sick grandchildren. Jesus replied that if he would believe in Him and be baptized, He would restore his grandchildren to health. He washed Jesus' feet, and gave Him the best he had for His refreshment. When the neighbors came in, he told them who Jesus was and what He had promised. He had a relative among them who was named Issacher.

After that he conducted Jesus to his sick grandchildren who, some from leprosy and some from lameness, had become quite deformed. Jesus commanded the children to rise, and they stood up cured. He visited some women also, who were sick of a bloody flux. Then He ordered a bath to be prepared. They got ready a large vessel of water under a tent. From one of the two flasks that He carried with Him strapped to His side under His outer robe, He poured into it some of the baptismal water from the Jordan, and blessed the whole. The sick were then ordered to bathe in it. They did so, and came forth cleansed and thanking the Lord. Jesus did not baptize them Himself, although this washing was equivalent to Baptism in case of death; but He exhorted them to go seek for the baptism at the Jordan.

When the people questioned Jesus, asking if the Jordan really possessed special virtue, He answered that the channel of the Jordan had been hollowed out and its course directed; that all holy places of this land had been allotted to special purposes by His Heavenly Father long before man had existed there, yea, even before the land or the Jordan had sprung forth from nothing. Very wonderful things spoke Jesus on this subject, and He instructed the women on marriage inculcating modesty and continency. He pronounced the degeneracy of the people of this place and the pitiful condition of the children, consequences of the illegitimate connections so common among them. He spoke of the parents' share in the corruption of their children, of arresting the evil by penance and satisfaction, and of the second birth in baptism.

Then He recounted to them all the kind offices they had performed for the Holy Family at the time of their flight, and gave them some information relative to the places at which they had rested and refreshed themselves. Mary and Joseph had with them on their flight a she-ass, as well as the ass upon which the Blessed Virgin rode. Jesus showed the people all their actions at the time of the flight, that is all the acts of kindness they had shown the Holy Family, as so many types of their present turning from sin to salvation. They prepared for the Lord a repast from the best they had. It consisted of a kind of milk thick like white cheese, honey, rolls baked in the ashes, grapes, and birds.

Accompanied by some of these men, Jesus left Ainon and, returning by another route, arrived toward evening at a city built on both sides of a mountain, through which ran a rugged valley full of deep ravines. Both mountain and city bore the name of Ephraim, or Ephron. The mountain faced straight toward Gaza. Jesus had come through the country of Hebron. At some distance from the road that He travelled could be described a ruined city with a tower still standing, whose name sounded like Malaga.[1] About an hour's distance from this place was the grove Mambre whither the angels bore to Abraham the promise of a son, Isaac; also the double cave that Abraham bought from Ephren, the Hethite, and which afterward formed his tomb. The field that witnessed David's combat with Goliath was not far off.

Jesus, His escort having taken leave, wended His way around one side of the double city and met His disciples in the rugged valley road which had been designated by Him as the place of meeting. He conducted them out of the winding ravine into a very spacious cave in the wildest part of the mountain, to which no path led. It had afforded a resting place, the sixth in order, to the Holy Family on their flight into Egypt, and here Jesus and His disciples passed the night.

Jesus told this circumstance to the disciples, impressing upon them the sacred character of the place, while they were busying themselves making a fire. They struck a light by revolving one piece of wood inside another. One of the Prophets had frequently spent some time in this cave, in order to give himself more unreservedly to prayer. I think it was Samuel. David, too, while guarding his father's flocks around here, had made the cave a place of prayer and there received commands of God through

---

1. Probably *Molada* is meant, or the *Malatha* of Josephus Flavius, 18, 7, 2.

the ministry of angels. It was while thus engaged that he was admonished to slay Goliath.

When the Holy Family reached this cave, they were dejected and exhausted. The Blessed Virgin wept sadly. They were in want of all things, because they had fled by unfrequented ways, shunning the great cities and customary inns. They spent a whole day here recruiting their strength, and several wonders were vouchsafed them for their refreshment—a fountain sprang up in the cave, and a wild goat bounded in and allowed itself to be milked.

Jesus spoke to the disciples of the great tribulations in store for Him and all His followers, of the hardships here endured by Himself and His Blessed Mother, of the mercy of His Heavenly Father, and of the holiness of the place. He added that at some future day there would be a church built on the spot, and He blessed the cave as if consecrating it. The disciples had brought with them some fruit and rolls, and of them all partook.

12. Jesus Goes Toward Maspha to Visit A Relative of St. Joseph

When Jesus and His disciples left the cave, they struck off in the direction of Bethlehem. On this side of Ephron they entered an inn that stood among houses built apart, and there, after washing their feet, took some refreshment. The people were good and somewhat inquisitive. Jesus instructed them on penance, the nearness of Redemption, and of what they must do to follow Him. They asked Him why His Mother took that long journey from Nazareth to Bethlehem, since she could have been so comfortably cared for at home. Jesus answered by telling them of the Promise and that He was to be born in poverty at Bethlehem among the shepherds, since like a shepherd He was to gather the flocks together. It was also for this same reason that now, after His Heavenly Father's testimony of Him, He visited these shepherd regions first.

From here Jesus turned His steps to the south side of Bethlehem about two hours distant, crossed a portion of the shepherd valley, and proceeded around the west side of the city, leaving Joseph's paternal house to the right. Toward evening He entered the now little city of Maspha, some hours from Bethlehem.

Maspha could be seen at a great distance, for on the highroads all around the city burned lights in iron lanterns. It was encompassed by walls and towers, and traversed by several streets. Maspha was long one of the principal places of devotion. Judas Maccabeus[1] had before battle held here a great prayer meeting in which he reminded Almighty God of all the outrageous decrees of the enemy, recalled to Him His own promises, and exposed the priestly garments before the assembled multitude. Then five angels appeared to him before the city and promised him victory. It was here also that Israel had assembled against the tribe of Benjamin, on account of an outrage and murder committed upon the wife of a travelling Levite. The infamous scene was enacted under a tree, which was afterward walled around, and no one went near it. In Maspha also Samuel had exercised his office of Judge; and here was found that Essenian cloister in which dwelt Manahem, who had foretold the scepter to Herod when the latter was only a boy. This cloister had been built by the Essenian Chariot, who lived about one hundred years before Christ. He was a married man from the country of Jericho. He had separated from his wife and both, he for men and she for women, had founded several communities of Essenians. He was a very holy man and died in a cloister founded by him not far from Bethlehem. He was the first to arise from his tomb at the death of Christ and appear to men.

---

1. *Mach.* 3:46.

Maspha was full of inns, and the arrival of a stranger was soon noised about the city; consequently Jesus had scarcely entered the inn when He was surrounded by a crowd. He was conducted to the synagogue where He explained the Law. Some of His hearers were spies whose intentions were insincere. They sought to draw Him out, because they had heard of His promise to lead the heathens also into the Kingdom of God, and that He had spoken among the shepherds about the Three Kings. Jesus' words on this occasion were very severe. He said that the days of the Promise were completed; and that all who would be born again in Baptism, would believe in Him whom the Father had sent, and would keep His commandments, should as well as His followers have a share in the Kingdom. But from the unbelieving Jews should the Promise be withdrawn and given over to the heathens.

I cannot repeat Jesus' words exactly, but they were to this effect: that He knew their intentions, that they were spies, that they might betake themselves to Jerusalem, and there tell all they had heard Him say.

Jesus had alluded to Judas Maccabeus and the several important events that had here taken place. His hearers boasted the magnificence of the Temple and the superiority of the Jews over the heathens. But Jesus explained to them that the end for which the chosen people had been called and their Temple erected was now attained, since the One promised by God through the Prophets was now come to establish the Kingdom of His Heavenly Father, and to raise to Him a new Temple.

After this instruction, Jesus left Maspha and went about an hour eastward. He reached first a row of houses, then came to a residence that stood alone and which belonged to one of Joseph's family. Joseph's father had married a widow with one son. This stepson had married and settled in this place, and his

descendants now occupied the house alluded to. They
had been baptized and had a family of children. They
received Jesus cordially and with every mark of deference. Several of the neighbors assembled at the
house. Jesus gave an instruction after which He partook of a repast with them. The meal over, He retired
with two of the men, Aminadab and Manasses. They
questioned Him as to whether He was acquainted
with their circumstances and whether they should
follow Him right away. Jesus replied no, that they
should for the present be numbered among His secret
disciples. Then they knelt before Him, and He blessed
them. Prior to His death, they publicly joined the
disciples. Jesus stayed here overnight.

13. Jesus Visits an Inn at Which Mary Stopped on Her Journey to Bethlehem

From here Jesus and His disciples went on for a
couple of hours till they came to a farmhouse which
had been the last stopping place but one on Mary's
journey to Bethlehem. It may have been about four
hours' distance from the city. The men of the house
came out to meet Jesus and, falling down before Him
on the road, begged Him to enter. He was very cordially received. These people went almost daily to
John's instructions and were all familiar with the
wonders connected with the Lord's baptism. A warm
bath was prepared for Jesus, also a repast, and a
beautiful couch was made ready for Him that night.
Jesus taught here.

The woman who had harbored the Holy Family
here thirty years ago was still alive. But she was
blind, and had been for many years almost bent double. She lived alone in the main building and her
children, who lived nearby, sent her her food. When
Jesus had performed His ablutions, He went to see
the poor, old woman. He spoke to her of compassion
and hospitality, of good works that bear no merit,

and of selfishness, placing her present afflictions before her as a punishment of the same. She was deeply touched, confessed her fault, and He cured her. He ordered her to bathe in the water He had just used. She did so, recovered her sight, and became straight and well. But Jesus commanded her to say nothing of her cure.

The people of this place questioned Jesus as to which was the greater, He or John. Jesus answered: "He of whom John gives testimony." Then they spoke of John's zeal and energy, also of the beautiful, manly figure of Jesus Himself. Jesus remarked that, three and a half years hence, they would see no beauty in Him, they would not even recognize Him so disfigured would He be. Of John's zeal and energy He spoke, likening him to one knocking at the house of a sleeping man, to rouse him for the coming of the Lord; to one breaking a path through the wilderness, that the king might safely travel over it; and lastly to an impetuous torrent that rushing along purifies the channel through which it flows.

14. "Behold the Lamb of God"

Next morning at daybreak Jesus departed with His disciples, followed by the crowd that had gathered around Him. They wended their way toward the Jordan, distant from this point at least three hours. The Jordan flows through a broad valley that rises on either bank for the distance of about half an hour. The stone in the enclosed space whereon the Ark of the Covenant had rested, and where the recent festival was celebrated, was about an hour's distance from John's place of baptism, that is, taking it in a straight line toward Jerusalem. John's hut near the twelve stones was in direction of Beth-Araba and somewhat more to the south than the stone of the Ark of the Covenant. The twelve stones lay one-half hour from the place of baptism and in the direction of Gilgal. Gilgal was on a gentle slope on the west side of the mountain. From John's baptismal pool the view up both the shores, which were very fertile, was most lovely. The most delightful region, however, rich in fruits and teeming with abundance, was around the Sea of Galilee. But here, and also around Bethlehem, there were broader meadowlands, more husbandry, and a greater abundance of dhurra, garlic, and cucumbers. Jesus had already passed the memorial stone of the Ark of the Covenant and was about one quarter of an hour beyond John's tent, before which the latter stood teaching. A gap in the valley disclosed this scene to the distant traveller, and Jesus in passing was for not longer than a couple of minutes visible to the Baptist. John was seized by the Spirit and, pointing to Jesus, he cried out: "Behold the Lamb of God, who taketh away the sins of the world!" Jesus passed, preceded and followed by His disciples in groups, the multitude lately gathered around Him in the rear. It was early morning. The people crowded forward at the words of John, but Jesus had already disappeared. They called after Him in acclamations of praise, but He was out of hearing.

When returned from their fruitless attempt to see Jesus, the people complained to John that Jesus had so many followers and that, as they had heard, His disciples had already begun to baptize. What, they asked, would be the outcome of all that. John made answer by repeating that he would soon resign his place to Jesus, since he was only a servant and precursor. These words were not at all acceptable to John's followers, who were somewhat jealous of Jesus' disciples.

Jesus now directed His steps toward the northwest, leaving Jericho on the right and proceeding to Gilgal about two hours distant from Jericho. He stopped at many places on the way. The children followed Him singing songs of praise, and ran into the houses to bring their parents out.

15. Jesus in Gilgal, Dibon, Socoth, Aruma, and Bethania

The region known as Gilgal comprised the whole of the elevated country above the low valley of the Jordan, and which was embraced by the inflowing streams of the Jordan for a circumference of five hours. But the city Gilgal, to which Jesus drew near before evening, lay scattered and interspersed by numerous gardens for the distance of about one hour, in the direction of the place to which John had retired to preach and baptize.

Jesus first entered the precincts of a sacred spot open to Prophets and Doctors of the Law. It was the place where Joshua had communicated something to the Children of Israel, namely, the six maledictions and six benedictions that had been revealed to Eliezer and himself by Moses before his death. The circumcision hill of the Israelites was nearby, and it, too, was enclosed by a wall.

I saw on this occasion the death of Moses. He died upon a low, but steep peak of Mount Nebo, which rises between Arabia and Moab. The camp of the Israelites flanked the mount, the outposts extending far into the valley around. A growth like ivy covered the whole mount. It was short and crisp, and grew in tufts like the juniper. Moses was obliged to support himself by it when climbing to the top of the peak. Joshua and Eliezer were with him. Moses had a vision from God that his companions saw not. He delivered to Joshua a roll of writing containing six maledictions and six benedictions, which the latter had to publish to the people when in the Promised Land. Then having embraced them, he commanded them to depart and not to look back. When they had gone, Moses cast himself upon his knees with outstretched arms, and gently sank upon his side dead. I saw the earth open under him and enclose him as in a beautiful grave. When Moses appeared at the

Transfiguration of Jesus on Thabor, I saw that he came from that place. Joshua read the six blessings and six maledictions before the people.

Many of Jesus' friends awaited Him in Gilgal: Lazarus, Joseph of Arimathea, Obed, a son of the widow of Nazareth, and others. There was an inn here, in which they set refreshments before the Lord and His companions after washing their feet.

Before the crowds here assembled, many of whom were on their way to John's baptism, Jesus gave an instruction. The spot chosen for the purpose was near the baths and place of purification built high up on the sloping, terraced shore of an arm of the Jordan. It was shaded by an awning, and all around were pleasure gardens ornamented with trees, shrubs, and green plots. Saturnin and two other disciples who had left John to follow Jesus baptized after Jesus had given an instruction on the Holy Ghost. He taught of the several attributes of the Holy Spirit, and pointed out the marks that distinguish one that has received Him.

John's baptism was preceded by only a summary confession of sins accompanied by proofs of contrition and a promise of amendment. But at the baptism of Jesus the acknowledgment of sin was not made in this general way. Everyone accused himself individually and mentioned his chief transgressions. Jesus exhorted to sincerity. He frequently proclaimed the sins of those that, through pride or false shame, concealed them thus to lead them to repentance.

Here also Jesus alluded to the passage over the Jordan and the ceremony of circumcision that had here been performed. It was in memory of this latter circumstance that baptism was now administered here and, through its efficacy, He said, they should henceforth be circumcised in their heart. He spoke likewise of the fulfillment of the Law.

The baptized on this occasion were not immersed in the water, they only inclined their head over it;

nor did they put on an entire baptismal garment, a white cloth only was placed on their shoulders. The disciples did not make use of a three-channelled shell like John's; but from the basin over which the neophyte inclined, they dipped up the water three times with the hand. Jesus had previously blessed it and poured into it some from His own baptismal well. About thirty were baptized at this time. They appeared radiant with joy after the ceremony, and declared that they truly felt that they had now received the Holy Ghost.

Jesus then proceeded with His followers amid the acclamations of the multitude to Gilgal, to celebrate the Sabbath in the synagogue, a very large, old building on the east side of the city. It was a four-cornered edifice, longer than broad, the angles filled in in such a way as to give it something of the appearance of an octagon. It contained three stories, in each of which was a school. A spiral, exterior flight of steps joined to the wall led up to each, and around each landing ran a little portico. High up in the rounded corners of the building were niches, in which one could stand and view the country far and near. The synagogue stood by itself with gardens cut off on both sides. In front of the entrance was a porch and a teacher's desk similar to that of the Temple in Jerusalem, and there was also an open court containing an altar upon which sacrifice had once been offered. There were likewise covered porches for women and children. One could easily detect the similarity of all these arrangements with those of the Temple, also that the Ark of the Covenant had once rested here and sacrifices had been offered.

The school on the lowest story was the most beautiful in its arrangements. At one end, in the spot corresponding to that occupied by the Holy of Holies in the Temple, stood an octagonal pillar around which were compartments containing rolls of writings. A table encircled the base of the pillar, and below that was a vault. Here it was that the Ark of the Covenant had once stood. The pillar was very beautiful, of polished white marble.

In the school on the first story, Jesus taught before the priests, the people, and the Doctors of the Law. Among other things He alluded to the fact that here the promised kingdom had been first established, but that idolatry so abominable had been practiced at a later period that scarcely could seven just souls be found among the inhabitants. Ninive, though five times greater, had been able to produce five just. Gilgal had been spared by God, therefore they should not now repulse Him who came to fulfill the Promise: they should do penance and through Baptism be born anew. Then taking the rolls from their places around the pillar, Jesus read and explained them.

After that He taught the young men in the school on the second story, and lastly the boys on the third. Coming down, He delivered another instruction to the women in an open space under a porch, and still another to the young maidens. To these last He spoke of modesty and chastity, of repressing curiosity, of modesty in dress, of veiling the hair, and of covering the head in the Temple and in the synagogue. He reminded them of the presence of God and the angels in holy places, and that the latter themselves veil their face before the Lord. He told them that in the Temple and synagogue there were myriads of angels hovering around the worshippers, and He explained why females should veil the head and hair. The children ran familiarly to Jesus. He blessed them and took them up in His arms. They were very much attached to Him. The joy and jubilation over Jesus were general in this place. As He left the school, the people ran from all sides to meet Him, crying out, and exclaiming: "The Promise is fulfilled! May it remain with us. May it never forsake us!"

When Jesus had finished His instructions, the people were anxious to bring their sick to Him. But He dismissed them, saying that it was neither the time nor the place for that, He must now leave them, for He was called elsewhere. Lazarus and the friends from Jerusalem returned to their homes and Jesus took leave of the Blessed Virgin, telling her that He would see her again before He retired into the desert. The Sanhedrin in Jerusalem again held a long consultation on the subject of Jesus. Everywhere they had spies bribed to give them information of His words and actions. The Sanhedrin consisted of seventy-one priests and doctors, of whom twenty were again divided into fives, thus forming so many subcommittees for deliberating and disputing together. They examined the genealogical register, and could in no way deny that Joseph and Mary were of the House of David and Mary's mother of the race of Aaron. But as they said, these families had fallen into obscurity, and Jesus strolled around with vagrants. He also defiled Himself with publicans and heathens, and sought the favor of slaves. They had heard, they said, of the familiar way in which He had spoken lately to the Sichemites, who were returning home from their work in the region of Bethlehem, and they thought that He must have designs to raise an insurrection with the aid of such hangers-on. Some gave it as their opinion that He was very likely an illegitimate child, because He had once proclaimed Himself the son of a king. Others declared that He must in some way receive secret training from the devil, for He often retired apart and spent the night alone in the wilderness or on the mountains. They knew what they were saying, for they had already inquired into all this. Among these twenty deliberators were some who knew Jesus and His family very well, who were most favorably inclined toward Him, who were indeed His friends in secret. Nevertheless, they did not contradict what was said against Him. They kept silence in order to be the better able to serve Him and His disciples and to

give them information of whatever might come to
their knowledge. The majority of the committee concluded at last that Jesus was in communication with
the devil from whom He received instruction, and
this was the opinion they publicly proclaimed and
which was spread throughout Jerusalem.

John's disciples announced to him the baptism that
had lately taken place in Gilgal, representing the
same as a usurpation of his rights. But in deepest
humility John again repeated what he had often told
them before; viz., that he would soon give place to
his Lord, whose herald and precursor he had been.
The disciples could not rightly understand his words.

With about twenty followers, Jesus left Gilgal and
moved on to the Jordan which He crossed on a raft.
All around on the beams of the raft were seats, and
in the center two concave spaces in which they were
accustomed to stand the camels that they might not
slip between the beams into the water. Three camels
could be so accommodated; but now there were none
on board, the Lord and His disciples being the only
passengers. It was night, and lighted torches stood
in the hollow spaces. Jesus related the parable of the
sower which, on the following day, He explained. The
passage over the river occupied fifteen minutes at
least, for the current at this point was very strong.
They had to row some distance up the river, and then
drift down to the spot at which they intended to land,
and which was not directly opposite their starting
point. The Jordan is a singular river; it cannot be
crossed at all in many places, and its steep shores
are pathless. It makes frequent and sudden bends,
and often appears to flow straight past a place around
which it is, in reality, running. Its bed in many places
is rocky and its course consequently arrested. Its
waters encircle numerous islands as they flow sometimes troubled, sometimes clear, according to the
nature of its bed, here and there forming falls. The
water of the Jordan is soft and tepid.

They landed near the settlement of the publicans. A highroad from the region of Kedar passed nearby and there, too, a lovely valley took its rise. The publicans, who had already received John's baptism, entertained Jesus; but several of His followers, surprised at their Master's intimacy with these despised people, stood shyly aloof. Jesus and His disciples spent the night here, accepting hospitality from the publicans, who were most deferential to them. Their houses stood on the side of the road that ran through the valley and not far from the Jordan; somewhat further on was the inn for the accommodation of merchants and their camels. There were many tarrying here at the time, on account of the next day's feast, that of Tabernacles; for although most of them were pagans, yet they were obliged to observe the festivals as days of rest. The publicans questioned Jesus as to how they should restore their unjustly acquired goods. He told them that they should be taken to the Temple, which however He meant only spiritually, for in reality He designated thereby His own community, the Church. There should, He said, be purchased with it a field near Jerusalem for the support of poor widows, and He explained to them why a field, illustrating by the parable of the sower.

Next day Jesus walked with them on the shore and in the country around, teaching again of the sower and the future harvest. He took His text from the feast of Tabernacles, which was then beginning, and which commemorated the vintage as well as the ingathering of the fruits of the field. From the publican village, Jesus pressed on further through the valley. On either side of the mountain slope, for the distance of half an hour perhaps, were rows of houses in which the Feast of Tabernacles was being celebrated. These houses extended as far as Dibon in the environs of which indeed they appeared to be. By their side were erected the booths formed of green branches of trees and adorned with bushes, festoons, and clusters of grapes. On one side of the road were the tabernacles and the little tents of the women; on the other, the huts in which the animals were slaughtered. All the food was carried across the road. The children, adorned with garlands, went in bands from one tabernacle to another, singing and playing upon musical instruments. These last consisted of triangles furnished with rings which they tinkled, triangles spanned by cords, and a wind instrument from which arose spiral tubes.

Jesus paused here and there to teach. Refreshments were offered to Him and His disciples, grapes on sticks, two clusters on each. At the further end of this row of houses stood an inn which Jesus entered. Not far from the inn, between it and Dibon, was a broad, open space in the middle of the road. Here, surrounded by trees, arose the large and beautiful synagogue of Dibon.

On the next day Jesus taught in the synagogue, taking again the parable of the sower, alluding to the baptism and the nearness of the Kingdom of God. He spoke also of the feast of Tabernacles and of its celebration here, taking occasion to reprove the people for mixing up heathenish customs in their services, for some of the Moabites still dwelt in this place, and with them the Jewish people had intimate relations. When Jesus left the synagogue, He found in the open court numbers of sick who had been borne thither on litters. They cried out as soon as they saw Him: "Lord, Thou hast been sent from God! Thou canst help us! Help us, Lord!" He cured many. That evening a banquet was prepared in the inn for Jesus and His followers. There were many of the heathen merchants near Jesus when He spoke of the call of the Gentiles, of the star that had appeared in the Land of the Kings, and of their going to visit the Child. Jesus left the place that night alone and went to pray on the mountain. He had engaged to meet His disciples the following morning on the road at the other side of Dibon. Dibon was six hours distant from Gilgal. It was rich in fountains and meadows, gardens and terraces, for it lay in the valley and up both sides of the mountain. Jesus next went to Socoth where He arrived toward evening. An innumerable multitude gathered around Him, among them many sick. He taught in the synagogue, and allowed Saturnin and four other disciples to administer baptism. It took place at a spring in a rocky grotto facing westward toward the Jordan which, however, could not be seen from it as a hill intervened. But the spring was fed from the deep waters of the river. The light fell into the grotto from apertures in the roof. In front of it was an extensive pleasure garden beautifully laid out with small trees, aromatic shrubs, and well-kept lawns. In it was an ancient memorial stone commemorative of an apparition of Melchisedech to Abraham.

Jesus taught here of John's baptism, which He called a baptism of penance, and which would soon be discontinued. In its stead would be received the Baptism of the Holy Ghost and the remission of sin. He received from them a kind of general confession of their sins, and then some separately disclosed their predominant passions and transgressions. Many trembled at hearing Jesus accusing them of sins that they thought secret. After the confession Jesus laid His hands upon them as if giving absolution. They were not immersed when receiving baptism. A large basin of water was placed on Abraham's memorial stone, and over it the neophytes bowed with bared shoulders. The baptizers poured the water thrice from the hollow of their hand over the heads of the baptized, who were very numerous at this place.

Abraham had once dwelt at Socoth with his nurse Maraha, and had owned fields in three different localities. Even here he had begun to share with Lot. It was here that Melchisedech first appeared to Abraham in the same way as did the angels. Melchisedech commanded him a threefold sacrifice of doves, long-beaked birds, and other animals, promising to come again and offer bread and wine in sacrifice. He told him what was going to happen to Sodom and to Lot, and pointed out to him several graces for which he should pray. Melchisedech at that time had no longer an earthly abode at Salem. Jacob also dwelt at Socoth.

From Socoth Jesus proceeded to Great Chorazin where, at an inn near the city, He had appointed to meet His Mother and the holy women. On the way thither He passed through Gersas where He kept the Sabbath, after which He went to an inn in the desert some hours from the Sea of Galilee. The proprietors dwelt nearby. The inn was still adorned as for the feast of Tabernacles, for the holy women had rented it some days previously and put all things in order. The necessary provisions were brought at their expense from Gerasa. Peter's wife was with them, also Susanna of Jerusalem, and all the others excepting Veronica. Jesus had an interview with His Mother alone. He told her that He was now on His way to Bethania, whence He would retire to the desert. Mary was grave and anxious. She begged Him not to go to Jerusalem for awhile, for she had heard of the council convened on His account.

Later on Jesus gave an instruction. The place chosen for it was a hill upon which was a stone seat formerly used for the same purpose. There were rows of people from the surrounding country and about thirty women present. They stood apart from the men. After the instruction Jesus told His followers that He must now leave them for a time and that they, as well as the women, should disband until His return. He spoke of John's baptism soon to cease, and of the bitter persecution awaiting Him and His.

Jesus left the inn with about twenty disciples and followers, and journeyed some twelve hours southwest toward the city of Aruma near which an inn for Him and His friends was always in readiness.

Martha, for whom the journey to Gerasa was her first expedition with the holy women, had prepared this inn for Jesus, and His friends in Jerusalem bore the cost. The steward and servants lived in the neighborhood. The holy women told Jesus of the inn before His departure. The city was about nine hours from Jerusalem and between six and seven from Jericho. Some Essenians dwelt near the inn. They went to see Jesus, conversed and ate with Him. Jesus went to the synagogue and taught of John's baptism, which was a baptism of penance, a preliminary purification, a preparatory action such as was prescribed in the Law. It was different from the Baptism of Him whom John heralded. They that were baptized by John I did not see again baptized, until after the death of Jesus and the coming of the Holy Ghost when, for the most part, the ceremony was performed at the pool of Bethsaida. The Pharisees of this place asked Jesus by what signs they should know the Messiah, and He told them. He gave an instruction on the subject of mixed marriages with the heathens and Samaritans.

Judas Iscariot, subsequently the Apostle, here heard Jesus preaching. He had come alone and not with the other disciples. After listening to His instructions for two days, and passing remarks on the same with the disaffected Pharisees, he departed for a neighboring village which did not bear a very good name. There he gave an account of what he had heard, talking with an air of importance to a pious man of the place. The latter in consequence invited Jesus to visit him. Judas carried on some kind of traffic. He was much occupied with writing, and held himself in readiness for general services of any kind.

When Jesus and His disciples arrived at the afore-named place, which had been lately built and which on account of its mixed population was not in very good repute, Judas had departed. Herod owned a castle in the neighborhood. Something connected with the Benjaminites must have happened in this place, for there was a tree close at hand surrounded by a wall, and no one went near it. Abraham and Jacob had each offered sacrifice here, and hither had Esau withdrawn when at variance with Jacob on the subject of the Blessing. Isaac at that time was living near Sichar.

The man that had invited Jesus to these parts was called Jairus; he belonged to the married Essenians. He had a wife and several children, among the latter two sons named Ammon and Caleb. He had also a daughter whom Jesus at a later period cured of some disease, but he was not the Jairus of the Gospel. He was a descendant of Chariot the Essenian, who had founded the convents near Bethlehem and Maspha, and he was familiar with many circumstances of Jesus' youth and family. He and his sons went forth to meet Jesus, whom they received with marks of deference. Jairus was, on account of his charity, the chief man of this despised place. He helped the poor and, on certain days, gave instructions to the children and the ignorant, for they had here neither schools nor priests. He likewise cared for the sick. As usual, Jesus taught of the baptism of John, setting it forth as a preparatory baptism of penance, also of the near coming of the Kingdom of God. With Jairus He visited the sick, and consoled them, but He would not cure any. He promised to return in four months and cure them. In His instructions He alluded to the events that had taken place here, namely, the estrangement of Esau in anger from his brother, and the consequences following upon his rage. It was this that had brought the place into ill-repute. Jesus told of the mercy of the Heavenly Father, who would realize all His promises in favor of those that would believe in the One sent by Him, would do penance, and be baptized and He showed how penance wards off the consequences of sin. Toward evening, accompanied about halfway by Jairus and his sons, Jesus went with His disciples to Bethania.

They stopped at an inn in the vicinity, and there Jesus gave His disciples a long instruction in which He alluded to the trials in store for Him and all His followers. He told them that they should now leave Him, and weigh well whether they would be able to stand by Him in His future sufferings.

Lazarus came out to meet Him. The disciples departed for their homes, Aram and Themeni alone accompanying Him to Bethania where many friends from Jerusalem were awaiting Him, among them the holy women and Veronica. Aram and Themeni were the nephews of Joseph of Arimathea on the mother's side. They had been John's disciples, but had followed Jesus when on His way to Gilgal He had passed John's place of baptism. Jesus gave an instruction at Lazarus' on the baptism of John, on the Messiah, on the Law and its fulfillment, and on the various sects among the Jews. His friends had brought with them from Jerusalem some rolls of writings from which Jesus explained to them the words of the Prophets relative to the Messiah. But only a few were present at this instruction, only Lazarus and some intimate friends.

Jesus advised with them on the subject of His future abode. They counselled Him not to remain in Jerusalem, telling Him all that was said of Him there. They proposed to Him Salem as proper for His residence, since but few Pharisees were in it. Jesus spoke of various places and of Melchisedech, whose figurative priesthood was soon to be realized. Melchisedech had laid out all the roads, founded all the places that in the designs of God the Son of Man was afterward to travel over and evangelize. Jesus concluded by telling them that He would be found mostly around the Lake of Genesareth. This conference was held in a retired apartment that opened upon a garden attached to the baths.

Jesus had an interview with the women in a chamber fronting on the road that led to Jerusalem, and which had formerly been occupied by Magdalen. In obedience to Jesus' direction, Lazarus brought his silent sister Mary and left her alone with the Lord, the other women retiring in the meantime to the antechamber.

Silent Mary's bearing toward Jesus was somewhat different from that of the last interview, for she cast herself down before Him and kissed His feet. Jesus made no attempt to prevent her, and raised her up by the hand. With her eyes turned heavenward, she, as once before, uttered the most sublime and wonderful things, though in the most simple and natural manner. She spoke of God, of His Son, and of His Kingdom just as a peasant girl might talk of the father of the village lord and his inheritance. Her words were a prophecy, and the things of which she spoke she saw before her. She recounted the grave faults and bad management of the wicked servants of the household. The Father had sent His Son to arrange affairs and pay off all debts, but they would receive Him badly. He would have to die in great suffering, redeem His Kingdom with His own Blood, and efface the crimes of the servants, that they might again become the children of His Father. She carried out the allegory in most beautiful language, and yet in as natural a manner as if she were recounting a scene enacted in her presence. At times she was gay, at others sorrowful, calling herself a useless servant and grieving over the painful labors of the Son of the merciful Lord and Father. Another cause of sorrow to her was that the servants would not rightly understand the parable, although so simple and so true. She spoke of the Resurrection. The Son, she said, would go to the servants in the subterranean prisons also. He would console them and set them free, because He had purchased their Redemption. He would return with them to His Father. But at His second advent, when He would come again to judge, all those that had abused the satisfaction He had made and who would not turn from their evil ways, should be cast into the fire. She then spoke of Lazarus' death and resurrection: "He goes forth from this world," she said, "and gazes upon the things of the other life. His friends weep around him as if he were never to return. But the Son calls him back to earth, and he labors in the vineyard." Of Magdalen too she spoke: "The maiden is in the frightful desert where once were the children of Israel. She wanders in accursed places where all is dark, where never human foot has trod. But she will come forth, and in another desert make amends for the past."

Mary the Silent spoke of herself as of a captive, for her body appeared to her a prison, and she longed to go home. She was so straitened on all sides; not one around her understood her and they were, as it seemed to her, all blind. But, she said, she was willing to wait, she would bear her captivity submissively, for she deserved nothing better. Jesus spoke to her lovingly, consoling her and saying: "After the Pasch, when I again come here, thou shalt indeed go home." Then as she knelt before Him, He raised His hands over her and blessed her. It seemed to me that at the same time He poured over her something from a flask, but I cannot say whether it was oil or water.

Mary the Silent was a very holy person, but none knew or understood her. Her whole life was one uninterrupted vision of the work of Redemption, of which she spoke like an innocent child. No one guessed her interior life, and she was regarded as a simpleton. When Jesus signified to her the time of her death, viz., that she should, freed from captivity, at last go home, He anointed her for death.

From this we may conclude that anointing is more necessary for the body than some people generally think. Jesus pitied Silent Mary who, as a reputed simpleton, would have received no embalming. Her holiness was hidden. Jesus dismissed her, and she returned to her abode.

After this Jesus again instructed the men on the baptism of John and that of the Holy Ghost. I do not remember any very great difference between the first named and that bestowed by the disciples of Jesus. The latter, however, was a little more like that which at a later period was to take away sin. Nor did I ever see any of those that had been baptized by John rebaptized before the descent of the Holy Ghost.

The friends from Jerusalem returned to the city before the Sabbath, Aram and Themeni going in company with Joseph of Arimathea. Jesus had told them that He would retire awhile in order to prepare for the painful mission before Him, that of teaching, but He did not tell them that He was going to fast.